Power and the Praise Poem

Southern African Voices in History

Carter G. Woodson
Institute
Series in
Black Studies

Armstead L. Robinson
General Editor

Power and the Praise Poem

Southern African Voices in History

by
Leroy Vail
and
Landeg White

University Press of Virginia
Charlottesville

James Currey
London

The University Press of Virginia
Copyright © 1991
by H. Leroy Vail and Landeg E.
White

First published 1991

Library of Congress Cataloging-in-
Publication Data
Vail, Leroy.
    Power and the praise poem:
southern African voices in history / by Leroy Vail and Landeg
White.
        p.   cm. — (Carter G. Wood-
son Institute series in Black
studies)
    Includes bibliographical refer-
ences and index.
    ISBN 0-8139-1339-X (cloth). —
ISBN 0-8139-1340-3 (pbk.)
    1. Oral tradition—Africa,
Southern—History and criticism. 2. Folk songs—Africa,
Southern—History and criticism. 3. Civilization, Western. I.
White, Landeg. II. Title. III. Series.
GR358.V35   1991
398'.0968—dc20   91-14065
                                        CIP

British Library Cataloguing in Publication
Data has been applied for.

0-85255-088-X (James Currey paper)
0-85255-089-X (James Currey cloth)

Printed in the United States of
America

**For
Jack Mapanje**

"Hope is our
only hope."

Contents

Illustrations

Preface

From the late nineteenth century until the 1960s anthropology was associated with both imperialism and colonialism because of its self-declared privileged expertise in explaining non-Western peoples to Westerners. As Western hegemony over colonial areas crumbled after World War II, as the hitherto colonized peoples increasingly refused to accept their status as dumb objects interpreted by anthropologists, and as the realization grew that even non-Western peoples had histories and were not chained by timeless "traditions" and "customs," the discipline was thrown into a prolonged crisis from which it has not yet emerged. As a consequence, anthropologists have devoted much effort to criticizing their discipline's basic epistemological and methodological assumptions, an endeavor which now appears to be assuming the proportions of a major academic industry.[1]

In some ways, this book can be placed within this stream of criticism. In the first half of chapter one we base our argument against the hegemony of "custom" on several studies already published by self-critical anthropologists. By now, however, we feel that their self-criticism has largely been heard and had its impact, and we have no desire to continue flogging the dead horse of past anthropological arrogance. Far more troubling has been the continuation of the old stark dichotomy between Westerners and Others, between "us" and "them," in the fresh guise of a psychologizing literary theory. It is this new opposition between literate culture and "oral" culture which we are most concerned with deconstructing in the second half of chapter one and to which our chapter two lays out an alternative approach that is explored in detail, case by case, in our remaining chapters.

A dehumanized stereotype known as "oral man" is now abroad and, paradoxically, seems to have gained widespread acceptance at precisely the time when anthropologists have been assiduous in rejecting such ahistorical simplicities. To cite but one example, much of the argument of James Axtell's recent prizewinning study of Eu-

ropean relations with Native Americans in the colonial era is based
on his acceptance of the notion of oral man as elaborated by the very
scholars we consider, in chapter one, to have failed to substantiate
their argument. For Axtell, Native Americans were at a disadvantage
in their early encounters with Europeans not so much because they
were politically weaker than the well-armed Europeans or because
their economies were more fragile but rather because, being nonliterate, they were encased in an oral culture which was by nature uncreative and unadaptive.[2] This was allegedly so, because, as Axtell
writes:

> An oral culture is intensely communal. . . . Knowledge and truth are
> not an individual matter so much as a corporate possession. Accord-
> ingly, oral man psychologically faces outward, toward the community
> from which he derives the meaning and veracity of his thoughts: to
> break with social values is to feel the shame of popular disap-
> proval. . . .
> By the same token, oral knowledge is relatively authoritarian, de-
> pending on tribal consensus rather than personal analysis. Due to the
> difficulties of acquisition, memory, and recall, oral knowledge is de-
> signedly uncreative, nonindividualized, and slow to change. It is
> stored in flexible units of memory, such as adages, proverbs, and repet-
> itive, thematic formulas, rather than being dependent upon verbatim
> recall. Mnemonic devices, such as condolence canes, wampum belts,
> and medicine sticks, release the memory of these units and help in
> their reconstruction.

He concludes that "oral man has little perception of the past except
in terms of the present. Myth and history tend to merge." Living in
cultures that were "tenaciously conservative," the Native Americans simply could not effectively adapt to the challenges presented
by the literate Europeans.[3]

In approaching our task of dealing with individual instances of
how nonliterate peoples of southern Africa, like nonliterate Native
Americans of centuries past, coped with change, whether brought
about by the presence of politically and economically powerful Europeans or by other causes, we have found the notion of oral man
useless. Instead, we have been struck with the flexibility of these
societies, not their changelessness, with their openness and sense of
history, not their conservatism, and with the sheer vigor of their
forms of expression. In sharp contrast with earlier accounts of oral
performance, our central argument is that it is the region's oral po-

etry, subject to the aesthetic we have described as poetic license, that gives access to the past and present intellectual life of the communities we describe. The poetry is the arena where competing "histories" clash, subjected not only to political reevaluation but to moral and spiritual reassessment.

This book has been many years in preparation and ranges far both geographically and linguistically and in the genres it discusses. Appropriately, it has many intellectual, personal, and financial debts. Although James C. Scott's pioneering books have been about southeast Asian societies, his warm humanity and willingness to listen to the people among whom he has lived and studied have provided us with one intellectual model.[4] Our second has been provided by the hundreds of men and women we have interviewed over more than twenty years or whose songs and poetry we have recorded. No stereotypes could survive the confrontation with their humor, their imaginative vitality, and their profound capacity for skepticism.

Those generous enough to have aided us with criticisms of earlier versions of various chapters or to have shared their own research materials include Anne Akeroyd, Karin Barber, Julian Cobbing, David Coplan, Tim Couzens, Jonathan Crush, Jill Dias, Mamadou Diawara, Carolyn Hamilton, Patrick Harries, the late Fernando Honwana, Richard Khonje, Gerhard Liesegang, Mbongeni Malaba, the late Ching'anya Mkandawire, Joseph C. Miller, Mapopa Mtonga, Sally Falk Moore, Anthony Nazombe, Anne-Lise Quinn, Terence Ranger, Antonio Rita-Fereira, William Rowe, Patricia Vail, Jan Vansina, Megan Vaughan, and Michael West. We are also deeply grateful to Eric Allina, C. S. Chanda, T. W. Kalusa, Monica Kangwa, Chipasha Luchembe, Marion Lwala, Hugh and Monica Macmillan, Venancio Mbande, Dick Middleton, Augustine Msiska, M. M. Musa, K. A. Mwenya, Mark Ncube, Kondwani Nyirenda, Andrew Tracey, Alice White, and Rebecca Zulu for vital help in carrying out our work in the field.

Financial support has been extended to us at various times and at various levels by Harvard University, the Social Science Research Council of the United States, the Southern African Studies Trust, the University of Malawi, the University of Zambia, and the Vilas Trust. Rhodes University, Grahamstown, South Africa, provided a generous research fellowship for work in its International Library of African Music. The Leverhulme Trust provided a two-year fellowship together with the costs of research trips to southern Africa and Portugal.

Finally, certain sections of the book have appeared in different forms in L. Vail and L. White, "Plantation Protest: The History of a Mozambican Song," *Journal of Southern African Studies* 5, no. 1 (1978): 1–25; L. White, "Review Article: Literature and History in Africa," *Journal of African History* 21, no. 4 (1980): 537–46; L. White, "Power and the Praise Poem," *Journal of Southern African Studies* 9, no. 1 (1982): 8–32; L. Vail and L. White, "Forms of Resistance: Songs and Perceptions of Power in Colonial Mozambique," *American Historical Review* 88, no. 4 (1983): 883–919; L. White and T. Couzens, "Introduction," in L. White and T. Couzens, eds., *Literature and Society in South Africa* (Harlow, Essex: Longman, 1984), 1–23; and L. White, "Of Chameleons and Clowns: The Case of Jack Mapanje," the *Southern African Review of Books*, Winter 1987–88, 26–27.

L.V.   L.W.

Concord, Alcabideche,

Massachusetts Portugal

Notes

1. Among the more notable of these writings have been, in chronological order, T. Asad, ed., *Anthropology and the Colonial Encounter* (New York, 1973); S. Diamond, *In Search of the Primitive* (New Brunswick, N.J., 1974); E. Said, *Orientalism* (New York, 1979); E. Wolf, *Europe and the People without History* (Berkeley and Los Angeles, 1982); J. Fabian, *Time and the Other: How Anthropology Makes Its Object* (New York, 1983); J. M. Clifford and G. E. Marcus, eds., *Writing Culture: The Poetics and Politics of Ethnography* (Berkeley and Los Angeles, 1986); G. E. Marcus and M. M. J. Fischer, *Anthropology as Cultural Critique* (Chicago, 1986); G. W. Stocking, Jr., *Victorian Anthropology* (New York, 1987); J. Clifford, *The Predicament of Culture: Twentieth-Century Ethnography, Literature, and Art* (Cambridge, Mass., 1988); A. Kuper, *The Invention of Primitive Society; Transformation of an Illusion* (London and New York, 1988), V. Y. Mudimbe, *The Invention of Africa: Gnosis, Philosophy, and the Order of Knowledge* (Bloomington, Ind., 1988), B. McGrane, *Beyond Anthropology: Society and the Other* (New York, 1989); J. A. Boon, *Affinities and Extremes* (Chicago, 1990); and M. Torgovnik, *Gone Primitive: Savage Intellects, Modern Lives* (Chicago, 1990).

2. J. Axtell, *The Invasion Within: The Contest of Cultures in Colonial North America* (New York and Oxford, 1985), 19.

3. Ibid., 14, 15. For a more convincing assessment of the reasons behind historical consciousness than the presence or absence of literacy, see D. E.

Brown's stimulating *Hierarchy, History, and Human Nature: The Social Origins of Historical Consciousness* (Tucson, Ariz., 1988).

4. J. C. Scott, *The Moral Economy of the Peasant: Rebellion and Subsistence in Southeast Asia* (New Haven, 1976) and *Weapons of the Weak: Everyday Forms of Peasant Resistance* (New Haven, 1985).

Power and the Praise Poem
Southern African Voices in History

1

The Invention of "Oral Man"
Anthropology, Literary Theory, and a Western Intellectual Tradition

In 1840, as part of the city of Leipzig's commemoration of the 400th anniversary of Johannes Gutenburg's invention of movable type, Felix Mendelssohn composed his Second Symphony, the *Lobgesang*, or "Hymn of Praise." Inspired by the challenge to produce a celebratory piece commensurate with the anniversary's importance, Mendelssohn wrote a work for three soloists, chorus, and orchestra taking some eighty minutes to perform. At the very heart of the symphony, as its musical and intellectual turning point, occurs a joyous transition of great emotional power written for orchestra and full chorus. This moment expresses the profound transformation literacy brought about in European history:

> The night has passed away
> and the day has come.
> So let us cast off the works of the darkness
> and put on the armor of light,
> and take up the armor of light.
> The night has passed away!

Lest printing's importance be in any doubt, however, Mendelssohn at once reinforces the chorus's message in a chorale of thanksgiving in which Gutenburg's invention is depicted as comparable to God's separation of day from night as recounted in Genesis. Mendelssohn's contrast is notable for its absoluteness: those possessing print literacy are truly blessed by God, while those without it are indeed benighted. Mendelssohn was not alone in this view. His symphony's message well reflected the feelings of his educated western European contemporaries about the basic differences between the literate and the nonliterate, and their enthusiasm for the symphony made it one of the most frequently performed musical works of the mid- and late-nineteenth century.

Mendelssohn's work not only appealed to his contemporaries, but, with its concern for drawing a sharp boundary between groups, it was also part of a growing preoccupation of European intellectuals with defining borders between peoples.[1] The aim was to establish differences between nationalities by describing allegedly national characteristics, but, at a time of growing racial consciousness, finding differences between the human races was also considered of cardinal importance. During the first six decades of the nineteenth century, the study of human physical characteristics—such as the shape of skulls, cranial sizes, and differences in anatomy—provided the most important data for specifying presumedly objective distinctions between races that were ranked in a hierarchy of presumed ability.[2] This research, called "ethnology," legitimized the period's growing racism by providing it with a pseudoscientific underpinning, and many were persuaded by its "findings" even to accept the radical notion, suggested seriously in the late eighteenth century, that the world's races had different origins and thus did not share a common humanity.

Several considerations prompted this concern with race. Black slavery, continuing in many parts of the world despite the attacks of abolitionists, demanded justification. Improvements in the means of travel brought Westerners into ever closer contact with non-Western peoples whose often puzzling or offensive practices undermined earlier idealizations of Noble Savages as sharers in a common humanity. A revival of Christian evangelism and missionary endeavor stressed the imperfect, unsaved nature of those without the Faith. Finally, and probably most importantly, the technological superiority of Western societies resulting from industrialization reinforced existing racist conclusions, making it seem obvious that whites comprised the clever, hardworking, successful race, while others were merely "savages" or, at best, "primitives." By mid-century, then, racism was a lens through which most educated Westerners perceived the world and their place in it.

From the mid-1850s onwards, however, an important shift of emphasis in writings about race began to occur. By then it was becoming clear that ethnology's preoccupation with finding physical differences between the races not only encouraged notions of polygenesis offensive to faithful Christians but, equally damaging, the study was yielding conclusions of highly doubtful scientific validity. As a consequence, racial theorists began to combine in a new synthesis earlier romantic preoccupations with the uniqueness of individual national cultures with the contemporary pride in technological progress arising from literacy and education. The earlier racism based on calibration thus yielded to a new racism based on cultural distinctions perceived as determined by and linked to racial identity.

That races with a common origin could possess fundamentally different cultures and ways of thinking was soon explained in terms of one of the major organizing ideas of the last half of the nineteenth century, evolutionism. The findings of the new science of archeology had transformed the Western perception of humankind's position in Time from biblical brevity to geological expansiveness.[3] Human history thus could be thought of as a gradual evolutionary development through a set of stages.[4] By being situated within the matrix of evolutionism, the old static hierarchy of races was given both a temporal dimension and a history. Some races were different from others because they had experienced greater cultural evolution from humankind's common origin than the others. Important cultural distinctions between races arose from their occupying different places along the path of dynamic evolutionary development, with technological advances—such as Gutenburg's invention of movable type—central to the accumulated differences. This evolutionist perspective allowed the new racism to coexist comfortably with Christian beliefs in human monogenesis.

The writings of Charles Darwin were critical in gaining a broad popular acceptance for the concept of a racial hierarchy governed by natural laws operating within an evolutionist dynamic.[5] This was not merely because Darwin's *Origin of Species* (1859) and *Descent of Man* (1871) legitimated "scientifically" the concept of evolution but also because he himself, backed by his immense scientific prestige, argued in his *Origin of Species* that his approach could be used to throw light "on the origin of man and history," explicitly suggesting its applicability to human "psychology."[6] His suggestion was quickly taken up by intellectuals such as Herbert Spencer and popularized as Social Darwinism. According to them, the races of mankind not only occupied distinct positions in a staged sequence of "development" over time but were also engaged in a natural conflict or struggle with each other. Thus, while it satisfied believing Christians by affirming the basic unity of mankind, Social Darwinism's strongest message was that the fittest were destined to prevail. This idea was especially welcome to the energetic racists of the later nineteenth century, for it justified the imperial expansion upon which they were then embarked, and it soon came to be one of the key intellectual assumptions of educated Westerners both in Europe and in America.[7]

It was in this intellectual climate, with its concern for constructing boundaries between "civilized" and "primitives," and with its wide acceptance of Social Darwinism, that the discipline of anthropology, dedicated to describing and explaining "their" cultures to "us," began to be professionalized.[8] At one and the same time, Native Americans, Australian aborigines, Pacific islanders, Asians, and Africans came to be the subjects of racist discourse, the victims of imperial expansion, and the objects of study of anthropology, the very existence of which was based on the assumption that "they" differed in fundamental ways from "us" and thus required explanation.

As anthropology took form as a discipline that claimed privileged expertise, evolutionism was perhaps the single most important influence molding it. As E. E. Evans-Pritchard has noted:

> Evolutionism . . . was more than a mere theory: it was a philosophy, a theodicy, a moral vision, a surrogate for religion. It saw in evolution and progress the key notions in which human life was to be interpreted. . . . Given such a vision it was quite inevitable that archaic "primitive" people would acquire a very special interest, no longer as curiosities, but as evidence about our own crucial evolutionary past. Anthropology, in effect, came into being as the time machine science.[9]

In addition to evolutionism, anthropology was also shaped by its embrace of the comparative method. This method involved comparing a range of presumedly similar items in an attempt to establish connections and relationships within the set. It had achieved marked successes during the first half of the nineteenth century in the fields of anatomy and zoology and in the study of philology and languages.[10] These significant achievements assured its appeal to practitioners of the new anthropology as they sought to establish linkages and relationships within the differing races of humankind.[11] Desk-bound anthropologists in London or Cambridge or Paris culled raw data from accounts of non-Western peoples written by explorers, travelers, traders, missionaries, and government administrators who were untrained as observers and predisposed to dwell upon the most exotic of strangers' customs. They then applied the comparative method to the material thus collected and drew from it a model of a developmental sequence of the history of human societies that was allegedly governed by "natural" laws of evolutionary change.[12] But it was not the evolution of techniques of fishing or of metallurgy or of agriculture that most fascinated educated Victorians. One aspect of human existence that preoccupied educated people of the time was the nature of kinship in non-Western societies, with its relationship to totemism and incest avoidance.[13] And, with the implications of Darwinian evolution then provoking a great crisis of religious faith among the educated, the intellectual life of "primitives," and especially their religious beliefs and practices, also attracted much attention.

Edward Tylor, the man considered the father of British anthropology, was typical, using both the evolutionist paradigm and the comparative method and being especially concerned with issues of "psychology." Having drawn his main ideas from a wide range of European scholars, Tylor published his seminal book on the mental life of nonliterate peoples, *Primitive Culture*, in 1871.[14] Tylor argued that the human intellect, like all of nature, was subject to organic laws that determined how it changed. Careful study of the phases of mankind's history as represented by peoples still living on earth could uncover these laws. These phases extended from the simple "savage," through the "primitive" and the "barbarous," and finally to the complex, apical, "civilized" stage, which, as it happened, was the bourgeois class of northwestern Europe during Tylor's lifetime: "The history of civilization teaches, that up to a certain point savages and barbarians are like what our ancestors were and our peasants still are, but from this common level the superior intellect of the progressive races has raised their nations to heights of culture."[15]

Of particular concern to Tylor were religion and morality, and, with *Primitive Culture* having laid out the basic priorities of the new discipline, Tylor's successors considered the exploration of the psychological lives of the people whom they studied as important as much for what they might indicate about Western people's own mental evolution as for their own sake. The broadly defined areas of "magic" and "religion" were especially fascinating, for it was widely believed that human intellectual development evolved along the "primitive"-"civilized" axis, from magic, through superstition and religion, to the scientific rationality so greatly admired by the positivist Western bourgeoisie of the nineteenth century. A central concern of anthropologists studying the races located at early stages of such progress on the lower levels of the racial hierarchy was, therefore, to find a general definition of "savage" or "primitive" *psychology*. In their evolutionist perspective, "savages" and "primitives" were "living fossils," the "living ancestors" of Western gentlemen, and therefore studies of contemporary "savages" based on the application of the comparative method had a special fascination to educated Westerners interested in learning about the roots of their own mental processes and psychology.[16]

Perhaps the most popular and influential of such evolutionist studies of supposed mental development was Sir James Frazer's *The Golden Bough*. Frazer believed that the proper approach to the study of "primitive" culture was through studying "primitives'" psychology for, he argued, all people formed the perceptions that governed their actions by exercising their mental capacities as they sought to explain the world in rational terms. Unfortunately, in Frazer's view, "primitives" had not gotten very far, and he depicted them as encased in a world of mystery and magic and with mental processes much inferior to those of his educated contemporaries.[17] Yet Frazer, an optimistic believer in the dynamism of evolutionary processes, also saw Reason as struggling with Superstition, with the ultimate victory guaranteed to Progress.

Toward the end of the nineteenth century, imperial expansion placed more and more reports of primitive peoples at the disposal of anthropologists and their synthesizing comparative method. In the process of establishing political control and trying to compel African peoples to work to produce goods for the world market, a profound shift in attitude regarding non-Westerners' capabilities occurred, moving swiftly from Frazerian optimism to dark pessimism. As this shift occurred, ever-more negative stereotypes of primitives and their presumed mental life and psychology arose. As we are concerned in this book with southern Africa, Dudley Kidd's *The Essential Kafir*, published in London in 1904 and enjoying wide circulation, can serve as an example of such anthropological reportage at the zenith of imperialism. In this book of over 400 pages Kidd sought to explain to whites the Africans of southeast Africa, an area defined as extending from the eastern Cape Province, northwards through Mozambique, the Rhodesias, and Nyasaland. He was very much a man of his times, accepting the evolutionist paradigm and using the comparative method. In commenting on certain African practices, he echoed Tylor's and Frazer's rejection of polygenesis and their acceptance of both human mental unity and differential development, noting that "when we come to understand the silliest of their customs we are surprised to find how it fits with human customs the whole world over, and forms some of the primordial stuff out of which modern European usages have evolved."[18]

Kidd's principal concern, however, was to explain the "essential spirit or personality of the Kafir," and he was convinced that he had managed to penetrate to the secrets of the Africans' mental life and psychology. The stereotyped African that emerged from his book must have satisfied the region's white settlers, as it conformed remarkably with the tenets of their own crude racism.[19] Kidd's notional African could not be trusted to be truthful, not out of malice, but simply because, "childlike," he could not grasp the importance of truth. His mental abilities were undeveloped. He had no sense of logic and was "capable of entertaining contradictory ideas at the same time." He lacked the ability to classify phenomena because he could not think in abstract terms. He was especially weak in grasping causal relationships.[20]

Kidd was not optimistic that Africans could "improve their minds" through Western-style education because the African was stalled irremediably at an early stage of development:

> Sometimes the native children are very precocious in the rapidity with which they absorb knowledge; but at puberty there generally comes a falling off in capacity, and the white boys then easily outdistance the black. The energy of the native seems to be absorbed in merely bodily functions—nutritive and sensual—as soon as he reaches the age of puberty, when the development of his brain, as a rule, comes to a standstill. . . . The fact of stunted mental development remains.[21]

As a significant corollary, Africans were not fit subjects for historical research because, being stunted and uncreative by nature, they neither possessed a history nor had any sense of change taking place with the passage of time. Although the evolutionist paradigm was explicitly situated *in* time, only the highest "civilizations" possessed a sense *of* time and were themselves dynamic.[22] Africans and other "primitives," by contrast, were hedged in by timeless, unchanging "customs" and "traditions." Kidd thought this fortunate because, being mentally stunted, the African could survive *only* through blindly following his society's customs:

From the moment that a Kafir baby is rocked, muling and puking, in
his mother's blanket . . . to the moment he is carried to his last long
home . . . his life is rigidly confined by the power of custom, as if by
some fated Destiny; all that is left for him is to spin more or less mer-
rily down the ringing grooves of custom.

Unsurprisingly, Kidd concludes with the complacent observation
that "the natives must be more or less the drudges of the white men,
owing to their inherent inferiority and incapacity." [23]

Kidd was undisturbed by the tensions implicit in his acceptance of
both a dynamic evolutionist model of humankind's history and a belief in Africans' intellectual stasis that was probably prompted by his
recognition of the needs of a rapidly industrializing South Africa for
cheap unskilled black labor for whom Western education would be
wholly "inappropriate." [24] Kidd was by no means exceptional. By the
turn of the century, with the establishment of colonial empires
throughout Africa, there was a growing feeling among whites that
"natives" differed essentially from them both psychologically and
intellectually and that earlier presumptions of possible African ad-
vancement were only well-intentioned illusions.

Such clearly racist ideas were not restricted to publicists for white
supremacy and colonialism. Just six years after the publication of
Kidd's *The Essential Kafir*, the eminent French philosopher Lucien
Lévy-Bruhl published his much translated and highly influential *Les
Fonctions Mentales dans les Sociétés Inférieures* (1910), a book significantly entitled in its English translation *How Natives Think*. Although far more scholarly in its trappings than Kidd's work, this
study nonetheless resonates strongly with Kidd's overtly racist formulations. Lévy-Bruhl had been influenced by the theory of "folk
psychology" that Wilhelm Wundt, the pioneer in experimental psychology, had developed at the University of Leipzig in the late nineteenth century.[25] This theory, derived from earlier romantic formulations of the "national soul," argued that the mental creations of a
"folk" community—its culture—could not be explained in terms of
the creative acts of individuals. They were, rather, the product of the
group, which cooperated actively both to transmit its traditions and
to constrain individuals to accept them.[26] Wundt's ideas about an
aggregate, nonpersonal folk consciousness directly influenced Lévy-
Bruhl's own intellectual development.

Lévy-Bruhl also used the comparative method in his work, marshaling as data whatever accounts of "primitive" peoples he could find. His aim was to explore the nature of the mental processes of peoples presumed to be characterized by "collective consciousness" and to compare these processes with those of "civilized" people, who thought individualistically. Following Wundt, Lévy-Bruhl claimed that the ideas of individuals counted for little amongst primitive peoples because they were necessarily overwhelmed by the collective consciousness: "Myths, funeral rites, agrarian practices, and the exercise of magic do not appear to originate in the desire for a rational explanation; they are the primitives' response to collective needs and sentiments which are profound and mighty and of compulsion." He concluded that Tylor and Frazer were wrong to assume that primitives possessed minds that sought—like "ours"—rational explanations for the world's phenomena and failed only because of mistakes that arose from their inferior positions in the hierarchy of races and on the path of evolutionary development.[27] For Lévy-Bruhl there was an essential, not merely accidental, difference between the minds of "us" and "them": "As soon as we take into consideration the collective nature of these ideas, the inadequacy of this [evolutionist] explanation is apparent. Being collective, they force themselves upon the individual; that is, they are to him an article of faith, not the product of his reason. . . . The mind of the 'primitive' has hardly any room for such questions as 'how?' and 'why?' "[28]

Primitives were also subject to what Lévy-Bruhl called "the law of participation," in terms of which they conceived of themselves as participating mystically in a universe permeated by magic.[29] This "law" shaped their mental processes in ways that did "not coincide with those which we are accustomed to describe in men of our type." Indeed, "the mentality of primitives, being mystic, is necessarily prelogical also: which means that, preoccupied above all with the mystic powers and properties of persons and things, it conceives of their relations under the law of participation without troubling about contradictions which rational thought cannot possibly tolerate." As Lévy-Bruhl said, "primitives perceive nothing in the same way as we do," and he would have readily agreed with Dudley Kidd's comment that "primitive" man was "as ignorant of logic as he is of the moons of Jupiter."[30]

Indeed, when, from his Parisian library, he turned his attention specifically to the Africans of South Africa in search of grist for his comparative mill, Lévy-Bruhl cited "evidence" from missionary and traveler accounts that might well have been used—or written—by Kidd. Of the Tswana:

> "To them thought is dead, so to speak, or at any rate they cannot raise it above the things of sense; . . . they are boors whose god is their belly."[31]

And of the "Hottentots":

> "Our friends in Europe would certainly regard the examples we could give of the mental sluggishness of these people in thinking, grasping and retaining, as absolutely incredible. Even I, who have known them so long, cannot help being surprised when I see how tremendously difficult it is for them to lay hold of the simplest truths, and above all, to reason anything out for themselves—and also how quickly they forget what they have taken in."[32]

It was from "evidence" such as this that Lévy-Bruhl, as Kidd had done six years earlier, concluded that "native children, especially where missionaries have succeeded in establishing schools, learn almost as quickly and well as our own, at least up to a certain age, when their development proceeds more slowly and then stops short."[33]

Although the ideas of Tylor, Frazer, Lévy-Bruhl, and others continued to shape popular Western perceptions of non-Western peoples for decades, contributing to the maintenance of boundaries between races and the perpetuation of racist stereotypes, by the beginning of the twentieth century profound methodological changes in anthropology altered the assumptions of its most serious practitioners. As colonial administrators began to take up their posts in the field, they found that the generalizations about "savages" and "primitives" that had been produced by the use of the comparative method were of little practical value. What they needed for effective administration was more precise information about specific peoples in actual colonial situations. Anthropologists, at that time becoming professionalized through new links with museums and universities, responded to this demand by shifting their emphasis from abstract theorizing toward gathering empirical evidence through intensive fieldwork within individual societies.[34]

This methodological "revolution" occurred on both sides of the

Atlantic. In America, Franz Boas vigorously attacked racist assumptions about "them," which he saw arising naturally from anthropology's acceptance of the evolutionist model and the comparative method. He argued that one could understand so-called primitives only if one situated them in their actual historical and material environment. Above all, one had to avoid shaping one's account of them to fit the demands of a preconceived model of a hierarchy of cultures assumed to be determined by the natural laws of evolutionist development.[35] For Boas, seeing non-Westerners on their own terms was crucial for understanding them, and it was largely through Boas's influence that the modern pluralist and relativist view of culture became dominant in American anthropology after World War I.[36] Paul Radin, one of Boas's students, for example, carried on his teacher's assault on the racism implicit in much of the anthropological writing of the time. Drawing on his own field experiences with Native Americans, he refuted Lévy-Bruhl's intellectualist notions of prelogicality and the commonly held view of primitives as being mere slaves of custom, arguing that "up to the present all attempts . . . to understand [natives], or to come to any reasonable adjustment with them, have met with signal failure, and this failure is in most instances due to the scientifically accredited theories of innate inferiority of primitive man in mentality and capacity for civilization quite as much as to prejudice and bias."[37] Radin and other anthropologists trained by Boas—such as Robert Lowie, Margaret Mead, and Ruth Benedict—went so far as to use the insights of cultural relativism to sustain a critique of American society as less rational and less humane than those of the much-spurned primitives.[38]

American scholars, whose field experience centered on the New World and the Pacific Basin, had, however, little direct impact on the study of southern Africa's people. Although Boasian ideas of cultural relativism were discussed in South Africa during the 1920s, the revolution that occurred in anthropological studies in this region flowed mainly from changes in Britain. Bronislaw Malinowski, who taught at the London School of Economics in the early 1920s, echoed Boas's call for intensive fieldwork. Culture had to be grasped as a coherent totality, he argued, and only by getting to know the practices and beliefs of a specific group of people at first hand could a student begin to understand its culture. From the 1920s onward, the British-ruled territories of southern Africa became important sites for the type of intensive fieldwork Malinowski advocated.

The shift from the primacy of theory elaborated in the library's armchair to fieldwork conducted in the village had, however, a contradictory impact upon formulation of the long-established opposition between "us" and "them." On the one hand, British anthropologists, like Boas's American students, quickly recognized that "primitives" were not primitive, possessing as they did complex systems of thought, language, and social institutions. In Malinowski's terms, these were both rational and logical, no matter how strange they initially appeared. The Boasian idea of cultural relativism was strongly reinforced by the demonstration that different cultures had different, but effective, ways of accomplishing common human goals. In this way anthropologists went far toward removing such pejorative tags as "savage" and "barbarous" from African cultures and toward undermining the hegemonic hold of the period's racism, at least on the minds of some better-educated people.[39]

On the other hand, Malinowski had also been trained by Wundt at Leipzig, and, like Lévy-Bruhl, he had largely accepted Wundt's notion of "folk psychology." This meant that Malinowski and his students tended to conceive of the societies they studied, not as aggregates of individuals, but in rather romantic terms as naturally integrated wholes—called tribes—that naturally resisted disintegration.[40] Thus the main focus of British social anthropology as it developed in southern Africa after World War I was on the society, not the individual, seeking to identify and analyze the *systems* of kinship, social relations, thought, and religion that served to reaffirm and preserve African "tribes." Their existence was governed by the normative "rules" and "laws" of their "tribal" systems, a notion at base not all that dissimilar to Kidd's "grooves of custom" and Lévy-Bruhl's "collective consciousness."

This emphasis on social cohesion, stability, and the pervasive importance of "custom" and "tradition" had profound implications for anthropological research in Africa. First, although the societies of southern Africa were in fact being rapidly and fundamentally transformed by capitalism and colonialism, anthropologists sought to uncover the enduring essence of the precapitalist, precolonial tribal systems, largely ignoring the impact of historical changes. So strong was this search for encompassing systems that A. R. Radcliffe-Brown, the doyen of British social anthropologists after Malinowski's death, explicitly rejected the need to study history when analyzing African societies, believing it was sufficient to study tribal systems synchronically to gain a correct understanding of tribal societies.[41] With a few exceptions, such as Max Gluckman, Hilda

Kuper, Isaac Schapera, and Godfrey Wilson, anthropologists operated on the working assumptions that tribal societies were naturally
"homeostatic" and that the more unaffected by change they were,
the more appropriate they were for study. For this reason they were
best observed in the isolation of their rural areas, where tribesmen
seemed to exist most purely outside time.[42]

A second implication of this emphasis was that issues of power
and power relationships were largely overlooked. In any society
power is subject to conflict, but because conflict is dynamic, working itself out over time, it did not readily lend itself to the synchronic
approaches that anthropologists favored or to any detailed analysis
during the relatively short periods of time devoted to field research.
Thus, aside from describing normatively defined ways of exercising
power, such as that of a man over his wife in a marriage relationship
or that of a chief over his people as judge and dispenser of land, there
was little attention devoted to the actual dynamics of power relationships. Indeed, conflicts over power were seen as dysfunctional to
the smooth operation of the systems that were assumed to regulate
tribal society and ensure tribal cohesion.[43]

The third effect of the anthropologists' use of the tribe as a unit of
study was to reinforce earlier tendencies to see Africans as lacking
individual initiative and creativity. The old oppositions of "civilized"-"primitive" and "European"-"native" were replaced by a new
one: "Westerner"-"tribesman." In effect, a new, less pejorative form
of the older stereotype was created in terms of which Africans were
defined as essentially rural people, out of place in the cities. It was
widely argued that they suffered when "detribalized" by city life and
that it was thus desirable to sustain tribal customs so as to ensure
that young Africans could be socialized into their proper tribal identities. These ideas have had a long history, underpinning indirect
rule throughout southern and central Africa until the end of the colonial period and then used in South Africa to legitimate the building of distinct ethnic ideologies molded during the era of segregation. Today these ideas continue to be used to justify apartheid and
"separate development."[44]

In sum, then, while the cultural relativism that arose from the acceptance of Malinowski's fieldwork methods and from Radcliffe-
Brown's emphasis upon the coherence of social structures weakened
the stigma that earlier anthropological work had placed upon being
primitive, it nonetheless continued the basic dichotomy between
them and us so central to nineteenth-century writings. By ignoring

history, by ignoring conflicts over power that were embedded in historical change, and by focusing on the systems that allegedly functioned to regulate tribal life, this work created idealized abstractions of "natives" whose cultures were molded by "customs" and permeated by stasis. Thus, when independence came to most areas of Africa in the late 1950s and 1960s, it came to peoples who were still conceived of as being essentially distinct from "us." In anthropology the terms of the binary oppositions used to express this division had changed from decade to decade, from "civilized"-"primitive," to "logical"-"prelogical," to "hot"-"cold," to "open"-"closed," and to "rational"-"irrational," among others.[45] But whatever the terms employed, the tradition of asserting a clear opposition between them and us had continued.

The movement towards political independence for much of sub-Saharan Africa that occurred after the Suez debacle of 1956 presented African studies with a profound intellectual challenge that its senior discipline, anthropology, was unable to handle. As sophisticated Africans negotiated their countries' independence in London and Paris, and as new states entered the United Nations as members of the world community, academic enquiry about Africa swiftly focused on the "roots of nationalism" and the nature of African politics. With its working assumption of African stasis, with its acceptance of the tribe as the appropriate unit of study, and with its preoccupation with kinship, anthropology could not explain what was behind the new African nation-state.

History could explain this, however, and it quickly became the dominant discipline within African studies. This shift is perhaps best symbolized by four publications that straddled British Prime Minister Harold Macmillan's famous "winds of change" speech and that, together, were crucial in establishing the primacy of history. Kenneth O. Dike, in his *Trade and Politics in the Niger Delta, 1830–1885* (Oxford, 1956), disproved the notion that precolonial Africans were "tribesmen" isolated from the wider world and stressed the importance of African initiative in shaping early relations with European imperialists. George Shepperson, in his *Independent African* (Edinburgh, 1958), showed that Africans had complex political and intellectual histories that careful research could uncover. In so doing, he inspired a host of studies exploring African resistance to colonialism and the sources of modern politics. The publication of the *Journal of African History* at the University of London from 1960 onward gave academic legitimation to African history, encouraging its establishment as a course of study in universities throughout Europe and America. And, finally, Jan Vansina's *De la Tradition Orale* (Tervuren, 1961) argued convincingly that even nonliterate Africans possessed recoverable histories and prompted scores of scholars to scour African villages to record oral traditions that were then used as the raw materials for new written histories. Following on these intellectual innovations and the spread of political independence in Africa came a broad change in attitude toward Africans and their history, with overt racism no longer publicly acceptable, even in white-ruled South Africa.

Anthropology also faced an additional political challenge from within Africa. With its long association with colonialism, its concern for the structures of the now irrelevant system of indirect rule and the tribe, and its oft-repeated rejection of the importance of African history for understanding the African experience, anthropology came under a cloud. Nationalists were frequently outspokenly hostile to it, and it was generally banished from the universities of newly independent African states unless relabeled with euphemisms such as "rural sociology." Plunged into a crisis of purpose, over the next two decades its practitioners came to accept the cardinal importance of historical changes and of dynamic struggles for power in shaping African societies.[46] They also sought to redefine anthropology's priorities, giving increased attention both to analyzing Western societies and, especially, to applying the approaches of the now hegemonic discipline of history to their studies of non-Western peoples. These changes undermined assumptions of static tribal systems regulated by functional rules, and anthropology's decades-old preoccupation with defining boundaries between us and them waned.[47] The concurrent achievements of oral historical research reinforced these changes, and the two disciplines gradually moved closer together, both in their methods and in their research agendas.[48]

Yet, despite the obvious advances achieved in the study of African history, scholarship's ancient project of defining boundaries between us and them has persisted down to the present, this time rooted in the unlikely field of literary criticism.[49] The starting point for this unexpected departure was Milman Parry's innovative research on the Homeric tradition carried out in the 1920s and 1930s. Because most of Parry's work remained either unpublished or not readily accessible, however, it was only in 1960, when his acolyte and disciple

Albert Lord published his *Singer of Tales*, that Parry's principal hypotheses were brought to the attention of a wider audience.[50]

Parry's original concern was the hotly debated question of the authorship of Homer's works.[51] Inspired by the earlier research of Meillet and van Gennep,[52] Parry analyzed the prosodic structure of the *Iliad* and the *Odyssey* and reached the startling conclusion that, in the words of Walter Ong, "virtually every distinctive feature of Homeric poetry is due to the economy enforced in it by oral methods of composition."[53] According to Parry's theory, the Homeric epics were composed *during performance* in a poetic language shaped by the requirements of singing in verse. What made this possible, given the constrictions of the Greek hexameter verse form, was that Homer could draw constantly on a wide repertoire of traditional and largely predictable verbal formulas.[54] Parry defined his centrally important notion of the "formula" as "*a group of words which is regularly employed under the same metrical condition to express a given essential idea.*"[55] At its simplest level, this meant that Homer had available to him a limited number of standardized epithets for "Achilles," or "wine," or "the sea," and that his choice of words was determined not so much by the sense as by the metrical needs of the moment. Parry also claimed that his oral formulaic theory was able to explain the dialect-mix of Homer's style and the apparent aberrations in his meter and that this made obsolete the old debate about single or multiple authorship.

Parry offered a vision of Homer's style that stressed naturalness, directness, and convenience. As Adam Parry stressed in a summary of his father's achievements, Milman Parry was very much a child of his age, his enthusiasm for a language "directly expressive of heroic ideals," reminding us "of Hemingway finding courage and beauty in the vision of the Spanish bullfighters, or of T. E. Lawrence (one of Parry's favorite authors) finding a more satisfactory theatre of self-realization in the austere simplicities of Arab life."[56] But he acknowledged that intuition and feelings were no substitutes for empirical evidence, and he sought to verify his theories about Homeric technique by studying contemporary Slavic epics, which he viewed as part of a "still living oral poetry" descending from the tradition in which Homer flourished. He discovered repeated phrases in the Slavic epics, proclaimed them "formulae," and asserted that "*oral poetry is formulaic and traditional.*" In one of his most influential essays, published two years before his death, he made the vital distinction that was later elaborated by Albert Lord and adopted by their many followers:

> The critics, groping for the rules by which they should group and separate the varied works of the world's literature, have come to see more or less clearly that literature falls into two great parts, but they have not yet agreed upon the real nature of these two parts, nor upon the terms which should be applied to them. "Heroic" is one of the attempts to find the term for the first part. Others have chosen "popular" or "primitive." "Natural" was one of the first tries, and was given up largely because of the romantic notions of those who sought to apply it. . . . There is surely much truth in each one of these names, but I think that no one of them goes deep enough: in each case there is the failure to see that literature falls into two great parts not so much because there are two kinds of culture, but because there are two kinds of *form: the one part of literature is oral, the other written.*[57]

The debate following Lord's persuasive presentation of Parry's theories has been enormously influential, generating a large bibliography and encompassing many literatures, both ancient and modern. In the process, largely as a consequence of ambiguities in Parry's original elaboration of his ideas, his work has inspired the growth of two strikingly different—but not necessarily wholly mutually exclusive—schools of interpretation, each claiming direct descent from Parry's work as interpreted and popularized by Lord.

The first of these schools is able to claim Parry as its founder because of the ambiguous manner with which he dealt with the relationship of style to thought. Parry defined his cardinal concept, the "formula," as expressing a "given essential idea." For him, style was "the form of thought."[58] Albert Lord describes it as "the offspring of the marriage of thought and sung verse. Whereas thought, in theory at least, may be free, sung verse imposes restrictions, varying in degree of rigidity from culture to culture, that shape the form of thought."[59] Thus Parry could readily be construed as conflating style with thought, and several scholars have used this idea to formulate a fresh opposition between "us" and "them" to replace the fading ones inspired by earlier anthropology.

The intellectual history of this first school claiming inspiration from Parry has been both complex and circuitous. In the late 1930s Marshall McLuhan, then an ardent disciple of I. A. Richards and

F. R. Leavis, supervised the Ph.D. dissertation of the Reverend Walter Ong, S.J.[60] At McLuhan's urging, Ong later turned to studying the Renaissance theologian Peter Ramus.[61] In his first major book, *Ramus, Method, and the Decay of Dialogue* (1958), Ong argued that, as a consequence of Gutenburg's invention of printing, Western culture shifted from a primarily aural mode of perceiving reality to a primarily spatial, or visual, mode.[62] Ong's idea appealed greatly to his former teacher, who, as both ardent Roman Catholic and committed social conservative, was appalled at the erosion of Western cultural values that he considered to be then taking place as a result of the attack on literacy by radio and television.

McLuhan was at the time working on a book surveying the cultural changes brought about by the introduction of printing and literacy, and he incorporated Ong's hypothesis as a central element in his interpretation. In 1962 *The Gutenburg Galaxy* was published. It is a squirrel's nest of a book that consists of a mass of direct quotations from almost two hundred authors with McLuhan's own ruminations interspersed to form a rough approximation of an argument.[63] Among the dozens of authors from whom McLuhan quoted were his own former student Walter Ong, the psychiatrist J. C. Carothers, and, giving them a central prominence, Milman Parry and Albert Lord. Indeed, McLuhan claimed in the book's very first sentence that it was "complementary" to the work of Parry and Lord.[64]

Parry and Lord had been primarily concerned with contrasting the styles of oral and written poetry and had dealt especially with the techniques of oral composition and the creativity of the oral poet. McLuhan, however, seized upon the idea implicit in Parry's notion that oral poets thought in a special way because they belonged to oral cultures and made his principal concern "the *forms* of thought and organization of experience in society and politics" that he thought he detected among oral peoples.[65] In effect, McLuhan moved from Parry's discussion of style in cultural forms to his own conclusions about group psychology and ways of thinking, a latter-day Lévy-Bruhl. Most especially, he wanted to explore the impact of the invention of printing and the spread of literacy upon Western culture as well as the contemporary deleterious influence of electronic media such as radio and television on literate culture.

As a device for forcefully presenting his argument, McLuhan created a notional nonliterate—or "oral"—man and a notional literate man, and his choice for the typical "oral man" was what he assumed to be a "typical" nonliterate African. Indeed, his stereotyped African was for him so compelling—and frightening—that he argued that the printed word had a "crucial role in staying the return to the Africa within" us all, a return to the intellectual darkness of the oral world.[66] He sketched an African that Sir James Frazer, Dudley Kidd, or, especially, Lucien Lévy-Bruhl would have easily recognized. Although McLuhan claimed the literary critics Parry and Lord as his principal intellectual mentors for his book, he actually cobbled together his caricature of oral man from a range of sources that had nothing whatsoever to do with literature or literary criticism.

Central among these sources was the work of J. C. Carothers, whose career had included being head of the Mathari Mental Hospital, near Nairobi, between 1938 and 1950, and who had elaborated his ideas about African intellectual life in *The African Mind in Health and Disease* (1953) and in a report produced for the Kenyan colonial administration, *The Psychology of Mau Mau* (Nairobi, 1954). McLuhan's decision to rely on Carothers as a major source was significant in that Carothers's own work had depended on earlier publications by, among others, Dudley Kidd and Lucien Lévy-Bruhl. For Carothers, as for Kidd, it was evident that the "psychology of the African is essentially the psychology of the African child. The pattern of his mental development is defined by the time he reaches adolescence, and little remains to be said."[67] Unquestioningly accepting such arguments, McLuhan quoted from Carothers that an African

"comes to regard himself as a rather insignificant part of a much larger organism—the family or the clan—and not as an independent, self-reliant unit; personal initiative and ambition are permitted little outlet; and a meaningful integration of a man's experience on individual, personal lines is not achieved. By contrast to the constriction at the intellectual level, great freedom is allowed for at the temperamental level."[68]

McLuhan concluded that "our notions of the 'uninhibited' native ignore the utter inhibition and suppression of his mental and personal life which is unavoidable in a non-literate world."[69]

Contrasting an African child's world with the orderly world of a literate Western child, McLuhan claimed that "the African child lives in the implicit, magical world of the resonant oral world. He encounters not efficient causes but formal causes of configurational fields such as any non-literate society cultivates." Should an African balk at the constraints of the "customs" he has imbibed in growing up, he would be in deep trouble:

> "Since all behaviour in such societies is governed and conceived on highly social lines, and since directed thinking can hardly be other than personal and unique for an individual, it is furthermore implicit in the attitude of these societies that the very possibility of such thinking is hardly to be recognized. Therefore, if and when such thinking does occur . . . it is apt to be seen as deriving from the devil or from other external evil sources, and as something to be feared and shunned."

McLuhan concluded that "nothing can exceed the automatism and rigidity of an oral, non-literate community in its non-personal collectivity."[70]

Ironically, given his self-proclaimed indebtedness to Parry and Lord, he was effectively standing them on their heads. Their work had been dedicated to demonstrating the creativity of the oral artist, beginning with Homer's masterpieces, while McLuhan's emphasized the paralyzing rigidity of oral man in dealing with anything beyond his personal relationships. McLuhan so thoroughly believed that Africans lacked imagination that he claimed that "the native of Ghana cannot accept a film about Nigerians. He cannot generalize his experience from film to film, such is the depth of involvement in particular experiences."[71] McLuhan's psychological caricature of the nonliterate African was based on no personal knowledge of or research about African societies. Yet his message enjoyed a wide readership, and, just as the old boundaries between peoples that had been derived from anthropology were falling, he was successfully erecting new ones, this time between the literate and the "oral." Ironically, his insistence on literacy as a determinant characteristic of human history occurred at precisely the moment when archeologists and anthropologists, who had so long argued for the crucial importance of literacy for "civilization," were themselves abandoning that position.[72]

The next major contributor to the construction of the novel notion of oral man was Eric Havelock, a classicist who was a colleague, friend, and advisor to McLuhan when both taught at the University of Toronto.[73] Havelock published his *Preface to Plato* in 1963. He sought to explain why Plato, although obviously a cultured man, wanted to banish poetry from his ideal republic. His conclusion was that Plato was the "prophet" of a new way of thinking to be based on literacy. Thus he repudiated the old modalities of thought that were embedded in oral poetry.[74] Havelock's conflation of the technology of writing with the human psyche was total and his debt to Parry clearly stated: "I turned to the work of Milman Parry and thought I saw the outline of the answer. . . . The formulaic style characteristic of oral composition represented not merely certain verbal and metrical habits but also a cast of thought, or a *mental condition*."[75] Havelock also credited Lévy-Bruhl with being an important influence upon his understanding of oral ways of thinking. Following Lévy-Bruhl, Havelock argued that the oral ambience of Greece before 430 B.C. stultified independent thought by making "a common consciousness and a common set of values" paramount.[76] The blame for this lay with the poets. It was poetry—and especially Homer's poetry—that served as the means of both education and indoctrination in pre-Platonic Greece: "Oral verse was the instrument of cultural indoctrination, the ultimate purpose of which was the preservation of group identity. It was selected for this role because, in the absence of the written record, its rhythms and formulas provided the sole mechanism of recall and re-use."[77] As such, Havelock stressed, the task of education in nonliterate cultures "could be described as putting the whole community into a formulaic state of mind." Plato became the resisted liberator of Greeks psychologically beguiled by the sorcery of their oral poets. For Havelock, the "Homeric audience submitted gratefully to the hypnotism of another." Homer was little better than a supplier of a psychological opiate, able to give his auditors "not only pleasure but a specific kind of pleasure on which they came to depend, for it meant relief from anxiety and assuagement of grief. It is this power . . . of which the poet is most conscious, and naturally so, for, although he might be consulted in his didactic role as a source of knowledge and guidance, he was far more continuously applauded as the great releaser."[78] As in the cases of Tylor, Frazer, Lévy-Bruhl, and McLuhan, Havelock had no direct experience of dealing with the oral men about whom all wrote with such remarkable confidence.[79]

By contrast, the next major contributor to the reification and mystification of "oral man," Jack Goody, is an anthropologist with a record of fieldwork in West Africa. Interested in reconciling anthropology with history and seeking to introduce a dynamic thrust into his studies, Goody, in his *Domestication of the Savage Mind* (1977), developed earlier ideas about literacy that dated to his work in the

1960s. Although critical of the long tradition of binary oppositions between us and them, his criticism was primarily directed, not at the fact of oppositions, but only at their absolute nature—their inflexibility—which had resulted in a neglect of dynamic social changes experienced by such peoples as they move from one condition to the next. Such oppositions as "logical"-"prelogical" or "hot"-"cold" simply were not subtle enough to account for the transitions that one found in actual history. The opposition between literacy and nonliteracy, however, avoids such inflexibility, Goody argued, because it allows for nonliterate people to acquire writing over time and to change fundamentally, albeit gradually. Literacy, in effect, "made it possible to scrutinise discourse . . . this scrutiny favoured the increase in scope of critical activity, and hence of rationality, scepticism, and logic. . . . It increased the potentialities of criticism because writing laid out discourse before one's eyes in a different kind of way; at the same time [it] increased the potentiality for cumulative knowledge. . . . No longer did the problem of memory storage dominate man's intellectual life." [80]

Goody's main concern was with the impact of writing itself, and he discussed at length lists, recipes, formulas, and other forms of writing.[81] His primary concern was *not* with assessing nonliterate, oral man. But he had to say something about the "before" stage of his evolutionist model. In line with earlier functionalist anthropologists, Goody argued that oral societies tend "towards cultural homeostasis"—towards cultural balance.[82] In approaching the centrally important question of whether or not creative intellectuals could exist in societies tending towards such stasis—the very core of the work of Parry and Lord—Goody wavered, observing that "one cannot imagine a novel or a symphony in a society without writing, even though one finds narrative and orchestra." [83] He then overcame his hesitancy and resolved his conflict, not by acknowledging that intellectuals do exist in oral societies, but by citing the work of Parry and Lord. Their argument that "oral narrative is composed during the performance" was sufficient for him to prove the existence of intellectuals in oral societies.[84] Once again, the emphasis was on form and technique, not content.

Unlike McLuhan and Havelock, Goody was extremely cautious, carefully avoiding generalizations about any notional oral man, aside from his assertion about the tendency of oral societies toward homeostasis. His true importance lies, then, in the fact that while McLuhan had only doubtful claims to respectability and while

Havelock wrote in a highly conjectural way about the distant world of ancient Greece, Goody gave scholarly legitimation to oral man as a contemporary phenomenon meriting serious attention, thereby encouraging scholars to continue to draw sharp boundaries between literate and nonliterate societies.

Walter Ong, McLuhan's former student, is the fourth significant figure in the contemporary evolution of the notion of oral man. As a consequence of his early study of Ramus, Ong became keenly interested in the interface of nonwritten and written languages, and he also came to acknowledge the work of Parry and Lord as seminal in shaping his own views.[85] Ong, seeing "a deeper stratum of meaning" in Parry's concept of the formula, agreed with McLuhan and Havelock that it should apply not merely to oral poetry but, far more tellingly, to the realm of thought. Seizing on Parry's words about a formula's expressing "a given essential idea," Ong moved beyond Parry's preoccupation with style and offered formulas that have little to do with meter and everything to do with thought. As in his earlier *Interfaces of the Word* (1977), his theme in *Orality and Literacy* (1982) was the "phenomenological history of culture and consciousness," and he sought to explain the "psychodynamics of oral cultures."[86]

He begins with the irony that everyone reading his book will be literate. He challenges the reader to enter a world in which there is language but no signs (and no dictionary). Knowledge is something quite separate from study, and thought is preserved in mnemonic patterns, in formulas and formulaic expressions that have to be repeated to keep thought alive. Oral expression is characterized by simple additive sentences rather than by complex subordinate ones. It prefers standardized epithets to original ones, and it ensures that its audience is keeping up with what is said by constantly repeating the main points. It is far more concerned with the conservation of knowledge than with speculation, sticking closely to human activity and showing little interest in or capacity for abstract thought. It tends to present the past in terms of simple conflict, but it lives very much in the present, tradition representing a codification of an oral society's present values rather than genuine curiosity about the past.[87]

Associated with these distinctions between literate people and oral man are even larger hypotheses. Following Goody—and echoing both Frazer and Lévy-Bruhl—Ong presents the shift from orality to literacy, though occurring at different stages in different societies, as representing *the* fundamental turning point in human history. "More than any single invention," he claims, "writing has transformed human consciousness." It underlies the shift from "magic to science . . . from the so-called 'pre-logical' to the more and more rational state of consciousness . . . from Lévi-Strauss's 'savage' mind to domesticated thought."[88] Ong's formulas, then—including "formulaic expressions" and "formulaic clusters," by which he means the often unconscious patterns of narrative and imagery—are the methods by which *knowledge* is preserved and transmitted in preliterate societies.

This theory has certain attractions for the student of Africa. By shifting the emphasis from form to content, it appears to place oral literature at the very center of African intellectual life. The shift is accomplished, however, only by overthrowing everything Parry and Lord had asserted about the creativity of the oral poet. Instead the poet assumes the role described by McLuhan and Havelock of preserver of the values of the ancestors, the stock figure of anthropologists of decades past. The formulas are not there to aid him in his composition but are the very substance of his performance. Though Ong denies implying a return to older ideas of the static transmitted text, he writes of "mnemonics," and the most he will allow the poet is a certain reshuffling of formulas under the pressure of new situations.[89] Thus, we have two contrasting descriptions of the oral performer, Lord's and Ong's, both accurately claiming Milman Parry's intellectual paternity.

The fact is that Ong—unlike Parry and Lord, but very much like McLuhan, Havelock, and Goody—is only peripherally concerned with oral literature. Not only does he impose on all its varied forms—the memorized proverb, the riddle coining new metaphors, the story narrated to entertain, the praise poem discussing power—a single, reductionist critical framework, he conflates it with orality in general, denying the validity of the term *oral literature* and making his version of the formula the basis of *all* nonliterate discourse.[90] He cushions the rough edges of his argument by showing that some oral habits continue in literate societies and by talking about the wisdom of the peasantry. But at bottom what Ong has crafted is yet another version of the old stereotype of oral man that claims to be a representation of reality. Citing Goody, he asserts that oral societies are "characterized as homeostatic," living "very much in a present which keeps itself in equilibrium or homeostasis by sloughing off memories which no longer have present relevance."[91] Ong's oral men worldwide are trapped in an endless cycle of repetition until, one day, their history takes off with the invention or importation of signs.

Plainly, the introduction of literacy to much of southern Africa during the nineteenth and twentieth centuries did mark an important shift in what could be done and by whom. Yet Ong's model offers us no handle on the history of orality until that point or on the subsequent development of oral performance (often in interaction with literates), and his vision of oral communities locked into traditionalism by a determining orality is hopelessly at odds with the actual history of southern Africa over the past two hundred years.[92] Ong's argument, in fact, is only a slightly more sophisticated version of McLuhan's preposterous reformulation of Mendelssohn's vision of 1840:

> Until WRITING was invented, we lived in acoustic space, where all backward peoples still live: boundless, directionless, horizonless, the dark of the mind, the world of emotion, primordial intuition, mafia-ridden. . . . A goose quill put an end to talk, abolished mystery, gave us enclosed space and towns, brought roads and armies and bureaucracies. It was the basic metaphor with which the cycle of CIVILIZATION began, the step from the dark into the light of the mind.[93]

The argument has indeed moved a long way since Parry, the romantic, identified Homer's *virtues* as those of preliteracy!

While McLuhan, Havelock, Goody, and Ong all invoked Parry's work in the creation of their various stereotypes of a homeostatic oral man, others have built on Parry's work to establish a second, far different, school of criticism. As the romantic title of Lord's book, *The Singer of Tales*, indicates and as Parry always insisted, the whole point of studying oral poetry is to understand and appreciate the individual oral artist's enviable genius:

> The art of narrative song was perfected, and I use the word advisedly, long before the invention of writing. It has no need for stylus or brush to become a complete artistic and literary medium. Even its geniuses are not straining their bonds, longing to be free from its captivity, eager for their liberation by writing. When writing was introduced, epic singers, again even the most brilliant of them, did not realize its "pos-

sibilities" and did not rush to avail themselves of it. Perhaps they were wiser than we, because one cannot write song. One cannot lead Proteus captive; to bind him is to destroy him.[94]

Albert Lord's book was immensely influential. Its positive, enthusiastic depiction of the literature of a non-Western society both caught the imagination of a generation of literary scholars and resonated well with attitudes of the 1960s, an era of decolonization and new respect for the cultures of Africa, Asia, and Latin America reflected by, among other things, the creation of the Peace Corps and other agencies extending foreign aid. Yet despite its clear superiority over the approach of McLuhan and his followers in the uses it makes of Parry's original ideas, the vision of oral poetry popularized by Lord is nevertheless flawed. Once again, the flaw arises from the imprecision of Parry's original formulations.

In his first research, Parry stated that he was specifically studying the southeastern European oral epic poem. But there was always a tendency for him to push beyond this narrow focus in pursuit of more widely applicable generalizations and towards a universal theory of oral literature. Lord, too, began with a narrow focus, but he has been similarly imperial in his writing, claiming first that Parry's oral formulaic theories are valid for "all story poetry"[95] and subsequently welcoming its application to all oral poetry/literature. What began as a hypothesis about the making of Homeric verse has come, since the 1960s, to be applied, first, to all oral poetry, whether composed in hexameters or their equivalent or not, and, second, to all oral literature—praise poems, songs, narratives, moralities, proverbs, tables, and riddles. Oral literature as a worldwide phenomenon has come to be *defined* as literature composed in performance through the manipulation of formulas and formulaic expressions. It has thus come to be seen as a genre in its own right and as an appropriate subject for a revival of the epistemologically unreliable comparative method. The link between the separate "literatures" of the world came to lie in their common techniques of composition, while criticism, in Ruth Finnegan's words, confined itself to the "study of detailed stylistic points and formulaic systems leading to statistical conclusions."[96]

With specific regard to Africa, most research on oral literature in recent years by scholars such as Harold Scheub, Jeff Opland, Isidore Okpewho, Donald Cosentino, and Elizabeth Gunner has been inspired by Albert Lord.[97] Despite their reservations on some issues, these scholars can be fairly described as working within the Parry-Lord tradition. Thus, just as Parry tested his conclusions about Homer by examining modern Serbo-Croatian narratives, Jeff Opland has used his study of performed Xhosa praise poetry to illuminate Anglo-Saxon literature, while Isidore Okpewho has attempted to extend the traditions of Balkan oral literature described in Lord's *The Singer of Tales* to include narratives from West Africa.[98] Even Ruth Finnegan, to whose monumental *Oral Literature in Africa* (1970) and *Oral Poetry* (1977) all scholars are deeply indebted, and who has subjected the Parry-Lord theories to the most searching empirical analysis, has been content as critic and anthologist to treat oral poetry comparatively as a worldwide phenomenon. Her role has been to debunk all reductive theories by demonstrating the endless variety of forms and practices oral poetry may assume. Martin Mueller, for example, has recently paid tribute to the "great service" Finnegan has done for Homeric scholarship "by proving that the Parry-Lord theory in its rigid form is a myth that does not fit the facts. She surveyed a wide range of oral literature, differing in genre, social function and geographical origin, and demonstrated beyond any reasonable doubt that it is impossible to identify a set of traits common to all oral literature."[99] Yet, as she repeatedly acknowledges, she has no new theory to put forward and in that sense has remained constrained by the tradition she is questioning.[100] Only in her first book, the delightful *Limba Stories and Storytelling* (1967), does she relate in any detail the literature to the society that values it.

The emphasis upon the creativity of the oral performer that has been stimulated by the work of Parry and Lord has revolutionized the study of praise poetry and narratives, shifting attention away from the stultifying realms of the "collective consciousness" and the timeless "text" and toward the individual artist and the act of creation. The oral poet or narrator is seen no longer as a mere "memorizer," but as an artist, improvising brilliantly within the formulas of his or her tradition. These are attractive arguments. Not only are they consistent with the obvious fact of the historicity of oral literary traditions, but they also insist forcibly on the nature of literature *as* literature, putting the creativity of the performer at the center of our attention.

Yet the problems in trying to apply oral formulaic theory to African oral poetry have persisted because of the lack of supporting evidence. As Finnegan has pointed out, the determining power of the Greek hexameter line for Homer has no equivalent in Africa. While

Opland has countered that "the quest for metre in southeastern Bantu is not yet concluded,"[101] no one has yet discovered a poem or narrative in an African version of Greek hexameters or Serbo-Croatian decasyllabics. On present evidence there seems to be no expectation that the poet should perform in strict meter and no need for him or her to have available formulas, in Parry's phrase, groups "of words . . . regularly employed under the same metrical conditions to express a given essential idea." Faced with such evidence, Albert Lord has shown himself willing to dispense with the need for "metrical conditions" and to redefine formulas as "any repeated word groups." These repeated words or phrases may occur within a single poem, or within a single poet's repertoire, or within the tradition to which the performer belongs. What makes such repetitions "formulas" is that they are "useful" to the oral poet as he composes his work in performance. As such, they are quite different from repeated phrases that may occur in written poetry. Formulas are those repetitions which are functional to oral composition and "are not marked as such by repetition alone."[102]

Lord is certainly correct in noting that oral poetry contains a high degree of repetition—more so even than is often apparent from written transcriptions, from which repetitions are often excised. But it is hard to see how their function can be identified with such confidence, or how they can be separated from other functions they may serve. No poems anywhere contain more straightforward repetitions than an ordinary African work song, in which a group of two or three lines may be repeated for half an hour at a stretch with only minimal variations. A written transcription of one of these songs would show a very high percentage of apparent formulas. Yet the "function" in this case is not stylistic but to provide a rhythm for communal labor, and the song lasts as long as the task does or until a different work song is taken up. In complete contrast, one of the most famous versions of the praises (*izibongo*; sing., *isibongo*) of Shaka, the founder of the Zulu empire, contains as the climax to a catalogue of Shaka's victories the following set of praises:

> He who while devouring some devoured others
> And as he devoured others he devoured some more;
> He who while devouring some devoured others
> And as he devoured others he devoured some more;
> He who while devouring some devoured others
> And as he devoured others he devoured some more;

> He who while devouring some devoured others
> And as he devoured others he devoured some more;
> He who while devouring some devoured others
> And as he devoured others he devoured some more.[103]

The repetitions here convey the same dramatic finality as King Lear's five trochaic "nevers" as he holds the dead Cordelia in his arms.

Between these extremes of the work song and the Nguni *izibongo* may be placed most African oral poetry, the repetition either serving some extraliterary function such as to provide the rhythm for pounding maize, paddling a canoe, or performing a communal dance, or, more frequently, being deployed for dramatic or aesthetic purposes. There is nothing surprising about this. Repetition—of words, phrases, phrase patterns, rhythms, or of sounds in the form of rhyme, assonance, or alliteration—is characteristic of *all* poetry, whether oral or written. Without some pattern of repetition, some underlying grammar or shape, it is doubtful whether one could recognize the piece in question as a poem. But such repetitions are never purely repetitive. Hearing a phrase for the second time is not the same as hearing it for the first time. In oral performance, the tone changes, the drumming has a different beat, the dance is at a different stage, a climax is being reached or has just receded, and so on. As in a Handelian da-capo aria, a concerto's cadenza, or a jazz solo (or, indeed, in a Tennysonian lyric), variation within the pattern for dramatic or aesthetic effect is one of the artist's main resources. To transcribe such a performance, counting the verbal repetitions to support a presumption about techniques of composition, is thus to misrepresent the performer's art. It is not surprising that a definition of the "formula" has proved so elusive.

Related to this central problem are two further issues. The first is that comparatively little African oral poetry is in fact performed in circumstances approximating those of Lord's traditional artist. African storytellers, their audience at their feet, obviously exist and their art has been widely studied.[104] But, allowing for the exceptions to all such generalizations, such storytellers normally operate in prose, not poetry, and the conventions governing their performance have more to do with the shape of the narrative than with repeated patterns of language. Of the oral poetry considered in this book, only the *migodo* (sing., *ngodo*) of the Chopi people of Mozambique were performed specifically to entertain an audience, and the performers were whole companies of musicians, singers, and dancers. The praise poems we discuss were chanted by professional or semi-professional praise poets (*izimbongi;* sing., *imbongi*) in a wide variety of situations but always with a social and political intent, the poet's art serving a public end. Finally, the work songs, dance songs, and songs of spirit possession that are dealt with in our remaining chapters were sung, or sung and danced, communally with no obvious demarcation between performer and audience.

The second additional problem with oral formulaic theory—and one that is also critically important in assessing the validity of the notion of oral man as elaborated by McLuhan, Havelock, Goody, and Ong—is that much of the oral poetry that we discuss in this volume was demonstrably *not* composed in performance.[105] It is curious that scholars have been willing to work with a definition of oral literature that, through its stress on extemporaneity, must necessarily result in the exclusion of so much African oral material. What are we to call the songs of the Chopi *migodo* or the Zambian *kalela* dance that are carefully composed well in advance of performance, meticulously rehearsed, and sung to musical accompaniment? Or the songs accompanying the rituals of spirit possession? Or, indeed, all those wedding songs, funeral songs, beer songs, pounding songs, work songs, dance songs, and satiric-political songs that are well known over wide areas or over long periods of time precisely because they have become popular?

In a paper presented at a conference on oral literature and the formula in 1974 Ruth Finnegan made a spirited attack on the "rigid distinction between written and oral poetry," demonstrating that the interaction between oral and written forms has been characteristic of several African cultures and providing a wealth of instances from Somalia, Gambia, Sudan, and Zambia of songs formally composed by experts and memorized for reperformance by others. Her argument drew from Albert Lord a reply that makes one blink in disbelief: "the kind of composition in which the singer makes up a song orally, and doesn't commit it to writing, but commits it to memory, may not be oral composition, but rather written composition without writing."[106]

Just how damaging the break oral formulaic theory makes with reality may also be illustrated more concretely by an episode reported in Opland's *Xhosa Oral Poetry.* Opland describes how, in March 1977, he arranged for Chief S. M. Burns-Ncamashe to perform as part of the ceremonials during the installation of Dr. Ian

Mackenzie as the new chancellor of Rhodes University.[107] Chief Burns-Ncamashe was asked to submit a text in advance to be printed in the official program, and, on the basis of the information provided to him about Mackenzie, he complied with a poem which Opland prints. At the actual ceremony, however, Burns-Ncamashe departed from his prepared text in two important ways. First, he commented on Cecil Rhodes, the university's eponym:

> You know him, you crowd of whites:
> Cecil's the beast of Rhodes,
> The thing who crossed the sea to come to this country
> Carrying a trowel and a shovel;
> He dug mines and money appeared,
> Gold appeared and was refined;
> He took the money and shut it in banks;
> When he scooped it, he did so with bowls and buckets
> And he built this village whose name we say:
> It is Rhodes University.

Second, he commented on the absence, in an apartheid society, of black students at the university:

> It is Rhodes University,
> A deep river with deep waters.
> There the children of the white swim.
> They go to it at the call of *gqoloma* and *chanti*
> And they leave it wearing gowns and hoods,
> And they leave it as experts and sages,
> Knowing everything from top to bottom.
> I plead for myself, then, homestead of the whites:
> I plead also for the black peoples;
> I say open the door, Zimwongile!
> The son of Henderson has finished with you.
> Open the door and let blacks enter,
> Let them drink from the fountain!
> Let them drink from this water!
> I disappear!

The occasion Opland describes is a bizarre one, made no less bizarre by his own explanatory note in the official program: "There is good reason to believe that in traditional Xhosa society the tribal poet's eulogy of his chief ensured the sympathetic attention of the chief's ancestors to the welfare of the chief and (through him) of the chiefdom." A Xhosa chief wearing academic dress and a headband of beads was being invited to invoke the Xhosa ancestors at a ceremonial at an all-white university before an audience to whom the performance, in the most charitable of interpretations, was little more than a piece of agreeable local color.

Yet Opland's discussion of the two texts focuses only on their contribution to oral formulaic theory. His program note records that "the Xhosa tribal poet today has no concept of a fixed text" and his comments treat Burns-Ncamashe's departure from the text submitted to the organizing committee as proof that the oral poet composes in performance. What eludes him and invalidates his argument is the obvious hypothesis: that Burns-Ncamashe, a well-educated politician, has his own game to play with Rhodes University—and that he may well have been unwilling to disclose in advance what he *meant* to say and that the two poems were never intended to be the same. Opland's preoccupation with oral formulaic theory became the camouflage behind which the poet outwitted his sponsors, using the occasion to attack economic injustice and educational apartheid in South Africa.

In the introduction to *The Singer of Tales*, Lord quotes from Parry's last, unfinished manuscript to the effect that his research is "a starting point for a comparative study of oral poetry which sought to see how the way of life of a people gives rise to a poetry of a given kind and a given degree of excellence." We have been tempted to present our own study as building on this foundation, especially given Lord's acknowledgment that this is a topic he has "not fully entered upon." [108] Yet the debate has been flawed from the beginning by the terms of Parry's original formulation. By insisting on the determinancy of *"form: the one part of literature is oral, the other written,"* Parry effectively broke the link between performance and history. That it is essential to restore that link in studying the oral poetry of south-central Africa is the theme of this volume.

For both the Homeric epics and the Serbo-Croatian heroic poems, where the notion of the "formula" began with the work of Milman Parry and Albert Lord, the task has already begun. Martin Mueller has stressed the originality of the author of *The Iliad* and rejected the leg-irons of formulaic theory. David Shive, in a recent study of Homer's work, has called into question the very reality of the formula, seeking "to help cure Homer of blindness and put a pen in his hand." [109] And the Yugoslav scholar Svetozar Koljevic has reexamined the traditions described by Lord and reviewed some of his conclusions. Koljevic's own conclusion is profoundly relevant to our own project in this book:

> Oral epic singing at its best was both a way of coming to terms with history and a means of getting out of it. That is why its ultimate significance cannot be grasped in the analysis either of the technique of its composition or of the diverse historical sources of its social concepts, motifs and themes. For a song about fighting is not the same thing as fighting or even as the recording of an actual response to it. Similarly, songs about great defeats, vassalage, outlawry or rebellions attempt to grasp in language not only their historical but also their moral significance. They interpret the actual in terms of what it means as a challenge to the human spirit and to the whole tradition of oral poetic language in which it expresses itself.[110]

Notes

1. For a stimulating assessment of one aspect of this concern, see M. Bernal, *Black Athens: The Afroasiatic Roots of Classical Civilization*, vol. 1, *The Fabrication of Ancient Greece, 1785–1985* (London, 1987).

2. The pages that follow are largely based on W. Stanton, *The Leopard's Spots: Scientific Attitudes towards Race in America, 1815–1859* (Chicago, 1960); P. D. Curtin, *The Image of Africa: British Ideas and Actions, 1780–1850* (Madison, Wis., 1964), 363–72; G. L. Mosse, *Toward the Final Solution: A History of European Racism* (New York, 1978); S. J. Gould, *The Mismeasure of Man* (New York and London, 1981); N. Stepan, *The Idea of Race in Science: Great Britain, 1800–1960* (London and Hamden, Conn., 1982); G. W. Stocking, Jr., *Victorian Anthropology* (New York and London, 1987); and R. Ackerman, *J. G. Frazer: His Life and Work* (Cambridge, 1987).

3. See B. McGrane, *Beyond Anthropology: Society and the Other* (New York, 1989), 88–93, for a discussion of the importance of Charles Lyell's *Principles of Geology* (1830) to the shaping of both evolutionism and anthropological theorizing.

4. G. W. Stocking, Jr., *Race, Culture, and Evolution: Essays in the History of Anthropology* (1968; rpt. Chicago, 1982), 114.

5. Ibid., 144–85.

6. C. Darwin, *The Origin of Species by Means of Natural Selection, or, The Preservation of Favoured Races in the Struggle for Life* (1859; rpt. Harmondsworth, 1968), 476.

7. As Stocking, in *Victorian Anthropology*, 237, notes, Social Darwinian notions of conflict and the "survival of the fittest" coexisted with "a more Lamarkian evolutionism" which asserted that nonwhites could change rap-

idly if given the opportunity to do so. It was such "liberal" assumptions that formed the intellectual basis of the notion of the "white man's burden." These two ideas—at once complementary and contradictory—remained in tension throughout the period of imperialism and colonialism and are far from dead now.

8. F. Eggan, "One Hundred Years of Ethnology and Social Anthropology," in *One Hundred Years of Anthropology*, ed. J. O. Brew (Cambridge, Mass., 1968), 121; McGrane, *Beyond Anthropology*, 93–102.

9. E. E. Evans-Pritchard, *A History of Anthropological Thought* (New York, 1981), xvii–xviii.

10. H. Hoenigswald, "On the History of the Comparative Method," *Anthropological Linguistics* 5 (1963): 1–11.

11. Ackerman, *J. G. Frazer*, 75.

12. As Ackerman notes, such "conjectural" history was widely practiced by savants of the Scottish Enlightenment of the eighteenth century and had a significant impact on the intellectuals of the nineteenth century before the influence of Ranke's approach to writing history made it unfashionable (ibid., 46–47).

13. A. Kuper, *The Invention of Primitive Society: Transformations of an Illusion* (London, 1988), 17–75.

14. Ibid., 78–82, for the intellectual influences on Tylor.

15. E. Tylor, *Anthropology* (New York, 1881), 75, quoted in Stocking, *Race, Culture, and Evolution*, 116.

16. Ackerman, *J. G. Frazer*, 78; Stocking, *Victorian Anthropology*, 185; McGrane, *Beyond Anthropology*, 93–96.

17. Frazer shared with Tylor an acceptance of a boundary between literate and nonliterate and believed that the height of intellectual achievement to date was attained by the European bourgeoisie. For him European peasants "remain barbarians or savages at heart" (quoted in Ackerman, *J. G. Frazer*, 212).

18. D. Kidd, *The Essential Kafir* (London, 1904), 3–4.

19. For one indication of the content of this "popular" racism, see B. V. Street, *The Savage in Literature: Representations of "Primitive" Society in English Fiction, 1858–1920* (London and Boston, 1975), which discusses a range of popular fiction set in southern Africa.

20. Kidd, *The Essential Kafir*, vi, 8, 74, 133, 5, 277.

21. Ibid., 278–81.

22. On this aspect of the creation of the stereotypical Other, see J. Fabian, *Time and the Other: How Anthropology Makes Its Object* (New York, 1983).

23. Kidd, *The Essential Kafir*, 66, 405.

24. Although largely outside the scope of this book, it is worth noting that Kidd's contradictory views reflected more widespread confusion amongst progressives in South Africa following the demise amongst South African

whites for the ideology of Cape Liberalism, which was characterized by mid-nineteenth century optimism that Africans could be educated, and the rise of the belief that Africans were placed in southern Africa primarily to provide cheap and malleable labor for white-owned mines and farms. See S. Trapido, "'The Friends of the Natives': Merchants, Peasants, and the Political and Ideological Structure of Liberalism in the Cape, 1854–1910," in S. Marks and A. Atmore, eds., *Economy and Society in Pre-Industrial South Africa* (London, 1980), 247–74.

25. A. Kuper, *Anthropology and Anthropologists: The Modern British School*, 2d rev. ed. (London, 1983), 11; T. K. Penniman, *A Hundred Years of Anthropology*, 2d rev. ed. (London, 1952), 139–41.

26. W. Wundt, *Völkerpsychologie* (Berlin, 1900) and *Elements of Folk Psychology: Outlines of a Psychological History of the Development of Mankind* (London and New York, 1916), English translation by E. L. Schaub of *Elemente der Völkerpsychologie* (Berlin, 1912); Penniman, *Hundred Years of Anthropology*, 287.

27. L. Lévy-Bruhl, *How Natives Think* (New York, 1926), English translation by L. A. Clare of *Les Fonctions Mentales dans les Sociétés Inférieures* (Paris, 1910), 24, 17–20.

28. Ibid., 25. See also Evans-Pritchard, *A History of Anthropological Thought*, 119–31, for a defense of Lévy-Bruhl's interpretation.

29. Lévy-Bruhl, *How Natives Think*, 69–104.

30. Ibid., 14, 104, 43–45; Kidd, *The Essential Kafir*, 277.

31. Lévy-Bruhl, *How Natives Think*, 23, quoting the missionary Frédoux.

32. Ibid., 25, quoting the missionary Robert Moffat.

33. Ibid., 26.

34. G. E. Marcus and M. M. J. Fischer, *Anthropology as Cultural Critique: An Experimental Moment in the Human Sciences* (Chicago and London, 1986), 17–19.

35. F. Boas, *The Mind of Primitive Man* (New York, 1911). See also Stocking, *Race, Culture, and Evolution*, 133–233.

36. Stocking, *Victorian Anthropology*, 287.

37. P. Radin, *Primitive Man as Philosopher* (New York, 1927), ix.

38. This point is made in Marcus and Fischer, *Anthropology as Cultural Critique*, passim, but especially in chapters 5 and 6.

39. In southern Africa, it should be noted, evolutionist ideas dating back to the mid-nineteenth century, and speculations about primitive mentality that are reminiscent of the ideas of Kidd and Lévy-Bruhl, remain strong among contemporary whites. Defenders of white rule never tire of explaining to visitors that "the natives will take centuries to reach the level of Europeans" and that "the natives simply do not think like we do!"

40. Kuper, *Anthropology and Anthropologists*, 26.

41. As discussed ibid., 65.

42. Fabian, *Time and the Other*, 20–21.

43. On the other hand, certain anthropologists did recognize the existence of struggle in societies they studied but, in keeping with the dominant functionalist perspective of their discipline, they interpreted such struggle as contributing positively to the sustaining of that society. The classic study is M. Marwick's *Sorcery in Its Social Setting* (Manchester, 1965), which saw witchcraft as functional in preserving Chewa society rather than as a symptom of social pathology. See also the discussion of Max Gluckman in chapter two of this book.

44. See, for example, P. B. Rich, *White Power and the Liberal Conscience: Racial Segregation and South African Liberalism* (Johannesburg, 1984); J. Sharp, "The Roots and Development of *Volkekunde* in South Africa," *Journal of Southern African Studies* 8, no. 1 (1981): 16–36; and several studies in L. Vail, ed., *The Creation of Tribalism in Southern Africa: Studies in the Political Economy of Ideology* (London and Berkeley, 1988).

45. As in Tylor, *Primitive Culture;* Lévy-Bruhl, *Les Fonctions Mentales dans les Sociétés Inférieures* (Paris, 1910); C. Lévi-Strauss, *La pensée sauvage* (Paris, 1962); R. Horton, "African Traditional Thought and Western Science," *Africa* 37 (1967): 50–71, 155–87; B. R. Wilson, ed., *Rationality* (Oxford, 1970).

46. For discussions of this "crisis," see, for example, Stocking, *Race, Culture, and Evolution;* T. Asad, ed., *Anthropology and the Colonial Encounter* (New York, 1973); S. Diamond, *In Search of the Primitive* (New Brunswick, N.J., 1974); E. Said, *Orientalism* (New York, 1979); E. Wolf, *Europe and the People without History* (Berkeley and Los Angeles, 1982); Stocking, *Victorian Anthropology,* 284–329; J. Clifford and G. E. Marcus, eds., *Writing Culture: The Poetics and Politics of Ethnography* (Berkeley and Los Angeles, 1986); and McGrane, *Beyond Anthropology,* 113–35, among others.

47. This point is cogently argued throughout Marcus and Fischer, *Anthropology as Cultural Critique.*

48. As, for example, in Jean Comaroff, *Body of Power, Spirit of Resistance: The Culture and History of a South African People* (Chicago and London, 1985); M. Sahlins, *Islands of History* (Chicago, 1985); S. F. Moore, *Social Facts and Fabrications: "Customary" Law on Kilimanjaro, 1880–1980* (Cambridge, 1986), among many other studies.

49. One should note, however, the continued influence within anthropology of the structuralism of Claude Lévi-Strauss's work, which, following a linguistic model of binary oppositions attempts to discover a "grammar" and "syntax" for culture. In this, following Lévy-Bruhl, Lévi-Strauss distinguishes between "us" as "hot" and "them" as "cold." See C. Lévi-Strauss, *Tristes Tropiques* (London, 1973) and, especially, *La Pensée Sauvage* (Paris, 1962).

50. Parry's major publications were *L'Epithète Traditionnelle dans Homère: Essai sur un Problème de Style Homèrique* (Paris, 1928) and *Les Formules et la Métrique d'Homère* (Paris, 1928). Parry's works were only made easily available in 1971, when Adam Parry's edited collection, *The Making*

of Homeric Verse: The Collected Papers of Milman Parry (Oxford), was published.

51. See, for example, M. Parry, *The Making of Homeric Verse*, xi–xxi, for a discussion of the debate over the Homeric Question.

52. Ibid., 8–9; see also D. Shive, *Naming Achilles* (New York and Oxford, 1987), 4.

53. W. J. Ong, *Orality and Literacy: The Technologizing of the Word* (London and New York, 1982), 21.

54. Parry's theory of the creativity of the oral artist rests on the rather odd assumption that the "oral" performance should be an *extemporaneous* one as well. There is no necessary reason why an oral artist should not prepare his or her text in advance, and ample evidence from southern Africa shall be presented in this volume that oral artists do in fact do just that.

55. Parry, *Making of Homeric Verse*, 272 (emphasis in original). See also A. B. Lord, *The Singer of Tales* (Cambridge, Mass., 1960), 30.

56. Parry, *Making of Homeric Verse*, xxvi.

57. Ibid., 440, 377 (emphasis in original).

58. Ibid., 272, 441.

59. Lord, *Singer of Tales*, 31.

60. W. J. Ong, "McLuhan as Teacher: The St. Louis Years," in *Marshall McLuhan: The Man and His Message*, ed. G. Sanderson and F. Macdonald (Golden, Col., 1989), 25.

61. The remainder of this paragraph and the next is based on P. Marchand, *Marshall McLuhan: The Medium and the Messenger* (New York, 1989), 59, 112, 153–55.

62. W. J. Ong, *Ramus, Method, and the Decay of Dialogue* (Cambridge, Mass., 1958), 295–318.

63. Marchand, *Marshall McLuhan*, 155, acutely observes that the structure is so loose that "almost any part of the text could have been placed in almost any other part without interfering with the development of the author's argument."

64. M. McLuhan, *The Gutenburg Galaxy* (Toronto, 1962), 1–3.

65. Ibid., 1.

66. Ibid., 45.

67. J. C. Carothers, *The African Mind in Health and Disease* (Geneva, 1953), 106.

68. J. C. Carothers, "Culture, Psychiatry, and the Written Word," *Psychiatry*, November 1959, 308, quoted in McLuhan, *Gutenburg Galaxy*, p. 18. It is worth noting that F. Fanon, in his *Wretched of the Earth* (trans. Constance Farrington [New York, 1966], 244–46), was pillorying Carothers's work at just about the same time that McLuhan was praising it.

69. McLuhan, *Gutenburg Galaxy*, 18.

70. Ibid., 19; J. C. Carothers, "Culture," quoted ibid., 20; McLuhan, *Gutenburg Galaxy*, 21.

71. Ibid., 39.

72. Cf. G. Connah, *African Civilizations* (Cambridge, 1987), 7.

73. T. W. Cooper, "The Unknown McLuhan," in *Marshall McLuhan*, ed. Sanderson and Macdonald, 49.

74. E. A. Havelock, *Preface to Plato* (Cambridge, Mass., 1963), vii.

75. Ibid., x (emphasis added).

76. Ibid., xi, 42.

77. Ibid., 100. See also pages 43–44, 60–86, 107.

78. Ibid., 140, 147, 153.

79. Havelock's ideas have been attacked as "woolly and grandiose" by the most recent authority on the subject of ancient literacy. See W. V. Harris, *Ancient Literacy* (Cambridge, Mass., 1989), 40–41, and passim.

80. J. R. Goody, *The Domestication of the Savage Mind* (Cambridge, 1977), 1–9; ibid., 37, quoted in Harris, *Ancient Literacy*, 40.

81. This theme is continued in Goody's recent work, *The Logic of Writing and the Organization of Society* (Cambridge, 1986).

82. Goody, *The Domestication of the Savage Mind*, 14.

83. Ibid., 26. Considering the large forces of up to sixty people involved in the performance of a Chopi *ngodo*, and considering that it is divided into distinct movements that can last well over an hour and that it has a distinct intellectual thrust, one questions Goody's ethnocentric rejection of the possibility of a "symphony" occurring in oral societies.

84. Ibid. Goody's acceptance of the current wisdom about the precise nature of the central creative processes in oral literature and for oral man is surprising, for immediately afterwards, he noted that the Parry/Lord formulation does *not* apply to the LoDagaa people of northern Ghana, amongst whom he did his fieldwork and where he observed composers working carefully in private before performance. Ibid., 27.

85. Ong, *Orality and Literacy*, 16–30.

86. Ibid., 31.

87. Ibid., 31–77 passim.

88. Ibid., 29.

89. Ibid., 42.

90. Ibid., 11.

91. Ibid., 46.

92. For similar critiques of the notion that nonliterate peoples have no concept of historical change, see R. Rosaldo, *Ilongot Headhunting, 1883–1973* (Stanford, Calif., 1980), and R. Price, *First Time: The Historical Vision of an Afro-American People* (Baltimore, 1983).

93. M. McLuhan, *Counterblast* (London, 1970), 13–14.

94. Lord, *Singer of Tales*, 124.

95. Lord, *Singer of Tales*, 6.

96. R. Finnegan, "What is Oral Literature Anyway?" in *Oral Literature and the Formula*, edited by B. A. Stolz and R. S. Shannon (Ann Arbor, 1976), 127.

97. As, for example, H. Scheub, *The Xhosa "Ntsomi"* (Oxford, 1975); J. Opland, "*Imbongi nezibongo:* The Xhosa Tribal Poet and the Contemporary Poetic Tradition," *Proceedings of the Modern Language Association* 90 (1975): 185–208, and *Xhosa Oral Poetry* (Cambridge, 1983); I. Okpewho, *The Epic in Africa: Towards a Poetics of the Oral Performance,* rev. ed. (New York, 1979); D. J. Cosentino, *Defiant Maids and Stubborn Farmers: Tradition and Invention in the Mende Story Performance* (Cambridge, 1982); E. Gunner, "Ukubongo Nezibongo: Zulu Praising and Praises," Ph.D. diss., University of London, 1984.

98. For instance, J. Opland, "Caedmon and Ntsikana: Anglo-Saxon and Xhosa Transitional Poets," *Annals of the Grahamstown Historic Society* 2, no. 3 (1977): 56–65; Okpewho, *Epic in Africa.*

99. M. Mueller, *The Iliad* (London, 1984), 10.

100. R. Finnegan, *Oral Poetry, Its Nature, Significance, and Social Context* (Cambridge, 1977), 272.

101. Ibid., 92–93; Opland, *Xhosa Oral Poetry,* 159.

102. A. Lord, "Perspectives on Recent Work in Oral Literature," *Forum for Modern Language Studies* 10 (1974): 187–210.

103. T. Cope, *Izibongo: Zulu Praise Poems* (Oxford, 1968), 96.

104. See, e.g., R. Finnegan, *Limba Stories and Storytelling* (Oxford, 1967); Scheub, *The Xhosa "Ntsomi";* Okpewho, *The Epic in Africa;* Cosentino, *Defiant Maids and Stubborn Farmers.*

105. As Goody noted for his LoDagaa example. Cf. Goody, *The Domestication of the Savage Mind,* 27.

106. Stolz and Shannon, eds., *Oral Literature and the Formula,* 176.

107. Opland, *Xhosa Oral Poetry,* 175–80. A fuller account is given in J. Opland, "The Installation of the Chancellor: A Study in Transitional Oral Poetry," unpublished paper presented at the Conference on Literature and Society in Southern Africa, University of York, U.K., 8–11 September 1981. See also Opland's "The Isolation of the Xhosa Oral Poet," in *Literature and Society in South Africa,* ed. L. White and T. Couzens (Harlow, Essex, 1984), 191–92.

108. Lord, *Singer of Tales,* 4.

109. Mueller, *The Iliad;* Shive, *Naming Achilles,* 139.

110. S. Koljevic, *The Epic in the Making* (Oxford, 1980), 320–21.

2

"Maps of Experience"
Songs and Poetry in Southern Africa

A conversation late in 1976 with a group of old men in a village on the banks of the lower Zambezi River is largely responsible for our writing this book. We were in Mozambique's Zambesia Province researching a book about the area's history, and we were discussing with the men certain work songs we had collected.[1] During our conversation, we found one song being singled out as being especially important. It was the song that is analyzed in detail in chapter six of this book, a song satirizing "Paiva," at the time the eponymous local name for the sugar company founded in part by José de Paiva Raposo that dominated the lower Zambezi for over eight decades, controlling the land and extorting male and female labor under Portugal's system of forced labor:

Paiva—ay,
  Wo—o—o, Wo—
Paiva—ay,
  Wo—o—o, Wo—
Paiva—ay,
  Paiva, ndampera dinyero ache,

  Nsondo wache!

Paiva—ay,
  Wo—o—o, Wo—
Paiva—ay,
  Wo—o—o, Wo—
Paiva—ay,
  Paiva, I have killed his money for him,
  His penis![2]

Two things said about this song especially intrigued us. The first was the claim that it was important because of its content. "This song," the men declared, "cannot be forgotten. Even our children will have to know it because it's about what people suffered. It is a map of our experience." The men were speaking in Podzo, the language of the lower Zambezi area, but to stress their point, they used the Portuguese word *mappa*. The second comment was in response to our question about how such a ribald, insulting song could be performed regularly in the presence of the very officials denounced in it when, under Portuguese colonial rule, Africans had no political rights and could be legally subjected to severe physical punishment in the name of worker discipline. It was "all right," the men said, because the complaint was expressed in song. To say such things outside the song "would be just insulting him . . . just provoking him," but so long as it was done through singing, "there will be no dispute."[3]

We have quoted these comments in other contexts, but over a decade of intermittent reflection on them has not lessened our appreciation of their significance. They summarize exactly what, in the course of collecting and studying other kinds of oral poetry, we have come to appreciate as an aesthetic, a set of assumptions about poetic performance held throughout southern Africa—and perhaps farther afield—over a period of at least the past 150 years.[4] Most descriptions of the region's oral poetry emphasize, intentionally or otherwise, its extreme fragmentation. There are collections of Tsonga drinking songs, Ambo hunting songs, Zambezi boating songs, Shona harvesting songs, Bemba praise songs, Chewa pounding songs, and so on: the twin determinants being the genres and the presumed "tribal" designations. It may appear from our own chapter headings that this book is not so very different. Yet despite the region's variety of genres and multiplicity of languages, the comments by the men in Zambesia in 1976 opened our eyes to the existence of a common aesthetic, an extremely adaptable but continuous poetic tradition extending over a long period of time and over a wide area. It is this aesthetic that links the different "poetries" of our separate chapters.

The first of the men's comments stresses the importance of the *Paiva* song *as history*, as a "map" of peoples' experience over eight decades that must be transmitted to the children because "it came from our fathers." The second comment describes the song's importance *in history* when, taking full advantage of the convention that criticism expressed in song is licensed criticism, the singers defined pungently and accurately the terms of their exploitation. The song draws its force from what is universally believed to have been the justness of the original accusation against the sugar company's official when singers at a named plantation denounced the individual they were confronting. But its ultimate importance is that it transcends that moment, turning a timely, bald intervention in history into a symbolic statement about what has always been the relationship between labor and capital on the banks of the lower Zambezi River.

Two separate claims are thus held in tension. The song declares in licensed fashion what was true at a moment in time. The song also transcends that original encounter, giving it a permanent significance. The individual originally targeted—"Paiva"—has become the totality of the sugar industry itself—"the store, the factory, the railway line, the compounds, the canefields."[5] The central hunting metaphor—"I have killed his money for him"—with its implicit demand that the proceeds of the hunt should be shared equitably, becomes a symbolic representation of the people's experience of company rule over four generations. The ribald jibe—"His penis!"—stands as a permanent repudiation of the company's values. Thus the song could be carried from the canefields and "danced in the village," where its license was not required because no company official was present, without any loss of relevance.[6] Like a legal precedent establishing a norm for subsequent judgments, it has long passed into the local culture as the bearer of a particular set of values. It can be extended, elaborated, reshaped, changed in tone, reapplied to different circumstances including, as we demonstrate, FRELIMO's (Frente de Libertação de Moçambique) victory, without ceasing to be "the Paiva song." But it draws its authority from the fact that everyone can refer back, specifically or by inference, to the occasion of its first performance. A historical intervention has become a reading of history and, hence, a way to transcend that history.

Some of the most interesting writing on African oral poetry in recent years has been provoked by encounters such as the one just described, when researchers with no theories to impose or methodologies to test were confronted with performances far outside their previous experiences and were forced to ask new questions to account for them. Karen Barber's work on Yoruba *oriki* and David Coplan's on Sotho *sefela* are good examples.[7] Perhaps it has always been the case that the most stimulating intellectual discoveries about African societies have been made inadvertently, when investigators were ambushed by information outside their immediate preoccupations and hence were open to its impact.

Alan Merriam's experience collecting songs among the Bashi people of the Belgian Congo's Kivu District provides a striking example. Merriam was a skilled musicologist, and his interests did not normally extend to the words of the performances he recorded. In

treatment was evolutionist, and they employed the comparative method: the forms of contemporary oral literature in nonliterate societies, they argued, were the best clues we have to the forms of those ancient oral literatures which preceded the earliest written texts. In the archeological search for the development of form, content was ignored.

Considerably more sophisticated in their approach were three studies of southern African oral performance by Hugh Tracey, Max Gluckman, and Clyde Mitchell that were published in fairly quick succession between 1948 and 1954. The first of these was Tracey's *Chopi Musicians*, a study based on observations and recordings made in the early 1940s of the massed xylophone orchestras of the Chopi people of southern Mozambique. *Chopi Musicians* is a minor classic. By paying serious attention to African music, Tracey was a generation ahead of his time, and in the Chopi orchestras he found a splendid subject. He was aware that many of the songs he was recording were highly satiric in content, and we adopt his usage of the neat term *poetic license*, which captures with more precision than its normal English usage the central feature of the region's oral poetry.[10]

Tracey was, however, first and foremost a musicologist. It was Chopi music, particularly the instrumentation of the orchestras, that commanded his most informed attention. He was equipped neither as a literary critic nor as a historian to examine the meanings of the songs he transcribed. Although his explanatory notes are frequently illuminating, his general comments range from the whimsical and patronizing to the totally erroneous. Two examples will suffice to demonstrate the need for a fresh look at the material he collected. The first is a song by Katini, of Wani Zavala's village, recorded in 1940:

> It is time to pay taxes to the Portuguese,
> The Portuguese who eat eggs
> And chicken.
> Change that English pound![11]

Tracey comments that the tax question "is an oft-recurring theme in native songs," and his explanation of the fourth line—that migrant workers returning from South Africa resented having to change their British-sterling notes to Portuguese escudos at the border at a 10 percent discount—is helpful. On the song's central eggs-and-chicken metaphor, however, he had only this to say:

> The rightness of reference to the Portuguese as those who eat eggs and chicken will be wistfully admitted by every good Portuguese house-wife in the district, of whom there may be a dozen or so. (The last census shows a total of 27 Europeans in Zavala district.) Had they added fish from the lakes as well, the picture of the available choice of proteins would have been complete! But with the memory of my host-ess vividly in mind I would gladly return any day to sample again the hundred and one delicious disguises she has conjured up for this culi-nary trinity.[12]

There is more in this vein, and while the song itself is almost forgot-ten, Tracey inadvertently helps to confirm the central complaint—which is, of course, that the Portuguese consume everything, "eggs and chickens," without regard to the future.

Equally disingenuous in his comment on lines that attack the use of the brutal *palmatoria*, a perforated paddle used for inflicting cor-poral punishment: "Here is a mystery, the Portuguese beat us on the hands / Both us and our wives!" Tracey's *mystery* is a weak word for what ought to be translated as "something arbitrary and inexplic-able," and his comment that this is a "very light-hearted lyric," aris-ing from his opinion that the Chopi feel they should instead be beaten on the "part specially fatted by nature for sacrifice," is typical of his refusal to take the words of these songs seriously."[13] Despite the huge advance *Chopi Musicians* represented in the context of its time, then, it fell short of understanding what the Chopi people themselves valued about their performances.

The second study that broke with earlier approaches was Max Gluckman's "Rituals of Rebellion in South-East Africa," originally delivered at the University of Glasgow as the Frazer Lecture of 1952. The focus of Gluckman's analysis was Hilda Kuper's recently pub-lished description of the Swazi *Ncwala*, or firstfruits ceremony, and, in particular, the highly abusive songs that Kuper had recorded as being addressed to King Sobhuza II during the *Ncwala* of the 1930s.[14] Gluckman appropriated these songs as further validation of what he believed was "a new contribution to anthropological theory," namely, that "African states contained within themselves a process of constant rebellion, but not of revolution." As he summarized his argument:

> I tried to connect together the following series of facts: the Swazi and Zulu had a stationary subsistence economy, without good communi-cations or highly productive tools, widespread trade, or luxuries to en-

able the ruling group to establish themselves as a "class" distinct from the commoners; the economy necessitated widespread dispersal of the population, and the division of the nation into counties; all men owned their own weapons, so every county had an army; these counties developed strong loyalties to their leaders and hence local power autonomy; leaders had to support followers for their own power and their own kin intermarried with these followers; these ensured a tendency towards hostility towards central government and hence towards independence; but Zulu and Swazi history showed that these provincial loyalties very, very rarely led to movements of independence, and in practice the different sections of the nation (as among Anuak and Shilluk) supported different princes in their struggles to gain the throne, and thus were involved in fighting for kingship, and not against it, even though they might be against a particular king; and this struggle was one of the important themes of the great national festivals.

Thus, for Gluckman, the *Ncwala* was an aspect of a timeless drama of kingship "acting out the powerful tensions which make up national life" in a ritual that could only occur "within an established and unchallenged social order."[15]

Gluckman's analysis was clearly imaginative. Accepting the challenge implicit in what the *Ncwala* songs actually declare and refusing to relegate them to the obscure corners of formalist literary debate, he attempted to explain them with reference to a total analysis of the Swazi political economy and its expression in Swazi myth. In so doing, he set formidable standards for subsequent analysts. His explanation, however, required that he abstract the songs from their historical context, the circumstances of Swaziland in the 1930s, and to assume the songs' great antiquity. This is a very curious assumption, given that Gluckman was fascinated by Kuper's account precisely because it contrasted sharply with his own earlier essay on the firstfruits ceremony of the neighboring Zulu people, which had been based on reports of missionaries and travelers.[16] He attributed these differences to "the great change in the data for our analysis brought about by modern field-work methods" and denied that actual historical change might be involved in the shifting emphasis from external enemies in the Zulu songs to the internal enemies in the Swazi ones.[17] In fact, nothing in Kuper's account of the *Ncwala* justifies Gluckman's suggestion that the songs are ancient. In her essay of 1944 and in her subsequent monograph, she does not describe them as timeless, noting only of one of them, the *Lihubo*, or "national anthem," that it "is said by some to be very old, but by others to be fairly recent." Not until her 1978 authorized biography of Sobhuza II, long after Gluckman's reinterpretation of her material, does she claim that some of the *Ncwala* songs were composed in the nineteenth century by the wife of Sobhuza I.[18]

The matter is complicated by the fact that a version of one of the *Ncwala* songs,

> Alas for your fate, Lord,
> They reject thee, Lord,
> They hate thee, Lord.

had been published in 1929 in R. C. A. Samuelson's *Long, Long Ago,* in which it is said to be a war song of Mphande.[19] Samuelson's volume, along with the various collections of Zulu *izibongo* published by James Stuart in the mid-1920s, was, as we show in chapter five, an important source for the revival of Swazi praise poetry on the Zulu model during the 1930s. But Gluckman's general description of the "Swazi and Zulu . . . stationary subsistence economy," and of their lack of a ruling class distinct from commoners, conforms in no way to the historical realities of the alienation of Swazi land to Europeans, of large-scale migration of Swazi men to the mines of the Witwatersrand, and of Sobhuza II's control over labor recruitment. Furthermore, his interpretation of the *Ncwala* as a ritual that could occur only in an "established and unchallenged social order" or a "stationary . . . repetitive social system"[20] is sharply at odds with the actual circumstances of the king's struggle for acceptance in the 1930s, when Kuper was recording her observations. Kuper's most recent work has demonstrated the historical evolution of the *Ncwala* ceremony in a context of political struggle. As for the *Ncwala* songs and Swazi royal praise poems (*tibongo;* sing., *sibongo*) in general, we are once again confronted with material that can better be interpreted in the light of the dynamic, dialectical relationship between "poetic license" and history.

The third contribution of this period was J. Clyde Mitchell's monograph *The Kalela Dance,* first presented in the same year as Gluckman's Frazer Lecture at seminars at the Rhodes-Livingstone Institute in Lusaka and at the University of Manchester. Modeling his study on Gluckman's earlier essay "Analysis of a Social Situation in Modern Zululand,"[21] Mitchell made the *kalela* dance the centerpiece of an analysis of ethnic relations in an urban environment, the

Zambian Copperbelt, where *kalela* was immensely popular at the time of Mitchell's research during the 1950s.

In *The Kalela Dance* performances of the dance itself are vividly described, sections of one lengthy song text are presented, and the social background of the dance troupe is cataloged in great detail. From these descriptions, Mitchell draws out the "paradox" that is the theme of his study. On the one hand, all the dancers in the group he discusses are of Bisa origin, most of them from the same home village, and the majority of their songs are satiric attacks on Lamba and Nsenga people. On the other hand, the basic imagery and the whole frame of reference of the performance is drawn from life on the Copperbelt, where such ethnic categories were assumed to be losing their relevance and hence breaking down. Mitchell's answer was that while "tribes" on the Copperbelt were no longer expressions of kinship networks, they remained for the lowest-paid workers natural and essential categories "of interaction in casual social intercourse."[22] As for the satire in the songs, this must be understood as the urban equivalent of the old interethnic "joking relations" of the rural area. The jokes are "licensed" in that no one takes offense, but they depend for their legitimacy on the re-creation in urban areas of "tribal" identities.

As with the studies of Tracey and Gluckman, Mitchell's monograph continues to stimulate. Working with African informants and trying to interpret African texts, including the movements and costume of the dance itself, Mitchell draws on labor history, sociological data, and anthropological theory to arrive at some plausible conclusions. Once again, it is the range of enquiry that is impressive, together with the assumption that most of the answers are to be found through enquiry on the spot and within a social context. His essay provided the inspiration for one of the finest extended investigations of the role of dance in African societies, T. O. Ranger's *Dance and Society in Eastern Africa, 1890–1970: The Beni Ngoma* (1975). Ranger shows that *kalela*, like the Tanzanian *mganda* dance and the Malawian *malipenga*, is one of a number of variants of the *mbeni* dance, which originated on the east coast in the late nineteenth century and was immensely popular throughout eastern and much of southern Africa from World War I until the 1960s. Ranger's sources are for the most part archival rather than oral, and his approach, unlike Mitchell's, is historical. Like Mitchell, however, he is able to demonstrate the complex interaction between dance and social processes, the *mbeni* having served in different places and at different periods as a means of dramatizing district rivalries (in the old Swahili towns), tensions between ex-slaves and freemen (in Ujiji), incipient class divisions (in rural Tanzania), and generational conflict (on Bukurebe Island), as well as a means of articulating "modernist" aspirations and, occasionally, resistance to colonial rule.

Where Mitchell's essay—and, to a lesser extent, Ranger's book—is flawed is in its failure to analyze the actual words of the *kalela* songs.[23] By treating the lyrics as merely modern versions of "joking relationships," he is in effect relegating them to the sidelines of his analysis, which focuses mainly on costume and ethnicity. Yet, the making of a *kalela* dance begins with the composition of the words of a song, which are then set to music with the choreography added last.[24] The words are of its very essence. Mitchell claims that the songs were dominated by Copperbelt concerns and that "there is no mention of planting crops and of reaping them, of building huts, of fishing and hunting and other rural activities we might associate with tribal Arcadia." Yet even in the short sections that Mitchell quotes (parts of six stanzas from a song of fourteen stanzas), the composer Luke Mulumba makes it clear that when his travels as a dancer are over, he will return with his wife to the "city of Matipa," where his uncle is chief, to continue his dancing:

> I will then go and say goodbye to Chief Katanga
> Who is my father-in-law
> And the one whose daughter I married.
> When I finish that work, mothers,
> I shall never stay in Lambaland,
> But I shall hasten to my motherland of Chief Matipa.[25]

Mulumba and his fellow dancers regard their presence on the Copperbelt as transient and look forward to returning home as a group.

Further research on the *kalela* dance, including interviews with former performers, has both clarified and amplified these points. A closer attention than Mitchell paid to the actual words of the *kalela* songs reveals no inconsistency between the celebration of a Copperbelt life-style and the maintenance of a rural base as the context for self-assertion. In fact, having originated on an island in Lake Bangweulu in the early 1930s out of the earlier *mbeni* dance tradition,[26] *kalela* had become by the time of Mitchell's investigations an important means of discussing the contradictions for Africans that arose out of their living on the Copperbelt as long-term labor migrants and yet possessing, out of necessity, ties with a countryside dominated by the "traditional" political structures of indirect rule.

Many of the *kalela* songs sung on the Copperbelt were indeed about rural activities, with the skills involved in hunting and fishing being described in words and mimicked in the dancing.[27] Equally significantly, *kalela* had a whole rural social dimension upon which Mitchell never touches, with many songs discussing the problems caused in the rural areas when migrants failed to remit money home or when they even abandoned their families wholly: "The groups of *kalela* were formed in different villages. This . . . comprised young men who had come from the Copperbelt and their future wives [*ba-kobekela*]. They wore nice clothes and joined *kalela* groups so they could show other people what they acquired. This forced a lot of young men to go to the Copperbelt to acquire nice clothes and then come back home."[28]

When these migrants returned home they also took the dance back with them and, at times, using the poetic license of song, directly challenged the patterns of authority and inheritance they encountered, with, for example, songs "about chiefs expressing pleasure or displeasure."[29] In dance competitions, in rural Bemba-, Bisa-, and Ushi-speaking areas, the dance leaders or "kings," attired in smart black suits, would be feted like chiefs, carried shoulder-high in canoes between villages competing in the dance.[30]

Later, and logically, *kalela* was appropriated by independent Zambia's United National Independence Party (UNIP), and the subject of the songs was changed to satire and self-praise in the context of the politics of the late colonial and early independence periods.[31] To this day, many *kalela* groups are organized from local party headquarters, the dance having become largely fossilized as an officially patronized part of public culture.

The first attempt to provide a literary account of what is, after all, a literary convention, came a decade after Gluckman's and Mitchell's papers with two articles by another anthropologist, Archie Mafeje. Mafeje's theme was the "role of the bard in a contemporary African community."[32] The context was the controversy in the early 1960s over whether the Transkei area should accept the "self-governing" status then being urged upon them by the South African government, and the "bard" concerned was Melikaya Mbutuma, *imbongi* to the Thembu paramount chief, Sabata Dalindyebo.

In his first article, "A Chief Visits Town," Mafeje describes the visit of Mtikraka Matanzima, Kaiser Matanzima's cousin, to Langa township, near Cape Town, in 1961. The purpose of Matanzima's visit was to raise funds and marshal support for the project of self-government, and his township audience was unsurprisingly hostile. The *imbongi* Mbutuma was in Matanzima's entourage, but when it appeared that the meeting's chairman, a clergyman, was attempting to suppress criticism from the audience, Mbutuma

> dramatically jumped forward onto the stage, and recited a praise poem, addressing himself to the chairman:
>
> > "Mlambo, you know how to handle royal affairs,
> > Refrain from giving ministers all the chance to speak,
> > For they are going to preach, as they are wont to.
> > Be advised and give way before the Thembu burn one another."
>
> He went on praising the chief and introducing him to the audience. After the *imbongi* had sat down, one of the Mgudlwa chiefs . . . said a few words of welcome to the chief. . . . The next speaker was a Joyi chief. He also welcomed Mtikraka. . . .
>
> This speech touched everybody, and most of all the *imbongi*, who stood up, and burst into a praise poem with great emotion:
>
> > "I have been wondering what is happening to everybody else,
> > That up to now nobody has made any reference to Joyi,
> > The dark bull that is visible by its shiny horns,
> > Horns that today are besmeared with streaks of blood.
> > It is for that reason that today he is not amongst us.
> > As I am talking to you now, he is far away in a lonely desert.
> > But, to me, it seems that even that loneliness will not stop his
> >   bellowing."
>
> The Joyi the *imbongi* was referring to is one of the Thembu chiefs who have been uncompromisingly opposed to such schemes as rehabilitation and stock limitation. He has been banished.[33]

Intrigued by what he had witnessed, Mafeje sought out Mbutuma, and in a second article he gave six examples of his performances between September 1959 and March 1963, explaining their interaction with current events. Mafeje begins by rejecting the term *praise poet* as a satisfactory translation for *imbongi*, preferring the title *bard* in order to stress that his role is not to eulogize but to "interpret public opinion and to organise it":

> The method of the South African bard, in carrying out his duties, is not unlike that of the European bards. Like them, he celebrates the victories of the nation, he sings songs of praise, chants the laws and

customs of the nation, he recites the genealogies of the royal families, and in addition, he criticizes the chiefs for perverting the laws and customs of the nation and laments their abuse of power and neglect of their responsibilities and obligations to the people. . . .

In summary it may be stated that (i) both the European and the South African bards came from the commoner rank; (ii) their positions depended on their general acceptance by the people; (iii) the roles of both types are characterized by some measure of freedom to criticize, whether subtly or openly, those in authority, i.e. Kings and Chiefs. In contemporary western societies this role seems to have been taken over by the newspaper cartoonist. The significance of all these public "critics" (the European bard, the medieval court jester, the South African bard, and the newspaper cartoonist) is considerable, since they serve as a check against abuse of power by those in authority; they represent the opinions of the ruled.[34]

The six texts that illustrate Mafeje's argument were provided by Mbutuma, some in written form and others taken down by Mafeje during public performances.[35] They chart in considerable detail and with a wealth of sarcastic eloquence the ruthless determination of the South African government to push the Transkei into "home-land" status. Being an *imbongi*, Mbutuma is first concerned with the unity of the Xhosa-speaking Thembu people under their chiefs. But as that unity erodes, with Matanzima openly siding with governmental policies and accepting the illegitimate position of "Paramount Chief of the Emigrant Thembu," Mbutuma first lashes out at Matanzima's ambition:

I came across the ancestors at the top of Xhalabile's Mountains,
They said we were subverting the country by our great desire for
    power.
Things are so critical because of Kaiser Matanzima's ambitions,
How could he strive to get a higher position than the Paramount
    Chief of the Thembu?
He has shocked me by unleashing such destructive forces.

He then attacks the inability of Sabata, the rightful paramount, to act for the nation:

He does not drink European liquor but he swims in it.
He says the difficulties facing him are alarming, and at times he
    dreads the thought of them.
I found him using brandy as a quencher of his worries.

He has found it a suitable substitute for traditional *amasi* [light
   beer].
I found this depressing and distressing.
What can one do? These people are born in their positions![35]

With chiefs failing the nation and with mediation impossible, the
imbongi assumes the role of people's spokesman. Mafeje records
that Mbutuma received several official warnings and one outright
summons and that he had been raided and interrogated four times by
the police. When he boycotted the inauguration of the Transkei assembly, his "absence was greatly felt by the people, who kept inquiring about him and remarking that 'he is the only *imbongi* who
speaks sense.' "[37]

Mafeje was the first writer since Andrew Smith to record with
such alertness the relationship between oral performance and politics. Mafeje's mentor was the Xhosa poet, novelist, and critic A. C.
Jordan, who in a number of influential papers insisted forcibly on the
praise poet's multiple responsibilities. His main role was not to
"shower flattering epithets on his chief" but to act as a chronicler of
a reign, "praising what is worthy and decrying what is unworthy." It
was in making "sharp criticism of the habits of their subjects" that
the "bard found the greatest scope for his wit."[38] More recently, Jordan's balanced and subtle description of the *imbongi*'s role has been
simplified and romanticized by writers such as Z. Pallo Jordan and
Mbulelo Mzamane, for whom the bard has become a man defying
authority. Mzamane calls the praise poet "the conscience of the nation. He cannot be censured. Not even an all-powerful king like
Shaka the great did it."[39] This idea has taken on a life of its own,
providing several literate contemporary black South African poets
with a definition of their own role in society. Thus Keorapetse Kgositsile insists that "the revolutionary poet concretizes the dreams of
people for a better life." Mazisi Kunene prefaces his epic poem *Emperor Shaka the Great* with the statement that the Zulu poets "defined social values, celebrating what was historically significant and
acting as democratic agents to reaffirm the approval or disapproval of
the whole nation."[40]

As Kunene's anachronistic terminology indicates, this vision of
the oral poet's role needs to be qualified before it can be used for
literary or historical analysis. On the basis of our interviews and of
the research that has gone into the subsequent chapters of this book,
we suggest three qualifications are needed. The first is that, histori-

cally, praise poets have not always acted as the autonomous spokesmen of the people. As we demonstrate in chapter three, Ndebele praise poetry changed significantly over the decades following Andrew Smith's visit to Mzilikazi, as the political economy of the kingdom changed. The praises of Lobengula, recorded in the 1880s, contain no evidence of dialogue between king and subjects. They insist instead on the legitimacy of the ruling group, and they preach to common people and subject peoples the virtues of national unity under the king. After the overthrow of the royal house and the establishment of white colonial rule, Ndebele praise poetry changed again. The praises of Mzilikazi, chanted at his grave in the Matopos Hills, became a means, not of debating national issues nor of bolstering national unity, but of asserting in nostalgic and exclusive terms an injured pride in an Ndebele ethnic purity.[41]

Similar evidence for the changing history of praise poetry and of a changing role for the poet is provided in our discussion of Swazi praise poetry in chapter five. The majority of the tibongo (praise poems) familiar today in Swaziland are the creation of the late 1960s by praise poets close to Sobhuza II. In the context of the political struggles of the period, they promulgate a royalist view of Swazi history and culture and were a key component in securing the king's eventual triumph as supreme ruler. They differ substantially from earlier tibongo recorded in 1929.

What is absent from A. C. Jordan's work, and especially from the work of those who have simplified and popularized his ideas, is a sense of the complexities and mutability of power relations in southern African societies. Power is a dynamic relationship between the relatively dominant and the relatively subordinate in any society, with the nature of the domination and subordination determined by a host of economic, social, political, technological, and cultural factors. The totality of such relationships within a society hold that society together, providing a web of connections that make participants members of a common group. At the same time, however, relationships between the dominant and the subordinate are necessarily ambiguous, for within them are the seeds of conflict and strife, or, to use Gluckman's terms, rebellion and revolution. It is this structured imbalance that goes far toward providing the dynamic element in power relationships, making them subject—even in situations where power is successfully maintained—to ever-changing reformulations of the relationship between ruler and ruled and thereby affecting the historical role of licensed poetry.

As was clear to Andrew Smith as early as the 1830s, divisions of class and gender complicated the relationship within southern African societies of the "chief" to the "people," and complicated also the position of the oral poet. In discussing oral poetry from this region over the last century and a half, it is always necessary to ask the question, "Who is speaking for whom?" and there can be no easy assumption that the "poem" is the popular voice. In the oral poetry discussed in this book a variety of voices will be encountered, both male and female, speaking from opposite ends of the various social spectrums. At its best, praise poetry is lively, mischievous, dense with history refined to metaphor, and capable of redefining the terms of authority and the qualities of the nation in a manner that can make the prevailing ruler, to employ Andrew Smith's description of Mzilikazi, "pensive." [42] At its worst, praise poetry can be obsequious in its content and profoundly conventional in its expression.

Our second qualification flows from this: there are dangers in focusing only on the elaborate traditions of royal praises found in the societies of the Nguni diaspora that occurred after Shaka's rise to power. The image of the *imbongi* confronting the king with the demands of the people is an attractive one, as seductive as Albert Lord's description of the traditional storyteller, and most collections of oral poetry from southern Africa published in recent years have been collections of *izibongo*. Mafeje rebukes Schapera and Lestrade for equating royal praises with entertainments and self-praises and with the praises of horses and cattle, arguing that the praises "composed for chiefs and notables" are "a more serious type of undertaking" with "greater political significance." [43] Mafeje is right that there are hierarchies of genre in the oral literature of south-central Africa, with oral poetry being regarded by most informants as a more serious matter than riddles or moralities or trickster tales. Yet court praise poets exist in only a minority of the societies of south-central Africa, in the politically centralized societies that evolved out of the Nguni diaspora. Elsewhere in the region there are few such court poets. But the phenomenon of "poetic license" occurs everywhere.

The fact is that Jordan and Mafeje were misled by Nguni practices into placing special emphasis on the role of the *imbongi*. As Andrew Smith's investigations made clear, it is not the *poet* who is licensed by the literary conventions of the region; it is the *poem*. Mafeje remarks, and our own interviews confirm, that anyone can become an *imbongi*, even a "white man." [44] If certain poets have acquired a special reputation, it is only because of the poems they have produced and not because of any special privilege vested in their "office." In this sense, the much-repeated comparisons with Celtic bards and medieval court jesters are misplaced. It is *not* the performer who is licensed; it is the *performance*—whether the poet is addressing the chief or protesting to an overseer or complaining while possessed by a spirit or mocking a husband in a pounding song.

The advantage of this emphasis is that it enables us to take into account the wide variety of different performances the prevailing aesthetic can encompass and to locate this broader range of poems in a more complex set of social circumstances than Jordan or Mafeje envisaged. It permits, for instance, the assumptions legitimating the *imbongi* to be carried not only into the village, the dancing arena, the homestead, the spirit-possession ceremony, but also into the plantation, the township, the mining compound, or the black trade-union meeting.[45] These assumptions have, as we demonstrate in chapter eight, also provided an aesthetic for the long-detained Malawian poet Jack Mapanje.

Our third major qualification concerns terminology. Jordan wrote of the praise poet as a "chronicler."[46] Mafeje stressed his role as political commentator. Both descriptions are excessively narrow. The oral poetry described in this book is, by its very nature, public poetry, and its range is as wide as a society's concerns. Some of it deals directly with military events or political hierarchies, drawing on the poet's historical knowledge to assert or praise or arbitrate or pass judgment on power. Much of it deals with the moral significance of events, and hence with religious truths or with assertions of identity. Much, too, is concerned with communal or personal feelings of anxiety, displacement, exploitation, or loss. Even those songs performed primarily for entertainment place a high premium on social comment or satire. The performers seek through poetic expression a language with the authority to marshal a public response, and the poetry confronts the changing panorama of African history with a stream of comment—heroic, celebratory, elegaic, satiric—always attempting to construct, as our Mozambican informants put it, "a map of experience."

This literature, then, is best understood through its interaction with historical experience. But there have been formidable obstacles to realizing this ideal.

One of the greatest of such obstacles to the recognition of the aesthetic we are trying to describe has been the belief held by most researchers in the region in the concept of a primal urtext from which later, degenerate poems have derived. From James Stuart, recording his Zulu *izibongo* at the turn of the century, to Cope, Schapera, Damane and Sanders, and Hodza and Fortune, editors in the 1960s and 1970s of volumes in the Oxford Library of African Literature, the subject has been dominated by the assumption that an "authentic" urtext may be reconstructed from a variety of recorded versions, oral transmission constituting an archive of diminishing efficiency.[47] Thus, in a throwback to the approaches of the comparative method, the splendid and terrifying *izibongo* of Shaka published in Cope's collection actually derives from a text assembled by Stuart from no fewer than thirty-three separate performances![48] Similar distortions appear in the Oxford Sotho and Shona collections. As we have shown in chapter one, it was precisely this assumption that came under such effective attack in the work of Milman Parry and Albert Lord, though with consequences that further obscured the nature of African oral performance.

In effect, researchers in this area must contend with three overlapping chronologies. The first is the *chronology of the events* or personalities that form the subject of the poems under consideration—the dates when things happened or when chiefs and headmen were alive. The second may be called the *ideological chronology,* as past events or the achievements of dead chiefs are constantly reinterpreted in the light of contemporary preoccupations. And the third is the *chronology of research,* as scholars of different generations and backgrounds have been drawn to investigating different features of African societies and in the light of different intellectual fashions, providing a distorting perspective on change. One result of this situation is that it can be exceedingly difficult to do what we attempt in several of our chapters—to provide a "history" of the forms themselves and of individual poems. Another result is that it is relatively unusual to have available recorded versions of the "same" poem from different periods.

Before returning to the discussion initiated by our comments at the start of this chapter, on the *Paiva* song and the aesthetic of which it is an expression, we should like to consider two further poems that provide significant evidence precisely because contrasting versions of them *do* exist, separated in time. These are the *lithoko* (praises) of Moshoeshoe I and the *izibongo* of Shaka Zulu, figures important enough to have triumphed over the varied preoccupations of different generations of researchers.

Our first instance contrasts two versions of the praises of Moshoeshoe I, founder of the Sotho nation. Both are available in Damane's and Sanders's collection of praise poems, but the first was taken down by Chief Molapo Maama at the dictation of his father, Maama Letsie (1848–1924), shortly after World War I. The second was written down in November 1968 by Chief Lishobana Mpaki Molapi, a great-grandson of Moshoeshoe, as the "text" of an earlier public performance.[49]

Of the 1919 version, the opening lines are as follows:

The child of 'MaMokhackane, Thesele,
Thesele, the enormous cleft:
The cattle have entered it, they've gone forever,
And the people have entered it, they've gone forever!
You who killed cattle for the Koena,
Please have cattle killed for you, grandmother,
Please have cattle killed for MaSetenane, that she may be adorned
And wear to the full the fat of cattle and of people.
The frog of the armies, the comrade of Shakhane and RaMakoane,
The one who set fire to the dust, which came from the bowels of the
    land of RaTsoonyane:
The child of the chief of Qhoai saw it,
It was seen by RaTjotjose, the son of Mokheti,
The cloud, the gleaner of shields.
When the Frog isn't present in the armies of men,
The lords of the armies continually cry:
"Frog and RaMakoane, where are you?"
The armies of men have turned back on the way,
Seeking the Frog and RaMakoane.
Moshoashoaile, Maphule's cow with white-streaked back,
Moshoashoaile, the white-streaked cow, the white-streaked cow of
    Maphule,
The cow of the man of Maphule has a white-streaked back.
It hasn't grown yet, it's still lean,
Its hair is still rough, the milk-cow,
The milk-cow of Setenane and his friends.
The spear of the child of Khoana, Thamae,
The spear was damaging:
The razor-sharp spear has come from the home of Khoabane or the
    Tramplers:

The spear was damaging the bowels of the child of Mphaphang,
Black cow of the salt, of the salt, black cow,
Black cow, go on, I am coming,
I am coming to catch you up on the way, right here at the home of
    Phototsa.
Thesele of the Binders of Mokhachane,
The wiper of dirt from his shields,
From his shields while they're still in the huts.[50]

Thesele means "the thumper" or "the beater," and in these praises
Moshoeshoe is presented purely as a military figure. Although
Moshoeshoe lived until 1870, all the allusions in the praise poem are
to battles fought before 1835, and there is no reference to his skills
in government and diplomacy. It is tempting to connect this emphasis on warriorship with Lesotho's circumstances immediately following World War I. Flushed with his success in seizing German
Southwest Africa (Namibia), South Africa's Prime Minister, Jan
Smuts, was pressing a claim to the High Commission Territories.

Chief Molapo Maama, however, has provided an alternative context in his charming and delightful description of the occasions
when his father, Maama Letsie, Moshoeshoe's grandson and celebrated warrior of the Gun War, would "regale his followers with beer
and meat after they had been working on his lands":

At such times everyone in the village would be happy and relaxed and
would look to their chief with an uplifting sense of gratitude and de-
votion. Perhaps the men would sing the *mokorotlo,* itself a deeply
moving experience, and then the Maama would rise and call for silence: *"Tsie, lala"* (literally, "Locust, go to sleep!"). Taking up his
weapons, he would begin chanting his own praises, and the people
would listen in rapt attention. At first he would walk slowly and recite
carefully, but gradually he would quicken both his movement and his
delivery, until after a while he would be almost trotting and would be
chanting half as fast again as normal speech. As he moved around,
some of his old comrades in arms would follow him, occasionally pat-
ting him on the back and calling out: *"Ke ne ke te teng! Ke ne ke te
teng!* ("I was there! I was there!"). Listening to his exalted language
and its evocation of a glorious past, many of his followers would weep
with emotion; and when at last he had stabbed the ground with his
spear, there would be deafening shouts and whistles from the men, and
long, trilling ululations from the women. Then the *lithoko* (praises) of

Moshoeshoe and Letsie would be chanted, perhaps by Maama himself, perhaps by one of his followers.[51]

Such infectious nostalgia is ample explanation of the version of Moshoeshoe's career that we are offered in the version of 1919. The emphasis is entirely on his actions in war—the cattle he has seized, the men he has killed, the rival chiefdoms he has subdued. The past tense is used when specific incidents are mentioned, such as the defeat of "the child of Mphaphang" (Chief Matiwane of the Ngwane people, defeated in 1827), and the present tense for "permanent" truths, such as the army's dependence on Thesele's leadership. The imagery insists on Moshoeshoe as the man who initiates action. He is Thesele, the thumper or beater; he is "the Shaver" (spelled here Moshoashoaile, but pronounced Moshweshwe; "shweshwe," is an ideophone describing the sound of a razor); later in the poem he is "The spear . . . / The razor-sharp spear"; he is "The one who set fire to the dust"; he is "the gleaner of shields," picking them up from his defeated enemies on the battlefields, and is so constantly ready for battle that he is "The wiper of dirt from his shields / . . . while they're still in the huts"; and so on.

At the same time, the 1919 version is clearly the poetry of a ruling group. Moshoeshoe's family are named, not because *he* needs to be legitimated, but because they are the ones who share the loot of battle "And wear to the full the fat of cattle and of people." His friends and comrades are named in the poem—Shakhane, Ra-Makoane, Setenane, RaPolile, and Lesaoana. These are companions in battle, again sharing the loot, yet their dependence upon him is stressed: without his presence the armies will simply turn back. He is the Frog—a symbol of prosperity, since frogs appear with the rains. He is the milk cow, the provider, the source of wealth. It is interesting in this context to note three lines of the praises of Makhabane, Moshoeshoe's young brother and staunch ally, the "support of the pot in the fire":

> The lion is standing on the Tsatsa-le'Meno,
> It's standing and scolding the Makaota,
> Saying that the commoners should acknowledge the government.[52]

The Makaota, the "lean ones," were people who were impoverished by the wars that occurred in the region in the early nineteenth cen-

tury and who lived as hunters and gatherers. They are outside the
charmed circle. This version of Moshoeshoe's praises, chanted seventy years ago at the beer parties of aging warrior heroes, is a clear
echo of the days when the "big men" and their regiments lived by
raiding and the task of state-building had scarcely begun.

The portrait presented in our second version—written down by
Lishobana Mpaki Molapo, a great-grandson of Moshoeshoe, in 1968
as the authentic "text" of his own version of Moshoeshoe's praises—
could scarcely be more different.

> You who are fond of praising the ancestors,
> Your praises are poor when you leave out the warrior,
> When you leave out Thesele, the son of Makhachane;
> For it's he who is the warrior of the wars,
> Thesele is brave and strong,
> He is Moshoeshoe-Moshaila,
> When Moshoeshoe started to govern the Sotho
> He started at Botha-Bothe.
> Thesele, the cloud departed from the east,
> It left a trail and alighted in the west,
> At Thaba Bosiu, at the hut that's a court.
> Every nation heard,
> And the Pedi heard him too.
> Moshoeshoe, clear the road of rubbish,
> That the Maaooa should travel with pleasure,
> And travel with ease.
> The Ndebele from Zulu's heard too,
> Lay down the stock, son of Mokhachane,
> Sit down:
> The village of the stick isn't built,
> "What can you do for me?" doesn't build a village;
> The village that is built is the suppliant's, Thesele,
> Great ancestor, child of Napo Motlomelo,
> Protective charm of the Beoana"'s land,
> The cave of the poor and the chiefs,
> Peete's descendant, the brave warrior,
> He's loved when the shields have been grasped,
> When the young men's sticks have been grasped.
> He's taken the hide of the ox of the Mafatle,
> He's made it a guard.
> By a guard I mean a shield,
> And with it he'll parry in the midst of war.
> The children of Napo are stubborn indeed,
> They want him to rescue the nation,

Saying that the government is of cattle and people.
He's the yellow cow of the regiments,
He's the comrade of Shakhane and Makoanyane,
The one who set fire to the dust:
The dust came out of the bowels of the land,
It was seen by RaTjotjose, the son of Mokhethi.[53]

What is rather obscured by our use of extracts is that these are indeed two versions of the same praises: of the final ten praise paragraphs of the 1968 version (beginning with the final paragraph of our extract), six are adapted from the 1919 version. There exists, in short, a common stock of praises on which both performers are drawing.

The second version, however, dates from a period when those "who are fond of praising the ancestors" are in danger of leaving out the warrior. All this is clearly ancient history. The state is established. Lesotho has been independent from British control for two years, and Chief Leabua Jonathan is firmly in control. The king, Moshoeshoe II, has been politically marginalized. The ancient wars have been almost forgotten. Even basic historical facts have to be explained by the poet—that Thesele is Moshoeshoe, that he began at Botha-Bothe Mountain and later led his warriors to Thaba Bosiu, where people of other nationalities such as the Pedi and the Ndebele (meaning the Zulu) gathered. But, although he is praised as a warrior, what a different warrior he is from "the Shaver" of the 1919 version. Moshoeshoe this time is a "Great ancestor"; he is one who "governs" from "the hut that's a court"; he is a "Protective charm"; he is "The cave of the poor and the chiefs," that is a refuge for all groups without distinction; he is "a shield, / And with it he'll parry in the midst of war." There is little attention paid to names of family or of comrades who fought with him in battle: the nation is conceived of as a unity. Hence the words attributed to Moshoeshoe in lines 20–21—"The village of the stick isn't built / 'What can you do for me?' doesn't build a village."

This, of course, is Moshoeshoe the administrator and diplomat, ruling through the consent of his subjects, who are attracted to him by what he has to offer. He has now become the founding father of the state of Lesotho, an ikon of national unity. Not surprisingly, therefore, Chief Molapo, as poet, encounters some difficulties when he comes to handle the common stock of praises presented in the earlier version. Yet he copes triumphantly, showing a splendid ingenuity in reinterpreting metaphors. The "cloud" that in the first

poem was the dust raised by Moshoeshoe's army on the march becomes the 1968 version the dust raised by the migration of people to
the safer fortress of Thaba Bosiu. The "cleft" that followed up the
defeated after their ambush in the first poem becomes a hiding place
for "the long-bearded people" and "the great horned cattle" in the
second. Instead of "gleaning" shields dropped by the fleeing enemy,
he has made his regiment, the Mafatle, into a shield to protect the
nation who look to him to rescue them, "Saying that the government is of cattle and people." Warfare in the second poem is later
described in terms more appropriate to a public cultural display, like
"traditional" dances at Independence Stadium:

> The women are trilling for Moshoeshoe:
> The men have lengthy spears.
> He's loved when the shields have been taken.

When at last, in the penultimate praise, people do actually get killed
by Moshoeshoe, we are told that "The loudmouths' villagers were
burnt." Even in the best-run states some regrettable police action is
occasionally necessary.

What the version of 1968 has accomplished is a reassessment of
Moshoeshoe's place in Sotho history. But in doing this, Chief Molapo has largely remained faithful to the original stock of metaphors
associated with Moshoeshoe, which were themselves the figurative
expressions, and hence evaluations, of historical events. Conceivably, in a different tradition, the poet might have devised a new poem
based on incidents in Moshoeshoe's history during the second half
of his reign, between 1835 and 1870, arguably the period of his greatest achievements. But even to suggest this is to underestimate the
degree to which, in the minds of the poet's audience, among whom
the metaphors remain current, Moshoeshoe *is* his praises and the
praises *are* the history. Reassessments of history must proceed from
the "evidence" by reinterpreting the stock of metaphors as Chief
Molapo has done.

Our second instance of this process of reinterpretation is even
more striking. It concerns a performance of the praises of Shaka recorded by E. W. Grant in 1927.[54] The performer was Gwebisa, an old
man of about eighty who had fought with the Kandempemunvu regiment against the British at the Battle of Isandhlwana in 1879. Later
he had been an *imbongi* to Chief Zibhebhu, a Mandhalazi chief who
fought against King Cetshwayo after the latter's restoration by the

British in 1883. Grant's description of the performance is reminiscent of Chief Molapo's description of his father performing Moshoeshoe's praises: "As the recital proceeded the *imbongi* became worked up to a high pitch of fervour, and was evidently living again in the glories of the past. His voice became loud and strong, his face was uplifted. Shield and stick would be suddenly raised and shaken in the air. Gestures became more frequent and dramatic."[55] With this background, one might have expected Gwebisa's version of Shaka's praises to place the same emphasis as the Sotho poem of 1919 on military ferocity, individual heroism, and the king's preeminence in a band of elite warriors.

Natal in 1927, however, was a place of rapidly shifting alliances. When Gwebisa fought at Isandhlwana, the Zulu were already sharply divided between those who were loyal to the Zulu kingdom of Cetshwayo and those who had converted to Christianity, the *amakholwa* or "converted ones."[56] After the defeat of the Zulu by the British in 1880 and the later return of Cetshwayo from exile, matters were further complicated by political divisions within the kingdom, and several chiefs opposed his restoration.[57] These included Zibhebhu, whom Gwebisa served as *imbongi*. But the bitterest divisions continued to be between Zulu living under the king and those connected to various mission stations. As late as 1913, John Dube, spokesman for the *amakholwa* and first president of the South African Native National Congress, the precursor of the ANC, could describe "the system of tribal segregation" as suitable to "a period when barbarism and darkness reigned supreme," as "being essentially opposed to all enlightenment and Christianity," and as lacking any means of "raising the native people out of the slough of ignorance, idleness, poverty and superstition."[58]

One of the consequences of the South African Native Lands Act of 1913 was a radical shift in sentiment on the part of Dube. By 1917 he had lost the presidency of the Congress, and recognizing that the grievances of peasants and sharecroppers displaced by the Lands Act were being directed in part against black Christian landowners like himself, he had begun to move closer to the Zulu royal house, a force for stability and conservative values. In 1922-23, acting as a spokesman for the *amakholwa*, Dube was active in the formation of the *Inkatha* organization, uniting royalists with "educated natives from outside" in the Zulu National Council. The agenda of the 500-strong meeting of *Inkatha* in 1924 included proposals for the formation of a Zulu National Church, the establishment of a Zulu National Fund,

the resolution of divisions within the royal family dating from
Cetshwayo's time, and the preservation of "the present means of
government through Solomon and the chiefs" in resistance to the
introduction of a council system on the Transkei model.[59]

It was in 1927, during the realignment of political alliances among
the Zulu, that Gwebisa performed at the royal court near Nongema,
two praise poems, the *izibongo* of Zibhebhu and the *izibongo* of
Shaka. The first of these, the praises of Zibhebhu, Gwebisa's old patron, are simply the praises of a much-admired but long-dead warrior—"the Slicer," "the Stabber," the "Long-armed One." The poem
is a celebration of military success, though it is significant that in
the long catalog of Zibhebhu's victories no mention is made of his
capture and destruction. of Cetshwayo's capital at Ulundi in 1883.[60]
Gwebisa was nothing if not tactful! His interpretation of the *izibongo* of Shaka confirms the old man's alertness to the requirements
of the new age of Zulu unity. The poem is a celebration of Zulu ethnic pride, with Shaka heralded for the first time ever in recorded
praises as the king who "welded together the Zulu nation." This is
the first *Inkatha* version of Shaka's praises.

Like Chief Molapo performing the Sotho poem of 1968, however,
Gwebisa had to work from the "evidence" in the form of the cluster
of metaphors long associated with Shaka's name. No praises of
Shaka were recorded during his lifetime. In the published record of
Zulu *izibongo*, Shaka first appears in the praises of Dingane that
were recorded during his lifetime (died 1840) by Arbousset and Daumas.[61] Unsurprisingly, Shaka is execrated as a tyrant, while Dingane,
his assassin, is hailed as a deliverer. Most praises of Mphande, Dingane's successor, however, stress his legitimacy as Shaka's rightful
heir, and it seems reasonable to assume that, under Mphande,
Shaka's *izibongo* were recreated. Further praises of Shaka were recorded by dictation, first by Lewis Grout in the 1850s, then by
R. C. A. Samuelson during his period as tutor at Cetshwayo's court
(though they were not published until 1929), by A. T. Bryant at an
unspecified date, and by James Stuart who, at the turn of the century,
recorded thirty-three versions in his ill-conceived pursuit of the urtext.[62]

Most of Grout's and Bryant's version and some 80 percent of Samuelson's are represented in Stuart's, but, given that Stuart, Bryant,
and Samuelson are known to have corresponded with each other, the
relationship between their "texts" is extremely problematic. Their

versions were not published until the 1920s, in time to play their part in the revival of Zulu ethnic consciousness (influencing as well the manufacturing of Swazi "traditions," as described in chapter five). They may, however, be employed to demonstrate two points of significance. First, although Stuart's megapoem is not the transcript of any actual performance, it does have status as a kind of anthology of Shaka's accomplishments that were current at the turn of the century and that had been made available to the creators of *Inkatha* in the 1920s. Second, as Grout's and Samuelson's versions make clear, the mixture of praise, assessment, and blame in Stuart's poem is not merely the consequence of assembling in one text contradictory attitudes to Shaka among the different Zulu clans but of the attempts by different *izimbongi*, acting as intellectuals in their societies, to assess Shaka historically and in terms of permanent human values.

Stuart's megapoem presents Shaka as a phenomenon, a natural force astounding in its impact, operating within history and changing history's course, but as impervious to moral assessment as a volcano. Much of the poem is taken up with the long litany of Shaka's victories, recorded impressively in passages tense with repetition and with astonishment at his military genius and his restless, unbounded energy:

> The old women were left in the abandoned sites.
> The old men were left along the tracks,
> The roots of the trees looked up at the sky.

At the same time, Shaka is criticized vehemently. He is accused of excesses, of "lack of control," of not knowing where and when to stop. Mapitha, one of his counselors, and Ngqengelele, his bodyguard, are asked to help in teaching Shaka skills he lacks, such as milking and cultivating:

> Help me, Mapitha and Ngqengelele,
> And give him a cow that he may learn to milk into the mouth,
> And give him a sharpened stick that he may dig for himself.[63]

The sharpest criticism of all is one that, from the nature of the address, *Nkosi* ("King"), it has been suggested dates from Shaka's actual reign:[64]

King, you are wrong because you do not discriminate,
Because even those of your maternal uncle's family you kill,
Because you killed Bhebhe, son of Ncumela of your maternal
    uncle's family.[65]

These judgments are unequivocal, but the poem recognizes that they
had no effect. It contains no moral scheme in terms of which Shaka
may be constrained or punished for his excesses.

With this in mind, there is one further aspect of the background in
Gwebisa's performance of Shaka's *izibongo* that must be noted.
Stuart's collection of praise poems includes a "text" of the praises of
Ndaba, Shaka's semimythical great-grandfather.[66] Once again, the
poem seems to have been assembled from several performances, and
there is no need to believe, as has been suggested, that it dates from
Ndaba's own day in the late eighteenth century.[67] Ndaba, who was
no more than a minor chief, is being celebrated, not in his own
terms, but as an ancestor of Shaka's. Given the wrangles about
whether Shaka was legitimate or not, a respectable line of descent
was obviously desirable and, in the Shakan mythology, Ndaba becomes the ancestor who foretold he would father a line of kings,
composing when he was still a herdboy the song "Ndaba is a king!
Oye! Ha! Oye!"[68]

Once these points have been made, however, the poem is wonder-
fully suggestive. The various *izimbongi* anthologized by Stuart have
set about their task of giving Shaka an acceptable ancestry by describing the days before his rise to power with a nostalgia so potent
that it becomes a reproach to Shaka's actions as a ruler. In Ndaba's
days, people lived in their clans tending their herds of cattle. Violence was expended in hunting, and Ndaba was a great hunter—so
successful that the forests themselves protested, though he did not
exhaust the game. He was a "big man" and had some of Shaka's at-
tributes. But as a warrior his task was to protect his people; he carried, not spears, but shields; the duty of the chief was to be on guard,
and Ndaba's final epitaph is "What wrong did he do?"[69] The contrast
with the praises of Shaka is explicit.

At this point, we may return to Gwebisa and his performance of
Shaka's *izibongo* for E. W. Grant in 1927. Whether Gwebisa knew
Stuart's version is uncertain, though successive volumes of *izibongo*
were published by Stuart in Zulu in the mid-1920s, in time to feed
into the revival of Zulu nationalism. There is no doubt, however,
that he knew the stock of metaphors. He looks back across the

ninety-nine years since Shaka's death and celebrates him as the king who "allied the regiments" and "welded together" the Zulu nation. This shift of emphasis from the earlier praises is managed in three ways. First, Gwebisa changes the order in which the praises occur in the versions recorded by Grout, Samuelson, Bryant, and Stuart. Gwebisa's opening praises are:

> I have blamed Zihlandhlo and Gewabe,
> They did not tell the chief of the drifts:
> They showed him a bad one which is still slippery.[70]

This praise, which occurs at lines 76–80 of the Stuart version, refers to the one occasion after his childhood when Shaka may be said to have been justifiably angry—he had been deliberately misled by Zihlandhlo and Gewabe about a ford on the Tugela River. By moving it to the start of the praise poem and repeating it later, Gwebisa introduces and maintains the notion of Shaka as a king more sinned against than sinning, exasperated into violence by the behavior of his subjects.

Second, and more problematically in terms of his poetic tradition, Gwebisa omits all material critical of Shaka. The praise "The kicking of this beast puzzles me," which occurs in all recorded versions of Shaka's *izibongo* from Grout onwards is omitted, together with other comments such as the lines quoted above about the old men and old women, where the point of view shifts to Shaka's disadvantage, and the "Help me, Mapitha and Ngqengelele" and "King, you are wrong" praises, where the criticisms are explicit.

Third, and most significantly, Gwebisa repeats the stock metaphors of earlier versions but adapts them to carry entirely different meanings. To consider just one of several possible examples:

> The hawk which I saw sweeping down from Mangcengeza;
> When he came to Pungashe he disappeared.
> He invades, the forests echo, saying, in echoing,
> He paid a fine of the duiker and the doe.
> He is seen by the hunters who trap the flying ants:
> He was hindered by a cock in front,
> By the people of Ntomazi and Langa.
> He devoured Nomahlanjana, son of Zwide;
> He devoured Mdandalazi, son of Gaqa of the amaPela;
> He was lop-eared.

The Driver-away of the old man born of Langa's daughter!
The Ever-ready-to-meet-any-challenge!
Shaka![71]

Gwebisa here has brought together several praises that in Stuart's megapoem belong to quite different contexts. Stuart's "hawk," for example, is a metaphor for the speed of Shaka's military maneuvers, which are too swift to follow ("They said, 'Hawk, there he is, here he is / Whereas he was silent in the forest like the leopards and lions.'")[72] Stuart's reference to the "cock" that "prevented him" refers to Shaka's attack on Nomogaga, when he arrived with his regiment (*impi*) at dawn, too late to attack in darkness. Finally, the image of the forests speaking and of a fine being paid is actually a praise from the *izibongo* of Ndaba, Shaka's ancestor, who is praised as a hunter so successful that the forest itself protested.[73] Gwebisa has appropriated these metaphors, including the one from Ndaba's praises, which, as we have noted, are implicitly critical of Shaka, and recombined them into a sequence that claims that Shaka disappeared into the forests to hunt, was manly enough to be extremely successful in hunting, as other hunters bore witness, but was then quite gratuitously interrupted in this peaceful activity by a "cock"— that is, in Gwebisa's version, the followers of Zwide. There follows a brief description of the war with Zwide, in which the long catalogs of the defeated in Stuart's (and Samuelson's) version have been cut to just two names, and which is described in purely defensive terms. This sanitized Shaka is "the cluster of stones . . . / Which sheltered elephants," "Ever-ready-to-meet-any-challenge," who "drove away Zwide" after his unprovoked attack—another praise that is repeated several times.[74] The poem ends with the nation's protector rallying the regiments for victory.

As with the two versions of the praises of Moshoeshoe, the program of reinterpreting Shaka's place in Zulu history has been carried out without introducing new material. Gwebisa has remained largely faithful to the stock of metaphors associated with Shaka's name, metaphors which draw their authority from the fact, or at least the belief, that they can be referred back to actual historical events by those who know best. Gwebisa's *izibongo* is constructed from the same "evidence" as earlier versions, but he has reinterpreted it to provide a historical and moral assessment appropriate to his audience, the Reverend E. W. Grant, and to his times.

We have now described with reference to three examples—the *Paiva* song, the praises of Moshoeshoe I, and those of Shaka—how certain metaphors, created at particular historical junctures, come to stand as the bearers of history and remain in the cultures concerned as evaluative precedents, the "evidence" to be deployed by subsequent poets as they reinterpret that history. It should be clear that these metaphors are not "formulas," either in the sense that they are repeated expressions, for the original diction need not be retained, or in the sense that they repeat given "essential ideas," for their value is precisely that they provide the currency for new ideas, for reassessment and for reevaluation. Metaphors, by fusing abstract concepts with concrete images, have the characteristic of uniting physical and metaphysical elements into a rich compound of meaning. Like theory, they transcend empiricism, but in an open manner, cherishing complexity and receptive to fresh experience and interpretation. The problem remains of establishing why such oral poetry should so depend on the convention we have termed poetic license that it is appropriate to term this literary convention an aesthetic.

It is very tempting at this point to simplify the argument by separating the "art" from the "history" and to declare that the public authority of this poetry derives from the creative eloquence of the individual poets and singers. The skills of the performers are obviously extremely important. A gift for the memorable phrase and a gift for the elaboration of metaphor are both integral to poetic creation, and the wordplay of the oral poet, his mischievous game with language, his skills in punning and double entendre, his manipulation of rhythm and of expressive sound, and his control of metaphors carrying different layers of meaning, are all crucial to the impression he makes on his audience—an impression in which delight, admiration, deep feeling, and intellectual consent are all combined.[75]

When listening (as we describe in chapter six) to retired laborers from the lower Zambezi sugar company singing the *Paiva* song, it is impossible not to appreciate the enormous pleasure they derive from the song's shape. Modeled on canoe songs, it is divided between the lead singer and the chorus, with Paiva's name denounced three times before the judgment—"I have killed his money for him."—is delivered. The old men who have been grinning through the long "*wo—wo—wo—*"s bring out the final thumping insult rhyme—"His penis!"—with great shouts of laughter, while the women giggle and stop their ears against the obscenity. Though the name of the poet

who devised the *Paiva* song appears to have been forgotten, the form
has clearly contributed to its popularity and memorability. Mafeje
also reports of the pleasure taken by the township audience in the
unfamiliar "oratory" of the *imbongi* Mbutuma, and our own interviews have emphasized repeatedly that the *imbongi* is "a man who
can speak well."[76] We do not underestimate the power of a well-
turned phrase to enter history.

Nevertheless, we have been describing our own account of oral poetry in south-central Africa as constituting *in itself* an aesthetic, at
the heart of which is the concept of poetic license. To relegate aesthetic considerations to felicities of expression and then raid the
content of these songs and poems for "history" would be to abuse
them profoundly. Damane and Sanders, writing of Sotho praise
poems, claim that "as a source of detailed historical evidence, the
lithoko are disappointing. . . . In general, accuracy and clarity have
been sacrificed for the sake of eulogy and aesthetic excellence." In
complete contrast, Schapera states that the praises of the Tswana
paramount Tsekedi were particularly admired by his Ngwato informants because they were "full of history," adding the comment that
"praises in general do seem to be appreciated more for what they say
about a chief than for how they say it."[77] Schapera's comment has
the merit of reflecting oral evidence, but in fact both assumptions—
that "history" is sacrificed in praise poetry for "aesthetic excellence," or that excellence of expression is less important than "history"—are thoroughly misleading.

It is instructive to open any volume in the Oxford Library of African Literature, to which the collections edited by Schapera and by
Damane and Sanders belong, and to set it alongside any volume, say,
in the Cambridge edition of Shakespeare's plays. An average page of
each Oxford or Cambridge volume will be made up of approximately
twenty lines of text and the rest of footnotes. The Shakespearian
notes contain a mixture of information—variant readings, literary
sources, cross-references to other plays, paraphrases of difficult lines,
comments on rhetorical devices, and occasionally, in the historical
plays, an indication of where the dramatist has invented or modified
his material. The notes to the Oxford volumes of praise poems consist almost entirely of historical paraphrase, the exceptions being
comments on linguistic usage. Individuals mentioned in the praises
are identified by date and lineage, regiments are named, places are
located, battles are dated, and succession disputes are explained. In

short, the notes are primarily concerned with decoding the alternative history of the text. The information thus provided is invaluable and is a necessary preliminary to interpretation. But by reducing the texts to a set of complex historical "allusions," the different editors in the series have missed the opportunity of demonstrating that history as metaphor is not simply history as code. It is history as drama, evaluation, and judgment: history with the metaphysics included. The metaphors, elaborated into patterns of interpretation, are not simply vehicles for the events themselves. They are the means of comprehending those events in terms of permanent or changing systems of values, a means of being equal to events and hence of transcending them.

Much the same could, of course, be said of a great deal of written poetry, and it is central to our argument that there is no essential difference between oral and written literature. Print, however, does create certain tendencies. There is a useful distinction to be made between print and performance, whether in Africa or outside, at the level of timing, for example. When a poem reaches its audience through print, we expect the poet to have revised and revised his work, producing something that is polished and yet effortless, like a fine piece of pottery or a skilled carving. We take it at our own pace, appreciating its completeness as a work of art. Even when the points it makes are topical, we tend to praise it for achieving timelessness. Some oral poetry resembles this. There are songs and poems that have been preserved over long periods because they express perfectly what people feel on certain subjects, the words remaining largely unchanged because "they come from our fathers." There are others composed well in advance of performance and polished to perfection in rehearsal. The songs of the Chopi *migodo* described in chapter four are good examples. In general, though, the tendency of oral poetry is for it to be concerned with the drama of the moment.

The oral poet's sentences are likely to be short and fairly simple in construction. The subject of the poem is often repeated over and over again. The time is usually the present. Even when describing historical events, the oral poet is never happy for long with past tenses, preferring the present because of its greater vividness. For the same reason, he keeps moving back from third-person pronouns to first and second persons. He jumps from reported speech to direct speech, the actual words used being quoted. If a phrase or image has gone down well with his audience, he will repeat it and enlarge upon it.

Sometimes it takes him a while to hit his stride, and there are moments when he almost dries up and pads his lines, waiting for inspiration. He cannot, like the poet with a pen, address his work to eternity, waiting to be appreciated by a later generation. The audience is there in front of him, and his first business is to hold their attention. It is this demand, as much as anything, that explains the liveliness of oral poetry, its directness and immediacy, the alertness of its comments. Implicit in the very mechanics of performance is an expectation that something of public interest is being said, and said in a manner worth attention.

At what point in history oral poets in southern Africa succeeded in formalizing such expectations into a convention of poetic license that privileges poetry and song above all other forms of oral discourse is impossible to establish. Much easier to demonstrate, as we show in the following chapters, is the number of guises in which this aesthetic can appear. At its simplest, in the testimony recorded by Andrew Smith and reiterated by the singers of the *Paiva* song, it takes the form of bald insistence on the right of anyone singing a song to incorporate any criticism he or she chooses. No special skills in composition or performance need be involved. Andrew Smith witnessed this convention being applied to what he calls "a lower order of songs" more "barren of ideas" and more "vulgarly expressed."[78] It is clear, however, that there are societies in which such license to comment is linked with poetic excellence, and perhaps in Africa as a whole, this is a more common emphasis. Commenting on Dinka poetry, for example, Francis Deng describes how a man may speak of his wealth in song, may accept his wife's praises in song, may discuss sexual experience in song, and may criticize his father in song, all of which topics would normally be proscribed in ordinary speech. Deng calls this candor "a medium of speech which is viewed as an artistic skill and minimises the violation of normal restrictions."[79] Similarly, the composers of the Chopi *migodo* discussed in chapter four emphasize the "mystery" of the composer's art that gives them the moral authority to rebuke wrongdoers within the community:

> We see you!
> We know you are leading that child astray.
> Katini sees but keeps quiet,
> Although he knows it all right, he keeps quiet, Katini, the leader of
>   the *timbilas*.
> We know you![80]

The warning comes at the end of Katini's *ngodo* of 1943, the theme of which has been the power of Chopi music to bring tears to the eyes of even the ruling Portuguese.

It is a short step from this to the conviction described earlier in our comments on Mafeje's pioneering work that the poetic license is vested, *not* in the poem or song, but in the poet or singer, certain figures having acquired quasi-constitutional authority as "spokesmen of the people." We argued that this belief is misplaced, as are also the parallels frequently invoked with Celtic bards and medieval court jesters. In practice, however, in some communities the idea has taken on a life of its own, the academic conclusions of one generation feeding the poetic practices of the next. In interviews conducted by Jeff Opland during the 1970s, his informants repeatedly made the point that "the praise singers or imbongis, they have a license of theirs which they give themselves." Although there are hints in some of the testimony that this development is a recent one—"nowadays people do say that the imbongi has freedom of speech"[81]—there is no doubt that in the contemporary apartheid state the belief in the right of the black poet to comment without redress has become fundamental to the creation of both oral and written poetry. Opland in an excellent essay has described the imprisonment of the Xhosa *imbongi* Mncedisi Qangula for protesting about the arrest and deportation of Kaiser Matanzima's old political rival, Sabata Dalinyebo, paramount chief of the Thembu. Continuing to chant poetry through the bars of his prison cell, Qangule was reported as saying, "This precious talent is bestowed on me by God. Nobody can arrogate to himself the dubious authority of telling me not to use it."[82] More recently, there are indications that this belief in the privileged status of the *imbongi* has been effectively superceded for the *Staffrider* generation, although not for "traditional" reasons, by a return to an older aesthetic in which poetic license is vested demographically in the individual poem.[83]

Poetic license may also be reinforced by appearing under the guise of spirit possession. It is significant that this should especially apply to performances by women. Women singing the *vimbuza* spirit-possession songs of rural northern Malawi or urban Zambia are not assumed to be "responsible" for comments they are addressing to their husbands or other relatives or neighbors or for those on the structures of authority within which they are disadvantaged. The "complaint" is viewed as being expressed by a spirit that has temporarily taken possession of her. This spirit may be that of a long-dead hunter or chief of a rival community threatening to drive her mad unless reparations are made that will bind her once more to her own community and people. In the *nantongwe* spirit-possession ceremonies of the neighboring Yao peoples, a spirit of a recently deceased relative might speak on her behalf. Whatever is sung during these ceremonies is licensed in the sense that the complaints are expressed with impunity and that the "free speech" of the possession songs is integral to the cure:

> Words in my heart,
> Words in my heart,
> E-e-e-e-e!
> I will bring them out.[84]

Our analysis of this phenomenon in chapter seven of this volume throws light on why the normal poetic license of these women's songs should require such powerful reinforcement.

As these guises under which poetic license may appear suggest, the aesthetic we are describing has itself been an arena of historical struggle. Andrew Smith argued in 1835 that the right to complain in song was welcome to Mzilikazi, who thereby "becomes acquainted with the sentiments, views and wishes of his subjects."[85] But not everyone in authority has been as wise and open-minded as Mzilikazi. The chronic imbalance in relationships of power sometimes tilts badly towards the ruler, and with this situation comes the censor. Our chapters give numerous examples of attempts to control poetic license, ranging from the banning of songs by missionaries or colonial radio stations or Bantustan authorities or national presidents to, at the opposite end of the spectrum, the appropriation of praise songs by rulers as a facet of state rituals. Among the Ndebele this appropriation seems to have occurred as early as the 1870s under Lobengula, Mzilikazi's successor, while the appointment of carefully vetted and trained court poets was a significant feature of Sobhuza II's struggle for political dominance in Swaziland in the decades up to independence. Against this background of a constant, although often distant, threat of censorship and retribution, it is not surprising that there should have been attempts to reinforce poetry's authority by emphasizing the mystery of the poet's art, by claiming for individual poets quasi-constitutional status, or by invoking religious sanctions in the belief that songs are the voices of powerful spirits speaking through their medium.

The problem for kings and chiefs and governors and presidents, as well as for employers and parents and husbands and senior wives, is that oral poetry is less amenable to censorship and control than poetry in print. Even in the Malawi of its dictator, Life President Hastings Kamuzu Banda, where government censors monitor opinion at every level, including newspapers, parliamentary debates, and published literature, and where, in the words of Malawi's finest poet, the old songs have been changed "to watered down propaganda to praise the new leaders with very little poetic insight,"[86] praise songs sung by members of the officially sponsored Women's League continue to influence the political agenda at public meetings. As we show in chapter eight, they can even on rare occasions redirect political debate in ways unwelcome to the Life President, demonstrating the continuing vigor of a long-established poetic convention.

The authority of oral poetry, then, is an aesthetic authority, a reflection of its public and protected role as a vehicle for heroic celebration or satiric comment or lament or entertainment, or any combination of these. The poet is expected to be eloquent, someone who can speak well. But he is above all expected to be knowledgeable. A poem is "a way of tracing one's roots—we've done this, we've done that." A good poet is "somebody who knows the history and can explain everything. . . . when something happens in the land he puts it in."[87] "Singing praises for a chief or anything, it's an inspiration. You talk about things, but you must have knowledge of the whole set up. . . . The *Imbongi* . . . they had knowledge of their history, where their nation came from, generation after generation. . . . Now the *imbongi*'s aims in criticising the chief were that, he even criticized the councillors, you know, that is why he was recognised as an important figure because he is the man who's regarded as intelligent."[88] Sharp distinctions are made between poets who merely recite familiar texts and those who "know the history," who can "build things up" and "include them in their praises."[89]

This emphasis enables us to perceive the continuity of a particular poetic tradition over a wide area of southern Africa, and probably further afield, and over a long period of time and to gain access to the past and present intellectual life of communities that have hitherto been assumed to have had few important ideas or whose ideas have had to be inferred mechanically through the analysis of institutions and patterns of behavior. Rarely in the writing of African history has it been possible to demonstrate in any depth the part played by African thinking in the unfolding of events. Yet the region's poets are in the profoundest sense the intellectuals of their societies. In addition to their intrinsic value, the resulting songs and poems are a constant source of historical insight.

Finally, this emphasis enables us to recognize the lines of continuity between oral and written poetry in southern Africa. As we demonstrate in chapter eight, the conventions of oral poetry remain available to writers like Mapanje to be reworked in written forms and in English, confirming yet again Mbulelo Mzamane's contention that "in practice the distinction between traditional oral modes and Western literary forms does not exist or, at least, is never clearly demarcated. Black writers often operate, unconsciously most of the time, within both traditions."[90] The result is an unusually interesting kind of poetry, one apparently distinguished by the originality of its "voices" in creating imagined worlds but in fact drawing its metaphors directly from recent events and providing for local readers a guide to contemporary history.

In the final analysis, the long popularity of the *Paiva* song in the lower Zambezi area has had little to do with its form—the simple language, the accumulative rhythm, the concluding ribald rhyme— enjoyable though those may be. It has depended on what is widely believed to have been the audacity of its original protest at a historical moment people still cherish, and on the absolute precision of its central metaphor in expressing the plantations workers' complaint about the sugar company. What the original, long-forgotten poet possessed was the imagination to address the company as Paiva, thus insisting that the new relationship between capital and labor remained at bottom a personal one imposing mutual obligations. He also had the imagination to establish the metaphorical link between hunting game and producing sugar, those two areas of male enterprise, the former ruled by strict conventions about the sharing of gain, the latter apparently governed by the right of the powerful to appropriate without just reciprocity. As the testimony shows, it was the exactness of the song's central metaphor in linking past values to present experience that established it as the history that "even our children will have to know."[91] The fact that the poet made use of an existing form, the canoe song, with its rhythms of cooperation, and that he showed skill in its deployment, only confirmed the quality of his vision. The song was audacious, pleasurable, and true. Endlessly adaptable, it remained in the culture over eight decades as a "map of experience" with reference to which the singers could celebrate FRELIMO's victory over Paiva and the opening of a new historical era in Zambezia.

Notes

1. L. Vail and L. White, *Capitalism and Colonialism in Mozambique: A Study of Quelimane District* (London and Minneapolis, 1980).

2. Sung by Charlie Vicente and the men of Chimbazo village, Mopeia, Mozambique, 13 August 1975.

3. Group interview, Pirira village, Luabo, Mozambique, 25 October 1976.

4. *Aesthetic* is a difficult word, laden with associations irrelevant to our purpose that have arisen from postromantic criticism. It was originally coined in the mid-eighteenth century as a term for the science of perceptions, for the process of our apprehension of the world through images and hence as a summation of the shared assumptions of artist and audience about the nature of artistic creativity. Its antithesis became *anaesthetic,* the suppression of all sensation. In the hands of Walter Pater and the aesthetes, who vulgarized Keats's equation of Truth with Beauty, its meaning was narrowed to the belief in Beauty as a sufficient end and hence to the doctrine of Art for Art's Sake.

Since the 1960s, in conscious rebellion against art per se, it has been reappropriated by African, Carribean, and African-American critics in an attempt to create a "Black Aesthetic," contending that all beauty is socially crafted. At times, this criticism has been crudely reductive, but one effect, welcome in the absence of meaningful alternatives, has been to reinstate more generally something of the term's original meaning. In our usage, we intend to sum up by it the common set of assumptions about the crafting of poetic images that we identify as prevailing in the societies of southern Africa. (See Raymond Williams, *Keywords: A Vocabulary of Culture and Society* [London, 1976], 27–28).

5. Personal communication, Luiza Drennon, 25 October 1976.

6. Group interview, Pirira village, Luabo, Mozambique, 25 October 1976.

7. K. Barber, "Documenting Social and Ideological Change through Yoruba Oriki: A Stylistic Analysis," *Journal of the Historical Society of Nigeria* 10, no. 4 (1981): 39–52, and D. Coplan, "The Power of Oral Poetry: Narrative Songs of the Basotho Migrants," *Research in African Literature* 18 (1987): 1–35.

8. A. P. Merriam, "Song Texts of the Bashi," *African Music Society Journal* 1 (1954): 51–52.

9. E. E. Evans-Pritchard, "Some Collective Expressions of Obscenity in Africa," in his *The Position of Women in Primitive Societies and Other Essays in Social Anthropology* (Oxford, 1965), 76–101.

10. H. Tracey, *Chopi Musicians* (London, 1948), 68.

11. Ibid., 10. The translation is Tracey's.

12. Ibid., 10–11.

13. Ibid., 15.

14. M. Gluckman, "Rituals of Rebellion in South-East Africa," in his *Order and Rebellion in Tribal Africa* (New York, 1963), 110–36; H. Kuper, "A Ritual of Kinship among the Swazi," *Africa* 14 (1944): 230–56, reprinted in chapter 13 of Kuper's *An African Aristocracy* (London, 1947), 197–225.

15. Gluckman, "Introduction," to his *Order and Rebellion*, 9, 19; Gluckman, "Rituals of Rebellion in South-East Africa," 125, 127.

16. Gluckman, "Introduction," 19. Gluckman's essay is "Social Aspects of First-Fruit Ceremonies among the South-Eastern Bantu," *Africa* 11 (1938): 25–41.

17. Gluckman, "Introduction" to *Order and Rebellion*, ix, 19.

18. Kuper, *An African Aristocracy*, 205; H. Kuper, *Sobhuza II: Ngwenyama and King of Swaziland* (London, 1978), 19.

19. R. C. A. Samuelson, *Long, Long Ago* (Durban, 1927; rpt. Durban, 1974), 278.

20. Gluckman, "Rituals of Rebellion in South-East Africa," 127.

21. J. C. Mitchell, *The Kalela Dance*, Rhodes-Livingstone Paper no. 27 (Manchester, 1956); M. Gluckman, "Analysis of a Social Situation in Modern Zululand," *Bantu Studies* 14, nos. 1 and 2 (1940): 1–30, 147–74.

22. Mitchell, *Kalela Dance*, 42.

23. We are grateful to Dr. Chipasha Luchembe and, especially, to Messrs. C. S. Chanda, T. W. Kalusa, M. M. Musa, and K. A. Mwenya for our own information on *kalela*.

24. Interview with D. S. Mwape, Samfya, Zambia, 1 April 1987. (Translations of all such interviews are by the authors.)

25. Mitchell, *Kalela Dance*, 9, 7.

26. Interviews with Seja Kashimba, Kitwe, Zambia, 13 April 1987, and with a group from the Msunda Cultural Team, Samfya, Zambia, 14 April 1987. Also see Mitchell, *Kalela Dance*, 9.

27. Interviews with G. Mulenga and Evaristo Kampinda, Ndola, Zambia, 8 April 1987.

28. Interview with Albert Chongo, Mansa, Zambia, 11 April 1987.

29. Interview with Saviour Ngandwe, Mansa, Zambia, 10 April 1987.

30. Interview with Mederty C. Kasese, Mansa, Zambia, 10 April 1987.

31. Interviews with Emmanuel Chipulu, Samfya, Zambia, 12 April 1987; Mwana Sejenno, Samfya, Zambia, 16 April 1987; and Andrew Mumba, Mansa, Zambia, 9 April 1987.

32. A. Mafeje, "A Chief Visits Town," *Journal of Local Administration Overseas* 2 (1963): 88–99, and "The Role of the Bard in a Contemporary African Community," *Journal of African Languages* 6, no. 3 (1967): 193–223.

33. Mafeje, "A Chief Visits Town," 91–92, quoted in J. Opland, *Xhosa Oral Poetry* (Cambridge, 1983), 58–59.

34. Mafeje, "The Role of the Bard," 195–96.

35. Opland, *Xhosa Oral Poetry*, 69, asserts that Mafeje tape-recorded all the poems, but Mafeje makes no such claim.

36. Mafeje, "Role of the Bard," 216.

37. Ibid., 221.

38. A. C. Jordan, "Towards an African Literature," *Africa South* 2, no. 1 (October-December 1957): 104–5, and 3, no. 2 (January-March 1959): 74. See also his *Towards an African Literature: The Emergence of Literary Form in Xhosa* (Berkeley and Los Angeles, 1973).

39. M. V. Mzamane, "The Uses of Traditional Oral Forms in Black South African Literature," in *Literature and Society in South Africa*, ed. L. White and T. Couzens (Harlow, Essex, 1984), 147–48.

40. Kgositsile quoted ibid., 148; M. Kunene, *Emperor Shaka the Great* (London, 1979), xxv–xxvi.

41. Kunene, *Emperor Shaka*, 54–58.

42. *Andrew Smith's Journal of His Expedition into the Interior of South Africa, 1834–36*, ed. W. F. Lye (Cape Town, 1975), 239.

43. Mafeje, "Role of the Bard," 194.

44. Ibid., 195; Interview with Mr. Hlabangana, Bulawayo, Zimbabwe, 8 April 1982.

45. See A. Wainwright, P. McAllister, and P. Wallace, *The Xhosa Imbongi (Praise Poet) as a Conveyer of Social Criticism and Praise in the Mining Industry*, Research Report 39/78, Johannesburg, Chamber of Mines and South Africa Research Organisation (1979). Songs were also featured in the organization of the strike that occurred at Wilson-Rowntree in 1985 and occur at virtually every political demonstration in contemporary South Africa. See also Mi S'Dumo Hlatshwayo and Alfred Tembo Qabula, "The Tears of COSATU" (Durban?, n.d.)

46. Jordan, "Towards an African Literature," 105.

47. I. Schapera, *Praise-Poems of Tswana Chiefs* (Oxford, 1965); T. Cope, *Izibongo: Zulu Praise Poetry* (Oxford, 1968); M. Damane and P. B. Sanders, *Lithoko: Sotho Praise Poems* (Oxford, 1974); and A. C. Hodza and G. Fortune, *Shona Praise Poetry* (Oxford, 1979).

48. Cope, *Izibongo*, 88–117.

49. Damane and Sanders, *Lithoko*, 65–69, 73–75. See also L. White, "Power and the Praise Poem," *Journal of Southern African Studies* 9, no. 1 (1982): 19–23.

50. Damane and Sanders, *Lithoko*, 66–67.

51. Ibid., 26–27.

52. Ibid., 78.

53. Ibid., 73–74.

54. Rev. E. W. Grant, "The Izibongo of the Zulu Chiefs," *Bantu Studies* 3

(1927–29): 201–44. The argument developed in this section of the chapter was first developed in L. White and T. Couzens, *Literature and Society*, 12–14, before being extended, elaborated, and qualified by Mbongeni Malaba in his excellent "Shaka as a Literary Theme," Ph.D. diss., University of York, 1986. See also E. Gunner, "The Pool of Metaphors: Poetic Language and Its Use in Zulu Praise Poetry," in *Memory and Poetic Structure: Papers of the Conference on Oral Literature and Literary Theory*, ed. P. Ryan (London, Middlesex Polytechnic, 1981), 168–78.

55. Grant, "Izibongo," 202. It is not wholly clear that the *imbongi* here is Gwebisa.

56. See N. Etherington, *Preachers and Politics in South Africa, 1835–80* (London, 1978).

57. Cf. J. Guy, *The Destruction of the Zulu Kingdom* (London, 1979).

58. Quoted in S. Marks, *The Ambiguities of Dependence in South Africa: Class, Nationalism, and the State in Twentieth Century Natal* (Baltimore and London, 1986), 53–54.

59. Ibid., 70.

60. Grant, "Izibongo," 229.

61. For a discussion of Shaka's promise, see Malaba, "Shaka as a Literary Theme," 6–15. A meticulously edited version of the text given in Arbousset and Daumas has been published by D. Rycroft in "An 1842 Version of Dingana Eulogies," *African Studies Journal* 43, no. 2 (1984): 249–74.

62. L. Grout, *Zululand: Or Life among the Zulu-Kafirs of Natal and Zululand* (1864; rpt., London, 1970), 197; Samuelson, *Long, Long Ago*, 260–66; A. T. Bryant, *Olden Days in Zululand and Natal* (London, 1929), 663; Cope, *Izibongo*, 88–117 (cobbled from material in J. Stuart, *uTulasizwe* [London, 1923]). Subsequent volumes of *izibongo* published by Stuart were *uHlangakula* (London, 1924), *uBaxoexele* (London, 1924), *uKulemetule* (London, 1925), and *uVusezakiti* (London, 1926).

63. Cope, *Izibongo*, 92, 106.

64. Malaba, "Shaka as a Literary Theme," 79.

65. Ibid., 106.

66. Cope, *Izibongo*, 72.

67. White, "Power and the Praise Poem," 19.

68. M. M. Fuze, *The Black People and Whence They Came: A Zulu View* (Pietermaritzburg, Natal, 1979), 73. The book was originally written in 1905. A full text of the song is given in Samuelson, *Long, Long Ago*, 254.

69. Cope, *Izibongo*, 72.

70. Grant, "Izibongo," 209.

71. Ibid., 211.

72. Cope, *Izibongo*, 98.

73. Ibid., 92, 72.

74. Grant, "Izibongo," 211.

75. One of our difficulties in writing this book, implicit in our argument as to the existence of a common aesthetic in south-central Africa over a

wide area and a long period of time, is that we have had to discuss poems in a multiplicity of languages and in several instances we have had to work from translations. If poetry is, as has been suggested, "what is left out in translation," then many of our comments and interpretations will need modifying by critics "versed" in the languages of which we are ignorant. None of the chapters that follow this one makes any claim to be definitive, and we must await the further intervention of those to whom the poems we discuss speak from deep inside their own cultures.

76. Mafeje, "A Chief Visits Town," 92–93; interview with Isaac Dlamini, Lobamba, Swaziland, 21 August 1985.

77. Damane and Sanders, *Lithoko*, 59; Schapera, *Praise Poems*, 15.

78. *Andrew Smith's Journal*, 238.

79. F. Deng, *The Dinka and Their Songs* (Oxford, 1973), 87–88.

80. Tracey, *Chopi Musicians*, 28–29.

81. Testimony of Justice Mabandla, in Opland, *Xhosa Oral Poetry*, 70; testimony of Max Khamie, ibid., 76.

82. Ibid., 267.

83. See M. Vaughan, "*Staffrider* and Directions within Contemporary South African Literature," pp. 196–212 in *Literature and Society in South Africa*, ed. L. White and T. Couzens (Harlow, Essex, 1984).

84. Quoted in L. E. White, *Magomero: Portrait of an African Village* (Cambridge, 1987), 189.

85. Smith, *Journal*, 238.

86. J. A. C. Mapanje, "The Use of Traditional Literary Forms in Modern Malawian Writing in English," M. Phil. thesis, University of London, 1974, 29–30.

87. Interview with Mr. Hlabangana, Bulawayo, Zimbabwe, 8 April 1982; interview with Isaac Dhlamini, Lomamba, Swaziland, 21 August 1985.

88. Interview with Nelson Tile Mabunu, quoted in Opland, *Xhosa Oral Poetry*, 81–82.

89. Interview with Isaac Dlamini, Lomamba, Swaziland, 21 August 1985.

90. Mzamane, "The Uses of Traditional Oral Forms in Black South African Literature," 147.

91. Interview with Jiwa Todo, Luabo, Mozambique, 2 November 1976.

3

The Development of Forms
Ndebele Royal Praises

In 1835, thirteen years after they had left Natal in the face of pressures from the area's growing trade in slaves and four years before they were driven north of the Limpopo River by the Afrikaner Voortrekkers, the Ndebele people, led by Mzilikazi Khumalo, were settled at the former Hurutshe town of Mosega, in the western Transvaal.[1] They had lived there for almost three years, longer than usual in their continuing anabasis. But the site was no more than a compromise, reflecting their predicament. Mzilikazi was anxious to maintain his contacts with traders from the east coast, but at the same time, he also wanted to be beyond reach of Dingane, the Zulu leader to the east, whose attacks were anticipated daily.

In June 1835, Mzilikazi was visited at Mosega by Dr. Andrew Smith, who was in command of a major expedition "to or towards the centre of South Africa" in 1834–35.[2] The expedition was sponsored by the Cape of Good Hope Association for Exploring Central Africa, and it included among its members an astronomer, a mapmaker, an artist, and a trader. Smith himself had earlier been a guest of Dingane at Bulawayo, in Zululand. Though he spoke no African languages, he proved to be an excellent observer and a persistent questioner, inquiring into matters "which other travelers either did not trouble to ask or did not bother to record."[3] During the visit to Mzilikazi, he was guided by the missionary Robert Moffat, who had met the Ndebele leader five years earlier. Moffat repeatedly records his admiration of Smith for being "persevering and most minute in investigation,"[4] and his own account of the meeting with Mzilikazi in letters to Mary Moffat provides a fascinating supplement to Smith's enormously detailed *Diary* and *Journal*.[5]

At the time of the expedition, all imperatives for the Ndebele were military. Responsible for this situation were interrelated changes that were then rapidly affecting the whole of southern Africa in addition to many of the areas to the north. The first of these was economic, involving the growth of long-distance trades in ivory and slaves from the interior of Africa to the Indian Ocean coast. Steady demand for ivory for the manufacture of piano keys, billiard balls, and objets d'art assured its continued high value throughout the nineteenth century. The British suppression of the slave trade north of the equator in 1807 pushed that trade south of the equator, and southern and central Africa became prime sources for slaves to work the plantations of the New World, Zanzibar, and Pemba, and Indian Ocean islands such as Réunion and Mauritius. To East African ports such as Zanzibar, Mozambique Island, Quelimane, and Inhambane slaves were brought and thence shipped overseas. This trade remained important for the region well into the 1890s, but sources of ivory and slaves moved steadily westward. In the decades after 1810, therefore, commercial frontiers of ivory and slave trading moved from east to west, sometimes separately and sometimes congruently. Competition for resources was often bitter, and the two commercial frontiers were accompanied by a frontier of violence fed by an increasing flow of guns and gunpowder into the region.

The second source of change was the pressure from the European settlement areas of South Africa as different groups of people moved northward from the Cape Colony in search of ivory, animal products, and labor, often in the form of slaves. Groups of people of mixed racial background, variously known at the time as Bastards, Korana, or, most commonly, Griqua, both challenged indigenous Africans for control over the land and its resources and sought slaves from among them. European frontiersmen, hunters, and pastoralists joined in this struggle. From the late eighteenth century onward, these culturally diverse groups established a set of small "states" in the interior of South Africa, trading for hides and hunting for ivory and frequently attacking their neighbors as they did so. Such initial pressures increased in the 1820s as a consequence of labor shortages in the Cape Colony that prompted British interests—both official and nonofficial—to venture toward the north and northeast in search of so-called Mantatee slaves.[6] Then, in the 1830s, thousands of Afrikaner Voortrekkers also migrated into the interior, spreading out over the veldt after their Great Trek from the eastern Cape Colony and establishing new republics that were characterized by their aggressive expansion into the territory of their African and Griqua neighbors.

From the late 1810s onward, then, the African peoples of Natal and

the deeper interior came to be caught up, in the words of Julian Cobbing, "in the trans-continental crossfire of interrelated European
plunder systems"—one from the east coast and one from the south.[7]
Their response to these novel pressures was to seek security wherever it could be obtained. Stockaded settlements—some of them
large towns offering protection to thousands, others no more than
villages hidden among the rocks of mountains or in the thickets of
papyrus along river valleys—soon dotted the entire region. In certain
areas new defensive states marked by increased centralization of authority and a high degree of military preparedness on the model of
Shaka's Zulu state were established. While these new states resisted
outside pressures upon them, they also fought among themselves for
land, cattle, and people. The struggle was long and arduous, and the
conflicts that resulted caused widespread dislocations of peoples and
conditions of chronic insecurity in the region for many decades.

As one consequence of these acute dislocations, African people
throughout the region, regardless of their own personal cultural
background or identity, were compelled to seek new, more secure political and social conditions for themselves and their families. Some
fled to the Cape Colony and became laborers on European farms.
Most, however, remained north of the Cape and, out of need, became
the clients of powerful patrons who, through their access to guns and
men, were able to provide them with a measure of security that was
otherwise unavailable. Large stockaded settlements came to dot the
entire region, and new and larger political entities centered upon
these protected zones took shape, replacing the scattered, smaller-
scale polities of earlier decades. In the process, new identities—such
as that of the Ndebele—crystallized.

During his journey in the mid-1830s, Andrew Smith discovered
that for "some time little or nothing was derived from the produce
of the soil" meaning that "the principal support of the natives . . .
was of necessity derived from their herds," which had to be protected
at all costs.[8] Despite the visible threats of ecological damage and disease, the people lived in large-scale settlements for the protection
they afforded, and it was the "ambition of the savage chief to be surrounded by as many of his people as he can collect." Moshoeshoe's
stronghold at Thaba Bosiu, for instance, was a natural bulwark so
secure that "a mere handful of defenders situated on the high cliffs
. . . and amply provided with large stones . . . may bid defiance to any
number of assailants."[9] There on the summit, where "all the most
sheltered situations" were "covered with groups of huts," the newly

constituted Sotho people lived, descending with the herds of cattle during the daytime and returning each evening, "winding their course up the rugged declivities of the mountain."[10] Another of these newly stockaded areas was Thaba Nchu, the fastness of the Tlokwa leader, Sekonyela. This was accessible only by one ravine in which a "stone wall of great thickness and not badly built had been carried across, from precipice to precipice," leaving "a small passage just sufficient to admit men and cattle."[11]

According to Moshoeshoe, Mzilikazi had himself "more than once expressed a wish to be permitted to retire to one of these hills with his people and live in peace." But by contrast, Mosega, Mzilikazi's capital, was on an open plain. Its only protection was that it was situated in a shallow basin so that "the traveller requires to arrive at its very brink before it can be seen and thus, . . . he may find himself in contact with hundreds of Zoolas before he would have any reason to believe himself near a human being.[12]

Although Smith describes these settlements as "tribes," he is thoroughly aware that they were composed of "very heterogeneous materials" and that cultural identity had become subject to the demands of survival. A strict division of labor had evolved, by the terms of which women were responsible for building houses and caring for children and doing whatever cultivation was possible, while the men performed "all the duties required for the cattle, besides engaging in hunting, war and plunder."[13] Cutting across this gender division, moreover, was a further division of "every tribe" into "classes":

> As far as South Africa is known, nearly every tribe is found to consist of three distinct classes of persons. First, the wealthy class. Second, a portion of the poorer class, disposed to reside with and serve the former, and third, the remainder of the latter class who either from disinclination to servitude or an inability to obtain it, trust for support to other means, and in pursuit of them remove from the haunts of their more settled countrymen and establish themselves in positions best adapted for the objects they have in view.[14]

Though most of Smith's encounters were with the "wealthy" chiefs and their clients, he remained throughout his journey acutely alert to the presence of his "third class," those who were not attached to the stockades or fortresses and whose protection was their poverty, their complete destitution being "their only safeguard," ensuring "anything like peace."[15] These people who possessed "literally nothing but what the earth or the chase afforded them" lived on the distant borders of the kingdoms to which they remained nominally subject. Frequently, as in the case of the various Tswana-speaking clans conquered by Mzilikazi, they were heirs of older political groupings that had been subdued and put to work as herders and tobacco growers for their new overlords. Smith paints a picture of poverty increasing in direct proportion to the distance from the new states' capitals of Thaba Bosiu, Thaba Nchu, or Mosega, with the most desperate people of all living on the very borders yet still fulfilling the political functions of maintaining their rulers' claims to territorial sovereignty and of acting as "spies," providing information about the movement of potential enemies.[16]

Smith's sympathies as a traveler are entirely with the "paupers." He records with indignation how Mzilikazi calls them "his dogs." He notes that if the Tswana men "wish any peace or favour," they must "exhibit the most supplicating looks, employ the most humiliating gestures and give utterance to the most endearing and at the same time most submissive expressions such as *Baba kosi* etc."[17] He was, all the same, hardheaded enough to argue that the solution to the problem of the region's acute political insecurity lay in the growth of new states of greater scale and power. These new groupings he called tribes. There already existed, he noted, a rough balance of power between Dingane and Mzilikazi, rulers of the two most powerful of the new post-Shakan states. Though this balance of power contained in itself the threat of a major war, it was for the time being a better guarantor of peace than the "general disorder" that followed upon the existence of many "separate independent hordes." His conclusion was that the "more speedily large tribes are formed the sooner will civilization be effected."[18]

His conclusion about the desirability of building up new "large tribes" led Smith into a series of reflections on the nature of chieftaincy and relationships of power in the new and still-fluid societies in the making. An extended conversation with Moshoeshoe had brought him to the realization that the chiefs were intelligent politicians as well as military leaders and that the most difficult thing to achieve in a newly established state was the continuing consent of the governed. Even the most powerful of the new leaders soon found that their people would desert them if the terms of survival under their leadership and patronage became too onerous. As Smith commented, "It is to the liability of chiefs to being forsaken by their subjects that the latter owe their principal privileges . . . otherwise there

would be no protection for them against tyranny and oppression."
The organization of food production, the distribution of the proceeds
of raiding, the levying of tribute, the hearing of cases, the balancing
of different interest groups and especially of the clans of the wealthy,
the management of the army, and the administration of subsidiary
settlements and headmanships all had to be undertaken in a manner
that ensured the consent of the governed. In the last resort, even a
powerful chief like Moshoeshoe was bound by the "caprice of his
subjects."[19]

In June 1835, as he approached Mzilikazi at Mosega, Smith was
preoccupied with the problem of how the autocratic rulers of the
new tribes could remain in touch with the concerns and wishes of
his subjects so as to ensure their continued loyalty. It was true, of
course, that the Ndebele were still at war and that Mzilikazi, as an
able general, enjoyed great popularity. The large questions of legitimacy and consent in government that were then preoccupying
Moshoeshoe had yet to arise amongst the Ndebele. For Smith's
guide, Robert Moffat, a man deeply prejudiced against African culture, there was no problem: Mzilikazi's government "was the very
essence of despotism."[20] But Smith was unconvinced by Moffat's
simplistic analysis, feeling that some channels of communication
had to exist between ruler and ruled, even among the militarized
Ndebele.

The conclusions he reached as he tried to unravel this problem are
doubly persuasive. Not only are they penetrating in themselves as
deductions from intelligent enquiry, but, inadvertently, and without
his fully understanding the fact, they were confirmed by the very
nature of the debate at Mzilikazi's court about his own and Moffat's
presence at Mosega. In his diary Smith explains briefly how Mzilikazi was customarily addressed: "They salute Masalacatzie by
'Ayaat, Kosi Immenao, Elephant Zoola, Son of Machaban,' etc. They
reckon that, though angry inclined, he leaves that disposition when
he hears these titles. When chiefs go with their people to dance in
hopes of getting food, they always appear with their shields, but at
other times they dance without them."[21] One can retranscribe
Smith's version as: "*Bayete* [Hail], *Nkhosi Elimnyama* [black chief],
Elephant, Zulu, Son of Mashobane!" These are extracts from Mzilikazi's official "praises," or *izibongo*. What Smith's cryptic note describes is the central political function the praise poem had in easing
the relations between Mzilikazi and his people and in providing a

medium through which they could press their requests upon him. In his *Journal* Smith elaborates on both these points. Although he was profoundly insensitive to the conventions of performance of what he witnessed, he was deeply responsive to their social and political implications. The passage is well worth considering at length.

It begins with a general description of the art of praising, in which are emphasized the social importance of the praise poets and their role as court historians:

> During the time we continued at the king's kraal he never visited our camp without being attended by his body guard and his dancing and singing men, but, when it happened that the latter did not actually accompany him, they were not long in making their appearance afterwards; they then instantly arranged themselves . . . near to whatever spot his Zoola majesty may have been stationed. On some occasions each of these people sang and danced at the same time, on others they simply sung when usually cross-legged on the ground, moving the body incessantly, and . . . they kept unceasingly raising and depressing the stick which each performer held in his right hand and pointing it in the direction of countries which on account of having been in some way connected with the history of their tribe were mentioned in the songs they were singing. Most of their songs being historical and by means of which the warlike feats of the tribe were handed down, it may readily be conceived that when they are sung by persons who took a prominent part in the events they describe no small enthusiasm is called forth.[22]

Smith continues by describing the performance of two such praise poems that had been composed since his expedition's arrival at Mosega:

> In some of the songs they sung while in attendance upon Musulacatzi they were very often simultaneously and with an expression of defiance pointed [*sic*] their sticks to the south and we supposed these passages to relate to Barend or John Bloom who lived in that direction and who formed prominent characters in their records.[23] On enquiry, however, we found this not to be the case. They were supposing the Amachosa would be driven from their country by the white men and that it was possible that they might attack the Zoolas to take their cattle, but, if they did, the show of sticks was meant to indicate that the spears of Musulacatzi's warriors were ready to oppose them. We naturally expressed our surprise that they would have so quickly composed a song on the Amakosa war but we were informed that this was not the only

composition they had completed since our arrival. Another had been produced describing the pleasure of the king at seeing so many Europeans, and particularly dwelt upon the circumstance of the white people "driving the Amakosie," and yet many of them were peaceably enjoying themselves amongst the Zoolas and watching their dances.[24]

These two songs clearly refer to the Sixth Xhosa War of 1835, when, following raids made by the Xhosa on the Eastern Cape at a time of drought and famine, Governor Benjamin D'Urban sent in troops to burn fields, seize cattle, and annex Xhosa territory.[25] While on the road to Mosega, the expedition had received news that the "power of the Kaffirs is broken" and that some 1200 Xhosa had been slain.[26] It is not absolutely clear from Smith's contorted syntax whether the praise singers anticipated an attack by the whites or by fleeing Xhosa, but the main point of the songs is perfectly clear. They express a deep anxiety about Mzilikazi's policy of welcoming Smith's expedition at the very time when Smith's compatriots in the Cape Colony were killing Africans and seizing their land. The second song, reinforcing the first, underlines the irony that Smith's men are actually sitting listening to these warnings "enjoying themselves amongst the Zoolas and watching their dances."[27] The singers were, of course, quite right to be concerned. Despite Mzilikazi's hopes of achieving an alliance with the English against his enemy Dingane, the Zulu king, when the Ndebele were attacked the following year, it was not by Dingane but by Afrikaner Voortrekkers.

Before commenting on Mzilikazi's reaction to this, Smith goes on to describe other types of songs sung, not by the official praisers, the *izimbongi*, but by "some of the least talented of the tribe." These "lower order of songs" were more "barren of ideas" and more "vulgarly expressed," but they served the important purpose that "Musulacatzie becomes acquainted with the sentiments, views and wishes of his subjects":

In the less important of the Zoola songs statements are made and feelings expressed with impunity which could not be conveyed directly to the ear of the king without involving the complaining parties, most frequently the composers of such songs, in trouble and danger. An instance of this occurred during one of their visits to us, and the singers showed no small judgement in the choice of a proper time for performing their song, which was immediately after we had formally handed over the cattle delivered from Mahoura. The object of the composition was to crave for animal food. The words were nearly these:

"Give us flesh that we may be strong to turn the cattle when John Bloom or Barend takes them from us. People who do not eat plenty of flesh are not fat nor in a condition to retake cattle when they are carried away. Corn is not a proper food, we must have meat."[28]

By this stage, through what must have been some very astute questioning, Smith has established five main points about Ndebele oral poetry. First, this poetry accepts that Mzilikazi's authority is supreme: whatever may be said, no challenge to the existing hierarchy is intended. Second, it serves to legitimate that hierarchy by celebrating its achievements: those who are prominent justify their position by boasting of their performance in battle. Third, there is nonetheless scope for comment on and even for criticism of aspects of Mzilikazi's leadership and the general direction of his policy. Fourth, supplementing the official praises (*izibongo;* sing., *isibongo*), there are songs in which ordinary people are able to present their requests and comments to the king, who is by this means kept in touch with popular sentiment. Fifth, and most remarkable of all, it is emphasized that all such comment is "privileged" in the sense that the song form itself carries with it a freedom of speech wholly beyond what would have been tolerated in other circumstances. The form legitimizes the content, such poetry constituting a medium free of censorship in an otherwise militarized and autocratic state.

Smith presents all this as a single day's entry in his *Journal,* though it seems fairly clear he must be including insights drawn from earlier occasions. He concludes his entry by describing Mzilikazi's reactions to all this:

During the time they sang, the king rarely appeared to attend to them, but there were moments when his attention became fixed upon the proceedings of his people and he then appeared a pensive listener or partook of the spirit of the performers and even condescended to resort to action like theirs and to hum the tune and words of the song in a low tone. When he merely listened he generally placed his elbows on his knees and his open hands upon his cheeks and thus supported the head. His look at such times indicated reflection and thought. We asked if anything was at such times expressed to make him behave so, but we could get nothing in answer but that when he did "his heart was full."

The following morning, Smith's party, whose motives the praise singers had questioned, received "no visit from Musulacatzi, the chief saying it was too cold for him to leave the house."[29]

It was two days before negotiations were resumed. Smith's explanation for the renewal of negotiations is that he sent a number of gifts to Mzilikazi, following which "perfect confidence in our intentions" was reestablished.[30] Robert Moffat's *Journal*, however, tells a different story. Moffat was making the second of what were to be five extended visits to Mzilikazi. Describing the first of these visits in 1829–30, Moffat had also emphasized, though with less specificity than Smith, the destructive aspects of the regional wars of the time. His reception by Mzilikazi, however, had been overwhelming and, to Moffat, mystifying and disturbing. Reluctant to explain it in political terms, he was inclined to attribute it to a kind of moral charisma he believed he possessed, and for long sections his *Journal* discusses little else than the power of his character over the Ndebele king.

Returning in 1835 with Smith's party, he returns to this theme. Gratified by Mzilikazi's rapture at seeing him again, he quickly decides that Smith's diplomatic approach as the representative of one government addressing the head of another is all wrong: "Smith's manner," he records, "is not calculated to win the esteem of savages." Though he continues to praise Smith's assiduity in research, it is difficult to avoid the impression that he regards investigation into Ndebele society a waste of time. When asked by Smith to help with negotiations for the proposed treaty of friendship, he refuses, feeling it his duty "to steer clear of subjects relative to Government." Only eight days later, though, his *Journal* notes disingenuously that Mzilikazi "seems to view me as a chief . . . the King of Kuruman," able to "collect and keep my people together, not by fighting, but by the power of doctrine."[31] Moffat's insight is not developed: it is simply part of the puzzle. He continues to ignore the possibility that his reception has any political dimensions or that Mzilikazi is anything but a savage tamed by the force of his character.[32]

Moffat had also been present during the praise singers' performance, though his only comment is that, as usual, it depressed him. An hour and a half after it ended, however, and unknown to Smith, Mzilikazi made a secret visit to Moffat's wagon, where he "talked very freely, made remarks about the doctor's intentions." He spoke, too, about Moshoeshoe, asking about the benefits of having missionaries at Thaba Bosiu and, obviously pumping Moffat for information, flattered him as the one man "who will tell me the truth." But he was unimpressed by Moffat's reassurances about the expedition. The following day, when negotiations on the treaty of friendship were suspended, Umnombate, Mzilikazi's most trusted adviser, arrived at court. His advice proved conclusive. On the Sunday when the negotiations were resumed, Moffat noted with sour satisfaction that Mzilikazi's "retinue, near a hundred in number, did not sing as usual."[33]

Five days later, after documents and a medal had been exchanged and Smith's party had moved on, Mzilikazi, accompanied by Umnombate, summoned a meeting: "After sitting himself down, he began a long harangue to his men (chief) on the respect paid to him by those whom he had proved to be his friends, and those who had proved him to be their friend, showing the fallacy of the reports which had been circulated by his enemies. Every sentence was hailed with eulogies and epithets of superlative but disgusting applause."[34] The matter was clearly settled, with the praise singers' doubts overruled. Moffat's *Journal* shows little awareness that he has just witnessed a fascinating interplay of politics and oral literature in a debate about foreign policy that directly concerned his own hopes and ambitions.

After Smith's departure, Moffat stayed on at Mosega for a further fortnight. Stimulated perhaps by Smith's own enquiries, he records in translation one of the poems addressed to Mzilikazi. One evening a group of six soldiers approached the king carrying shields, a sign that they intended to ask for food:

> The principal one then sallied out, walking quickly to and fro over the ground between his men and the king, talking away with all his might, now and then manoeuvring with a small rod he had in his hand, and addressing himself with great vehemence to Moselekatsie, recounting his mighty deeds as well as those of his forefathers. The following are some of the fragments of his speech: "Jan Bloom came with his commando to Kena (the Yellow River). We came to Kena. The Bastards fell and died at the battle of Kena. We also died at Kena. They fell and we fell at the battle of Kena, therefore we must eat and be fat (for tomorrow we die?) The Bastards and Corannas fell upon the Matsetse (youths taking care of the outpost). The Bastards fell and the Matsetse fell. They died. Barend fought against us with the great commando. We fell and died. They died. They will not hear (feel), though they are always killed. We must slaughter cattle and eat and be fat and strong for battle. Our father must feed us. Great is our father, the Great Elephant, the Lion, the King of Kings. His friend and companion has come to see him. His friends who have known him have come to see him. Heavens! Our father's heart is white."[35]

This was the first *isibongo* performed after the events of the previous week. For all its inadequacies as a "text," it is interesting for helping to confirm Smith's observations about their use as a medium for privileged complaint and for being the only contemporaneously recorded Ndebele poem from the period before their settlement north of the Matopos hills.

For the next examples of Ndebele poetry we must jump three decades to the closing years of Mzilikazi's life and to the writings of Thomas Morgan Thomas, who worked with the Matabeleland Mission from 1859 to 1870. By this time Ndebele society had entered a new phase in its history. The court had settled at Inyati, north of the Limpopo River and well away from the Ndebele's enemies. The refugees and captives of earlier decades had coalesced into a nation. With these changes came changes in the contents and tone of the *izibongo*, with the changes reflecting the new political realities.

Commenting that the Ndebele songs record the "history of such past events as they deem important, . . . Mr. Moffat's first visit to their king, . . . the attacks made upon themselves, and their victories over their foes, . . . their adventures in the hunt, and all journeys of any importance ever taken by them," Thomas transcribes a few examples. One of them concerns Moffat:

> This wind whence comes it?
> From Moffat from Kuruman.
> Some rejoice while others grieve. E!, E!, E!
> Some rejoice while others grieve.[36]

This suggestively ambiguous song is said to have referred initially to the bovine pleuropneumonia brought by traders from Kuruman, which had killed off cattle and created a temporary surplus of cheap beef.

The second of Thomas's examples is described as "Part of a Song in Honour of Mzilikazi":

> Thou tiger of kings, standing erect,
> Defeater of monarchs, surviving alone;
> Eaters of nations, consumer of men.
> Devourer of 'Nyoga, Umhatjo, Umzila,
> Utulwane, Sipihle, Sibindi, Ulanga;
> Devourer of Umjipa, Sikali, Pahlapahla,
> Ulituba, Kwali, Pilana, Makabe, Mafuta,

> Thou has finished the nations,
> Longing for war, with whom wilt thou fight?[37]

The provenance of this extract is not entirely clear, and no Ndebele text is provided. It appears alongside the praises of Senzangakhona, Shaka, and Dingane, which are described as having been supplied by "Mr Grout of Natal." The praises of Mzilikazi, however, refer to wars against the Zulu, the Boers, and the Griqua, which suggests that it must have been recorded at Inyati, perhaps by Thomas himself. He adds the further tantalizing comment that the poem sets up the claim that Mzilikazi is the rightful descendant of Mashobane and that the latter was the rightful descendant of ancient Zulu kings—a comment not borne out by the extract quoted and presumably referring to other parts of the praise poem.

Thomas provides a third poem, which he describes as "two lines of a lengthy song composed by Umatjobana [Mashobane] in praise of himself," which "the Amandabele seem never to weary in singing . . . nor their king of listening [to]":

> Come and see at Matjobana's, come and see!
> Come and see at Matjobana's, come and see!
> Here is the display, display of the spear;
> Come and see at Matjobana's, come and see![38]

The importance of this song is emphasized repeatedly by subsequent writers. A. C. Bailie, visiting Mzilikazi's successor, Lobengula, in 1876–78, heard the initial words as "Nausi indaba" [sic]. He describes it as the Ndebele "national anthem," claiming that it was sung only at sundown on state occasions such as the *Nxwala*, or "first fruits" celebrations.[39] Later, in a letter, he describes what he has heard of the song's origins in high romantic fashion:

> As Mzilikazi and the Ndebele left Zululand, after a war over the cattle dispute, the Ndebele regiments succeeded in recapturing the cattle— and on the fifth day, the last regiment reported back, "Naysi Indaba. Hosa Bone!" ["This is our news. Come and see!"]
>
> What a grand savage scene this presents when one pictures to the imagination the rugged peaks and precipitous defiles of the Drakensburg traversed by 1000s of victorious warriors clad in their picturesque costumes and urging with their spears the cattle before their chief, their exulting and excited women joining in the refrain and the whole scene lighted up and tinted by a sunset such as is seldom seen in other

parts of the world. . . . Mzilikazi, on this occasion, seemed to be carried away by his emotion. He made a speech to his people, telling them that they should become a great nation and assuming there and then the chieftainship. He proclaimed the chant Nauci Indaba [*sic*] to be their national anthem, and the name of the regiment who first sung it in his presence the "Swangindaba" ["Returned with the news"]. He further proclaimed that it would not be lawful to sing Nausi Indaba [*sic*] except on state occasions and then only at sunset.[40]

A similar account was given by the Jesuit missionary H. Depelchin, who, within a fortnight of arriving at Bulawayo, was disconcerted by the spectacle of a war dance in which the soldiers wore Protestant Bibles in their head plumes![41] Father Depelchin's colleague, Father C. Croonenberghs, transcribed the most complete of the different versions of this song:

> Here is the news, dzi, dzi!
> Oho! Oho! here is the news.
> Dzi! Dzi! here is the news.
> The news of the assegais, dzi, dzi!
>
> Come and see us, the Zulus.
> Come and see news from other peoples,
> Oho! no other people will come, dzi, dzi!
> (Repeat *Natzi indaba*, etc.)
>
> News of the people of Matchoban, dzi, dzi!
> Come and see, come and see!
> Here is the news of Matchoban!
> No other people will come, dzi, dzi!
> (Repeat *Natzi indaba*, etc.)
>
> Matchoban is the chief, the black lion!
> The black lion is Matchoban, dzi, dzi!
> The black lion is Matchoban.
> The great chief Matchoban.
> (Repeat *Natzi indaba*, etc.)
>
> Ah, it kills men, oho! oho! oho!
> Ah! it kills men, dzi, dzi!
> The chief's spear, oho! oho! oho!
> Yes it kills men, dzi, dzi!
> (Repeat *Natzi indaba*, etc.)[42]

He comments that when sung and danced "with complete uniformity" by thousands of young men the effect was both "striking and terrible."

By the 1880s the *Song of the Assegai,* as it was now known, had become one of the tourist attractions of the trip to Bulawayo. Montague Kerr transcribed a few lines routinely on his visit in 1884, adding the information that the chorus "Sh-Shu-Shu" (i.e., *dzi, dzi*) literally means "we stamp out—we will conquer." But Kerr was more impressed by the praises of Mzilikazi's successor as king, Lobengula, both by the quality of the poetry and the "disinterested" loyalty that the performance demonstrated. He transcribed the *izibongo* of Lobengula as follows:

> Black king!
> Calf of a black cow!
> Man eater!
> Lion!
> Thou art as great as the world!
> Thou who appeared when men spoke confusedly!
> Star that shot through the firmament in the day of
>   Zuangandaba!
> Thou are in the plains!
> Black mystery!
> Thou who pierceth the sky that is above!
> Calf of the terrible!
> The Letter destroyer!
> He crossed the great desert!
> The black duck of Mzilikazi!
> The black calf of Bulawayo![43]

These three poems (the praises of Mzilikazi, *Nansi Ndaba,* and the praises of Lobengula) dating from the time after the Ndebele settled north of the Matopos Hills, in what is today southwestern Zimbabwe, constitute a very small selection, and any conclusions drawn about them must necessarily be tentative. It seems reasonable to point out, though, that all three appear to be very different from the kind of songs described by Andrew Smith. The praises of Mzilikazi, if we may trust Thomas's comment, were in the late nineteenth century primarily concerned with establishing the legitimacy of the king's descent by laying claim to roots in the ancient Zulu "royal house." *Nansi Indaba,* originally a praise poem, is clearly a song around which a great deal of national and ancestral myth has accumulated, while the praises of Lobengula similarly emphasize the rightfulness of the succession ("Calf of a black cow . . . / The black duck of Mzilikazi") and dwell upon the circumstances of his assumption of the chieftainship in the days "when men spoke confusedly": the reference is to the civil war following Mzilikazi's death, when the Zwengendaba regiment supported the claims of Nkhulumane, the pretender sponsored by Theophilus Shepstone, the Secretary of Native Affairs in the British colony of Natal, whose schemes Lobengula ("The letter destroyer") frustrated. In none of these poems is there any element of criticism or debate. The issues are now settled, the nation is established, and the themes are the power and legitimacy of the ruling house and the unity of a nation that has emerged from an earlier period of insecurity and disruption.

Julian Cobbing's research has thrown a great deal of light on why this change in the songs' nature should have occurred.[44] Cobbing has challenged the racist myth of Rhodesian white settlers that the Ndebele were a wholly militarized people who lived by raiding their neighbors for cattle, grain, and women and who were subject to the fickle rule of a despotic monarch. While acknowledging that they were better organized militarily than their neighbors, he demonstrates that, in general terms, the Ndebele lived in a manner very similar to other African peoples in the region. Their settlements were not, as a rule, organized regimentally, nor were they very large, consisting for the most part of groups of villages under separate chieftaincies. Although cattle were important to the economy and the culture, the "primary branch of production was cultivation and the main part of the Ndebele diet was grain rather than beef." Raiding was essentially a punitive activity, intended not so much to feed the raiders as to safeguard the integrity of the state built up by Mzilikazi. Though the king was indeed the focus of national unity and although without him "there would have been an inchoate collection of feuding chieftaincies," he was far from being the absolute and arbitrary tyrant of European travelers' tales. The separate subsidiary chiefs and headmen (indunas) maintained a great deal of independent wealth and power, including cattle of their own. The king administered justice, maintained a monopoly over the important long-distance trade to the south, and distributed the proceeds of tribute and of raiding. But his importance is best described in ritual terms. He was "the rain-maker in chief" and "a collector of charms and medicines designed not only to secure rain but to protect the state against the machinations of its enemies."[45]

Cobbing's research covers the period between 1820 and 1896, but it mainly deals with the settlement at Bulawayo, and the bulk of his supporting evidence refers to the 1870s and 1880s. What is somewhat obscured by the energy of his assault on the self-serving Rhodesian myths is the profound change that overtook the Ndebele state once it had found a settled and secure homeland. Whatever Mzilikazi may have become in his old age, he can hardly be described in his youth as being primarily a rainmaker administering a system of grain production and heading a cult of ancestor worship. Robert Moffat's *Journals,* with their inadvertent noting of important details, illustrate something of the process of the change. During his third visit to Mzilikazi, in 1854, this time to the settlement at Matlokoloka, he found the king crippled by dropsy and leading a fairly sedentary existence.[46] He notes with approval that many of the soldiers had been permitted to marry and build villages for themselves and that there had for some time been no offensive wars, claiming for himself and for God the credit of what was plainly the result of more settled circumstances. Mzilikazi had become involved in the ivory trade, exercising a royal monopoly over it, and he was deeply interested in the possibility of a new trade route to the east coast by way of the Zambezi River, which Moffat's son-in-law, David Livingstone, was then exploring. But among the things that irritated Moffat about the king was an entirely new claim that "he, and only he, gives rain. . . . tell one of his subjects that the last rain that fell was not the production of Moselekatsie's power and he will look on you as a mad man.[47]

These are the changes that Cobbing notes became increasingly important after Lobengula's succession. While the public ideology of the state remained aggressively military, the actual relations of power had shifted as control of the means of production superseded control of the means of raiding as the base of wealth and privilege. Cobbing examines eighteen chiefly families, showing that by the 1870s the power structure had acquired a "firm genealogical basis, power passing from father to eldest son." The indunas (important advisers) "competed with each other to marry daughters of the king," while the king chose wives from the most important and wealthy subjects, leading to the emergence of "an aristocratic caste" quite different from that which had held power because of its military prowess in the 1820s and 1830s. As the power of this group increased, the king's position became correspondingly ritualized through a process of "ideological glorification." It was his ancestors who were invoked in ceremonies as the state's protectors, and "prayers to them lay at the root of tribal cohesion." [48]

The clearest expression of these new political and spiritual themes was the annual *Nxwala*, or "firstfruits" ceremony, held in January or February, when the green crops were ready. This ceremony, which had its origins back in Zululand, had "become refined over the years to assume a profusion of meanings and purposes." [49] It was a New Year ceremony, with the king ritually tasting the firstfruits of the harvest and hurling a spear to announce the new year's birth. These two symbolic actions, uniting the two strands of Ndebele history, dominated the proceedings. On the one hand, *Nxwala* was a festival of regeneration, a renewal of the bond between the king's ancestral spirits and the earth, having implications not only for rainfall and harvests but also for female fertility and national potency. At the same time, it was a great military display, an awesome demonstration of Ndebele power when people came to renew their allegiance to the state and when to be absent was tantamount to rebellion. One observer in 1889 described a "corn dance" in which the word *mabele* (millet) was rhythmically chanted while the crowds sang and danced, "waving their sticks backwards and forwards representing . . . a field of waving corn." [50] But the most important song of the festival was *Nansi Indaba*, the *Song of the Assegai*, with its invocation of the royal ancestor Mashobane and its celebration of the decades of achievement of the spear.

Against this background, we can understand what appears, on the limited evidence available, to be a distinct shift in the practice and purpose of praise poetry among the Ndebele, from the kind of performances described by Andrew Smith to the kind of texts recorded by subsequent visitors. The Ndebele state in the 1880s was not what it had been in 1835. The king was no longer a wandering warrior who had raised himself from nothing, practicing a variety of strategems to retain the loyalty of groups of refugees of different origins. A state had been established and inherited: the problem was to prevent its disintegration. A group of powerful and wealthy leaders had emerged: the problem was to prevent them from quarreling. There were incipient tensions between the various groups of aristocrats as well as between them and commoners, both captive and tributary, with the civil war following the death of Mzilikazi having provided an ominous warning. The praise poems played their part in promot-

ing a version of national unity based on the figure of the king who
was the "true" descendant of the founding ancestor and the central
figure in all national myths.

When Thomas Baines visited Lobengula in April 1870, however,
he watched a military display: "The warrior at this time has also the
inestimable privilege of speaking his mind to his king: 'Look at me
and at us all! Are we not your dogs who fight for you and keep you in
safety from your enemies? And now you starve us. Give us beef, you
niggard, that we may eat and be strong, and we will fight to the death
for you!' "[51] It is important to note that the older convention of truc-
ulence in performance had not entirely died away and that "praises"
could still work from the bottom up as well as from the top down.

After Lobengula's defeat at the hands of Cecil Rhodes's British
South Africa Company's army in 1893 and his subsequent death,
there were no further public performances of the praise poems or of
Nansi Indaba. Although the final defeat of the Ndebele did not come
until 1896, and although in a secret ceremony at the height of the
Chimurenga Uprising of 1896–97 Lobengula's successor, Nyamanda, was proclaimed the new king, the *Nxwala* ceremony was not
revived, and there is no record of any praises addressed to Nyamanda.
The establishment of colonial rule and the defeat of the Ndebele political hierarchy in the 1890s marked Ndebele society's entry into a
third phase of its history. With this transition came a new role for the
izibongo.

In the aftermath of defeat, the legend grew that the *Nansi Indaba*
song had been sacred, being performed at sundown as the climax of
the *Nxwala* but otherwise kept as a state secret. Mtompe Khumalo,
quoted in *My Friend Kumalo,* explains that it "could never be sung
at any other time under any circumstances whatsoever"; the words
would be "known some day" but never "from the lips of a Kumalo."[52] Modern testimony makes the same point: "After celebrations, the song was strictly forbidden and forgotten. . . . The Nxwala
song was taboo," and "he who knows it and tries to sing it becomes
mad." Meanwhile, missionaries had appropriated *Nansi Indaba* for
their own purposes:

> Come and hear the good news
> Not of the spear.
> The books have arrived
> The words of God

> They tell us about Jesus
> They tell about love
> Come and hear the good news
> Not of the spear.[53]

By World War I a new formulation of Ndebele ethnic nationalism was beginning to emerge amongst certain Ndebele, defined initially very much in accordance with the concepts and standards of the European conquerors. In 1915 the Amandebele Patriotic Society campaigned against prostitution in Bulawayo, arguing that it was against "the Christian law and the law of Mzilikazi" and demanding legislation against it.[54] More significantly, a short time later Nyamanda, Lobengula's eldest son, together with a cousin, Madholi Kumalo, with the advice of the South African Native National Congress's Richard Msimang, founded the Ndebele National Home Movement to press for a revival of the Ndebele monarch under the European principle of primogeniture.[55] On the death of Lobengula's queen, Loskeyi, Nyamanda demanded to inherit his father's cattle, but the government refused him, arguing that the cattle should pass to the offspring of his half brother Njube, who, the British argued, was Lobengula's legitimate heir according to Ndebele "custom."[56] Soon afterwards, Nyamanda presented a petition, this time demanding the return of Ndebele land:

> The members of the late King's family, your petitioners, and several members of the tribe, are now scattered about on farms so parcelled out to white settlers, and are practically created a nomadic people living in scattered condition under a veiled form of slavery, they not being allowed individually to cross from one farm to another, or from place to place except under a system of permit or Pass, and are practically forced to do labour on these farms as a condition of their occupying land in Matabeleland.[57]

When this petition, too, was rejected, Nyamanda sought to purchase land, explaining that this was how land was acquired these days, and he launched a successful appeal to raise funds for a homeland for "the tribe."[58] The success of this appeal startled the administration, which feared that he had hit upon the "one grievance" around which the Ndebele might unite.[59]

This new Ndebele nationalism differed greatly, however, from the older Ndebele patriotism of the early- and mid-nineteenth century, which had sought to ease the absorption of refugee soldiers and captives from widely different cultural backgrounds into a single unified state. Its proponents were, at heart, the aristocratic caste that had grown up in the latter half of the nineteenth century, who felt that they and other Ndebele were being left behind during a period of rapid social and economic change that was eroding the old structures of local patronage. Educated South African Xhosa speakers were taking positions of leadership in Matabeleland, while Shona people from northeastern Zimbabwe were successfully competing for ordinary jobs in Bulawayo.[60] The spokesmen of Ndebele ethnic pride thus preached a version of Ndebele ethnic purity that was exclusive as they sought to mobilize support.[61] In the work of Mtompe Khumalo, this note of Ndebele exclusivity and the rejection of Shona influence are harsh and strident. Ndebele religion had originally been simple and dignified, but "when Lobengula succeeded . . . all was changed. The rain-making ritual practised by the indigenous natives began to make insidious inroads in Matabele custom." Similarly, with marriage customs, the "Matabele have taken all sorts of customs from the Shona people, some of whom even pay *lobola* for girls when they are still children. They have made it a business." Khumalo even goes so far as to suggest that the Chimurenga Uprising of 1896–97, which involved the Ndebele in their final defeat, was deliberately instigated by the Mwari oracle of the Shona-speaking Karanga people "as a means of revenging themselves on the Matabele."[62]

One expression of the new ethnic consciousness orchestrated from above was a revival of praise poetry. The main poet (*imbongi*) involved was Ginyilitshe Hlabangana, and the purpose of the praises was an entirely new one. They neither debated national issues, as in the time of Mzilikazi, nor bolstered national unity, as during Lobengula's reign. Rather, they asserted an injured pride in Ndebele identity. In effect, praises were to become part of a newly found, newly defined "Ndebele culture." Lobengula's surviving wives also became objects of reverential pilgrimages: "When we went there we would meet them as royal people. . . . When we went there, the person who was our praise poet was Ginyilitshe. Ginyilitshe would praise until the Europeans in admiration would remark 'these people can make history.' Lobengula himself, though, was a slightly tarnished hero. He had both compromised Ndebele traditions and been defeated by Cecil Rhodes's forces. There were few praises addressed to him. Mzilikazi, on the other hand was eulogized—not now as a king, but as the exemplar of an abstract vision of Ndebele virture. His grave in the Matopos Hills also became a center of pilgrimage, and a plaque was erected there: "We used to assemble at Matopos in large numbers . . . we assembled here in Bulawayo and then went to Matopos in cars. We wanted to remind our people where the king was buried. We even suggested the place should not be sold, but a college should be built. We placed Gula Kumalo to look after the place, it is still there, near a big tree. We used to say our problems and praise-poems when we got there." [63]

Eventually one of these new praise poems was inscribed on the plaque at Mzilikazi's grave:

> The vari-coloured one with a black mouth, praised in tears of men.
> Our short one whose bunches of cats' skins may not be trampled,
> and yet those of tall ones are trampled: those of tall ones are
> Shaka's of Senzangakona. Those of tall ones are Zwide's of
> Langa.
> The tall conspicuous, early morning star in the south-east
> preceeding the constellation Pleiades.
> The sun that rises from the ear of an elephant, it rose and starlings
> cried one to another.
> The black fighting stick that beats cattle, it beats men.
> The tall grass in the Kalahari desert. The year it burns it'll burn with
> men's leather loin cloths.
> The up and coming leader of cattle: leaders of cattle lead them by
> driving them with a whip.
> The bush-buck that steps carefully on the rocks. It's afraid of its
> claws being spoilt.
> He dug with a spear. He dug with a knobkerrie.
> The obtainer of leopards and lions.
> One with spotted eyelashes,
> King of the Abantungwa and the Abatwakazi.
> The crab that moves on its side round my father's huts.
> He plundered the cattle of the Amalala, he plundered those of
> Sidhalamlomo, those of Reverend Dausim. He plundered those
> of Malibaliba, plundering them through his young brother Beje,
> of the household, in charge of the Impi.
> He who unlocks the way against elephants. He calls them and they
> refuse and keep a safe distance.
> The sender who sits with a young sable antelope in the wide plains
> of Lohasa and Lobulane. [64]

In 1971 another set of praises, the *izibongo* of Lobengula, Mzilikazi's successor, was recorded by T. J. Hemans. The *imbongi* was

Mtshede Ndhovu, whom Hemans describes as having been born when Mzilikazi was still alive:

> It roared like a calf.
> He who has books is at the river crossing.
> The cumulus cloud which rains from overcast sky.
> The words of a mountain, King of Mgabi Ndwandwe.
> The bird that built with its beak pointing to a pool of water, some
>   said catch it some said leave it that is the way it builds.
> The Black Lion of Mabindela.
> Grass does not burn in the Kalahari, some burns and bends.
> He was furious and then the tribes and the commoners were angry.
> Spoor of the leopard that disappears in rivers.
> The bush buck that strikes with its hooves and damaged the stones.
> Watch him, the destroyer, because he destroyed the commoners.
> He who is food they feed from for many many years, when he dies,
>   where will they feed from, they will eat jackals and roots.
> He whose majesty is like that of his father Matshobana.
> Cattle have popularity, they are lowing and attract afar.
> He whose path is winding like that of ants.
> The small bird of the spear, so small it can sit on the spear.[65]

The first thing to be said of these two praise-poems is that they are by far the most interesting and impressive examples of Ndebele oral poems published thus far. This point needs emphasis because, although they are twentieth-century praises, they are, both in the range and power of their imagery and in the complexity of their historical references, probably much more representative of the Ndebele tradition than the earlier examples we have actually been considering above. This observation is strengthened both from comparison with other praise poems in the Nguni tradition (such as the Zulu *izibongo*) and from a consideration of the circumstances in which nineteenth-century travelers actually recorded texts, without benefit of tape recorders or a knowledge of the language.

These are, nevertheless, twentieth century *izibongo*. The praises of Lobengula, for example, clearly reflect the ambiguity of his reputation after 1893. His legitimacy is emphasized—he is (as in Kerr's poem) the "calf" and his "majesty is like that of his father Matshobana." He is praised as rainmaker ("the cumulus cloud") and as "food they feed from." Cobbing has amply explained such tributes. But the praise poem contains no references to any positive achievements. There are no victories in battle or in raiding, no enlargement of the nation's wealth. No military virtues are mentioned at all. Lobengula is praised, a little conventionally, as the "black lion." Other images suggest diminutives—birds, grass, the ants. Several praises are in specific contrast to those of Mzilikazi. Mzilikazi is called the "tall grass in the Kalahari desert" that will "burn with men's leather loin cloths." Lobengula, by contrast, is the grass in the Kalahari that does *not* burn, or burns only feebly, bending over. Mzilikazi was "the bush buck that steps carefully on the rocks," implying diplomatic skills such as wariness, while Lobengula becomes the "bush buck that strikes with its hooves and damaged the stones."

All Mzilikazi's victories are against enemies of stature (Shaka and Zwide), but Lobengula's anger is directed against the "commoners." One is tempted to claim that some of these praises are the record of dissatisfaction during Lobengula's own time. If the *imbongi* Mtshede Ndholovu really was born before 1868, making him, as Hemans suggests, some 105 years old, he was certainly old enough to have witnessed contemporary disputes, and the line "The bird that built . . . , some said catch it some said leave it that is the way it builds" may well reflect debate at the time about Lobengula's performance as king. But the main current of the praise poem dates from the period when the Ndebele were looking for cultural heroes and, assessing Lobengula's career in the light of their twentieth-century predicament, found it lacking in important heroic aspects. To the nation whose anthem was *Nansi Ndaba*, Lobengula was "the small bird of the spear, so small it can sit on the spear."

Not so with Mzilikazi in the *izibongo* inscribed by the National Home Movement on his grave. There is no mention now of Mashobane or of ancient Zulu kings. The question of legitimacy does not arise, for nothing has been inherited. This is in sharp contrast both to Lobengula's praises and to the version of Mzilikazi's praises transcribed by Morgan Thomas. We have returned to Mzilikazi the warrior, the king who achieved kingship by his own heroic efforts. He is the man who, as Moshoeshoe put it to Andrew Smith, "raised himself into importance."[66] Thus Mzilikazi becomes "our short one" who, against all odds, defeated the tall ones of Shaka: the reference is to the legendary dispute over cattle when Mzilikazi sent back the impi with their head plumes cut. He is the "sun that rises from the ear of an elephant" causing consternation as the "starlings cried one to another." He is credited with tact and diplomacy, stepping "carefully on the rocks" or moving crablike "round my father's huts." But there is nothing remotely ritualistic about his kingship: there is nothing of Cobbing's rainmaker in these praises. The emphasis is on Mzilikazi's exploits as a warrior leader, on the exercise of power and the creation of wealth: he is "The black fighting stick that beats cattle, it beats men."

It is once again tempting to argue that Mzilikazi's praises are authentically of the period of history to which they refer and that they may well have been transmitted more or less intact. The fact that not all the historical references can be explained reinforces the probability that *some* of these praises date from Mzilikazi's lifetime and have been reused in creating new *izibongo*. Yet, as we have seen from Andrew Smith's account of the power relations at Mzilikazi's court, the *imbongi's* portrait of this king as a man who alone made history is true neither of the period nor of the period's poetry. In its other details, this praise poem clearly reflects twentieth-century concern with the creation of a cultural dimension for a new Ndebele ethnic consciousness being crafted to oppose European domination. The long catalog of enemies defeated by Mzilikazi, which dominated the extract quoted by Morgan Thomas, has been reduced to a single line: these details are of little relevance to a people conscious of their own defeat. On the other hand, there is considerable emphasis on cattle raiding, with Mzilikazi praised repeatedly for having built up the nation's wealth: the theft of these cattle by the white victors of 1896 is still a bitter complaint. Most interesting of all is the image of Mzilikazi as one who did not do his cultivating with a hoe but "with a spear . . . with a knobkerrie." To a people looking back from the humiliations of colonialism to their settlement as farmers under Lobengula and their earlier migration under Mzilikazi, the poetic expression of the simple military virtues had an irresistible appeal.

Notes

1. The events surrounding the so-called *mfecane* period (a period of political and social disruptions in South East Africa in the 1820s and 1830s) in South African history are currently being reassessed by Julian Cobbing, to whom we are grateful for access to his unpublished essays on the topic.

2. R. Moffat, *The Matabele Journals of Robert Moffat, 1829–1860*, ed. J. P. R. Wallis, 2 vols. (London, 1945), 1:33.

3. R. Kent Rasmussen, *Migrant Kingdom: Mzilikazi's Ndebele in South Africa* (London, 1978), 165.

4. Moffat, *Matabeleland Journals*, 1:48.

5. *The Diary of Dr. Andrew Smith 1834–36*, ed. P. R. Kirby, 2 vols. (Cape Town, 1939–40), and *Andrew Smith's Journal of His Expedition into the Interior of South Africa, 1834–36*, ed. W. F. Lye (Cape Town, 1975).

6. J. Cobbing, "The Mfecane as Alibi: Thoughts on Dithakong and Mbolompo," *Journal of African History* 29, no. 3 (1988): 492–95.

7. Ibid., 509.

8. *Andrew Smith's Journal*, 92.

9. Ibid., 110, 71.

10. Ibid., 70.

11. Ibid., 89.

12. Ibid., 76, 214.

13. Ibid., 93.

14. Ibid., 25–26.

15. *The Diary of Dr. Andrew Smith*, 2, 38.

16. *Andrew Smith's Journal*, 108–9, 184–85.

17. Ibid., 215, 264.

18. Ibid., 118.

19. Ibid., 65. See also p. 93.

20. R. Moffat, *Missionary Labours and Scenes in Southern Africa*, 6th ed., (New York, 1844), 357.

21. *Andrew Smith's Journal*, 279, quoting from his personal diary.

22. Ibid., 237.

23. Barend(s) and Bloom were Griqua "chiefs" dwelling to the south of the Ndebele. Their principal concerns were hunting for elephant ivory and raising cattle, but they repeatedly raided the Ndebele. See Rasmussen, *Migrant Kingdom*, for a discussion of their activities.

24. *Andrew Smith's Journal*, 238.

25. J. D. Omer-Cooper, *History of Southern Africa* (Portsmouth, N.H., 1987), 68–70.

26. Moffat, *Matabeleland Journals*, 1:50.

27. *Andrew Smith's Journal*, 238.

28. Ibid., 238–39.

29. Ibid., 239.

30. Ibid.

31. Moffat, *Matabele Journals*, 1:82, 78, 87.

32. It is worth recalling here that Robert Moffat was one of the sources cited by Lévy-Bruhl in his development of the notion of the "prelogical" mind of nonliterate peoples, as discussed in chapter one of this book.

33. Moffat, *Matabele Journals*, 1:75–77, 80.

34. Ibid., 1:85.

35. Ibid., 1:89–90.

36. T. M. Thomas, *Eleven Years in Central South Africa* (London, 1972), 206, 205–6.

37. Ibid., 204.

38. Ibid., 205.

39. A. C. Bailie, "Journal," folio 25, Zimbabwe National Archives, Harare (ZNA), BA 10/2/1.

40. Ibid., folios 42–44.

41. H. Depelchin, S.J., and C. Croonenberghs, S.J., *Journal to Gubulawayo* (Bulawayo, 1979), 199. English translation by Moira Lloyd of *Trois Ans dans l'Afrique Australe: Le Pays des Matabélés debuts de la Mission du Zambèse* (Brussels, 1882).

42. Ibid., 342–43. See also pp. 181, 222.

43. W. M. Kerr, *The Far Interior*, 2 vols. (London, 1886), 1:58–59.

44. Unless otherwise indicated, the four paragraphs that follow are based upon J. Cobbing, "The Ndebele under the Khumalos, 1820–1896," Ph.D. diss., University of Lancaster, 1976.

45. Ibid., 152–53, 51, 55.

46. The section that follows is based on Moffat, *Matabele Journals*, 1:229–333.

47. Ibid., 1:319. See also 1:288.

48. Cobbing, "The Ndebele under the Khumalos," 81–82, 54–55.

49. Ibid., 232.

50. Quoted ibid., 234–35. See also E. P. Mathers, *Zambesia: England's el Dorado in Africa*, 3d ed. (London, 1895), 176.

51. *The Goldfield Diaries of Thomas Baines*, ed. J. P. R. Wallis, 3 vols. (London, 1946), 2:332.

52. Mhlagazanhlansi, *My Friend Kumalo* (1944; rpt. Bulawayo, 1972), 70.

53. Interview with Mafima Ncube, Ntabasinduna, 9 October 1981, Bulawayo, ZNA. This interview explicitly identified *Nansi Indaba* as the *Nxwala* song that was considered taboo.

54. This paragraph is based partially on notes from the Zimbabwe National Archives generously shared with us by Michael West: statement of Amandebele Patriotic Society, Bulawayo, dated 15 December 1915, encl. in Superintendent of Natives, Bulawayo, to Chief Native Commissioner, 15 January 1916, ZNA, N/21/1.

55. Chief Native Commissioner, Salisbury, to Superintendent of Natives, Gwelo, 11 April 1919, and Native Commissioner, Umzingwane, to Superintendent of Natives, Bulawayo, 18 August 1919, ZNA, N3/19/4. For a full discussion of Nyamanda and the Ndebele National Home Movement, see T. O. Ranger, *The African Voice in Southern Rhodesia, 1898–1930* (London, 1970), 64–87.

56. Native Commissioner, Inyati, to Superintendent of Natives, Bulawayo, 29 July 1919 and 31 March 1920, ZNA, N3/19/3. See also, Southern Rhodesia, *Report of the Chief Native Commissioner for the Year 1919* (Salisbury, 1920), 1.

57. Sir Drummond Chaplin Papers, Native Affairs, A3/18/18/5–6, petition dated 10 March 1919, ZNA.

58. Nyamanda to Chief Native Commissioner, 11 June 1919, ibid.

59. Chief Native Commissioner, Salisbury, to Secretary, Department of Administrator, 1 April 1920 and 16 February 1921, ZNA, N3/19/4.

60. Cf. R. S. Roberts, "The End of the Ndebele Royal Family," seminar paper, History Department, University of Zimbabwe, 1988, 7–8; I. Phimister and C. van Onselen, "The Political Economy of Tribal Animosity: A Case Study of the 1929 Bulawayo Location 'Faction Fight,'" *Journal of Southern African Studies* 6, no. 1 (October 1979): 1–43.

61. It should be noted that not all Ndebele intellectuals espoused such exclusivism. See, for example, an account of the Matabeleland Home Society conference in 1945 in the *Bantu Mirror*, 29 December 1945, in which it is reported that Shona chiefs attended and that the president, Cephas Hlabangana, "speaking in English," denounced tribalism and urged that, as "workers let us rally to the banners of trade unionism." Ironically, it was left to the white government's spokesman to outline "the ancient Matabele system of Government" and call for an increase in chiefly powers.

62. Mhlagazanhlansi, *My Friend Kumalo*, 64, 77, 111–12.

63. Interview with Mafima Mcube, Ntabasinduma, 9 October 1981, ZNA.

64. T. J. Hemans, "Praises Given to the King of the Amandebele," *NADA* 10, no. 3 (1971): 95.

65. Ibid., 96.

66. *Andrew Smith's Journal*, 64.

4

The Development of Forms
The Chopi
Migodo

In late July 1871, the people of a stockaded African town southwest of the old Portuguese Indian Ocean port of Inhambane entertained St. Vincent Erskine, a British explorer mapping possible trade routes from Inhambane into the interior of Mozambique. From the start of his trip, the area had impressed him favorably. The land was fertile and densely settled. The people were "one and all industrious and capable of improvement" and demonstrated "great agricultural abilities." Now, having stopped at "the kraal of a principal man," Erskine counted himself doubly fortunate, for not only was he provided with ample food and drink but he was also pleasantly entertained by the "really effective music" played for him.[1]

This music was performed by an orchestra of xylophones, which Erskine called "native pianos" and which the performers themselves called *timbila*. These were large instruments of varying sizes with wooden keys positioned over large calabash resonators and carefully tuned so they could be played in harmony with each other.[2] The keys were struck by rubber-tipped hammers, and the orchestra was accompanied by drums and rattles:

> Instruments of one kind were played in conjunction with each other, each in their turns, and at intervals, as was deemed necessary; a clash of the whole came in chorus together. The effect was good, and the music very regular. At times it died away almost to silence, and they gradually grew louder as each instrument chimed in, till the big drums, hand-rattles, leg-rattles, bass voices and chorus came to the final *crescendo*, and then as gradually died away again. I never heard the native music again so effective.[3]

What Erskine heard was an *ngodo* (pl., *migodo*), a set of songs and instrumental pieces arranged into a composition lasting for as long as an hour or more. His attention to the music was appropriate, for it constituted an important cultural marker that set off those who maintained the orchestras as members of a distinct and self-conscious ethnic group that was then coming into increasingly clear focus. This group was known as the Chopi. They lived in a band of territory that began some seventy miles south-southwest of Inhambane and extended along the Inharrime River valley and among the chain of lakes that lay just behind the coast, extending southwards to the valley of the Limpopo River. In a situation similar to that of many other parts of southern and central Africa in the mid-nineteenth century, groups of refugees of widely diverse origins had been added to the local population and this mixture in no way formed a culturally homogeneous ethnic group or "tribe."[4] To understand how such different people gradually came to identify themselves as a distinct group one must situate them within the larger historical processes then affecting southeastern Africa.

In 1821, Zwide, the leader of the Ndwandwe group of Natal's Northern Nguni peoples, was defeated by Shaka, king of the Zulu. Many groups of fugitives were spun off from this defeat. One of these was led by Soshangane, a general in Zwide's army who had adopted the administrative and military practices of the victorious Zulu state and then led his following into southern Mozambique, where they became known as the "Gaza."[5] This invasion resulted in the conquest or disruption of the fragmented societies of the area, with many of the conquered sold into the burgeoning transatlantic and Indian Ocean slave-trading systems. Many of those who escaped slavery fled as refugees to seek security wherever they could find it.[6] The Gaza consolidated their position quickly, and their Afrikaner and Portuguese neighbors soon recognized that it was more advantageous to trade peacefully with the Gaza than to challenge them militarily.[7] From this trade the Afrikaners of the Transvaal were able to obtain large numbers of slaves for their use,[8] while the Portuguese settlements at Sena, Sofala, Inhambane, and Lourenço Marques came to be almost entirely dependent on the Gaza as the source for the slaves and ivory vital to their commercial prosperity.[9] Throughout Soshangane's reign, then, his state was based on a combination of military power readily deployed and control over the important slave and ivory trades between the interior and the coast.

On Soshangane's death in 1858 a civil war broke out between two contenders for the throne. In the course of this struggle, one of the disputants, Mzila, moved his capital north of the Sabi River, while the other, Mawewe, fled to Swaziland and there obtained Swazi support against his rival. The ensuing conflict, which continued until the end of the 1860s, especially affected the southern marches of the Gaza state, areas from which many refugees fled.[10] Once Mzila defeated his rival, however, he had to face serious economic problems. British actions against the slave trade along the Indian Ocean coast, combined with the decimation of most of the area's elephant herds, were rapidly undermining his state's economic foundations. To compensate, the Gaza elite regularly sent its armies out to levy tribute from those living on the periphery of their state or to raid them for slaves, who were then set to work within the Gaza state itself.[11]

While many people between the Limpopo and the Sabi rivers came directly under the control of the Gaza, and while some came under the authority of the Portuguese authorities at Inhambane, those settled in a band of territory along the Inharrime valley were able to remain independent for several decades. This area, which included some of the richest and most fertile land in all Mozambique, supported a population large enough to resist effectively both the Gaza and the Portuguese.[12] While no single leader came to be as powerful as Mzilikazi of the Ndebele, local leaders did succeed in organizing their followers into a set of large stockades (khokholwene), each of which was capable of sheltering several thousand people. These stockades were especially effective in thwarting Gaza armies, which lacked artillery power.[13] Despite the fact that relations with the Portuguese were often contentious to the point of conflict, many leaders were also able to negotiate treaties of "vassalage" with the Portuguese, thereby obtaining an ally against possible Gaza attack.[14] Probably most tellingly, however, the people of the area perfected the use of six-foot bows and poisoned arrows.[15] Protected by their stockaded villages and their skill as archers, they were able to avoid the direct rule of the Portuguese and the Gaza long enough to achieve a sense of themselves as having an identity distinct from that of neighboring African peoples. It was their military capabilities that gave the mixture of local people and recently arrived refugees their new tribal name, as vaChopi meant, in Northern Nguni, "the bowmen" or "the archers."[16] In effect, the Chopi came to be seen as "those who resisted—and succeeded."[17]

As this coalescence of peoples of varied origins occurred, a common culture and language that was based for the most part on the culture and language of the autochthons of the area emerged. Prominent among the cultural markers that set these people off from other peoples of the region were the large xylophone orchestras and the elaborate *migodo* that had been reported by European visitors to the coast as early as 1562 and that had so interested St. Vincent Erskine in 1871.[18] These orchestras, which in the late nineteenth century were sponsored by the stockade leaders, were militarily important in that they inspired bravery in Chopi soldiers and celebrated Chopi victories.[19]

But their skill as archers, their large stockaded towns, and their growing self-identification as Chopi ultimately proved insufficient to ensure their permanent independence. The emergent Chopi ethnic unit was very much a *cultural* unit, *not* a political unit. There was no single Chopi leader who could unite them into a single people, and political power was shared out unevenly between the leaders of the major stockades.[20] Conflicts broke out between various Chopi groups as readily as they did between the Chopi and the Gaza, and Chopi leaders often sought outside help against their fellow Chopi from both the Portuguese and the Gaza.[21] Politically fragmented, the Chopi were ill-prepared for the surge of fresh challenges they faced after 1875.

The first problem was the Portuguese. In the early 1860s, inflation in the cowrie-shell currencies of West Africa had prompted European firms trading for vegetable oils there to seek alternative sources of supply elsewhere.[22] The Mozambique coast was identified as one such source, and French and Dutch firms soon set up trading posts to trade for copra, sesame seed, peanuts, and other oil-bearing produce as well as for other tropical products, such as rubber and beeswax.[23] The opening of the Suez Canal in 1869 strengthened the trade, and Chopi territory gradually became a major source of vegetable oils. In 1875 the Portuguese, eager to tax the Chopi, launched a series of military campaigns that extended Portuguese control further into Chopi country, and the negotiation of further treaties of vassalage continued Portuguese expansion in succeeding years.[24]

After 1886, this gradual erosion of Chopi independence was accelerated by their old enemies, the Gaza. In 1886 Gungunyana, Mzila's successor, began raiding Chopi country, and in 1889 he moved his capital from north of the Sabi River to Manjacaze, a place south of the river and near both the Chopi and the Portuguese settlement at Inhambane. Intense competition for grazing land between the Gaza and the Chopi soon led to further conflict. Meanwhile the Portuguese, apprehensive about British designs on territory that Portugal claimed in the interior, concluded a formal alliance with the Gaza to forestall any possible Gaza alliance with the British. As part of the terms of this agreement, the Portuguese traded modern weapons to the Gaza, thus laying open those Chopi who were not already vassals of the Portuguese to renewed Gaza attack.[25] In 1891 a great massacre of the Chopi took place at the hands of Gungunyana's troops, and this was followed up by additional punishing raids in 1892, 1893, and 1894. As a consequence, the majority of slaves taken by the Gaza in the late 1880s and 1890s were Chopi.[26]

By 1894, however, European competition for African territory was pressuring Portugal to demonstrate unambiguous authority in Mozambique, and the government initiated a policy of "portugalizing" the territory it claimed. Central to this effort was the expansion of Portuguese control from their old coastal enclaves into the interior. In the south their major opponents were also their "allies," the Gaza.[27] Soldiers were raised from the population near Inhambane for the military effort, and these included several thousand Chopi men eager for revenge. In November 1895 the conflict was carried to the heart of the Gaza state, where the Portuguese defeated the Gaza armies at the Battle of Coolela. Many of the Gaza's tributary peoples deserted Gungunyana's cause, and, at last, in December 1895, the Portuguese captured him at the Battle of Chaimite. He was sent to Lisbon to be paraded through the streets in the fashion of an ancient Roman triumph and then was exiled to the Azores, where he died in 1906. The Chopi now had their revenge, but, for the first time, Portugal had control over all southern Mozambique.

The military conquest of southern Mozambique was followed up by Portuguese enquiries into the ways of life of the people there, including the Chopi. It is in this context that we find the next description of the Chopi xylophone orchestras. In 1907 Augusto Cabral, a colonial administrator, compiled a book about the people of Inhambane district and their customs.[28] Cabral's interests were many-sided, but (like Erskine before him) he was particularly fascinated by the Chopi xylophones, not least by the skill that went into their manufacture, and his description is much fuller than Erskine's. Slats carved from the stinkwood tree, the only type of wood used, were fastened in position on a wooden frame with leather thongs, and under each slat were two gourd resonators—one large and one small—their mouths forming a figure eight, and held together by beeswax. In the mouth of each gourd was a filament, an article of great value cut from the intestine of a type of pig. Most of these xy-

1. Chopi xylophone orchestra, Chief Zavalla's area, Inhambane district, Mozambique, probably photographed shortly before World War I. The orchestral performers are in the prime of life. (By permission of Jill Dias.)

lophones, which were played with drumsticks capped with rubber, had several eight-note scales, but there were also bigger four-note xylophones, which were used to provide the heavy bass for large performances. Each of the principal Chopi chiefs maintained a large orchestra made up of sixteen or seventeen ordinary xylophones and three or four bass xylophones. Each orchestra was under the control of a master musician, who was assisted by a master choreographer in charge of dancing.

Cabral's description of the *migodo* he witnessed is brief but compelling:

The natives form a circle in front of the orchestra, armed and costumed in the manner already described for the Landins [Gaza]. They first sing and then, at a certain moment, beating the ground with their shields, they begin a series of leaps and gestures, pretending they are fighting the enemy. At given moments, they all throw themselves on the ground, pretending to be dead, and some of the women step forward from a group, searching among them for those who belong to them, after which they get up again and resume the songs.[29]

The themes of the songs are indicated by the following titles: "The whites who defeated Gungunyana"; "The steam launches the whites brought to the rivers and that vomit fire"; "The steamers that came from the land of the whites and took away many people"; "No longer can they conquer lands and women by force of arms." According to Cabral, some of these songs were extremely old, while others were composed for the occasions of their performance. The vast majority, says Cabral primly, were extremely obscene.

The three examples he gives of the *migodo*'s song texts are flawed by imperfect transcriptions of the Chopi words and by his preference for broad paraphrase over direct translation. The first song describes an incident "when the chief of Zavala sent emissaries to the Gaza inviting them to join him in an attack on a neighboring Chopi chief, Chisoko. These emissaries were abused and killed by Chisoko, and a son of one of the victims demands of one of Zavala's generals, 'Why was my father killed on account of the worthless people of Chisoko?' Chief Nyakutowo, another neighboring Chopi chief, sent gifts to the whites, and his people preferred to remain with him. In Gungunyana's time, the women of Zavala fled from a raid and were captured by Chisoko's people. The soldiers of Zavala went out to fight Chisoko and also demanded to know why gifts had been sent to the whites instead of to the chief of Zavala."[30]

The second song is the earliest recorded text of a song still popular throughout Mozambique in the 1950s, namely "My mother is as sweet as *aguardente* [firewater]."[31] The third of Cabral's song texts is paraphrased as follows: "The Commandante ordered Nandedo to seize hold of the women and throw them into prison. They killed my husband and the money that he paid for me, where is it?"[32]

Cabral's account occupies only two pages, but it provides fascinating clues to the development of the Chopi *migodo* in the early years of colonial rule. The orchestras were well known as a peculiarly Chopi phenomenon, and they were well established, with every important chief investing in and maintaining an orchestra and a band of musicians. The instruments were expensive and manufactured with skill. In the actual performances of the *migodo*, themes of warfare continued to be prominent, with battles described and mimicked and with the shifting alliances of the precolonial period well represented. The Chopi took understandable pleasure in the defeat of Gungunyana. However, these *migodo* by no means glorified warfare. Questions were raised as to the justification for fighting as opposed to diplomacy, and the slain were poignantly commemorated during the break in the dance when the women stepped forward to search among the mimic dead for their husbands and sons.

Such songs obviously looked backward to the days before the Portuguese conquest. But there were already others dealing with the actions of the new white rulers who had put on the rivers steamers that carried people away to work as migrant laborers in distant places. The last song quoted by Cabral anticipates the type of theme that was increasingly to preoccupy the Chopi in the following years. What is described was clearly an early colonial tax raid. The commandant had sent out his police to seize Chopi women as hostages to compel their husbands to pay the new hut tax.[33] The singer's husband had been killed by the Portuguese, apparently after paying the tax, but the money had not been returned. In the first years of colonial rule, then, the composers of the *migodo* reflected the new circumstances of the Chopi, turning away from their former preoccupation with survival in warfare and applying themselves to the problems of surviving under the new realities of Portuguese colonial rule.

As early as 1892 the Portuguese government had granted a concession to speculators behind a proposed new "Companhia de Inhambane," which had announced its intention to grow tea, sugar, coffee, and other tropical crops. Because of the years of warfare in the area between 1892 and 1896, however, the company failed to take up its concession and no plantations were established.[34] With this failure, it initially seemed that the Portuguese had no choice but to leave the area's economy in the hands of the small-scale African producers and Indian and mestizo traders who had dominated it since the early 1860s. Yet there were problems. For example, a lack of adequate transport facilities inhibited the opening up of the interior to agricultural production.[35] Even worse, export tariffs imposed in 1892 to raise revenues for a bankrupt public treasury were rapidly stifling the agricultural production already established near the coast.[36] These taxes on vegetable oils came at a particularly unfortunate moment, for the international price of vegetable oils, already depressed during the 1880s, was at the time being driven even lower by the European trade depression of 1892–95.[37] As a consequence, by 1895, when

Gungunyana was captured, Inhambane was already mired in an economic depression.

Gungunyana's defeat, however, paved the way for the Portuguese not only to create a bureaucratically controlled colony in Mozambique south of the Sabi River but also to reconsider their economic policies in the area. Chopi territory was made a part of the district of Inhambane and administered from the town of Inharrime. Inhambane, however, was also a part of southern Africa, and it could not avoid being affected by what was occurring at the region's economic center, South Africa. The discovery of diamonds at Kimberley in the late 1860s and the growth of a sugar-plantation economy in Natal in the 1860s and 1870s had created a need for large amounts of unskilled labor, and as early as the 1870s men from north of the Limpopo had begun to travel as migrant workers to these and other areas to work for money and goods unobtainable in Mozambique.[38] The establishment of the Witwatersrand's gold industry increased the demand for migrants, and the intense competition for workers there pushed wages higher and higher during the 1890s, luring more and more workers away from the economically depressed Chopi area.[39]

This labor migrancy to South Africa caught the attention of the new generation of Portuguese colonial officials sent out to administer Mozambique after 1895. With most of Mozambique carved up between chartered companies exercising quasi-sovereign rights, their own work as administrators was largely restricted to the district of Moçambique in the north and the area south of the Sabi River in the south. Their vision of development for these areas, however, was only that the migrants should be made to produce income for the state. Workers, they argued, should be traded to South Africa in exchange for the payment of capitation fees and for the guarantee of a certain percentage of Transvaal-bound traffic through the port of Lourenço Marques. Such official reasoning prompted the Portuguese to agree as early as 1897 to suggestions made by gold mine-owners that the free flow of labor to the mines be replaced by controlled recruitment.[40] By 1901, the creation of the Witwatersrand Native Labour Association (WNLA) and the granting to it of exclusive recruiting rights within those areas of Mozambique under direct Portuguese administration had ended the costly competition for migrant workers, causing wages to drop precipitously.[41] By 1907 Inhambane's governor was publicly complaining that WNLA had established a "state within a state" in his district and that local people considered its 750 recruiters, wearing their smart uniforms, more important than his own 240-strong police force.[42] Having become a fiefdom of WNLA, Inhambane's agricultural exports plummeted to almost nothing and remained there until the end of the 1930s.[43]

The destruction of the free market in labor in South Africa naturally made mining less attractive to Chopi men. Nonetheless they had little choice but to continue as migrant workers. They urgently needed money to pay their taxes; to secure bridewealth (lobola), a prerequisite for starting families that was rapidly inflating during the first two decades of this century; and to purchase clothing and other goods they required.[44] Moreover, in 1899 the Portuguese had promulgated a labor code that obliged all male Africans between the ages of fourteen and sixty to work and permitted local officials to compel this labor as they saw fit.[45] This system of forced labor, known locally as *shibalo*, was used to supply public-works projects and inefficient local private enterprises with forced labor at greatly depressed wages. Given the choice of working under the *shibalo* system or working as a migrant laborer at a substantially higher wage in the South African mines, most Chopi men recognized that they had no real choice.[46] They chose the mines and have continued to work in them to the present day, leaving behind them their wives and children, who have always been legally forbidden from accompanying their husbands and fathers. Given the relentless pressures of the *shibalo* system of underpaid forced labor if they remained at home, most Chopi men saw no alternative but to return to the mines repeatedly. Migrancy thus rapidly became an entrenched part of their lives.[47] The Portuguese government recognized this situation formally in 1911 by designating Chopi country a "Native Reserve," in effect designating it an integral part of the South African gold-mining industry's labor infrastructure.[48]

This situation pleased both mining magnates and highly placed Portuguese colonial officials, but it was less satisfactory for the Chopi. The local problems caused by labor migrancy were deplored by the district's governors and local Portuguese settlers alike.[49] Their central grievance was certainly self-serving: that the flow of men restricted the colony's agricultural growth. But their other complaints reveal the social problems associated with migrancy. The district's widespread alcoholism, they claimed, was caused by it. The position of women, isolated from their husbands for long periods of time, had also been injured by it, they argued, with the marital bonds between Chopi men and women seriously weakened. They noted that infanticide committed by women who had borne children from adulterous unions while their husbands were absent also seemed to be increasing. In 1920, Inhambane's governor assessed migrancy as nothing less than a "cancer " on his district.[50]

In fact, however, this picture was overdrawn. Chopi men did not lose touch with their homes. Recruitment was by contract, and at the end of one's contract—customarily twelve or eighteen months—one legally had to return home, where, after a few months "rest," a man would be engaged under a new contract. Furthermore, the Portuguese state required that a proportion of the money earned by Chopi workers be deferred and remitted to Mozambique at the end of the worker's contract.[51] Thus, only by returning home could a worker obtain all the money his labor had earned in South Africa. Therefore, workers oscillated back and forth between their workplaces and home villages, with officials hoping that the limited presence of the men in their home areas would guarantee that rural society would not collapse.

Moreover, the workers' own long-term interests necessarily lay in the rural areas. It was there that they would eventually return when their working life was over. Even while absent from their homes, therefore, the workers' attentions were sharply focused on them. While accepting the inevitability of migrancy, they nonetheless felt they had to try to preserve the basic structures of Chopi rural society, if only so they would have something to which to retire when their working life was over. By coordinating their absences with kinsmen or friends who agreed to do necessary agricultural work on their behalf and by investing some of their earnings in tools to improve productivity, or in lobola, so as to increase the exploitation of female and child labor, Chopi men were able to maintain much of their rural economy during the first four decades of the twentieth century despite their long absences.[52]

It is in the context of the institutionalization of such migrancy within the political economy of Portuguese colonialism that we must consider the later development of the Chopi xylophone orchestras. Because of the lack of educational opportunities in Inhambane district, there were few intellectuals with a Western-style education among the Chopi. Yet, despite the overall lack of literacy, the Chopi, as with all peoples, had intelligent, thoughtful men who served their society as intellectuals even though they were not literate. Western-educated African intellectuals in other parts of southern Africa disseminated their ideas by producing written works about history, literature, and linguistics, by writing for newspapers, and, eventually, by participating in the Western-style politics of anticolonialism.[53] For the Chopi, who lacked the literacy needed for such projects, the place in which intellectuals aired their ideas were the songs composed for the *migodo*. They seemed ideal places for such comment, not only because they were extremely popular as entertainment but also because public competitions held annually to determine the year's most effective *ngodo* ensured a general hearing for them throughout Chopi country.[54] As the songs of the *migodo* enjoyed the same licensed freedom of speech that other oral songs and poetry of southeastern Africa enjoyed, Chopi men took the opportunity to use the *migodo*, literally, to give public voice to their own concerns. By so doing, they carried on the tradition of Chopi resistance to the enemy established during the nineteenth century.

It was between 1940 and 1943 that the South African musicologist Hugh Tracey collected materials for his study *Chopi Musicians: Their Music, Poetry, and Instruments*.[55] Tracey recorded seven complete *migodo* for his book, six of them in Inhambane district and the seventh in Johannesburg. He was fortunate in encountering the *migodo* at what appears to have been a high point of their development and in being able to study the work of two of the most accomplished and most famous Chopi poets and musicians: Katini weNyamombe, leader of the orchestra at the court of Paramount Chief Wani Zavala, and Gomukomu weSimbi, who held the same position for Filippe waMdumane Banguza at Mangene.

It is clear that such musicians enjoyed their reputation, and several of the songs stressed the specialist skills of the musician and the mystery of the composer's craft. "To play the *mTimbila* you must dream about it," sings Gomukomu. Or, as another composer puts it, "You must dream to compose music." Katini's is the most vivid statement of this theme:

> Wani Zavala!
> Hush, you people of Zavala,
> Cease your chatter
> At this court of Chiefs!
>
> *Timbila* music is so moving it brings tears,
> This music of Katini's *Timbila*
> Singing and dancing.

> Wani Zavala!
> Hush, you people of Zavala,
> Cease your chatter
> At this court of Chiefs![56]

The social aspects of professionalism and patronage should not, however, be overstressed. Composers and musicians had to cultivate their gardens and build their own houses like everyone else. Like everyone else too, they were subject to taxation, to forced labor and recruitment for the Rand, and to ill-treatment at the hands of the police and court messengers acting under the authority of the Portuguese administration. When they complained in the songs about such treatment, they were speaking not just for an elite but for the community as a whole.

Significantly, their protest centered on the role of the chiefs in Chopi society. Because the Chopi had been Portuguese allies during the war against Gungunyana, the Chopi leaders of the 1890s were recognized as chiefs in the new colonial administrative system, while Gaza chiefs were being sent into exile or deposed. As there was a sharp distinction in law between "natives" and "non-natives," with the former subject to "customs" and "native usage," the way was opened for the Chopi chiefs to exercise a considerable amount of authority in land allocation and divorce cases.[57] For labor migrants the actions of their chiefs were thus crucial for the maintenance of rural Chopi society and were naturally of central importance to those who composed the songs for the *migodo*.[58]

Until the early 1940s, the Chopi were able to retain a relatively centralized political life with strong and genuine chiefs who played a key role in looking after the interests of the absent migrants.[59] When Gomukomu complains on the subject of chieftaincy "You elders must discuss affairs: / The one whom the white man appointed was the son of a commoner," he is distinguishing between those chiefs who were chiefs by legitimate succession and those who were mere puppet creations of the Portuguese. His own patron and brother-in-law, Filippe Banguza, would have been flattered by the comparison. Similarly, when Gomukomu protested about the use of the *palmatoria* by court messengers, his real outrage was that "Even Chiefs are beaten on the hands . . . / The arrogance of Julai in beating even the hands of Chiefs!" Such was the respect of these musicians for the legitimate hierarchy that derived from the nineteenth cen-

tury that Sipangani Likwekwe even turned on his own patron, Chu-
gela Chisiko, a creature of the Portuguese:

> You, Chugela, you are proud of your position, yet you are only a chief
>   made by the white man.
> Oh, the chieftainships of Nyaligolana and Chugela!
> Oh, the chieftainships of Nyaligolana and Chugela!
> It is a shame that should be hidden from Wani.
> Chugela is always asking for presents from his brother.
> Sitiki is excluded from the council. They saw they don't know him.
> The country of Mawewana is full of troubles.[60]

"Wani" is the important Chopi chief Wani Zavala, patron of Katini,
whose music Sipingana Likwekwe also admired.[61]

Because the *ngodo* was an established genre, its set form to some
extent imposed demands on the content of the songs. It had, in other
words, to fulfill certain roles and to respect audience expectations.
One very obvious limitation of the genre was its male domination.
Not only do the *migodo* described by Tracey had no women participants, but in only two of the forty-six songs is any attempt made to
represent women's experience. One is the brief opening song of Sauli
Ilova's *ngodo:*

> My husband tells me when he's drunk.
> My husband tells me when he's drunk.
>   You bitch![62]

The other, again a brief dance song, is by Gomukomu:

> I am most distressed,
> I am most distressed as my man has gone off to work,
> And he does not give me clothes to wear,
> Not even a black cloth.[63]

These two themes, especially the second, with its complaint about
the migrant-labor system, are very common in women's pounding
songs throughout southern Africa. Apart from these two moments,
however, nothing in these *migodo* express the concerns of women.

Each *ngodo* is comprised of a sequence of more or less established
features. The order of the different sections in Katini's *ngodo* of 1940,
for example, is given by Tracey as follows:

1. *Musitso wokata*	First Orchestral Introduction
2. *Musitso wembidi*	Second Orchestral Introduction
3. *Musitso woraru*	Third Orchestral Introduction
4. *Ng'geniso*	Entry of the Dancers
5. *Mdano*	Call of the Dancers
6. *Joosinya*	The Dance
7. *Joosinya cibudo combidi*	The Second Dance
8. *Mzeno*	The Song
9. *Mabandla*	The Councillors
10. *Citoto ciriri*	The Dancers' Finale
11. *Musitso kugwita*	The Orchestral Finale[64]

Allowing for slight variations in, for instance, the number of orchestral introductions, this is the basic shape of six of the *migodo* Tracey recorded. The demands of this structure are frequently referred to in the songs themselves: "Nguyusa, my young brother, help me compose my music. / I have no 'Great Song' for my *Timbila*."[65] Certain stock phrases recur, and certain issues, such as the question of facial tattoos, are repeatedly aired as the composers maintain running arguments.[66] Quite clearly, the composers found these structural patterns satisfying, providing some unity in diversity. But the need to fulfill the requirement of form does affect the content of the songs. Just as there are sections where the orchestra plays alone, so there are others when the dancing takes precedence over the words, and vice versa. The high points of each *ngodo* in terms of the lyrics are the *mdano*, the Call of the Dancers, and, especially, the *mzeno*, The Song, which is sung by the composer himself.

Tracey placed considerable emphasis on the overall unity of each *ngodo*, and he explained the origin of this unity by describing how the sections were composed. The composer, he said, began with the words (presumably, although he did not say so, the words of the *mzeno*). The music was suggested by the flow of the words, as the Chopi language is tonal and "the sounds of the words themselves almost suggest a melodic flow of tones." This melodic kernel was then transferred to the xylophone, and contrapuntal melodies were elaborated. Those melodies then became the themes both of the orchestral accompaniments to the songs and of the orchestral introductions. Finally, the dance leader listened to the music and began to devise dance routines for other sections.[67]

What Tracey did not note, and what is somewhat obscured by his procedure of examining the forty-six songs one by one, is that each *ngodo* has a particular subject. Katini's *ngodo* of 1940, for example, opens, after the orchestral introductions, with the Entry of the Dancers to the words already discussed briefly in chapter two:

> It is time to pay taxes to the Portuguese,
> The Portuguese who eat eggs
> And chicken.
> Change that English pound!

The next section, the Call of the Dancers, describes an incident when Katini and his aged wife were beaten by Kapitini, the court messenger. The section that follows, The Dance, is accompanied by these words:

> O—oh, listen to the orders,
> Listen to the orders of the Portuguese.
>
> O-oh, listen to the orders,
> Listen to the orders of the Portuguese.
> Men! The Portuguese say, "Pay your pound."
>
> Men! The Portuguese say, "Pay your pound."
> This is wonderful, father!
> Where shall I find the pound?
>
> This is wonderful, father!
> Where shall I find the pound?
>
> O-oh, listen to the orders,
> Listen to the orders of the Portuguese.[68]

By this stage, the subject of Katini's *ngodo* of 1940 is clearly established. Its theme is Portuguese colonial rule. The complaint thus far is about the prodigality of the Portuguese settlers, about official violence and taxation. The next section, The Second Dance, contains lines already noted about the use of the *palmatoria*—"Here is a mystery, the Portuguese beat us on the hands, / Both us and our wives."[69] This is followed by the *mzeno*, which attacks the state's ignoring of legitimate procedures in the selection of chiefs and deals with some of the problems that arise when the wrong man is appointed. The next section carries this point further, complaining about Portuguese interference in matters of Chopi succession. Running through the whole *ngodo* are words like "orders," "threaten," "beat," "whip," "avenge," and "make trouble" and lines like "I heard them trying to

hush it up" and "Fambayane was brought bound before the judge."
The songs are full of peremptory instructions—"Change that English pound!" and "Pay your pound!" and "Don't waste your time
with *Timbila*!" and "If you come across Chimuke, greet him with a
'Good Day' / Greet him well because he likes to be in amongst the
chiefs."[70] Chimuke was the district administrator, the source of all
these orders and the local representative of the colonial system,
which is being criticized from so many different angles. Only in the
final song of the *ngodo* does the mood relax, with a brief amusing
song about the rather dilatory courtship of Katini's sister-in-law, an
attractive widow, by her suitor.

In Katini's next *ngodo*, however, performed in early 1943, the subject is quite different. There is no mention of taxation or the *sjam-
bok* (hippo-hide whip) or the *palmatoria* or the state-appointed
chiefs. Kapitini, the court messenger, reappears very briefly, but only
to be ridiculed in the context of an amusing little scandal. The dominant theme of the *ngodo* of 1943 is not the nature of Portuguese
colonial rule but pride in Chopi culture and in the triumph of Chopi
music. The first song accompanied the Entry of the Dancers:

> Hey, Dawoti!
> Dawoti, go and ask Madikise.
> He will tell you about our grandfathers.
> Chitombe, behold Madikise.[71]

Dawoti was a court messenger attached to the office of the administrator Luiz de Vasconcelos (*Madikise*, "Law-giver"), and Chitombe is
one of the great ancestors of the Chopi people. The song's double
irony is, first, that, instead of being ruled by Chitombe, the Chopi
are now ruled by the Portuguese and, second, that, for flunkies like
Dawoti, Chopi history and culture exist only through the antiquar-
ian researches of the Portuguese administrator! This is a sarcastic
beginning to the *ngodo*, but in the next section, the Call of the
Dancers, Katini describes how in July 1939 the Chopi musicians
were summoned to entertain Portuguese President Carmona on his
state visit to Mozambique:

> Come, you people of Zavala,
> Come, you people of Zavala, and go to Magule.
>
> The Song of Madikise,
> It is wanted by Ngungwanda at Magule.[72]

"Magule" is the Chopi name for the place of Gungunyana's defeat at Lake Coolela in 1895. Now, at Magule, the Chopi and Gaza were again in competition, this time before the Portuguese president and in terms of culture.[73] The encounter is described in The Dance, which juxtaposes two quite distinct events. The first four and the last two lines refer to Chopi experiences working as migrant laborers in the mines of the Witwatersrand and encountering prejudice on the part of the African "boss boys" like Malanje simply because they speak Chopi; lines 5–8, however, in a nice juxtaposition, refer to the performance of Chopi songs at the meeting with the Portuguese president:

> Malanje says, "You swear at me if you speak chiChopi,"
> So I will speak chiSotho.
>
> Malanje says, "You swear at me if you speak chiChopi,"
> So I will speak chiSotho.
>
> Katini will come to Magule to play the *Timbila.*
> The President is glad to see the WaChopi.
>
> The Shangaans are left to sing their "Ho-ho siyana"
> Until very late for the President.
>
> Malanje says, "You swear at me if you speak chiChopi,"
> So I will speak chiSotho.[74]

To the delight of Katini, as lines 6–8 make clear, in the cultural competition the Chopi defeated the Gaza, commonly known as the Shangaans, at the very place where the Portuguese defeated the Gaza.

But meanwhile, what happened to the Portuguese? This emphasis on entertaining the Portuguese president may seem ignoble, but Katini was interested in the nature of the encounter. Although the Portuguese now ruled over the Chopi, it appears from the *ngodo* thus far that they investigated Chopi history and were fast succumbing to Chopi culture and, especially, to Chopi music. These triumphs were not secured by open confrontation and resistance, such as the Gaza had once so disastrously attempted at Magule. Rather, they were achieved by stealthy accommodation of the type illustrated in the song by the vignette of ethnic relations on the Rand: when the Sotho-speaking "boss boy," Malanje, refused to listen when addressed in Chopi, Katini spoke to him in Sotho, a small concession where there were other, more substantial advantages to be gained.[75]

With these points established, Katini reached the climax of his argument in the *mzeno*. Its principal theme is the visit that Katini and his orchestra paid to Lisbon in 1940, when they performed in the celebrations of Portugal's tricentennial anniversary of independence from Spain: "We made new tunes for the *Timbila* in the midst of the sea / As we passed foreign lands."[76] Chopi ethnic pride could have had no greater triumph than this victory of music over politics and warfare, celebrated in Portugal itself.[77] Although the events of the *ngodo* were three or four years out of date by the time it was performed in 1943, Katini did not, as Tracey suggested, comment haphazardly on topical events; instead, the composer pursued a complex argument about the nature of one type of response to the realities of Portuguese rule, drawing on recent Chopi history to make his point about the power of Chopi music to conquer the conquerors. Appropriately, therefore, this *ngodo*, in the section following the *mzeno*, contains the song "*Wani Zavala!* / Hush, you people of Zavala" about the power of Katini's music to bring tears. Appropriately, too, the *ngodo* closes with a demonstration of Katini's moral authority within the community, as he used The Dancers' Finale to deliver a stern warning about the attempted seduction of an underaged girl.[78]

As these two examples by Katini have demonstrated, the *ngodo* is an extended and complex poetical form. Because the *migodo* were performed by professional musicians rather than by laborers and cultivators, and because they were devised for lengthy public entertainment rather than to accompany communal or work-gang activity, they are much more thematically and aesthetically ambitious than, say, the *Paiva* song described in chapters two and six. The world of the *migodo* is a relatively big place, including the village and the city, the plantation and the mine, Mozambique and South Africa (and even, briefly, Lisbon). It takes into account two different versions of colonialism and a variety of different Europeans—Portuguese, English, Dutch, Italians, and Germans. It records Chopi contact with other African peoples, the Gaza in Mozambique and the Sotho and Xhosa on the Rand. The Chopi did not have a single enemy present in all these locations or among all these choices. The *migodo* contain no uniform explanation of why things have gone wrong. They do exhibit, however, a definite pattern of concern. Although the forty-six songs of the seven *migodo* Tracey collected are the work of at least five different composers, so that the first impression is one of variety and contrast, they all share one central and passionate preoccupation.

This point can be most effectively established by an examination of how these *migodo* from the early 1940s deal with the potentially radicalizing experience of labor migration to the Rand. Little in these songs suggests that working in the mines was an unpleasant experience. "I'll go to the mines to work for money so that when I come back I can buy cider to drink," states one song. "If we go to the City we see wonders as we pass Pretoria," states another, from a *ngodo* actually recorded on the Rand. Only one line from one song— "If I go to the mines, where shall I find the courage to get into the cage?"—gives us any impression of what it might be like to work underground.[79] Most of the songs that refer to the Rand deal with the setting of the mining compound, and the subject is usually ethnic rivalries:

> Cast off your [dancing] skins!
> There is no relish left, you Shangaans, it has been eaten by the Sotho.
> It has been eaten by the Sotho and the Xhosa, and we will not get it.[80]

On the Rand, the Chopi's enemies tend to be, not the Portuguese or the Randlords, but other African peoples who, in working situations that encouraged ethnic rivalries, are in competition with them. For a fuller analysis of what is damaging about the migrant labor system, we must turn to Gomukomu's *ngodo* of 1942–43.

Gomukomu introduced the subject in the Call of the Dancers, apparently as a joke:

> It is Filippe's opinion
> That the girls also should sign on and go to the mines.
> It is Filippe's opinion.
> What a good idea!

"Filippe" is Filippe Banguza, the paramount chief, who was Gomukomu's patron. In the next song of the *ngodo*, however, a second Call of the Dancers, the joke suddenly turns out to be serious:

> Ha! We quarrel again! The same old trouble.
> The older girls must pay taxes.
> Natanele, speak for me to the white man to let me be.[81]

The complaint is about the notorious circular of October 1942 from the governor-general of Mozambique, which, while reinforcing forced labor as a requirement to meet rapidly growing labor demands within Mozambique's economy, gave local administrators no guidance on how this was to be accomplished.[82] One consequence among many was an intensification of tax collection, including the taxation of women. Filippe Banguza's duties, as a state-recognized chief, included tax collection—and the joke about sending women to the mines (Natanele was a mine labor recruiter)—suddenly becomes most bitter.

As the song accompanying the dance itself, the *ngodo* contains the complaint noted earlier of the woman whose husband has gone off to the Rand, leaving her with no clothes to wear, not even the "black cloth" of mourning. The *ngodo* thus comments from more than one angle on the position of women in the labor system. Gomukomu's argument is then brought to a head in the *mzeno*. He complains that he himself has been forced to give up playing the *timbila* to go to work as a laborer on the Incomati banana plantations. He complains that the administrator is troubling everybody "with his constant calling" to enlist. And he complains that the police are now beating people indiscriminately—"even the hands of chiefs" and "even women"—as the new labor regulations are enforced. The Portuguese "turn their backs" when any question of the people's welfare is raised:

> We got on the train and arrived at Sewe,
> And when we spoke about the matter of food,
> About the matter of food, they turned their backs,
> We overheard the Portuguese speaking about food,
> Speaking about food while their backs were turned.[83]

Significantly, the incident described here occurred during President Carmona's visit in 1939. Gomukomu, in effect, was retorting to Katini's argument that the Portuguese have been seduced by the appeal of Chopi culture by emphasizing how badly his own orchestra was treated when fulfilling an official engagement. Finally, Gomukomu explained that the whole problem of increased labor demands has to be understood in the context of "the German war": "The bloody fools of white men are fighting. / Mutijawo says that they are like four-legged beasts."[84] The presentation of the whole issue with a great deal of humor not represented in our selective quotations only reinforces the power of this *ngodo* and the quality of its analysis.

This *ngodo* deals only with the local effects of migrant labor. It does not mention what life was like on the Rand and makes no comment about whether working conditions there were very unpleasant or whether the pay was far too low. Instead, it focuses on the consequences for the local community of recruiting methods, of state-sponsored violence, and of the men's absence for such long periods of time.[85] The threat to the Chopi community is what matters. We noted earlier that the world of these *migodo* is comparatively large. By contrast with the songs from Mozambique's Quelimane district, which show little awareness of a bigger world outside the immediate relations of power in which the people were trapped, the *migodo* seem to encompass great diversity and individuality. The impression, however, is misleading. Underlying the surface variety of opinion and of mood, the *migodo* express a fundamental concern for the health of the Chopi nation. Although the word itself appears only once in the forty-six songs (and then as a language designation), Chopi identity, the good of the Chopi people, is the single major preoccupation to which all else relates.

The *migodo* of the early 1940s, then, express a feeling of ethnic nationalism in which the legitimate chiefs are the symbols of the nation's history and integrity. In the *migodo* themselves, no distinctions are made between those who were inside and those outside the circle of power, as, for instance, are repeatedly made in early Zulu, Swazi, or Sotho praise poetry. There are no appeals to national unity and no attacks on individuals for failing to respect chiefly power, as again occur in later Zulu, Swazi, or Sotho praise poetry. There is no straining of any sort after audience attention or audience agreement, and song after song proceeds on the assumption that the performance of the *migodo* is a community entertainment ("Come together with your wives" and the like).

Clearly most important of all is the positive, anticolonial aspects of Chopi nationalism. The targets for the most fierce attack in the *migodo* are consistently those that represent Portuguese authority, such as the court messengers—"You, Lekeni, you are as black as coal, / Son of Nyamandane, you are a terror!—and the labor recruiters—"Listen, they are off to their kraals as they are afraid that they will be signed on"—and the state-appointed officials with their new demands for "respect":

Just listen to the sons of Chigombe's village,
To keep on saying "Good Day" is a nuisance.
Makarite and Bubwane are in prison
Because they did not say "Good Day." . . .
They had to go to Chisiko [prison] to say "Good Day" there
    instead![86]

And, of course, the Portuguese, as the colonial rulers, were targets.
The Chopi songs, in short, attack a wide range of targets from a belief in a Chopi nation that is perfectly capable of managing its own
affairs. Running through all the songs of the *migodo* are references
to two contrasting systems of authority. On the one hand, representing the Chopi nation, are their genuine chiefs advised by their coun-
cils of elders and their professional musicians who speak through
their *migodo.* On the other are the usurpers of power—the administrators and *chefes do posto* (station chiefs), the court messengers, the
police, the labor recruiters, the tax collectors, and the puppet chiefs
and headmen. The fundamental problem is, "They have taken the
country, we know not how, and shared it out."[87] In the total absence
in the 1940s of any likely military or political solution to this problem, the *migodo* demonstrate continuing confidence in Chopi institutions and revel in the special skills and vitality of Chopi culture.

Tracey's study was published in 1948, and within two years he was
back in Inhambane recording further *migodo.*[88] He was struck immediately by profound changes in both the form and content of the
migodo since the early 1940s, and although he was to continue visiting Mozambique over the next fifteen years, accumulating an impressive archive of Chopi recordings, his task became increasingly
one of preservation. In 1960 António Rita-Ferreira, then administrator of the Chopi area of Homoine, lamented that the *migodo* appeared to be a dying form. By contrast with the groups studied by
Tracey, most of the dancers were by then middle-aged or even old
men, and the indifference of the young men to the xylophone music
was obvious:

The musicians we questioned (also men of age) never ceased to lament
the lack of interest in the art of the *timbilas.* The orchestras survive
under the patronage of tribal chiefs in whose investitures and other
ceremonies they take part, assuming, in their art, a type of music
purely formal. This role was accentuated by their eventual conscrip-

tion by high officials of the Administration, for visits of high dignitaries, inaugurations, etc. The Islamic community of Homoine also at times contracted them to add luster to certain showy occasions such as weddings.[89]

Tracey had succeeded only too well in drawing the wider world's attention to the pleasures of Chopi music.

These changes could scarcely have occurred, however, without powerful changes in Chopi society itself, some of them long in developing, other specific to the immediate postwar period. These combined to undermine the strong sense of community and of the nation's identity that, until the 1940s, had been the Chopi answer to Portuguese rule and the demands of migrant labor. The first of these changes occurred in 1942 when the Portuguese first began to take seriously the advantages of indirect rule. Addressing this theme in his annual report, Governor-General Tristão de Bettencourt complained of the large number of chiefs in Mozambique who ruled no more than 100 or 200 huts and who were much too poor themselves to command respect: "prestige," he declared, "goes together with the economic position of the person who exercises the authority."[90] There was a need to create an elite class of conservative chiefs, and by 1948, after six years during which the number of chiefs and headmen throughout Mozambique were cut by 60 percent—the unsatisfactory or uncooperative chiefs being dismissed—the administration felt able to pay the remaining chiefs a monthly salary of 350.00 escudos "to free them from the precarious life they live and stop them being dependent on their population."[91] Meanwhile, following a speech in Lourenço Marques by the Portuguese Colonial Minister, Marcello Caetano, which condemned forced labor,[92] the Portuguese were compelled once again to rethink the methods by which they broke their own laws to recruit labor. The requirement of the infamous circular of 1942 that administrators and *chefes do posto* should furnish labor was withdrawn, and, although African men remained subject to six months of forced labor each year, the responsibility for enforcing this requirement passed officially to the new class of chiefs. By 1950, chiefs were also being paid for a fixed percentage of the taxes they collected and were allowed to retain what was effectively a capitation fee on all labor recruited from their areas.[93]

Nothing, however, alienated the Chopi people from their chiefs so thoroughly as the chiefs' responsibility, from the early 1940s onward, for directing the forced cultivation of cotton and rice. A concession system for the cultivation of cotton on the model of the Belgian Congo had been devised for Mozambique as early as 1926,[94] but it was not until 1938 that a cotton board was established with the responsibility of supplying the textile industry of northern Portugal with its raw material.[95] The holder of a cotton concession held monopoly rights over the labor and produce of his area. In practice, this meant that all men could be compelled to cultivate one hectare of cotton and all women half a hectare to produce cotton for compulsory purchase at derisory prices. Most of this cotton was grown in concessions north of the Zambesi River, but in the districts of Gaza and Inhambane the company Algodeira do Sul de Save held ten concessions, including ones in Zavala and Muchopes. The speedy success of the system in furnishing the bulk of Portugal's annual demand for cotton and a shortage of rice caused by the fall of southeast Asia to Japan in 1941 prompted the government to create a similar concession system for rice.[96] A rice propaganda division was created in 1942 to oversee the operation of *circulos orizicolos* (rice zones) within which concession holders had the same rights over labor and the same purchasing rights as existed in the cotton concessions.[97] It was the introduction of this new rice-concession system, superimposed on both the cotton-concession system and the need to supply labor to the mines of the Witwatersrand, that brought the labor problems of the early 1940s to a head and prompted the governor-general's circular of 1942, which effectively doubled the supply of labor to be available within a year.

Once again, the chiefs were drawn into implementing the administration's policies. As early as 1942, an attempt was made to involve them in enforcing cotton production. Chiefs who actively assisted the concession holders were rewarded with gifts of houses built of corrugated metal.[98] From 1948, they were made legally responsible for enforcing the concession holders' rights to compulsory labor, and from the early 1950s they were permitted to hold small cotton concessions themselves that were cultivated by forced labor and tax defaulters.[99] By then, the chiefs had become a fully extended arm of the administration in all its main activities: tax collection, labor recruitment, and cotton and rice growing. By the early 1950s it was no longer possible for a poet and musician like Gomukomu to make distinctions between state-appointed puppet chiefs and "real" Chopi chiefs as he had done in his *ngodo* of 1942–43. Nor could he any longer conceive of the "real" chiefs as the true representatives of Chopi nationalism and symbols of Chopi survival.

These changes in the role of chiefs were specific to the 1940s. But there were other social changes that had been gathering pace since the 1920s or even earlier which also worked to undermine the unity of Chopi society. By the 1950s, Chopi men had been migrating to the Rand's mines for three generations, and although the initial effects of this had been in some ways to strengthen the existing hierarchy of Chopi society by making money available for lobola and for tools to improve agricultural production, there were longer-term consequences that undermined these hierarchies and encouraged the growth of class differences and of the nuclear family in place of the extended family.

Earlier in the century, the pattern had been for young men to grow up and establish themselves within the family village where fathers and uncles lived as neighbors.[100] The bride-price paid to fathers at their daughters' marriage usually was made available to the young men as a means of arranging their own marriages. The shift towards the payment of lobola in cash, rather than in cattle, which occurred as money from working on the Rand became available, coupled with the effects of taxation and forced labor on making people increasingly responsible for their own economic survival, seems to have led by the 1940s to more and more young men's being responsible for finding their own bridewealth. These men lived in their own houses, separate from their fathers. This tendency was reinforced by the emergence of a pattern of life in which young men worked on the Rand, successively, to obtain money for lobola, then money to obtain land, and then money for tools and oxen to work the land. Men who had succeeded in establishing themselves by such means and through their own and their wives' labor came to perceive their investments in highly individualized terms. The notion that property belonged to individuals, not to the extended family or lineage, was only further strengthened when money was used to buy such goods as sewing machines, bicycles, radios, cement-built houses, and furniture. Local labor, which had formerly been shared within the extended family itself for agricultural purposes, also became commoditized, and professional craftsmen—builders, carpenters, tailors, and the like—became common.

Linked with these developments was increased concern by men about control over women, especially as men were required to remain away from home for very long periods of time and relied upon

2. Chopi dancers in a performance of an *ngodo*, circa 1950, when chiefly patronage was becoming an increasingly dubious asset. (By permission of Jill Dias.)

women to protect their interests at home. Women, however, were being pushed by the tax and labor laws into becoming economically responsible individuals, and it was the women who in practice bore the brunt of the cotton and rice concessions. Men who had paid lobola with savings from a sixteen-month contract on the Rand and who had established their wives in houses and on land purchased with money from successive contracts, were not prepared to risk losing their investment through their wives' infidelity or recklessness. Ridicule of women guilty of adultery and invocations to women to observe "traditional" Chopi values and remain chaste, loyal, and obedient thus became common in the *migodo* of the 1950s and afterward.

All these male concerns are evident in Gomukomu's *ngodo* for 1955, an *ngodo* so different in emphasis from earlier compositions we have considered by him that it would not initially appear to be the work of the same man.[101] The themes of the *ngodo* are forced labor and labor migrancy for the men, female adultery, taxation, and forced labor for women on the local rice concessions. But running through the whole performance is anger and contempt for the venality and corruption of the chiefs, including chiefs previously regarded as true representatives of the Chopi, like Filippe Banguza, Gomukomu's own patron.

The *ngodo* begins with the usual three orchestral introductions, followed by a brief song that states that a Chopi migrant worker, Madaŵani, has been unexpectedly repatriated from South Africa, from which the authorities were then sending back many migrant laborers who had overstayed their contracts. Having set the scene, Gomukomu proceeds immediately in the *mdano* section to the first of his assaults on Filippe Banguza:

Chibhanda wushaka ngene Rute amahoko chivusa mbango. Ngene Rute amahoko chivusa mbango.	In this breaking up of the relationship, it is Ruth who is the real culprit. Indeed, it is Ruth who is starting the trouble.
Nguyuza, mwanathu, khuni vuneti timbila tamakono? Hinasika nhuhayini timbila tamakono natisiya?	Nguyaza, my brother, why are you not helping me compose for this year's *timbila?* But where can we go to compose for the *timbila* (for we have had to leave it all behind to go for *shibalo* work?)
Mahungu aFilippe akuna ng'ola mdende ŵasihoranana. Mahungu aFilippe akutala mawuya ni mdende!	Filippe's system is to grab all the young girls because of this repatriation business. Filippe's new system is just one of the things stemming from this repatriation business!

In the first of the three verses, Ruth, one of the chief's wives is criticized for ruining the marriage's harmony by trying to dominate her cowives. In the second verse, the composer's brother, Nguyaza, has no time to help to compose music for the *timbila* because of the demands of *shibalo*. In the third, Filippe Banguza turns out to be instituting his own system of registration, rounding up unmarried girls of sixteen years of age to be taxed to increase his income. Linking the three verses are the themes of dislocation and the abuse of power. The *mdano* is followed by the *mchuyo* movement, which deals, in a humorous fashion, with the amazement of NyaVoto, the wife of the repatriated miner Madawani, at her husband's unexpected return, which has rendered her "dumbstruck" (*dibhembaa*). Since in his absence she has borne a child by another man, Madawani demands the return of lobola so he can find other wives and "make children with them instead" (*nichiweleka nacho*). In the next song, the *cibudo,* or The Second Dance, Gomukomu voices a complaint of the repatriated workers: that they are being forced to pay taxes for all the years of their absence in South Africa.

Then comes the *mzeno,* the centerpiece of the entire *ngodo:*

Hambukani ŵatingamu kunene anagapinda Penselo! Waŵasikati ndiŵaŵatsambulele tinguwo ŵana ŵeka Likhuluni.

Oh, open a path through the crowd so Pensil can pass through! There the women are, stripping off their clothes so that they can clean the drainage sluices that run into the Likhuluni River.

Mavurute ahetile chiwumbe ngukuduketela liŵilo. Achitsula achagela Ndhumbe achikhane Likhuluni kubihile motsenu. Malalani, namigela maseko. Ningawona mkoma ni kukutuma, haaaa!

Running very fast, Mavurute just managed to get across the valley. He's gone in to tell Ndhumbe that the Likhuluni is a difficult river to cross. Keep quiet and I'll tell you a story that will make you laugh. I have seen a chief running, all panting and out of breath.

MaShangana maŵuka wukwele ngukuwomba-womba chiChopi. Mhayayiya yopwata mkoma khaditsuri ma6ayetha kaŵaChopi.

The Shangaan people are very jealous of us when they hear us chatting in Chopi. The Shangaan people have no chiefs to rule them, and so they must salute the Chopi.

Kwalakanya nguyateka maleyangu
mamana ni chisaŵa chikotela!
Njoninga ŵakoma ŵachitsaka
ŵachiningwa nguMathavi Zavala.
Achikhene ŵanatsaka
ngukomichi.
Njoninga ŵakoma ŵachitsaka eyo
male.

Oh, I think about the money I
spent to buy the chief an empty
tin for *him* to enjoy. The gift
for the chiefs' enjoyment has
been given by Matthew Zavala.
He said that it's for their
enjoyment in a cup. It's for
chiefs to enjoy themselves with
others' money!

Komukomu arukilwe—mtima
nkwambisamba govani!
"Uhakayiya yombasamba govani!
Ngunarukwa mtima
ngumahorana—
'ghaaa!!! thu!!,'"

Komukomu is being slandered—
he is disgustingly filthy
because he does not wash in the
river! "Oh, my habit of not
washing in the river! I have
no luck with the girls and they
all ridicule me, saying—
'ghaaa!!! pftuuu!!'"

Mafumane athaŵile awonako
maphoyisa mangahoka. Zavala
ŵamdana mahungu. Atsute
achaaka Mbandeni awonako
kutalelwa nguŵalungu.

Mafumane has run away because
he has seen the police coming.
They are calling a meeting at
Zavala. He has gone off to
stay at Mbanda because he has
white people calling at his
house constantly.

Hambukani ŵatingamu kunene
anagapinda Peniselo!
Wawasikati ndiŵaŵatsambulele
tinguwo ŵana ŵeka Likhuluni.

Oh, open a path through the
crowd so Pensil can pass
through! There the women are,
stripping off their clothes so
that they can clean the
drainage sluices that run into
the Likhuluni river.

Typical of Gomukomu's work, this *mzeno* touches with deceptive
lightness and good humor on a wide range of serious Chopi concerns. The overseer of the local rice concession, derisively nick-
named Pensil because of his self-important officiousness, is mocked
in the opening line. A crowd has gathered to see the women stripping
off their clothes to clean the sluices between the rice paddies and the
river, and Pensil, too, is eager to watch them. The women, of course,
are working under compulsion and were frequently subject to sexual

abuse by overseers such as Pensil. Gomukomu has succeeded marvelously in making Pensil look both comic and contemptible. In the second verse, he turns his mockery on the chief, Filippe Banguza, retelling an anecdote that has been the subject of local gossip. The chief had been given a field at Chidumbe by a friend, and he had gone there to see how his crops were doing. While there he seduced his friend's wife and was discovered in the act by his friend. He managed to escape "by running very fast" (*ngukuduketela liŵilo*), and when he reached home, he explained to his wife that the reason he was panting and out of breath was that the Likhuluni River was a difficult river to cross.

The next verse looks like an anachronism, repeated from the *migodo* of the early 1940s when the Chopi were proud of their chiefs and maintained their ethnic rivalry with the Gaza. Coming as it does in the *mzeno* of an old man and situated conspicuously between two verses that ridicule his own chief and patron, Filippe Banguza, its impact is sharply ironical. The attack on Filippe in the next verse returns to the theme of the repatriated miners and deals with the deep resentments of men like Matthew Zavala, who are expected to make gifts to the chiefs on their return. These gifts, says Gomukomu, have been squandered in drinking and hence were worthless—an "empty tin." Significantly, the verse begins with Filippe Banguza but ends with an attack on all chiefs ("It's for chiefs to enjoy themselves with others' money"), revealing how deep the divisions have now become between chiefs and the people as a consequence of Portuguese policies.

The fifth verse is meant to be paired with verse one. In it, the composer disingenuously ridicules himself, when, in fact, his victim was understood by his auditors to be Pensil, the rice-concession overseer.[102] Although keen to have success with women, he is contemptuously rejected by all of them (*ghaaa!!!, tuu!!*), and they accuse him of being filthy and unwashed despite his power over the Likhuluni River, where ordinary people usually bathed. The *mzeno* concludes, first, with a criticism of neighboring chief Zandamela ("Mafumane"), who spends so much of his time cooperating with the Portuguese after his appointment to the Chiefs' Council in Lourenço Marques that he has been forced by his unpopularity to shift his home to a remote village at the very edge of his chieftaincy, and, then, with a repetition of the opening sarcasms about Pensil.

Following the *mzeno*, the *ngodo* concludes with a further four movements. The first, the *msumeto*, is a complaint about taxation and the poverty of the people. The second, the *kutokoza*, is a shouted comment by the dancers in which Filippe Banguza is again attacked, this time for his compliance with "the white man." The fourth is The Orchestral Finale. The third, however, the *mabandla*, is a song that sums up what is happening to Chopi music now that it has become popular with the Portuguese:

Vusa mbango makono! Hinanguma ŵaBanguzi, hinanguma ngutimbila.	Oh, this year's troubles are starting! We people of Banguza will be finished off by the *timbila!*
Hambuzana chichangasika timbila, udanani ni maphoyisa hichisika timbila.	If we are going to compose for the *timbila*, you'll need the police to bring us all together for the work.

The complaint is that they are now being forced so often to perform for visitors by the Portuguese that composing and playing their music has become a kind of forced labor and that it soon will require the police to bring the *timbila* players together.

Gomukomu died in 1962, seven years after composing this *ngodo* on the state of his community and of his art. In the closing years of his life, he devoted much of his time to reviving the music of Katini, which he played with great authority, in particular the famous *mzeno* of 1943 dealing with the death of Katini's friend Manjengwe, a piece of music long revered by the Chopi for its beauty.[103] The combination of the licensed privilege of the *migodo* songs and his own personal reputation made his position impregnable, and he could attack his patron without fear of redress. But his role as social and political critic was not easily inherited by the next generation of *timbila* composers.

From the time when St. Vincent Erskine first described Chopi xylophone music down through the 1940s, it had flourished under chiefly patronage, the chiefs meeting the expenses of performance and the composers enjoying all the advantages of working in a small community where oblique comments and allusions to people and events or to rival performers were understood. The cooptation by the Portuguese of, first, their chiefs and, then, their *timbila* music for official occasions created a crisis for Chopi musicians.[104] One response reported by Rita-Ferreira in 1960 was to abandon playing music for the *migodo* altogether.[105] The young people he described as

3. Chopi xylophone orchestra, Homoine Inhambane district, Mozambique, circa 1962. By the 1960s most performers were old men, with younger musicians increasingly shunning earlier performance styles. (Copyright, António Rita-Ferreira.)

being completely uninterested in the *migodo* were instead forming what he called "jazz" bands, using stringed instruments brought back from South Africa together with other instruments of their own manufacture. Such bands had two categories of performance, namely *litsako*, when they played without charge at weddings, baptisms, and other family occasions, and *bisimuso* (derived from the English word *business*), when they performed at dances, earning a 200-escudos fee for playing the whole of Saturday night and from 6:00 P.M. to midnight on Sundays. Alternatively, they would hire a hall and charge dancers an entrance fee of up to 2.50 escudos. Though the bands Rita-Ferreira describes sang in Chopi, they drew their repertoire from many sources, Portuguese, Cuban, Brazilian, Ronga, Shangaan, Tonga, or even Xhosa.

The other response was to seek out alternative patrons for the orchestras on the gold mines of South Africa. It is not known exactly when the *timbila* were first taken to the mining compounds, but they were certainly there by 1920. The mining managements have always followed policies of divide and rule for their work forces, housing the different ethnic groups separately and encouraging competition between them.[106] Such competitions included "native dances," and the acknowledged leaders in the early dance competitions were the Chopi orchestras and their *migodo* dancers.[107] When the University of the Witwatersrand held a "Monster Native Dance" to raise funds in 1928, four rival teams of Chopi and Gaza musicians competed before a crowd of 5,000 spectators. The Chopi teams presented two complete *migodo*.[108] These *migodo* are interesting because they deal almost entirely with South African themes, such as the Rand Revolt of 1922, Hertzog's victory over Smuts in the 1924 election, the local weather, and other mine workers. One song was summarized in the program as follows: "There goes the East Coast train; it goes to the land of the Portuguese, who are treating us so badly."[109] This song drew a vehement protest from the Portuguese government's curator of labor in the Transvaal, who wrote to the Chamber of Mines as follows:

> The fact is that the funds of the University of the Witwatersrand profited considerably by the use of the Portuguese Natives at this function, but it is regrettable that instead of staging their natural dances they were made to choose items which constituted a libellous and unfair comment against the authorities of their own Government and a detrimental propaganda among the white population of the Union against the good name of the Portuguese Authorities and consequently of this Department in the presence of many thousands of spectators.[110]

By contrast, the *migodo* that are performed nowadays in the mining compounds seem tame affairs. The best known of the *timbila* players since the death of Katini and Gomukomu have been Shambini Makasi Chiseki, who was born around 1918 and who spent fifty years on the mines, his age-mate Sathayane waBokiso Makamo, and, most famous of all, Venancio Londolani Mbande. Mbande was born in Zavala in 1928 and learned to play the *timbila* at the age of six, being taught by his grandfather, Mahoho. He went to work on the Van Dyk Consolidated Mine in 1948 and immediately joined their established orchestra. In 1953 he met Hugh Tracey and on several occasions accompanied him to Mozambique, where Tracey recorded his *migodo*. In 1967, he moved to the Marievale mine to take charge of its orchestra. By this stage in his career he was exercising certain powers of patronage himself in finding employment for fellow Chopi workers. Finally, in 1978, he moved to his current post at Wildebeestfontein Mine where his patron, Dick Middleton, the hostel manager, made efforts to maintain the art of *timbila* playing by establishing a workshop for their manufacture and recruiting new Chopi players to join his team on the mine. Mbande has also lectured and demonstrated his art at universities in South Africa and the United States, has taken part in several films, and, in 1969, was the winner of the University of California's African Arts competition.

Venancio Mbande is a musician of great skill, but the patronage of the South African mining industry and his current life-style are far removed from the circumstances of the *timbila* players of an older generation. He himself regrets the loss of the closed community "in which people can know all the allusions that are made in the songs" and in which "a truly effective *ngodo*" is possible.[111] The words of his songs contain little that would give offense to anybody. A good deal of time is taken up with commenting on the sweetness of the *timbila* music and his own skills as a composer. His fellow workers are advised about the benefits of working for the whites and advised, too, not to spend their money on the local Tswana prostitutes. Local incidents are occasionally discussed, and the old tradition of using the *migodo* to comment on the ethnic rivalries that are encouraged by the mining companies also surfaces. But lacking a social context in which the freedom of poetic license can have much meaning, the songs have become merely bland adjuncts to the instrumental music. Significantly, the exceptions are deeply personal songs in which Mbande relates tragic incidents from his past life.

Meanwhile in Mozambique during the 1960s and 1970s, it was still possible to witness performances of *migodo*, and recordings continued to be made by musicologists Andrew Tracey, Curt Wittig, and Gai Zantzinger, who filmed two *migodo* in 1976. Most of these *migodo* are, however, mélanges by several composers, often brought together solely for the purposes of the recording. They lack the thematic unity of the *migodo* of the 1940s and frequently lack the topical relevance, being little more than anthologies of old favorites, including pieces by the long-dead Katini. A common complaint, however, is that the musicians are being forced to perform repeatedly at Portuguese functions, where they are made to sit for hours in the hot sun and play without remuneration.[112] The degree to which the chiefs had been able to take control of the content of the songs is revealed in the *mzeno* of one of the *migodo* filmed by Zantzinger, composed by Sathanyane waBokiso Makamo:

> To compose for *timbila*, Sathanyane, start by telling the chiefs, or
> they may be angry.

That time you tell them about the *timbila* they are happy.
Meet together, people of Mbanguzi, it is he, the Chief, the Governor
  who has arrived.
Come, Chopis, let us greet the Chief.[113]

It is scarcely surprising that Sathanyane found greater opportunities for performance in South Africa.

The advent of independence for Mozambique in 1975 did not reverse the decline of the *migodo*. FRELIMO's abolition of chieftainship as a "reactionary institution " has meant that the residual patronage required for organizing the large xylophone orchestras and manufacturing the xylophones was no longer available. FRELIMO, it is true, did decide to preserve some of the orchestras through state patronage in order to coopt them into new, official "national culture." But more importantly, the FRELIMO government also pressured its chosen orchestras to produce patriotic anthems and songs in praise of state policies and the FRELIMO party, in effect revoking the poetic license that had long lain at the core of the music's existence.[114] Worst of all, however, and destructive of all cultural life—ethnic and "national"—is the simple fact that the ordinary life of the Chopi people has been disrupted by the savage civil war that has been fought throughout Inhambane district between the FRELIMO government and the Resistência Nacional Moçambicana (RENAMO) guerilla movement. With daily life in the area disrupted and the economy shattered, survival itself is the only important issue. Prospects of the future revival and development of the *migodo*—so long the most striking example of Chopi culture—seem bleak indeed.

Notes

1. St. Vincent Erskine, "Journey to Umzila's, South-East Africa, in 1871–1872," *Journal of the Royal Geographical Society* 45 (1875): 56–57.

2. See H. A. Junod, *The Life of a South African Tribe*, 2d rev. ed., 2 vols. (1927; rpt., New York, 1962), 2:280–82.

3. Erskine, "Journey to Umzila's," 56–57.

4. F. Elton, "Journal of an Exploration of the Limpopo River," *Journal of the Royal Geographical Society* 42 (1872): 18; H. P. Junod, "Some Notes on Tshopi Origins," *Bantu Studies* 3, no. 1 (1929): 57–71; D. Earthy, *Valenge Women* (London, 1933), 3–10; M. L. Correira de Matos, "Origens do Povo

Chope Segundo a Tradição Oral," *Memorias do Instituto de Investigação cientifica de Moçambique* 10, ser. C (1973), 1–85, passim.

5. J. D. Omer-Cooper, *The Zulu Aftermath* (London, 1966), 33.

6. P. Harries, "Slavery, Social Incorporation, and Surplus Extraction: The Nature of Free and Unfree Labour in South-East Africa," *Journal of African History* 20, no. 3 (1981): 314–16.

7. G. Liesengang, "Notes on the Internal Structure of the Gaza Kingdom of Southern Mozambique, 1840–1895," in *Before and after Shaka: Papers in Nguni History,* ed. J. Peires (Grahamstown, 1981), 179; R. Pélissier, *Naissance du Mozambique: Résistance et révoltes anticoloniales (1854–1918),* 2 vols. (Orgeval, France, 1984), 2:538–39.

8. Harries, "Slavery, Social Incorporation, and Surplus Extraction," 317.

9. W. G. Clarence-Smith, *The Third Portuguese Empire, 1825–1975: A Study in Economic Imperialism* (Manchester, 1985), 36: Harries, "Slavery, Social Incorporation, and Surplus Extraction," 309–18; Omer-Cooper, *Zulu Aftermath,* 57–58; Pélissier, *Naissance du Mozambique,* 1:79–89.

10. St. Vincent Erskine, "Journey of Exploration to the Mouth of the River Limpopo," *Journal of the Royal Geographical Society* 39 (1869): 262; Elton, "Journal of an Exploration of the Limpopo River," 1–38 passim.

11. Liesegang, "Notes on the Internal Strucutre of the Gaza Kingdom," 180; Elton, "Journal of an Exploration of the Limpopo River," 18ff.; Richards to Bebout, 21 May 1885, ABC 15.4, vol. 12, American Board of Mission Papers, (ABMP) Houghton Library, Harvard University, Cambridge, Massachusetts.

12. On the fertility of the soil and the density of population, see Erskine, "Journey to Umzila's," 56, 80–85; A. A. Caldas Xavier, "O Inharrime e as Guerras Zavallas," *Boletim de Sociedade da Geographia de Lisboa,* 2d ser., nos. 7–8 (1880): 481–86; Mozambique, *Department of Agriculture: Bulletin no. 1* (Lourenço Marques, 1909), 9–13.

13. Caldas Xavier, "O Inharrime e as Guerras Zavallas," 482.

14. Pélissier, *Naissance du Mozambique,* 2:547–8, 558–61; Erskine, "Journey to Umzila's, South-East Africa, in 1871–1872," 124; Caldas Xavier, "O Inharrime e as Guerras Zavallas," 487.

15. St. Vincent Erskine, "Third and Fourth Journeys in Gaza, or Southern Mozambique, 1873 to 1874, and 1874 to 1875," *Journal of the Royal Geographical Society* 48 (1878): 45.

16. H. P. Junod, "Some Notes on Tshopi Origins," 57; Earthy, *Valenge Women,* 9; P. L. F. dos Santos, *Gramatica da Língua Chope* (Lourenço Marques, 1941), 9.

17. C. Correira Henriques, *Relatório do Governador do Districto de Inhambane, 1913–1915* (Lourenço Marques, 1916), 243.

18. A. P. deP. Pona, *Dos Primieros Trabalhos dos Portugueses no Monomotapa* (Lisbon, 1892); H. A. Junod, *Life of a South African Tribe,* 2:280–82.

19. The military function of the nineteenth-century orchestras is clear

even today from the nature of the costumes that the dancers wear, which include shields and spears, and in their often aggressive posturings. For photographs of the dances, see H. Tracey, *African Dances of the Witwatersrand Gold Mines* (Johannesburg, 1952), 124–40. See also H. P. Junod, "The Mbila or Native Piano of the Tshopi Tribe," *Bantu Studies* 3, no. 3 (1929): 283; B. Marques, *Musica Negra: Estudos de Folclore Tonga* (Lisbon, 1943), 11–93 passim; Tracey, *Chopi Musicians*, 85–90, 146.

20. Richards to Bebout, 21 May 1885, ABC 15.4, vol. 12, ABMP; H. P. Junod, "Some Notes on Tshopi Origins"; Correira de Matos, "Origens do povo Chope."

21. A. Cabral, *Raças, Usos, e Costumes dos Indigenas do Districto de Inhambane* (Lourenço Marques, 1910), 28–36; Pélissier, *Naissance du Mozambique*, 2:558.

22. G. Schnapper, *La Politique et le Commerce Français dans le Golfe de Guinée de 1838 à 1871* (Paris, 1961), 190–91.

23. Report of the Governor-General of Mozambique, 29 November 1875, pasta 29, Arquivo Historico Ultramarino, Lisbon; G. A. Pery, *Geographia e Estatistica de Portugal e Colonias* (Lisbon, 1875), 371–72.

24. Caldas Xavier, "O Inharrime e as Guerras Zavallas," 484–87; Pélissier, *Naissance du Mozambique*, 2:558–61.

25. Richards to Bebout, 21 May 1885, ABC 15.4, vol. 12, and Ousley to Smith, 7 March 1890 and 29 July 1890, ABC 15.4, vol. 20, ABMP; D. da Cruz, *Em terras da Gaza* (Porto, 1910), 49; Pélissier, *Naissance du Mozambique*, 2:567–69, 571–78.

26. Harries, "Slavery, Social Incorporation, and Surplus Extraction," 321; Cabral, *Racas, Usos, e Costumes*, 33–35. For an interpretation that sees Chopi resistance to the Gaza as wrongheaded and reactionary, see W. Rodney, "The Year 1895 in Southern Mozambique: African Resistance to the Imposition of European Colonial Rule," *Journal of the Historical Society of Nigeria* 5, no. 4 (1971): 525–27, 534–35.

27. The conquests of southern Mozambique are well analyzed in Pélissier, *Naissance du Mozambique*, 2:589–624.

28. The five paragraphs that follow are based on Cabral, *Racas, Usos, e Costumes*, 111–15. All translations from the Portuguese are by the authors.

29. Ibid., 111.

30. Ibid., 114–15.

31. Ibid. *Mother* would be better understood as "sweetheart" or "girl-friend."

32. Ibid.

33. A similar incident is related in Report by Evelyn F. Clarke, 6 September 1905, ABC 15.6.3, ABMP.

34. Ousley to Smith, 5 February 1892, ABC 15.4, vol. 20, ABMP; W. Churchill, *Report for the Year 1891 on the Trade of the Consular District of Mozambique*, Consular Series no. 995, C.6550 (London, 1892), 7; Gregory

R. Pirio, "Commerce, Industry, and Empire: The Making of Modern Colonialism in Angola and Mozambique. 1890–1914," Ph.D. diss., University of California, Los Angeles, 1982, 82.

35. T. de Almeida Garrett, *Um Governo em Africa: Inhambane, 1905–1906* (Lisbon, 1907), 79–92.

36. *Pautas das Alfandegas da Provincia de Moçambique: Comprehendendo as de Lourenço Marques e Cabo Delgado: Approvados por Decreto de 29 de Dezembro de 1892* (Lisbon, 1893), 4.

37. J. F. Munro, *Africa and the International Economy, 1800–1960* (London, 1976), 71; A. Enes, *Moçambique*, 3d ed. (1893; rpt., Lisbon, 1946), 88.

38. Harries, "Slavery, Social Incorporation, and Surplus Extraction," 321. H. H. Johnston, *Report for the Year 1889 on the Trade of Mozambique and District* (Consular Series no. 742, C.5895 [London, 1890], 8), reports large numbers of migrants recruited in Inhambane for military work in Tanganyika and for the sugar plantations of Réunion.

39. A. Cardoso, *Relatório do Governador do Districto de Inhambane, 1907–1909* (Lourenço Marques, 1909), 73–75.

40. The various negotiations between the Portuguese and representatives of South African mining interests are outlined in S. Katzenellenbogen, *South Africa and Southern Mozambique: Labour, Railways, and Trade in the Making of a Relationship* (Manchester, 1982), 36–78 passim.

41. For a discussion of the creation of the Witwatersrand Native Labour Association, see A. H. Jeeves, *Migrant Labour in South Africa's Mining Economy: The Struggle for the Gold Mines' Labour Supply, 1890–1920* (Kingston and Montreal, 1985).

42. A. Cardoso, *Relatório do Governador do Districto de Inhambane, 1906–1907* (Lourenço Marques, 1907), 46. For reports of South African-inspired forced-labor recruitment in Inhambane, see enclosures in Selborne to Elgin, 16 July 1906, FO 367/19, Public Record Office, London.

43. De Almeida Garrett, *Um Governo em Africa*, 107–12. See C. A. dos Santos, *Relatório do Governador do Distrito de Inhambane nãos annos 1931, 1932, 1933, e 1934* (Lisbon, 1937), and A. de Figueiredo Gomes e Sousa, "Recolonização do Distrito de Inhambane," *Boletim da Sociedade de Estudos da Colonia de Mocambique* 5, no. 31 (1936): 171–87, for laments during the 1930s about Inhambane's long-continuing economic depression.

44. Because of the great rinderpest epizootic of the mid-1890s that destroyed the large cattle herds of southern Mozambique, the payment of lobola, which had earlier been made by the transfer of cattle, came by the first decade of the twentieth century to be paid in cash. De Almeida Garrett, *Um Governo em Africa*, 150; Cardoso, *Relatório do Governador . . . , 1907–1909*, 14.

45. J. M. da Silva Cunha, *O Trabalho Indígena: Estudo de Direito Colonial*, 2d ed. (Lisbon, 1955), 147–48.

46. Jeanne M. Penvenne in "A History of African Labor in Lourenço Marques, Mozambique, 1877 to 1950" (Ph.D. diss., Boston University, 1982,

161–67) points out that other Chopi men escaped *shibalo* by traveling to Lourenço Marques and accepting sanitation jobs there that others would not take.

47. Cardoso, *Relatório do Governador . . . , 1906–1986*, 43.

48. De Matos, "Origens de Povo Chope," 12–13. For a discussion of the reasons for creating a native reserve in the area, see J. R. Pereira Cabral, *Relatório do Governador do Distrito de Inhambane, 1911–1912* (Lourenço Marques, 1912).

49. E. g., Cardoso, *Relatório do Governador . . . , 1906–1907*, 43ff. J. R. Pereira Cabral, *Relatório do Governador do Distrito de Inhambane, 1910–1911* (Lourenço Marques, 1912), 62–67; Correira Henriques, *Relatório do Governador . . . , 1913–1915*; and E. d'Almeida Saldanha, *Desnacionalização de Moçambique* (Lourenço Marques, 1911) and *João Belo e o Sul do Save* (Lisbon, 1928), among many others.

50. J. Botelho de Carvalho Araujo, *Relatório do Governador do Distrito de Inhambane, 1917* (Coimbra, 1920), 129.

51. Katzenellenbogen, *South Africa and Southern Mozambique*, 101–19.

52. David J. Webster, "Kinship and Cooperation: Aganation, Alternative Structures, and the Individual in Chopi Society," Ph.D. diss., Rhodes University, Grahamstown, South Africa, 1975, chap. 3; and Jeanne Penvenne to authors, 26 December 1981. Also see da Cruz, *Em Terras da Gaza*, 154–74, 225–73; E. H. Haviland, *Under the Southern Cross: or, A Woman's Life Work for Africa* (Cincinnati, 1928), 306–12; Earthy, *Valenge Women*, 20–60; and Charles E. Fuller, "An Ethno-Study of Continuity and Change in Gwambe Culture," Ph.D. diss., Northwestern University 1955, 150–51, 180.

53. See L. Vail, ed., *The Creation of Tribalism in Southern Africa* (London and Berkeley, 1988).

54. Earthy, *Valenge Women*, 172–73.

55. For a useful assessment of the second printing of Tracey's book, see D. J. Webster's review in *African Affairs* 32, no. 1 (1973): 53–54.

56. H. Tracey, *Chopi Musicians: Their Music, Poetry, and Instruments* (London, 1948), 28. All English translations quoted here of Chopi songs discussed in Tracey's book are by Hugh Tracey.

57. A. H. Wilensky, *Portuguese Overseas Legislation for Africa* (Braga, 1968).

58. See Earthy, *Valenge Women*, 11.

59. Webster, "Kinship and Cooperation," 16.

60. Tracey, *Chopi Musicians*, 43, 48, 68.

61. For songs that imitate Katini's *ngodo* of 1940, see, for example, Tracey, *Chopi Musicians*, 68, 75.

62. Ibid., 53. The exact flavor of songs such as this one, as recorded by Tracey, must be considered problematic, for it seems Tracey bowdlerized the songs he presented in his published work, removing obscenities. In this song, for example, Tracey translated the words "*Ngongo wako!*" as "You bitch!" although they literally mean "Your cunt!"

63. Tracey, *Chopi Musicians*, 46. The black cloth refers to mourning garments.

64. Ibid., 10. While this sequence is typical, other movements—such as the *mchuyo*, the *msumeto*, and the *kutokoza*—may occur.

65. Ibid., 35.

66. Ibid., 32, 58.

67. Ibid., 4–7.

68. Ibid., 10, 14.

69. Ibid., 15.

70. Ibid., 16.

71. Ibid., 20.

72. Ibid., 21.

73. Webster, "Kinship and Cooperation," 14.

74. Tracey, *Chopi Musicians*, 23. The remark of Malanje, a Sotho-speaking "boss boy" on the mines, would be better translated "Oh, whenever you speak Chopi you are really cursing me!"

75. The proliferation of clandestine schools after 1939 to teach people arithmetic and, among other subjects, Portuguese also attests to the Chopi's sense of realism. See Fuller, "An Ethno-Study of Continuity and Change in Gwambe Culture," 242.

76. Tracey, *Chopi Musicians*, 25.

77. Interwoven with the theme of cultural victory is a second theme, the death of Katini's close friend and associate Majengwe, who was also a claimant to the chieftainship of Wani Zavala. He died in Lisbon, and his death in a foreign land at the moment of triumph, coupled with Katini's suspicions that his death was not wholly unwelcome at court, brings human folly and weakness back to the center of the argument and turns the *mzeno* into a haunting dirge.

78. Tracey, *Chopi Musicians*, 28–29.

79. Ibid., 73, 80, 68.

80. Ibid., 30.

81. Ibid., 41, 43.

82. T. de Bettencourt, *Relatório do Governador-Geral de Moçambique, 1940–42*, 2 vols. (Lisbon, 1945), 1:45–47.

83. Tracey, *Chopi Musicians*, 48.

84. Ibid., 47.

85. For a discussion of the long-range effects of prolonged labor migrancy from Chopi country, see Fuller, "Continuity and Change in Gwambe Culture," and D. J. Webster, "Migrant Labour, Social Formations, and the Proletarianization of the Chopi of Southern Mozambique," *African Perspectives* 1 (1978): 154–74.

86. Tracey, *Chopi Musicians*, 41, 59, 55.

87. Ibid., 74.

88. A. Rita-Ferreira, " 'Timbilas' e 'Jazz' entre os Indigenas de Homoine

(Mozambique)," *Boletim Investigação Cientifica, Mozambique* 1, no. 1 (1960): 69.

89. Ibid., 78.

90. de Bettencourt, *Relatório do Governador-Geral de Moçambique, 1940–42,* 1:45–47.

91. Report for the Council of Quelimane, 1948, maço 31, Arquivo do Governador de Quelimane, (Mozambique).

92. *Noticias* (Lourenço Marques), 7 February 1945.

93. Report for Ile, 1951, maço 99, Arquivo do Governador de Quelimane, (Mozambique).

94. *Diário do Góvernor,* 1st ser., 165, 30 July 1926.

95. Ibid., 53, 5 March 1937; C. F. Spence, *Moçambique (East African Province of Portugal)* (Cape Town, 1963), 78.

96. *Boletim Oficial* do Governo de Moçambique—*Suplemento,* no. 24 of 1941; Spence, *Moçambique,* 81.

97. Colonia de Moçambique, *Cultura Industria e Comercio Arroz* (Lourenço Marques, 1941).

98. L. Vail and L. White, *Capitalism and Colonialism in Mozambique: A Study of Quelimane District* (London and Minneapolis, 1980), 307.

99. Interview with Shambini Makasi Chiseka, Witgoud, Transvaal, 8 September 1983; A. Isaacman et al., "Cotton Is the Mother of Poverty: Peasant Resistance to Forced Cotton Production in Mozambique, 1938–1961," *International Journal of African Historical Studies* 13, no. 4 (1980): 590.

100. The two paragraphs that follow are based on R. First, *The Mozambican Miner: A Study in the Export of Labour* (Maputo, 1977), 100–108, 126–28.

101. The complete *ngodo* for 1955 by Gomukomu appears on the *Music of Africa Series* of recordings, number TR5. The transcription and translation from this disk, as well as those for all other songs that follow in this chapter with a Chopi version, are, unless otherwise noted, the responsibility of the authors, who also hold the copyrights for those translations.

102. The explication of this and other of the *migodo* songs was done with the great help of Shambini Makasi Chiseki, Satyayane waBokiso Makamo, and other *timbila* players at Witgoud, Transvaal, South Africa, in August and September 1983. Many of these *timbila* players were at the original performance of Gomukomu's *ngodo* and remembered with amazing precision the allusions in the songs.

103. I. Rocha, *A Arte Maravilhosa do Povo Chope* (Lourenço Marques, 1962), 15, 26.

104. See, for example, *Festival do Povo Chope, Zavala, 6 de Outobro de 1963,* at the time of the visit of Governador-Geral Manuel Maria Saramento Rodrigues.

105. Rita-Ferreira, "'Timbilas' e 'Jazz,'" 74–75.

106. Cf. "Competitive Dances among Portuguese Natives in Mine Com-

pounds," leaflet of WNLA, September 1920, GNLB 125 2201/13, Transvaal Archives, Pretoria. Our thanks to Patrick Harries for this item.

107. D. B. Coplan, *In Township Tonight: South Africa's Black City Music and Theatre* (New York, 1985), 22.

108. GNLB 373, Transvaal Archives, Pretoria. Thanks are due to Professor Dunbar Moodie for making available to us copies of the *Programme* for this event and of official correspondence it generated.

109. *Explanatory Programme of Monster Native Dance at the Wanderers*, song 5 of the second Chopi team.

110. A. Ferrão to General Manager, Chamber of Mines, 23 April 1928.

111. Interview with Venancio Mbande, Witgoud, Transvaal, 29 September 1983.

112. As, for example, in the *migodo* for Mavila of 1963, for Nyakutowo of 1970, and for Mavila of 1970. The *migodo* of *Mavila* is contained in the Music of Africa Series, records TR198 and TR199. The other two *migodo* were recorded by Curt Wittig in 1970 and are available in taped versions in the Archives of the International Library of African Music, Rhodes University, Grahamstown, South Africa.

113. A. Tracey and G. Zantzinger, *A Companion to the Films "Mgodo wa Mabanguzi" and "Mgodo wa Mkandeni"* (n.p. [Roodepoort], 1976), 23.

114. Cf. I. Rocha, "A Morte dos *Ngodo* Chopes—Uma Dramática Forma de Resistência Cultural," in Institute of Anthropology, University of Coimbra, *Moçambique: Aspectos da Cultura Material* (Coimbra, 1986), 37.

5

Swazi
Royal Praises
The Invention
of Tradition

In what she terms "an essential introduction" to her officially authorized biography of *Sobhuza II, Ngwenyama and King of Swaziland,* Hilda Kuper prints the English text of a "traditional song," or
tibongo, in praise of the king. The poem was recorded in 1967 on the
eve of Swaziland's independence, and it summarizes key events in
Sobhuza's long reign since his accession in 1921—his voyage to England when he conquered the oceans, his challenge to King George
when "Twice the heavens flashed / Within the palace of the English,"
and his rise to preeminence within Swaziland, "devouring herds of
men" from his administrative capital at Lozithehlezi on "the ridge
of Lancabane." Above all, he is presented as a warrior king:

> They are calling you, they are giving you a message.
> King of the inner circle!
> They are not calling you for nothing,
> They are calling you to a war of nations, stabbing and killing.

The reference is to the king's dispatch of the 1991 Company, made
up of the Emasotja and Sikhonyane regiments, to join the British
Eighth Army in North Africa and Italy during World War II. Metaphors for the king are "claw of the lion," "strength of the leopard,"
"bushy tail of the bull," and "male elephant of the Swazi /Old one
whom age does not diminish."[1]

No Swazi-language text of this *tibongo* is provided by Kuper, but
the English text is by Thokozile Ginindza, former curator of the National Museum of Swaziland. Dr. Ginindza recorded the praise poem
as one of a collection of some thirty-five such praises of the Swazi
royal house. These begin with the *tibongo* of the mythical Landzandzalukane (Sidvwabasilutfuli) and continue with the praises of
Ndvungunye (1770–1815), Sobhuza I (1815–36), Mswati (1840–68),

Ludvonga (1872), Mbandzeni (1875–89), and Bhunu (1890–99). The collection also includes the *tibongo* of the Queen Mothers, or *ti-Ndlovukazi*, of whom the most famous is Labotsibeni, the *Ndlovu-kazi* during the minority of Sobhuza II. A selection of these praises were afterwards published by Dr. Ginindza under the title *Tibongo teMakhosi netetiNdlovukazi* (Praises of the chiefs and Queen Mothers).[2] This volume contains the Swati version of the praise poem printed by Hilda Kuper. The *imbongi* is Mabuntane Mdluli. These praises, as well as others, are also discussed in Ginindza's doctoral dissertation, "SiSwati Oral Poetry."[3]

As we shall see, most of the oral poets from whom these thirty-five *tibongo* were recorded belonged to the king's own generation and most of them, too, were members of the royal house. It is not going too far to say that they represent an official history of the kingdom of Swaziland's ruling house during the mid-1960s. Two features of these poems have suggested the argument of this chapter. The first is the extremely neotraditional character of the content and the language. To take illustrations from the *tibongo* already quoted, Sub-huza II is described as "devouring herds of men" from his adminis-trative capital at Lozithehleni as though ruling the Swazi of 1967 was no different from ruling them in the days of Mswati, in the mid-nineteenth century, when warfare and cattle raiding were indistin-guishable. Similarly, World War II is called a war of "stabbing and killing," as if weaponry had not changed since the 1820s, when Zwide and Dingane were the enemies. Linked with this is the odd contrast between the military history invoked for Swaziland by these *tibongo* and the actual facts of Swaziland's byzantine dealings with Afrikaners and British and, more recently, with the Republic of South Africa, in which any Swazi victories have been gained only by stealth and compromise. In contrast with chiefly praise poems from Lesotho, Botswana, or contemporary South Africa, some of these modern *tibongo* seem only distantly in touch with reality.

The second point of interest is that although these *tibongo* are de-scribed as having been handed down with little change over the gen-erations,[4] they have in fact little in common with the earliest collec-tion of Swazi praise poems. In 1929, P. A. W. Cook, of the University of Cape Town, took down by dictation the *tibongo* of Ndvungunye, Sobhuza I, Mswati, Ludvongo, Mbandzeni, and Bhunu. Contrasting Cook's English translations with the later collection (allowing for conscious transmutations of metaphor within the line) shows only 6 percent of praises in common between his *tibongo* and their equivalents in Ginindza's collection.[5] The praising of Swazi kings has changed significantly since 1929, and Swazi oral poets appear no longer to be drawing on traditions of inherited metaphor despite their archaic language.

Nkhotfotjeni, the infant son was to become King Sobhuza II, was chosen as King Bhunu's successor in 1899. The monarchy he inherited was in a desperately precarious position, for it had lost much of the authority built up so painstakingly in the middle of the century by Mswati, the Swazi state's eponym. It was also unpopular, having over the three decades since Mswati's death forfeited much of its credibility with the Swazi people.

The most serious reverses occurred during the reign of King Mbandzeni (1875–89), whose failures were far-reaching. In the realm of foreign affairs, he proved unable to deal effectively with the designs on his state's territory crafted by his Zulu, Sotho, British, and, especially, Afrikaner neighbors.[6] Thus he had to endure the ignominy of accepting border demarcations imposed jointly by the British and Afrikaners, first in 1881 and again in 1884. These drastically reduced the size of Mswati's kingdom and left many thousands of Swazi stranded under white rule in the eastern Transvaal.

It was in the area of domestic affairs, however, that Mbandzeni was seen as especially weak, for he was held to be largely responsible for selling off what remained of his country to a host of white concession hunters during the 1880s. According to Hilda Kuper, Mbandzeni was a good and generous king who was duped by unscrupulous adventurers. According to Philip Bonner, he was a weak, vain man who, while being subjected to relentless pressures from beyond Swaziland's borders, enjoyed the illusion of power within Swaziland as he conferred gifts on the white men crowding his residence.[7] In any case, between 1876, when he granted his first concession of grazing rights over 36,000 acres in southern Swaziland, to his death in 1889, Mbandzeni succeeded in signing away his entire kingdom.

The story of the Swazi concessions has been told many times, but no one has surpassed the sarcastic eloquence of the first, and as yet unpublished, account by the British resident commissioner in Swaziland, de Symons G. M. Honey.[8] In addition to awarding numerous grazing and mineral rights, often for the same patch of land, Mbandzeni also sold the rights to collect taxes and customs duties; to build railways and bridges; to maintain monopolies for importing such items as tobacco, wines and spirits, medicines and machinery;

to manufacture cement, gunpowder, dynamite, and cotton; to sell
licenses and insurance; to run banks, lotteries, and auctions; and to
establish mints. Finally, in Honey's words, there was a concession
"in consideration of a payment of £100 per annum that the independence of the country would not be given up to any foreign power to
which two gentlemen named Julius Porges and Hermann Eckstein
might object." [9] How far Mbandzeni profited from these deals is de-
batable. Honey estimated his annual income at £20,000, but Bonner
stresses the ambiguous role of Theophilus (Offy) Shepstone, Jr., the
king's shady resident advisor, demonstrating that much of the
money found its way to Shepstone's wife in Natal. [10]

The injuries to the Swazi monarchy that occurred under Mbandzeni were compounded during the reign of Bhunu, his young and
inexperienced son (1890–99). A protocol to the Anglo-Afrikaner
Convention of 1894, under the terms of which Swaziland had finally
lost its independence, downgraded the king's title to "Paramount
Chief." Subsequently Bhunu tried to rebuild the monarchy's power
over dissident local chiefs within Swaziland by asserting earlier royal
prerogatives, but, in so doing, he often acted both arbitrarily and
with great cruelty, alienating many. [11] In 1898, he was charged with
murdering one of his senior indunas and released with a fine of £500
only because the court was unable to establish its legal jurisdiction
over him. [12] This incident led to an additional protocol's being added
to the 1894 Convention, which made the Swazi king himself subject
to the colonial courts. When Bhunu died suddenly during the
Ncwala, or firstfruits, ceremony of 1899, there were widespread rumors that he had actually been poisoned by his mother, Labotsibeni,
the Queen Mother.

Later, in June 1903, when a British order-in-council placed the
kingdom temporarily under the government of the Transvaal, the
paramount chief's residual powers to judge criminal cases were an-
nulled and the very survival of the monarchy seemed doubtful. The
combination, however, of the existence of British guarantees of
Swazi independence made in 1881 and 1884 as part of their strategy
to deny the Afrikaners of the Transvaal access to the sea, official sen-
sitivity to British philanthropic concern with the fate of Swaziland,
and fears about the possible breakdown of public order that were
prompted by the Bambatha Rising of 1906 in neighboring Zululand
and by growing Swazi resistance to local taxation, prevented the
monarchy from going the way of its Ndebele and Gaza counter-
parts. [13] Thus, in December 1906, when Swaziland became a high

commission territory, the British preserved both the role of the aristocracy and the title of paramount chief. It was nonetheless a hollow title, and there seemed to be little of substance to which the boy Sobhuza might succeed.

The decline of the monarch's popularity was, moreover, accelerated by the sharp decline in the living standards of ordinary Swazi people as a consequence of a series of ecological disasters that struck the country between 1894 and 1904.[14] In both the 1894–95 and 1895–96 growing seasons, drought and locusts struck, and many Swazi starved. Crops again failed in 1896–97, and locusts and poor crops contributed to the outbreak of epidemics of malaria and smallpox and to still more starvation in the first years of the twentieth century. Perhaps most devastating of all, because the Swazi regarded cattle as their wealth, was the decimation of Swazi cattle by rinderpest in the late 1890s and the ravaging of the remaining herds by an outbreak of East Coast fever in 1902. As a consequence, in the decade between 1894 and 1904, the number of Swazi cattle declined by an estimated 90 percent.[15] This catastrophe not only impoverished the Swazi people but also led to the erosion of Swazi agriculture and to the start of large-scale labor migrancy to work in areas outside Swaziland. The extravagant claims of monarchical grandness in the *tibongo* of the 1960s by oral poets of the king's own generation, then, must be measured against the inauspicious political and economic realities at the beginning of Sobhuza's reign.

With such dramatic economic problems affecting Swaziland at the turn of the century, the new British colonial authorities addressed the question of the actual ownership of the land that arose out of Mbandzeni's precolonial concession giving as a matter of some urgency. In 1905, Lord Milner, the governor of the Transvaal, appointed a commission that was charged with settling the land question. When the commission reported in 1907, it recognized the legality of all but a fraction of Mbandzeni's concessions and concluded that the whole of Swaziland had been signed away in perpetuity. But the commissioners also accepted that the Swazi people had to live *somewhere*. Their solution to the problem proved of immense importance to the later development of the monarchy. They decided that one-third of each concession should be turned over to the trust of the king, areas that became known as the "Swazi Nation," and that the remainder would remain private or Crown land. In drawing the boundaries of the Swazi reserves in 1909, the surveyors were mindful of the monarchy's sensibilities, carefully including all royal villages, royal graves, royal cattle kraals, and chiefs' homesteads within the reserves of the new "Swazi Nation." The "Nation" came to consist of some 687,635 hectares scattered across 1,750,000 hectares of the country in a patchwork arrangement resembling a contemporary Bantustan. Those Swazi who found themselves resident on the private estates had five years in which to make a deal with their landlords or face eviction.

It fell to Labotsibeni, Queen Regent after Bhunu's death, to formulate a response to the British acceptance of the binding legality of Mbandzeni's concessions. A deputation was sent to London to argue the Swazi case with the colonial secretary, Lord Elgin, who appeared sympathetic to their appeals. When Lord Selborne, who had succeeded Milner as British representative in South Africa, decided to sell Crown land to finance the costs of local administration and to attract white settlers to the country, thereby reneging on Lord Elgin's promise that Crown land would soon be added to Swazi Nation land, it provoked further Swazi anger and frustration. The council discussed armed resistance, and for a time Labotsibeni considered trying to bypass the eight-year-old Sobhuza and have her own adult son, Malunge, proclaimed king.

Ultimately, Labotsibeni decided to pursue several interrelated policies calculated to strengthen the monarchy. The first was to pin her hopes on Sobhuza as future king, sending him for primary and secondary education at Lovedale, the region's preeminent school for Africans, something she had earlier refused to accept for Malunge. This decision not only ensured that Sobhuza would receive a Western-style education but also that the Swazi monarchy's links with the educated "progressive" black political leadership of the Union of South Africa would be strengthened and that wide publicity and support for the Swazi position on the land issue would be gained.[17]

Second, in 1911, she set up a "National Fund" under her own control to buy back alienated land. As an essential part of this strategy she sought to control the flow of migrant laborers from Swaziland by linking migrancy to the old Swazi regimental system and providing labor to selected white labor recruiters. As early as 1903 she had established relations with the Witwatersrand Native Labour Association, and from 1914 onward, she was able to extort up to a quarter of Swazi migrants' earnings on the Witwatersrand for her National Fund.[18]

Labotsibeni's third strategy was less consciously formalized as she set about to create a mystique for the weakened Swazi royal house on the model of the British monarchy. The Queen Regent had little more than symbolism to play with, but she did so with consummate skill. In 1914, when the resident commissioner, de Symons Honey, was compiling a history of Swaziland "from native sources," he was persuaded that the Swazi royal family extended back no fewer than twenty-two generations, to Umatalatala in 1550, who was succeeded by Mswati I in 1565. The Swazi nation had not been created with the flight of Sobhuza I from Dingiswayo in the early nineteenth century, and the House of Dlamini had actually ruled longer than the House of Hanover![19]

In many ways British officials proved easier to persuade than ordinary Swazi people themselves, for they were caught between the financial demands of the British, Labotsibeni, and the Swazi aristocracy on the one hand and the dismal realities of migrant labor and declining agricultural productivity on the other. In 1921, when Sobhuza was proclaimed king, Labotsibeni made a speech to the nation that a police spy translated as follows:

> She stood up and said to Sobhuza come and stand in front of me. Less noise and listen you Swazis. Here is your king. . . . You must not misbehave yourselves because of the Whites and despise him, thinking the authorities will interfere. He is also under whites—he shall also do likewise. . . .
> Look here you Swazis—you cowards—you have a very bad way of doing things. Whenever you fight with sticks you deliberately use a spear as well and you don't obey or respect those put in authority over you.[20]

Altogether different in content and tone were the imperial accents of Labotsibeni's letter, in Josiah Vilakati's translation, to the Resident Commissioner:

> This is the day I have always longed for. It has now come at last like a dream which has come true. King Mbandzeni died in October 1889 (32 years ago). As from that day my life has been burdened by an awful responsibility and anxiety. It has been a life full of the deepest emotions that a woman has ever had.
> . . . Bhunu died after only a very short life, leaving me with the responsibility of bringing up his infant son and heir. I rejoice that I now present him to Your Honour in your capacity as the head of the Adminis-

4. Swazi Queen Regent Labotsibeni, the canny strategist of the Swazi monarchy's revival, circa 1919 (from Owen O'Neil's *Adventures in Swaziland* [London, 1921]). (Courtesy of Jonathan Crush.)

tration of Swaziland. . . . I have brought him up as a Swazi prince ought
to be brought up. His spirit is in entire accord with the traditions and
feelings and aspirations of his countrymen. . . .
In conclusion, I desire to introduce to your Highness, in your capacity
as head of the Swaziland administration, this my grandson, Sobhuza II
and Paramount Chief of Swaziland and King of the Swazi nation. . . .
The Administration will henceforth address all its communications
direct to him. Sobhuza II gets his name, title and position by right of
inheritance from his ancient house and kings who have ruled over the
Swazi nation from time immemorial.[21]

Significantly, Labotsibeni insisted on the twin titles Paramount
Chief of Swaziland (the country as a whole) and King of the Swazi
Nation (the 687,635 hectares not in the hands of concessionaires).

Most of Sobhuza's earliest attempts to fulfill the role created for
him by Labotsibeni were deeply frustrating. He and his councillors
decided to approach the British directly on the land issue. A deputation to Cape Town to meet with the new High Commissioner,
Prince Arthur of Connaught, was followed by another to London in
1922, when Sobhuza had his encounter with George V. On both visits legal arguments were presented about the Order-in-Council of
1903, but both initiatives ran up against British obduracy. In January
1924, Sobhuza decided to pursue the matter through the courts. The
king and his advisors carefully chose their test case: the Unallotted
Lands Concession, granted by Mbandzeni in 1889 to John Thorburn
and Frank Watkins. The concession was to last for fifty years and
included a clause protecting the rights of those Swazi resident on the
land. Mbandzeni's secretary and adviser at the time was Allister M.
Miller, who later married Thorburn's daughter and became manager
of the Thorburn-Watkins farm. Following the concession commission's report of 1907, the land in question became Crown land, but a
portion of it was granted freehold to Miller as a farm. In 1922, Miller
began evicting Swazi residents from his land.

Sobhuza II vs. *A. M. Miller and the Swaziland Corporation, Ltd.*
ended with an appeal to the privy council and a ruling in 1926 that
the Order-in-Council of 1903 was an act of state that could not be
questioned in a court of law. The British government was ruled to be
beyond the court's jurisdiction. Swazi outrage at this blatant injustice was coupled with a feeling of helplessness, and Sobhuza lost further ground with his subjects when the costs of his travels and legal
action had to be met with another special levy on the people.[22] When
he built his new residence and administrative center following La-

botsibeni's death in 1925, he gave it the name Lozithehlezi, "sitting surrounded by enemies."[23]

The kingship itself, as Labotsibeni had begun to elaborate it, seemed his one remaining weapon, and there were comic maneuvers during the visits of Prince Arthur of Connaught and the Prince of Wales in 1922 and 1925, respectively, with the Swazi regiments refusing to give the royal salute, *Bayethe!* unless Sobhuza himself was present. But symbolism based on the traditions of the past seemed a rapidly declining asset. Labor migrancy was fast changing Swazi rural society. There were growing divisions between educated and uneducated and between Christians and non-Christians, while chiefs in outlying areas were resisting control from the center.[24] And ordinary Swazi remained unhappy with the constant demands of the aristocracy for more and more taxes. It was not surprising then, that attendance at the *Ncwala* ceremonies, revived in 1921 after a hiatus of over two decades, was meager during the 1920s.[25]

When P. A. W. Cook recorded his praise poems in 1929, it was also not surprising that he found no one familiar with the genealogy worked out "from native sources" by Honey in 1914 and that no one had heard of Umatalatala. As for the poems themselves, these were "fast disappearing, and if it is a matter of extreme difficulty to find men who know them, it is even more difficult to find men who can interpret the highly-particularized allusions with which the *izibongo* [*tibongo*] abound."[26]

The provenance of the *tibongo* recorded by Cook is not entirely clear. Only six texts are provided (the *tibongo* of Ndvungunye, Sobhuza I, Mswati, Ludvonga, Mbandzeni, and Bhunu), and the praise poets are not identified. Even so, Cook had difficulty in collecting his material and not merely because "these *izibongo* are fast disappearing." Working without a recording machine, he took down the praise poems by dictation. But, as he explained: "The praises were not recited in an ordinary voice, but were called out at the top of the voice in as rapid a manner as possible. Indeed so rapidly are these *izibongo* called out that, from habit, those who know them are unable to say them slowly, and to write them down entails countless repetitions." He concludes by thanking his assistant, David Dlamini, "who knows what a trying task it was to keep our *imbongi* from lapsing into slumber after starting off like a fire-engine several times."[27]

Plainly, it would be dangerous to put too much trust in Cook's work, and there were complaints afterwards from the resident commissioner's office about the quality of his transcriptions.[28] Nevertheless, Cook's texts are all we possess from any period of Swazi praise poetry earlier than World War II, and his comments are inadvertently suggestive. He describes the forms of these praise poems as "permanent."[29] The task of his informants was not to perform them but simply to recite them from memory. Some years ago Jeff Opland made a sharp distinction between praise poets capable of extemporizing inspired performances of their *tibongo* and people who had merely memorized other poets' praises.[30]. Swazi informants make the point in slightly different terms by distinguishing between poets who know both the *tibongo* and the history and others who merely recite the praise poems without understanding them. Cook, it will be recalled, had trouble getting his informants to explain the "highly particularised allusions."[31]

Fortunately, this argument may also be turned to advantage. The "memorisers" may not rank high with literary critics, but they do offer material to the historian. If the *tibongo* recorded by Cook in 1929 were not inspired performances, this is because they represented something older—the ghosts of earlier performances alive now only in memory. Some support for this suggestion lies in the length of Cook's *tibongo*. In their book *Lithoko: Sotho Praise Poems*, Damane and Sanders argue that praise poems may be dated by their length, the shortest being oldest, oral transmission constituting an archive of diminishing efficiency.[32] In fact, this is not normally true. It does not apply, for example, to Ginindza's collection of *tibongo*. It may have some relevance, however, in cultures experiencing great changes and where traditions of praising are in decline. The longest of Cook's *tibongo* (sixty-seven lines in the English translation) is Bhunu's, the second longest (fifty-six lines) Mbandzeni's, and so on backwards through the whole sequence to Ndvungunye's (six lines), and then silence. There is some justification, therefore, in treating Cook's small collection as representative of older traditions of praising. Certainly, it predates the revival of the monarchy under Sobhuza II, and it does not engage any of the themes thrown up by that particular campaign.

One further hypothesis should be clarified. As was noted earlier, there is very little continuity of metaphor between Cook's and Ginindza's collections, the proportion of lines in common or of deliberate adaptations being only some 6 percent. The most recent praises, in other words, are substantially new praises containing only a trace of older content. As we demonstrated in chapter two, with Zulu *izibongo*, and to a lesser extent with Sotho *lithoko* (praises), it is possible to trace the development of particular praises through different periods from the 1840s onwards, showing how metaphors familiar to both poet and audience are progressively modified as the past is reinterpreted within the framework of common tradition. In the absence of similar evidence for the Swazi *tibongo*, our suggestion is that a similar tradition may well have remained in some people's minds up until the time of Cook's recordings, and that the break has occurred since, the newest *tibongo* representing for the most part a fresh beginning related to the revival of the monarchy under Sobhuza II.

The point cannot be proven, but our reasoning for suggesting it is not simply the analogy with neighboring traditions of praising. Six percent is a small degree of continuity, but is is not entirely insignificant, and at that level the same processes of adaptation and reinterpretation are taking place in the recent Swazi *tibongo* that are represented in fuller terms elsewhere. To take two examples, Mbandzeni is criticized in Ginindza's collection with the comment:

> You abandoned the oxen
> And bought doves.[33]

The praise has been modified from Mbandzeni's 1929 *tibongo:* "He gave up cattle and paid for regiments of young men."[34] Similarly, the opening lines of the attack on Bhunu as recorded by Ginindza,

Ngwane waDlamini	Ngwane, son of Dlamini
Owadla galu	Who ate the meatless foreleg
Bathi udl 'umlenze.	Was blamed for eating the fleshy thigh.
Ngwane odl 'ezinye	Ngwane who ate others
Wadla ezinye.	And ate others.[35]

deliberately reverse the opening of Bhunu's *tibongo* in Cook's collection, which reads:

> What wrong does Ngwane do?
> They slay cattle and give to each other.
> Where can I find an ox that is big as Ngwane?[36]

As this comparison suggests, the most interesting contrast between the *tibongo* of 1929 and those of the 1960s and 1970s lies in their differing view of Swaziland's history. The contrast is not an absolute one. Praise poetry by its very nature regards history as divided into reigns, each dominated by a single personality, and the room for maneuver within such a view is circumscribed. Nevertheless, there are two differences of emphasis between the two sequences of praises, which are interesting both in themselves and in their implications for the writing of Swazi history.

In Cook's sequence there is no sharp distinction between the characters of individual kings. The kings are not "characters," and there is little sense of history having changed from one reign to another. Each king is described in turn as having been a good fighter and cattle raider, and as having offered the nation protection and guaranteed its survival. In addition, the *tibongo* elaborate the metaphors suggested by specific but essentially anecdotal incidents during each king's reign. But the record is a chronicle rather than that of the teleological process of nation-building chartered, as we shall see, in Ginindza's collection. The kings do not differ much from each other, and where differences do occur, they are regarded as departures from a norm and deserving of comment in those terms. Only in the case of Mswati and Mbandzeni are there any surprises. Mswati is remembered as a warrior king, but the tone is one, not of excited admiration, but of faint surprise that he should have found it necessary to behave as he did:

> News of war eats the child still in the womb,
> If a person can walk he should have run away. . . .
>
> Our chief who can stab,
> I never saw a man who could stab like him,
> He stabs with an assegai until he tires.[37]

Mbandzeni is abnormal for the opposite reason that his weakness left the nation without protection. But even Mbandzeni is praised for the most part, and in the 1929 version there is little of the later blistering sarcasms we shall soon be considering. The other kings from Ndvungunye to Bhunu are described as having done what is required of kings.

The second point following from this is that the standards of judgment implicit in the Cook collection have less to do with the military virtues and political power than with the king's mythic and ritual importance as one dealing with issues of ecological well-being through the *Ncwala* ceremony:

We were hoping, chief, it being easy to hope,
They say a chief is born like the old kafir corn
They are hungry in the kraals and they want a chief to be born
The news of him is sweet to the people.[38]

There is no need to take the metaphor "they are hungry" literally to understand the force of the connection. *Corn* and *hungry* are not words that occur in the sequence of *tibongo* recorded by Thoko Ginindza. The older *tibongo* of the days before widespread labor migrancy describe a Swaziland of rivers, watering holes, and green pastures, in sharp contrast with the later *tibongo*'s landscape of rocks, fords, caves, forests, and mountains. The kings are fighters, but they are also providers, the guarantors of protection and survival. Even the "fire" of warfare occurs in the context of night followed by dawn and of the dry season followed by rains. Ndvungunye is both a shield and a dish. Sobhuza I is rainmaker, for "the cow with many teats / Gives suck to ten men." Bhunu, in a sharply compressed metaphor, becomes "Shield that has the udder of a cow."[39]

Swaziland is, after all, a country of small farms and cattle pastures supporting a population that lives by migrant labor both within and beyond the national boundaries. By emphasizing the king's ritual importance, these *tibongo* of 1929 point to an alternative—and by now suppressed—Swazi history in which warfare takes a place secondary to the more enduring struggles against drought and disease and in which real problems of land alienation lay not in the threat to the king's prestige but in the threat to the very survival of his subjects.

When Cook collected his texts, Sobhuza's concerns were, however, clearly political, not ecological. He was then involved in a continuation of Labotsibeni's struggle to restore the monarchy's power and authority. Help for the king arose out of some rather unexpected trends that were then taking shape outside the country. The first was an increase of interest in the preservation of so-called traditional culture on the part of Western-educated African intellectuals who were distressed by what they viewed as the rapidly accelerating breakdown of southern African rural societies after World War I. These people increasingly saw the establishment of alliances with "traditional" leaders as one way of both mobilizing popular support against the colonial situation and counteracting the corrosive impact of capitalist "modernization" on local society. This tendency was perhaps best exemplified by the revival of Zulu ethnic pride that was taking place just to the south of Swaziland, a movement briefly discussed in chapter two. It was symbolized there by Dr. John Dube, who, in 1929, despite his having been president of the openly antitribal South African Native National Congress, the founder of the Ohlange Institute (which was modeled on America's Tuskeegee Institute), and the leading spokesman for the mission-educated African elite of Natal, was inviting the Governor-General to unveil a monument at Stanger to commemorate Shaka, "the founder of the Zulu nation and power."[40] Sobhuza, educated at Lovedale and in close touch with South African black intellectuals such as Dube, was himself keen to bring about such a revival of "traditions" within Swaziland and was well aware of the need for an alliance with Western-educated Swazi intellectuals to achieve it.[41]

Whites had played their part in shaping the "revival" of Zulu "tradition," both in official capacities and unofficially, publishing such influential books as A. T. Bryant's *Olden Times in Zululand and Natal*, R. C. A. Samuelson's *Long, Long Ago*, and various volumes of Zulu *izibongo* published in the vernacular by James Stuart.[42] Sobhuza also found his white supporters, both official and unofficial. Official support grew out of the South African state's increasing urgency during the 1920s to strengthen segregation and "separate development" by encouraging the continuation of so-called traditional customs.[43] In Swaziland, such a program was pressed by the Resident Commissioner, T. Ainsworth Dickson, who, after his arrival in 1928, became deeply concerned with the increasing class differentiation taking place in Swazi society. To blunt the impact of proletarianization he tried to strengthen Swazi ties to the land. As part of his program, Dickson sought to bolster the monarchy preparatory to introducing a form of indirect rule, urging Sobhuza and has advisors to produce a constitution of Swaziland according to the customs of earlier times for use in the 1930s. As a partial cultural dimension of this effort, the Swazi National High School was founded in 1931 at Matshapa, thus giving royalists an educational institution that was beyond the control of white missionaries hostile to Swazi customs and values and that was explicitly devoted to the cultivation of the "spirit of Swazi tradition and all that went with it."[44]

Central to the actual formulation of a set of Swazi "traditions" for the use of the royal house in strengthening its legitimacy within Swaziland was the surge of specifically academic interest in Swazi history and customs on the part of white anthropologists, many of

5. Swazi King Sobhuza II, instrument of the revival of the Swazi monarchy, Lozita, July 1931. (Photographed by W. M. Macmillan; copyright Mona Macmillan.)

whom were South African liberals in search of evidence demonstrating that Africans could rule their peoples rationally in accordance with "traditional" pinciples.[45] In 1931, Mrs. Winifred Hoernlé of the University of the Witwatersrand wrote to the Resident Commissioner with a proposal to study the *Ncwala* ceremony. She was, as she explained in a subsequent letter, "convinced that we have in the present performance a fusion of many different cultural strands," and she proposed to investigate sociological factors and the "psychological satisfactions or releases."[46] Mrs. Hoernlé was not quite the first academic to take an interest in Swazi culture. Cook had already collected his *tibongo* and P. A. van der Byl, of the University of Stellenbosch, had collected texts of some of the *Ncwala* songs. But her approach marked the beginning of a long and close involvement between professional anthropologists and the Swazi royal house extending over several decades and culminating in Hilda Kuper's classic studies of Swaziland and her hagiographic authorized biography of Sobhuza II.

As it happened, however, Mrs Hoernlé was unable to travel to Swaziland until 1933, and the 1931 *Ncwala* was instead attended by J. van Warmelo, a government anthropologist who was collecting material for his projected ethnographic survey of South Africa. Van Warmelo almost ruined the prospect of future research by ignoring the king's specific prohibition against taking photographs of the calabash dance.[47] There was a similar near disaster in 1933, when, after Mrs Hoernlé had been given a carefully selected program of events she would be allowed to witness, a journalist wrote a sensationalized account of the *Ncwala* for the Johannesburg *Star* that linked the ceremony with human sacrifice. The article, in fact, has its uses, combining personal observation with unpublished interpretive notes that the journalist had coaxed out of the Resident Commissioner, A. G. Marwick. But the allegations of ritual murder were not forgiven, and the *Star* had to publish a retraction.[48]

King Sobhuza seems to have learned from these episodes the need to exercise personal control over academic research. But he was also aware of the clear advantages to be gained from white academic validation of the Swazi "customs" central to his political program. In 1933, he proposed that the nineteenth-century Swazi regimental military system (*emebutfo*), which had become almost wholly moribund as a consequence of labor migrancy and the weakness of the monarchy, be revivified and made the basis of a new national educational system. Western education, he argued in an eloquent memorandum, "is causing the Swazi scholar to despise Swazi institutions and his indigenous culture" and "releases him from the wholesome restraints which the Swazi indigenous method of education inculcated." The proposal provoked a storm of protest from the Christian missions, but Sobhuza gained the support not only of British officials, including the Resident Commissioner, A. G. Marwick, but of Winifred Hoernlé, who collaborated with another anthropologist, Isaac Schapera, in compiling a long report outlining the advantages of the regimental system, and also of the great Bronislaw Malinowski, who visited Swaziland in 1934 accompanied by the young Hilda Beemer (later Mrs. Kuper).[49] The plan was put into practice at the Swazi National High School, where many who were later to form Swaziland's conservative elite received their education.[50]

Further academic support came in 1935 when P. J. Schoeman published a description of the Swazi rain ceremony. Schoeman's article emphasized especially the role of the *Ndhlovukazi* (Queen Mother) as keeper of the rain medicine and the function of the royal praises in producing rain when chanted at times of drought before the kings' graves. He was able to quote testimony by Mkehleni Mdhlovu, former *imbongi* to King Bhunu, saying of these *tibongo*: "They are lauding them thus so that they (the spirits) will rejoice and get soft, i.e. get in a generous mood, and grant the rain. They (the spirits) in their turn announce the request and offering from son to father right down the generations, till the earliest Swazi king, who is nearest Mkhulumqganti [God], addresses the last mentioned."[51] Schoeman's article was published at a time when Swaziland was experiencing its worst drought in a generation and when the dry earth and dying cattle were being widely attributed to Sobhuza's inability to make rain. His research drew a blistering response from Hilda Beemer, who accused him of describing ceremonies that he had never witnessed and of relying upon the "least reliable class of informants." Her riposte was prefaced by a statement signed by King Sobhuza II corroborating her corrections, and it concluded with Beemer's remarkable insistence that the thirty-six year old Sobhuza was the supreme authority in these matters and that, with the advent of indirect rule, it was the anthropologist's duty to "co-operate with those leaders who are in a position to judge for themselves the value and quality of his work."[52] Beemer had little difficulty in exposing errors of fact and interpretation in Schoeman's essay, and her attack was largely justified. Yet what Schoeman had collected was testimony illustrating the expectations of people outside Sobhuza's royal

circle. His nonofficial view of the role of Swazi kingship bears striking resemblances to the themes and images of the *tibongo* collected
by Cook in 1929.

The dispute was repeated in modified form nine years later, in
1944, when Hilda Kuper published her vivid and seminal account of
the *Ncwala* ceremony. Rejecting interpretations by Cook and Schoeman that had emphasized the place the *Ncwala* ceremony had in the
cycle of agricultural production and the king had as rainmaker, Kuper described the ceremony she had witnessed in 1934, 1935, 1936,
and 1941 as "first and foremost a ceremony which, as the Swazi say,
aims at 'strengthening kingship.' . . . The Ncwala unites the people
under the king and at present there is a fairly general appreciation of
its nationalising value." [53] Kuper was able for the first time to quote
songs sung during the *Ncwala* in which Sobhuza was insulted and
abused:

> Shi shi ishi ishi—you hate him,
> ishi ishi ishi—mother, the enemies are the people.
> ishi ishi ishi—you hate him,
> Mother, the people are wizards.
> Admit the treason of Mabedla
> ishi ishi ishi—you hate him,
> you have wronged,
> ishi ishi—bend great neck,
> those and those they hate him,
> ishi ishi—they hate the king.

And:

> Jiiya hhohho ye ye Nkosi, Alas for your fate
> Jiiya hhohho ye ye Nkosi, They reject thee
> Jiiya hhohho ye ye Nkosi, They hate thee. [54]

Despite her generally strong historical awareness, she made no attempt to relate these songs to the king's circumstances in the early
1930s, a time of ecological disaster for Swaziland and political and
economic weakness for the king. Her account subsequently became
the basis of Max Gluckman's influential *Rituals of Rebellion in
South East Africa*. Gluckman's analysis removed the songs from immediate history and presented them as part of an annually enacted
drama of kingship and a type that only occurred "within an established and unchallenged social order." [55] In her essay of 1944, how-

ever, Kuper did not claim these songs as timeless, noting only of one of them, the *Lihubo* or "national anthem," that it "is said by some to be very old but by others to be fairly recent."[56] Not until her 1978 biography of Sobhuza II does she slip into suggesting that some of the *Ncwala* songs were composed in the nineteenth century by the wife of Sobhuza I.[57] For Kuper, as for Sobhuza, the *Ncwala* was first and foremost a political statement on behalf of the monarchy of "traditional" support.

Meanwhile, as Sobhuza and his supporters tried to legitimate an increase in the authority of the monarchy by the manipulation of such "tradition" and by the compilation of a monarchy-oriented history, his position was bolstered by another unexpected external influence, the effect of World War II on Swaziland. Responding to a request from Britain, Sobhuza dispatched two regiments, the Emasotja, formed in 1929, and the Sikhonyane, formed in 1934, to fight as the 1991 Company. The soldiers were presented with a "national flag" (designed by the wife of the headmaster of the Swazi National High School, which was later to become the flag of independent Swaziland), were treated with traditional war medicines, and attended a ceremony at which they all sang the royal *tibongo*.[58] Sobhuza addressed them in the costume of Swazi warrior, drawing parallels between his actions and the help given to the British by Mbandzeni in the war with Sekhukhuni's Pedi people in 1879. His motive, he explained, was to remind the British of the guarantees they had given in 1881 of Swaziland's independence. The parallel was reiterated constantly over subsequent years, and in 1944 Sobhuza held ceremonies to bring back to Swaziland the spirits of ancestors who had died in 1879. The 1991 Company served with British forces in the Middle East before joining Montgomery's Eighth Army at Tobruk and Anzio.

During the last two years of the war, the 1991 Company published a cyclostyled newsletter called the *Swazi Gazette*. The paper, which ran to fifty numbers, is a fascinating document demonstrating, among other things, how successful the king had been in appropriating to the royalist cause a constituency thrown up by social and economic changes that elsewhere in Africa were undermining custom and "tradition." The soldiers came to view themselves as Swazi warriors and regretted that back home "even the old people neglect to tell tales of old or fables. I think much of their time is spent at beer drinks." Much space in the correspondence columns was taken up with rival versions of the royal genealogy until an anonymous correspondent eventually halted the discussion with the names of twenty-seven Swazi kings—five more than Labotsibeni had pressed on de Symons Honey—beginning with Landzandzalukane (Sidvwa-basilutfuli), who, from this date onward, became accepted as the founding ancestor. There were repeated reminders that all soldiers must attend *Ncwala* as their way of honoring the king and remaining in touch after the war. "The praise of the nation is tantamount to a praise of its king," remarked another correspondent, noting that So-bhuza II had been recently awarded the Order of the British Empire.[59]

Such manifestations of loyalty served as the context for stating other concerns. There were many letters urging that the king should take action against unfaithful wives, and a list of the names of sol-diers' suspected wives was sent to Sobhuza, who replied promptly with a promise of action. There were proposals to establish a reserve fund on which soldiers could draw after the war to establish small businesses or go into commercial farming. Just as the regiments who fought Sekhukhuni were rewarded with cattle, so the present sol-diers deserved their booty. The demand for booty alarmed the Swa-ziland censor, who seems to have envisaged Swazi impi raiding Ital-ian smallholdings for cattle. A letter from one correspondent noted that many soldiers had become literate for the first time in Swazi, the *Gazette*'s very existence being proof of the fact. The significance of this remark was that Swazi was not the language of education in Swaziland, schoolbooks being published in Zulu. This correspon-dent suggested the establishment of a printing press at the royal kraal to continue what the *Gazette* had begun. Finally, among many exhortations about hard work and discipline and the need for black people to develop, the *Gazette* expressed great concern about the land question, taking it for granted that the king was their appro-priate proxy spokesman on this issue.[60]

By the end of the war, the monarchy, with its passionate tradition-alism, had clearly succeeded in making itself the representative of new nationalist forces. A list of grievances presented to the High Commissioner in May 1945 began with the land question and the duplicity of the British on the fate of the Crown lands. But it moved on swiftly to complaints about the dominance in the educational system of textbooks in Zulu and Xhosa ("Our language is disappear-ing and we ask for ways to safeguard it"), about low wages for work-ers and the rising cost of living, about conditions for Africans in the civil service, about the treatment of African customers at post of-fices, about the cost of trading licenses, about the fact that soldiers were expected to pay taxes, and about the terms under which mining concession were granted resulting in Africans being denied opportunities they witnessed in places like Malaya.[61] In effect, for his soldiers the king had made himself into the Swazi equivalent of the anticolonial Native Associations and African National Congresses that existed in other British southern African colonial territories. The High Commissioner's reply in November 1945 showed that he was well aware of this fact. "We know that the people of Swaziland feel strongly for the Swazi nation and feel proud of its history and customs. We want to encourage that feeling. We hope that you many individuals will continue to feel as a tribe and act as a tribe. To encourage that feeling of being one tribe has been British policy throughout Africa. . . . Our system is, I assure you, to maintain the tribe and maintain the feeling of the people for the chiefs."[62] Sobhuza clung to this policy, aimed at preventing "what had happened in other parts of Africa where the tribal feeling has gone" even when, later, the British decided to try to force him to abandon it.

Over the next five years, Sobhuza seized the opportunity to expand the power of the monarchy within the context of a rapid expansion of Swaziland's economy. He had bitterly opposed the Native Authorities Proclamation of 1944, which reduced the paramountcy to a bureaucratic post under the High Commissioner, and in 1950 he succeeded in having the proclamation modified in the Native Authorities Act so as to give him the powers to issue legally enforceable orders, to hear cases in his own courts, and to gain control over the Swazi National Treasury, which had hitherto been under the control of the High Commissioner.[63] At the same time, he sought to strengthen alliances between himself and important forces in Swazi society. In 1948 Sobhuza established the Swazi Commercial *Amadoda* (Men) to encourage participation by Swazis in retail trade and to set up district committees to advise the King and Council on the granting of trading licenses.[64] In the same year, he struck a fresh deal with the Chamber of Mines. By its terms he was allowed to place his personal representative at the Native Recruiting Corporation (NRC) headquarters in Johannesburg, strengthening his influence over labor migrants there, and was given the right to deduct taxes for the monarchy from mine workers' pay. In return, he endorsed NRC labor-recruitment campaigns in Swaziland. Framed photographs of Sobhuza were subsequently displayed in all NRC offices, with the intention of stressing " 'to natives . . . the obviously close liaison that exists between the Paramount Chief and the Corporation.' "[65]

Central to his political program was the land issue. He distributed land obtained from purchase of concession lands to returning war veterans, thus both rewarding them for their loyalty and building up a stable rural bourgeoisie.[66] He subsequently continued to campaign for more land for the Swazi Nation, establishing the Lifa Fund in 1946, to which cattle owners contributed one head in ten to buy up estates as they came on the market. By 1950 the monarchy had purchased 269,003 additional acres, increasing the Swazi National land from one-third to one-half of the Swaziland's territory.

While not wholly unopposed in his policies, especially with regard to those that resulted in cattle destocking or the forced resettlement of people,[67] the support mustered by these various initiatives carried Sobhuza successfully through the political turmoil of the late 1950s and early 1960s, when the British imposed on Swaziland a legislative council subject to the authority of a Queen's Commissioner. Trying, as he put it, "to extricate Africa from this idea of one man one vote,"[68] Sobhuza first petitioned the British Parliament to rescind the constitution, then won a referendum denouncing it, and finally took the bold step of forming a royalist political party, the *Imbokodvo* ("Grind Stone"), to support his position.[69]

To British officials like the Resident Commissioner, Brian Marwick, who supported the constitution, and Michael Fairlie, who was then trying to organize the trade-union movement, Sobhuza's message seemed ridiculously anachronistic. The new generation of politicians—men like J. J. Nquku of the Swaziland Progressive party (SPP), Simon Sishayi Nxumalo of the Swaziland Democratic party, or Dr. Ambrose Zwane and Dumisa Dlamini of the Ngwane National Liberatory Congress (NNLC)—could mobilize support on particular issues, such as the Havelock Mine strike of May 1963 or the public demonstrations of domestic workers in Mbabane in June. What they were unable to do was to rival the comprehensiveness of Sobhuza's nationalist program, which was presented as the cancellation of colonial humiliations and a return to nineteenth-century greatness. Furthermore, the king seemed to have the most immediate answers for the land problem, so important to the semiproletarianized migrant workers of the country. As a consequence, only once, in the general election of 1972, did the *Imbokodvo* lose control of a single constituency, and within the year Sobhuza abolished the independence constitution and assumed supreme power as king of Swaziland.[70]

Hilda Kuper has given a fascinating account of the way in which these political changes were expressed in the *Ncwala* ceremonies of the 1960s.[71] Attendance at the *Ncwala* for the years 1959 to 1963, the year of the imposed constitution, was very poor, despite Sobhuza's efforts to marshal support. The *Ncwala* of 1964 followed *Imbokodvo*'s victory in the first election, and attendance showed a marked increase. The *Ncwala* of 1966, which Kuper witnessed, was held at a moment when Botswana and Lesotho had already gained independence and when negotiations over Swaziland's independence constitution were held up in a dispute with the British over mineral rights. For eight weeks Sobhuza effectively withheld himself from British negotiators while he demonstrated his authority ritually. Kuper records that "the Ncwala of 1966–67 drew a larger and more enthusiastic attendance than any Incwala which I had previously attended," noting that there were at least 3,500 participants and over 100 foreign spectators. By contrast with ceremonies of the 1920s and 1930s, the participants in 1966–67 included members of Swaziland's educated elite, such as teachers, civil servants, prominent members of the legislative council, and former members of the opposition parties, all taking their place in *Ncwala* costume "beside the ordinary Swazi citizens in the traditional age—regiments."[72] Equally significant, the *Ncwala* was now structured to appeal to Christians by an addition to the ritual on its sixth day, when two priests of the African separatist Church of Zion planted in front of the *Ncwala* sanctuary the shining silver rod known as the "Moses Rod," which had been created following a dream that came to Stephen Mavimbela, an early Zionist leader. In the *Ncwala* dance itself, seven priests from three Christian Zionist churches were conspicuous.[73]

From the 1930s onward, building on Labotsibeni's earlier campaign, Sobhuza had espoused a particularized version of Swaziland's history. Ultimately, the power of his vision lay in his increasing control over the land through his administration of the Swazi Nation, but he also showed considerable sophistication in articulating it. This sophistication showed itself not only in his manipulation of symbols, such as his warrior's dress, or in his identification of powerful allies, such as Malinowski and Kuper, or in his use of the educational system and, later, the broadcasting system to inculcate traditionalist values, frequently through the use of official *tibongo* praises that were increasingly a part of the symbolic assemblage of monarchical history, but also in his appropriation as early as the 1950s of the techniques of the oral historian.

Isaac Dlamini was employed by Sobhuza in 1939 as an electrician and repairman at the royal residence. From about 1945, he was made responsible for arranging loudspeakers whenever the king addressed large audiences, and soon afterwards he became responsible for recording all speeches, council meetings, and royal audiences. From the mid-1950s, he was sent out periodically with one of the princes to record oral history from the indunas. The recordings were brought back to Lobamba and played to the king, who commented, with his councillors, upon what had been said. Sometimes the king would summon the induna concerned for discussions. Sometimes he would send the recording back with the statement that he "didn't agree" and that the induna must "do it again." According to Mr. Dlamini, who possesses an extensive archive of royal tape recordings, each induna now has his own recorder and tapes with the corrected version of his chiefdom's part in the nation's history.[74]

The king's own official version of history is also reflected in a good deal of modern writing about Swaziland. From the early 1930s Hilda Kuper's work has been dominated by an extreme sense of respect for the royal house, which she accepts as extending back thirty generations, though without giving a source for this statement.[75] The writing of her authorized biography of Sobhuza was supervised by an editorial committee appointed by the king that included Polycarp Dlamini and Msindazwe Sujati, both of whom had attended the Swazi National High School during the 1930s, and J. S. M. Matsebula, the king's private secretary and official historian, whose own *History of Swaziland* is very much concerned with glorifying Sobhuza's rule and does not pretend to detachment.[76] Her central role in building up the position of the monarch was publicly recognized when—after having become a Swazi citizen in 1970 by swearing allegiance (*kukhonta*) to Sobhuza—she was given the signal honor in 1982 of delivering the initial eulogy at his funeral ceremonies.[77]

Even Philip Bonner's *Kings, Commoners, and Concessionaires,* by far the finest account of nineteenth-century Swaziland, is not entirely immune from such fixation on the monarchy. Despite using a mode-of-production paradigm, Bonner's book is for long sections preoccupied with migrations, battles, cattle raids, and kinship, the very stuff of Swazi aristocratic nostalgia, and the "commoners" of the title are not easily found in the text. This may, perhaps, reflect to some degree Sobhuza's interference in the oral record through his taped "corrections" to local history or, more generally, the broad sympathies of his informants. But it also reflects Bonner's interviews with the key figure of Maboya Fakudze, whom he describes as possessing a "seemingly inexhaustible fund of knowledge about Swazi history" and being "my single most important informant."[78]

Maboya Fakudze was the most prolific and most talented of the praise poets at Sobhuza's court during the last two decades of his long reign. Of the sixty-nine Swazi *tibongo* we have so far managed to assemble from published, private, and archival sources—the majority of them from Dr. Ginindza's collections—no fewer than twenty-one are Fakudze's.[79] His are not only the most numerous but are also by far the longest and most comprehensive, describing every king from Landzandzalukane (Sidvwabasilutfuli) and Ngwane III to Bhunu. Like Sobhuza II, Fakudze was a member of the Balondolozi regiment, and the king's confidence in him led to his serving for many years as regent of Nkanini royal village, near Lobamba. The link between the Fakudzes and the royal house derives from the earliest days of Swaziland's history. A Fakudze had been one of Sobhuza I's most famous generals, defeating Dingane at the battle of Lubuya, and another had been one of Mbandzeni's two principal councillors. In recent years, the family has been responsible for arranging ceremonials at Lobamba, including the *Ncwala* and the Reed Dance.

A further nine of the sixty-nine *tibongo* are by Ndinda Mavuso, also of the king's own generation and a member of the Balondolozi regiment. They are briefer texts than Fakudze's, some of them only five to seven lines long, and although they have few praises in common with his, they do not differ in their historical themes. The remaining praises poets include Mutsi Dlamini, a son of the king's elder brother, Sosiswa; Mcoshwa Dlamini, another member of the Balondolozi regiment and one of the grandsons of Mbandzeni; and Makhosini Dlamini, another grandson of Mbandzeni and the first prime minister of Swaziland. Mabuntane Mdluli, the praise poet responsible for the *tibongo* of Sobhuza II quoted by Hilda Kuper, is related to Labotsibeni and descended from Matsafeni Mdluli, Mswati's induna at Hhohho and later commander of Mbandzeni's army. The affinity of all these praise poets with the royal house is self-evident.

The texts of these *tibongo*—chanted at Sobhuza's royal court during the latter part of his reign, recorded for use by the Swaziland Broadcasting Service, and published to be read in schools—are the poetic history of the Swazi kingdom according to the royal house. The sequence begins with Landzandzalukane (Sidvwabasilutfuli), whose name was first featured, without prominence, in a list of early Bembo-Nguni chiefs drawn up by Offy Shepstone, but who, by the 1940s, had been elevated to the position of first ancestor. In Fakudze's *tibongo*, Landzandzalukane, whose name means "long-distance traveler," is described as leading a migration into southern Swaziland, the earliest area of settlement:

Sidvwaba silifuli!	Dusty oxhide skirt!
Singaba ntolo sibang' indlala.	Once wet, it causes famine.
Sekufihla lababi	It is for hiding the ugly ones
LabangemaLangeni.	Who are children of the Sun.
Longaweli ejubukweni lelishonako.	Who crosses not by the deep ford.
Uwela ngelesihlabathi.	He crosses by the shallow sandy one.
Mlawulela sizwe sakho ngendlela.	You directed your nation along the journey.
Inga iya eMagubheni, iNkayaneni.	Leading to Magubheni, to Nkayaneni.
Ngokuncobela izizwe zikuhlasela KulaseMzimbayeni.	By defeating nations attacking you At Mzimbayaneni.[80]

The "ugly ones / Who are children of the Sun" are the Ur-Swazi who are said to have followed Dlamini after he broke with his lineage and demonstrated his independence by breaking with taboo and eating food at noon. Having led his group northward along the Mozambique coast ("Dusty oxhide skirt . . . shallow sandy one"), he captured territory east of the Lobombo mountains. There followed further disputes within the lineage, coupled with attacks by the Nguni until, at last, Landzandzalukane accepted the entreaty that he should assume the chieftainship:

Umthekelethile Ngwane.	You bound the people of Ngwane together.
Ngendula enguDlamini,	The (dead) deaf one who is Dlamini
Ethanda Kunya malala	Who has recently disappeared.
Wasala wedwa kaHlathikhulu!	Alone you remained at Hlathikulu!

With the concluding lines, *"Nkosi! / Wena waseMavaneni!"* ("Hail King! You of Maveni!"), the Swazi royal house has been established, with Ngwane as the legitimate heir:

Wamnika Ngwane indvuku.	You gave Ngwane the stick,
Wachubeka nesive semaLangeni.	He perpetuated the nation of emaLangeni.[81]

The story then jumps generations to Ngwane III, Sobhuza I's grandfather. From this point onward, the kings are described as individuals, and it is important to emphasize how sharply their characters are distinguished. Ngwane III is presented as quite irrationally violent:

Ngwane lonelulaka ekhaya netsafeni,	Ngwane who rages at home and on the plains,
Emathunzini ezintaba.	In the shadows of the mountains.
Mbetsi wetidzandza emasekweni	You strike girls against hearth stones
Kwetfuke emadvodza.	Frightening men.
Bonina bangekho	The mothers are away
Basematsefeni.	Gone to the fields.[82]

Then, proceeding on his migration, he comes to Ngwane's Rock, a boulder on the border between Swaziland and South Africa, where the desolation of the scene of dying cattle, bare rocks, and vultures attracted by the smell of decaying meat brought him to his senses ("Then he remembered"—*Wakhumbula*) and he began to govern properly ("Before you knelt officials and ordinary men."—*Wagucelwa jizinduna nemadvodza.*) In Ndinda Mavuso's version, which begins with the same images of violence, the change is an absolute one:

Ngwane etinkhabini	Ngwane, among oxen
Ngingamfanisa nalesiphundvulu.	I would compare him to a hornless beast.
Etindleleni, Ngwane,	Among paths, Ngwane,
Ngingamfanisa naletivundlako.	I compare him to crosspaths.[83]

With the next king, Ndvungunye, the lineage reaches the father of Sobhuza I. Ndvungunye is presented first as a hunter (in lines that are borrowed from the praises of Ndaba, Shaka's ancestor, first pub-

lished by James Stuart in the mid-1920s)[84] and then, second, as a
warrior. But this is a Swazi warrior with a difference:

Mniki wamphi kumaLangeni.	You gave the war to the Malangeni.
Was' ukhala tinyembeti,	Then you wept,
Uyayihawukela.	Feeling pity for the regiment.
Wakhumbula tihlangu letidzala	You remembered old war shields
Yemakhosi asendulo.	Of ancient kings.[85]

The point is not simply to draw a contrast with Ngwane III. The
point is that the father of Sobhuza I, who some might believe to be
the founder of Swaziland, was already overwhelmed with a sense of
"ancient" history and the pity of warfare.

The praises of Sobhuza I occupied an important place in the reign
of his namesake and imitator, Sobhuza II, and they exist in several
versions, including *tibongo* by Maboya Fakudze, Ndinda Mavuso,
and Mutsi Dlamini, the king's cousin. Significantly, a further set of
Sobhuza I's praises, performed privately for Bonner in 1970, is almost
identical with those recorded by Cook in 1929, the only instance of
one of the older *tibongo* surviving into the new era.

Dlamini's *tibongo* begins with a reminder of Sobhuza's ancestry
among the Simulane and Mdluli peoples and by reminding them of
their debt to the king:

> You are crooked
> You bent before the king arrived.[86]

Sobhuza is described as rescuing his people, ensuring their safety
and survival by hiding them in the forest of the Drakensburgs until
Zwide's invading armies had withdrawn:

> They buried you in large forests
> On the Mdzimba mountain,
> And in them, Masikasale,
> And in them, Mangukube,
> There's no facing one another.
> It's dim,
> You count branches.

> * * *

> I can't praise you enough
> Child of Ndaba.

> Up to this day
> Tears drip down onto the pillow.
> Gleaned he stands!
> Still stands the army.
> Out he emerges
> From a wooden rampart
> And trees broke.
> Hail, your Majesty!
> Great as Matshapa and Delude,
> Together with Nkothake.
> You of the inner circle!
> Emerge!
> Let's bask in you,
> We've basked with you in the clouds![87]

Key verbs that appear within this poem are *arrived, escaped, buried, stands, emerges,* and *emerge!* Key images are of things threatened surviving and of things buried coming to light. Thus, the emergence of the king and the army from the forest becomes the broader metaphor for the emergence of "the inner circle" and of the nation from the darkness of the past history like "the little morning star." It is also a poem full of warm affection (We all like you / Calf of the elephant") for Sobhuza I's memory.

Fakudze's and Mavuso's versions echo this warm affection but supplement it with an emphasis on Sobhuza's role as rainmaker and provider. He is the "udder with numerous teats" that "suckled ten men." He is "grass on a high mountain," suggesting provision as well as refuge. Dlamini's image of Sobhuza I as "little morning star" is expanded by Fakudze into:

Abuk' ikhwezi nesilimela,	They could look at the morning star and Pleiades,
Azi ukuthi ikhwezi liyasibikela.	Know that the morning star foretells.[88]

The appearance of the constellation Pleiades marks the beginning of the plowing time, while the timing of the firstfruits ceremony is indicated by the position of the morning star.

The contrast with the praises of Mswati, Sobhuza I's successor, could hardly be greater. There are seven modern versions of Mswati's *tibongo* by six different poets, but they all share the same emphasis. Mcoshwa Dlamini's begins:

> You of the inner circle!
> Agitator of Mbelebeleni
> Cutter with a spear
> And blood overflowed.
> Constantly armed,
> Never tired of being armed.[89]

Maboya Fakudze's opening praises are similar:

Lodungandaba waseMbelebeleni.	Causer of strifes of Mbelebeleni.
Owadunga izindaba.	Who causes strifes,
Nalamuhla sihlalele kuMswati.	Up to this day we are on guard, Mswati.
Mswati, ngimbone ekhala Izinyembezi.	Mswati, I saw him shedding Tears.
Abekhalela kulwa nekulanyulwa.	He wept to fight and to be stopped from fighting.[90]

These *tibongo* are very long (Fakudze's has over 100 lines in Ginindza's translation). They record the long list of Mswati's victories and the extent of the kingdom he consolidated, from the sea to the Drakensburgs and from Zululand to the north. The images are of spears and shields; of his stockade surrounded by human heads; of thunder roaring even in the fog; of the elephant, the black bull, the mamba from the forest; and of fire thawing even the snow on the mountains:

> Where Mswati is
> They're burning,
> They burn inside houses,
> The mountainsides burned,
> Makhonjwa burned,
> Lufafa cooked.[91]

This is not seen as equivalent to the irrational violence of Ngwane III, and there is none of the bewilderment at Mswati's doings that is occasionally expressed in the Zulu *izibongo* of Shaka. Mswati is "admired" and "conspicuous" and

> Constantly being discussed
> By royal wives,
> Scared of the sting
> Of sharp whiskers.
> For your whiskers, Mswati,

> I've counted,
> They're multiples of tens and tens
> And more.[92]

The poem, then, is a straightforward and uncomplicated celebration of military ferocity. Perhaps it is not surprising that as the Swazi aristocracy tussled with the British in the closing years of the colonial period, Mswati should have been the most popular of the hero kings. Ndebele praise poets also responded to colonial defeat and humiliation by celebrating in the figure of Mzilikazi the simpler military virtues in contrast to the complications of Lobengula's administration. The appeal, then, in these *tibongo* chanted at Sobhuza's court before and after independence is "Oh, return, Mswati!"—*O, buya, Mswati!*)

Mswati nguloyo wakaLobamba,	Mswati is the one of Lobamba,
Angasi wakalokothwayo.	Being the daring one.[93]

Passing over the praises of Ludvonga, who died when only fifteen, there are two more of this sequence of *tibongo* that are illuminating to discuss before drawing some conclusions. Both are by Maboya Fakudze, and each is profoundly critical. The *tibongo* of Mbandzeni are a catalog of national disasters. This, once more, is a very long praise poem, but the opening section is worth considering in detail:

> Eater at noon,
> By eating in the sun
> When the nation,
> The descendants of Langa,
> Eat in the shade.
> Madeya of Ndaba,
> You gave up the oxen
> And bought doves.
> The men against you rebelled.
> Where you pass they burn
> You of Mavuso.
> The aged are lazy.
> You twirled a stone,
> And fire kindled.
> You dressed up in white snow
> Which had clothed the mountains.
> Scarcely would I have slept
> Had it clothed me, a menial.

> Chest that from commotion grumbles,
> Out came weaver birds and chirped noisily.
> Mourners you don't mourn,
> For you they'll remain mourning.
> Ndaba, spotted like a leopard
> For at creation he spoiled you.
> For in the gall of the heavens you bathed
> When people bathed in the portions of their
> ancestors.[94]

The accusations are explicit—of Mbandzeni's laziness, unconcern, and irresponsibility: eating in the sun while the nation was in the shade; bathing in the "gall of the heavens" while the nation had to consume their ancestral inheritances; relinquishing the nation's cattle for mere doves; wearing garments of snow when even a menial would have acted differently; and, when roused, producing only the empty chatter of weaverbirds. Later, Mbandzeni becomes

> Lazy one of Mavuso,
> You fed on other people's harvest. . . .

> Dove which flew on wings
> Flapping them,
> Spying on Mabhedla,
> Hare that ran fast to the *isigodlo* [harem]

> You were tricked by the English and the Hollanders.
> They tricked you by subduing nations
> With the chains of the south. . . .

> You called upon howling dogs
> And out came weaver birds
> And made a noise for you.

Sarcastic to the end, Fakudze reminds us of Mbandzeni's heritage:

> Here is the calf spoiling calves.
> It's the red one,
> King that should have been,
> Of Mswati, of Somhlolo, of Tikodze of Ngwane.
> Lion!
> You devoured enemies, calves and young heifers.
> Hail, your Majesty![95]

The images in this *tibongo* draw greater force from their context in the sequence of Maboya's praises. Doves, hares, dogs, and weaver-birds contrast forcibly with lions, elephants, mambas, and bulls. Mbandzeni is dressed in snow, but Mswati's fires thawed the snows on the Drakensburgs. Even the "leopard" metaphor (Sobhuza II was "a leopard" in Mdluli's *tibongo*) is turned against him: Mbandzeni's leopard is "spotted . . . / For at creation he spoiled you." Fakudze's poem is a powerful and contemptuous indictment of the king who sold off Swaziland to the concessionaires.

Finally, occupying the gap between Mbandzeni and the infant Sobhuza II comes the interlude of Bhunu. "A cruel and bloodthirsty man," de Symons Honey has been told "from native sources" in 1914,[96] and this is surely the theme of Maboya's *tibongo*. To Bhunu are applied the same appalling metaphors used earlier for Ngwane III:

> Flock of vultures,
> They come flying,
> Coming to the wooden rampart
> Smelling the scent of meat
> You licked with a broad-bladed spear,
> The mouth did nothing.
> Painfully, you ripped off,
> We're the buck's entrails.[97]

With Bhunu's murder toward the end of the poem, the stage is set for the coming of Sobhuza II.

It will be appreciated how close these *tibongo* are to the version of Swaziland's history outlined earlier—a history of migrations, conquests, and state formation under the monarchy. By contrast with the chronicle nature of the *tibongo* recorded by Cook in 1929, these praise poems chart the process of nation-building, each king being sharply distinguished by character but judged ultimately by his success or failure in advancing Swazi destiny. Swaziland itself is no longer a landscape of rivers and sweet grasses nourishing milk-swollen udders as it was in Cook's collection of 1929. It is instead a place of forests and dark caves, paths and fords, a place for stratagems, and finally—with its rocks and vultures and stinking entrails—a battlefield. The contemporary message is that the nation was betrayed by Sobhuza II's immediate predecessors, Mbandzeni and Bhunu, leaving to him the task of restoring former greatness.

From this perspective, the archaisms of style and reference in the different versions of Sobhuza II's *tibongo* have a certain logic and appropriateness. One by Mabuntane Mdluli, already quoted, with its emphases on military prowess and conquest, resonates with the achievements of Sobhuza I and Mswati. A second, by Mtjopane Mamba, focuses on Sobhuza's despatching of the Emasotja and Sikhonyane regiments during World War II:

> They are calling you, sending you messages,
> Montgomery and his party,
> They are calling you to Italy
> Tears fell from Mussolini who was born in Italy
> All nations have heard the crying. . . .
>
> The pile of spears
> It was too heavy on Mussolini
> It was too heavy on Rommel
> It was too heavy on Hitler
>
> Your arrow-coldness spears
> They are like an open grave
> You are the lion that eats men
> Hail, Bayethe![98]

However, the most interesting and certainly the most substantial of the *tibongo* of Sobhuza II was recorded by Ginindza from a performance by Makhosini Dlamini, Sobhuza's cousin and Swaziland's first Prime Minister. Dlamini's poem begins:

Banelusongo!	They are full of threats!
Bayakusongela!	They threaten you!
Bayasonga!	They threaten!
Ngebezitheni nebekhaya	It is the enemies and those at home.
Benamanga -ke.	They are wrong.[99]

With this image of Sobhuza as a king surrounded by enemies established, Dlamini rehearses the whole history of Sobhuza's reign. Even as an infant he was in danger, but he made the perilous journey from his grandmother's home at eZikhotheni to Labotsibeni's court at Zombodze safely, Dlamini combining the account of this journey with others made by Sobhuza in his youth, when he swallowed the insults of Madanda Mtsetfwa, governor of Zombodze, and survived the attempt of Mabhula at Langeni to feed him poisoned meat. Arriving at Zombodze as a child to be trained for kingship, his enemies laughed at him:

Zathi: 'Uyaphi yemntakaNdaba,	And said, "Where are you going, child of Ndaba,
Loku live laboyihlo liyadvungutela?'	For the country of your fathers is in turmoil?"[100]

As he grew up, Sobhuza was criticized for insisting on going to Lovedale School for his education, but his decision was correct, and he came back with the "white mud" necessary for modern kingship. The rumors that he was associating too much with the colonial administration are answered with the insistence that he

Longayembats' ingubo	. . . wears no blanket
Lowembatsa lugugo lwengwenyama.	Who wears the skin of a lion.

The story of the crisis of 1935, when Sobhuza's enemies accused him of responsibility for the great drought, is retold, along with the list of royal officials whose advice became necessary to resolve it:

Gijimani ngazo zonke izindlela	Run along all paths
Niye niyombikela uJokovu eNyakeni	And report to Jokovu at Nyakeni
UJokovu eNyakeni	Jokovu at Nyakeni
Ayekombikela uMshengu eMashobeni	To report to Mshengu at Mashobeni
UMshengu eMashobeni	Mshengu at Mashobeni
Ayekombikela uBhozongo koMabonya	To report to Bhozongo at Mabonya's
Ukuthi uSobhuza akalaz' izulu	That Sobhuza knows not the rain
Waz' ilang' eliphezulu kuphela	He knows only the sun above
Ngoba libalele labushis' utjani namanzi	Which scorched the grass and dried up water
Nalamuhla loku belusi bezihuku bazingcongcile.	To this day, the shepherds have lost their flocks.

Even the complaints about Sobhuza's support after 1945 for the colonial administration's afforestation schemes, which involved much resettlement, are recalled in the line "Dlodlobezel' abant' eqobheni" ("You force people into the thorny thickets."[101]

For long sections, then, this *tibongo* sounds like a catalog of weaknesses and shortcomings, with the attempts to undermine or destroy Sobhuza recalled in detail. But this is only the context for a celebration of his victories. Two features are especially significant. The first is the insistence that Sobhuza is still under threat, still surrounded by enemies. The *tibongo* as a whole is addressed to his most recent opponents, the leaders of the SPP, SDP, and NNLC, who are fighting Sobhuza in the 1960s' postindependence elections. The poem is a warning that Sobhuza has always had to struggle against enemies and has always been victorious, and it presages his assumption of full political power in 1973 after suspending the constitution. The second significant feature is the *tibongo*'s style. Sobhuza is presented throughout as the very model of a nineteenth-century warrior king. He is "Shaka, the dark one" (*Shaka lomyama*). He is "the attacker at noon, of Zwide at Ngobe at Tanga's, / Stick that points at the Nguni and the Swazi" (*Mganda mini kaZwide kaNgobe koYanga / Mzac' okhomb' abeNguni nemaSwazi.*):

Ngabe kuze kuse ngitfutfumela	Till dawn I would tremble
Ngemehlw' akho -ke Shaka	It is your eyes, Shaka,
Ngobe ayesabeka	For they are fearsome.
Ingani angangewembube	They are as large as those of a lion
Kantsi ngewengwenyama	They are those of a lion.[102]

Only once is there a concession to the twentieth century, with brief reference to Swaziland's railway.

In many of the essays in this volume there has been an emphasis on the role of oral poetry and song as a mechanism for dialogue between those who exercise power and those who are subordinate to them. In the case of the Swazi *tibongo*, however, it is clear that dialogue became ever more one-sided as the role of the *tibongo* was redefined, especially as Sobhuza, in the period after World War II, pressed for a general acceptance of his own vision of a traditionalist and royalist Swaziland of the future, with the monarchy firmly in control. In the process, the *tibongo*, so often misunderstood in the past as being *merely* "praises" became precisely that, with virtually no element of criticism or dialogue.[103] And the audience also shifted. Sobhuza was not so much "praised" to his face as to the Swazi people through public recitations, use in Swazi schools, and over the Swaziland Broadcasting Service. In effect, Sobhuza captured poetry, and it became a "traditional" means of propaganda in the service of a state that overtly espouses "tradition" in support of a "traditional" monarchy.[104]

Notes

1. H. Kuper, *Sobhuza II: Ngwenyama and King of Swaziland* (London, 1978), 14–16.

2. T. T. Ginindza, *Tibongo teMakhosi netetiNdlovukazi* (London, 1975).

3. T. T. Ginindza, "SiSwati Oral Poetry," Ph.D. diss., International College, Los Angeles, 1985.

4. Ibid., 158.

5. P. A. W. Cook, "History and Izibongo of the Swazi Chiefs," *Bantu Studies* 5 (1931): 181–202.

6. For a discussion of events down to 1889, see P. Bonner, *Kings, Commoners, and Concessionaires: The Evolution and Dissolution of the Nineteenth Century Swazi State* (Cambridge, 1983).

7. Kuper, *Sobhuza II*, 24–25; Bonner, *Kings, Commoners, and Concessionaires*, 161. Bonner's account is fair to Mbandzeni, showing, for example, that he succeeded for a long while in playing Boers off against British by his concession-granting policies and that many of his councilors were key supporters of the granting of more and more concessions.

8. Files S30 and RCS 115/14, Swaziland National Archives (SNA), Mbabane, Swaziland.

9. Ibid. Honey was certainly being disingenuous in not pointing out that Eckstein and Porges were two of the most important mining capitalists in South Africa. For a discussion of their position, see R. V. Kubicek, *Economic Imperialism in Theory and Practice: The Case of South African Gold Mining Finance, 1890–1914* (Durham, N.C., 1979), 53–85. Bonner, *Kings, Commoners, and Concessionaires*, 199–206, analyzes the role of Eckstein and Porges as stalking-horses for the South African Republic in its efforts to undermine the Swazi state and why Mbandzeni yielded this concession.

10. Bonner, *Kings, Commoners, and Concessionaires*, 183.

11. J. Crush, *The Struggle for Swazi Labour, 1890–1920* (Kingston and Montreal, 1987), 43–44; B. Lincoln, "Ritual, Rebellion, Resistance: Once More the Swazi Ncwala," *Man* n.s. 22, no. 1 (1987): 141.

12. Files S30 and RCS 115/14, SNA.

13. See M. Fransman, "The Colonial State and the Land Question in Swaziland, 1903–1907," in University of London, Institute of Commonwealth Studies, *The Societies of Southern Africa in the 19th and 20th Centuries*, vol. 9 (London, 1978), 30; J. Crush, "Colonial Coercion and the Swazi Tax Revolt of 1903–1907," *Political Geography Quarterly* 4, no. 3 (1985): 178–90; and Crush, *The Struggle for Swazi Labour*, 139, 147, 150–154.

14. This paragraph is based on A. R. Booth, "Homestead, State, and Migrant Labor in Colonial Swaziland," *African Economic History* 14 (1985): 115–16, and Crush, *The Struggle for Swazi Labour*, 38–41.

15. There is great uncertainty as to the number of Swazi cattle involved. Booth ("Homestead, State, and Migrant Labor" 116) indicates a reduction from 300,000 to 40,000, while Crush (*The Struggle for Swazi Labour*, 41) estimates the decline as "100,000 or approximately 80 to 90 per cent of the country's stock." R. Packard ("Maize, Cattle, and Mosquitoes: The Political Economy of Malaria Epidemics in Colonial Swaziland," *Journal of African History* 25, no. 2 [1984]: 125) more cautiously contents himself with the comment that the herds were "decimated."

16. Crush, *The Struggle for Swazi Labour*, 136–38.

17. H. Macmillan, "A Nation Divided? The Swazi in Swaziland and the Transvaal, 1865–1986," in L. Vail, ed., *The Creation of Tribalism in Southern Africa* (London and Berkeley, 1989), 294–96.

18. Booth, "Homestead, State, and Migrant Labor," 123; Crush, *The Struggle for Swazi Labour*, 56–61, passim.

19. RCS 115/14, SNA.

20. Report of Swaziland police, 23 December 1921, RCS 756/20, SNA.

21. Queen Regent to Resident Commissioner, 22 December 1921, ibid.

22. Ginindza, "SiSwati Oral Poetry," 312–13.

23. Kuper, *Sobhuza II*, 96.

24. Macmillan, "A Nation Divided?" 300. See also Crush, *The Struggle for Swazi Labour*, 191–94.

25. Crush, *The Struggle for Swazi Labour*, 192.

26. Cook, "History and Izibongo," 184.

27. Ibid., 183–84.

28. Acting Resident Commissioner to A. W. Hoernlé, n.d., 518/31, SNA.

29. Cook, "History and Izibongo," 184.

30. J. Opland, "*Imbongi Nezibongo:* The Xhosa Tribal Poet and the Contemporary Poetic Tradition," *PMLA* 90 (1975): 185–208.

31. Interview with Isaac Dlamini, Lobamba, Swaziland, 21 August 1985; Cook, "History and Izibongo," 183–84.

32. M. Damane and P. B. Sanders, *Lithoko: Sotho Praise Poems* (Oxford, 1974), 18–33.

33. Unpublished manuscript of translations of *tibongo* collected by T. T. Ginindza in the possession of Dr. Hugh Macmillan, pp. 28, 46. (henceforth

cited as Ginindza Collection). The *imbongi* were Maboya Fakudze and Mcoshwa Dlamini.

34. Cook, "History and Izibongo," 201.

35. Ginindza, "Siswati Oral Poetry," 264. The *imbongi* was Maboya Fakudze. Wherever the Swazi version is available and the transcription is sound, we will include both the Swazi and English versions.

36. Cook, "History and Izibongo," 187.

37. Ibid., 193.

38. Ibid., 197.

39. Ibid., 195, 187.

40. S. Marks, *Ambiguities of Dependence in South Africa: Class, Nationalism, and the State in Twentieth Century Natal* (Baltimore and London, 1986), 73.

41. J. S. M. Matsebula, *The King's Eye* (Cape Town, 1983), 22.

42. A. T. Bryant, *Olden Times in Zululand and Natal* (London, 1929); R. A. C. Samuelson, *Long, Long Ago* (Durban, 1929); J. Stuart, *uTulasizwe* (1923), *uHlanqakula* (1924), *uBaxoxele* (1924), *uKulumetule* (1925), and *uVusezakiti* (1926)—all published in London. E. W. Grant's "The Izibongo of the Zulu Chiefs" appeared in *Bantu Studies* 3, no. 3 (1927–29): 201–44.

43. For a discussion of this development, see S. Marks, "Patriotism, Patriarchy, and Purity: Natal and Politics of Zulu Ethnic Consciousness," in *The Politics of Tribalism in Southern Africa,* ed. L. Vail (London and Berkeley, 1989), 216–19, and pp. 64–70, above.

44. Matsebula, *The King's Eye,* 15. See also H. Macmillan, "Decolonisation and the Triumph of 'Tradition,'" *Journal of Modern African Studies* 23, no. 4 (1985): 648–53, and "A Nation Divided?" 300. On attitudes of Christians towards "traditional ways," see H. Kuper, "The Swazi Reaction to Missions," *African Studies* 5, no. 3 (1946): 177–88.

45. See, for example, P. B. Rich, *White Power and the Liberal Conscience: Racial Segregation and South African Liberalism, 1921–60* (Johannesburg, 1984), 54–76, for a discussion of anthropology's role at this time.

46. Timetable of 1931 *Ncwala*, RCS 958/31, SNA; A. W. Hoernlé to Resident Commissioner, 16 November 1933, RCS 912/33, SNA.

47. Swanepoel to Inspector in Charge, Mbabane, 7 January 1931, RCS 958/31, SNA.

48. Cuttings from the *Star* (Johannesburg) for 13 January and 6 February 1934, 195/34, SNA.

49. Joint report of A. W. Hoernlé and Dr. I. Schapera on "The advisability and possibility of introducing the *ibutho* system of the Swazi people into the educational system," [1933], 328/33, SNA. The file also contains Malinowski's letter of support, dated 13 August 1934, and the undated memorandum of Sobhuza II that began the debate. The same memorandum was read by the minister of education on Swaziland television on 18 August 1985 as a guide to the current educational policy.

50. Macmillan, "A Nation Divided?" 301; Matsebula, *The King's Eye*, 15–20.

51. P. J. Schoeman, "The Swazi Rain Ceremony," *Bantu Studies* 9 (1935): 171.

52. H. Beemer, "The Swazi Rain Ceremony (Critical Comments on P. J. Schoeman's Article)," *Bantu Studies* 9 (1935): 273–80.

53. H. Kuper, "A Ritual of Kingship among the Swazi," *Africa* 14 (1944): 255–56.

54. H. Kuper, *An African Aristocracy* (1947; rpt., London, 1961), 204–5.

55. M. Gluckman, *Rituals of Rebellion in South East Africa* (Manchester, 1954). See also A. Apter, "In Dispraise of the King: Rituals 'against' Rebellion in South East Africa," *Man* 18, 3 (1983): 521–34.

56. Kuper, *An African Aristocracy*, 205.

57. Kuper, *Sobhuza II*, 19.

58. Ibid., 139.

59. "Swazi Gazette," file 885, SNA.

60. Ibid.

61. Meeting of the Resident Commissioner with the Paramount Chief and Council, 28 May 1945, File 772ᴵᴵ, SNA.

62. Meeting of the High Commissioner and Resident Commissioner with the Paramount Chief and Ndlovukazi at Lobamba, 12 October 1945, ibid.

63. H. Kuper, "A Royal Ritual in a Changing Political Context," *Cahiers d'etudes africaines* 12, no. 48 (1972): 599.

64. Macmillan, "Swaziland: Decolonisation and the Triumph of 'Tradition,'" 655.

65. A. Booth, "Capitalism and the Competition for Swazi Labour, 1945–1960," *Journal of Southern African Studies* 13, no. 1 (1986): 138.

66. Kuper, "A Royal Ritual," 599.

67. Cf. Ginindza, "Siswati Oral Poetry," 312–19.

68. Quoted in Kuper, *Sobhuza II*, 217.

69. See, for example, C. P. Potholm, "The Ngwenyama of Swaziland: The Dynamics of Political Adaptation," in *African Kingships in Perspective*, ed. R. Lemarchand (London, 1977), 129–59. According to Ginindza ("Siswati Oral Poetry," 200), *Imbokodvo* refers to the grind stone used in making potions for the *Ncwala* ceremony.

70. See Kuper, *Sobhuza II*, and R. P. Stevens, "Swaziland Political Development," *Journal of Modern African Studies* 1 (1963): 327–50.

71. This paragraph is based on Kuper, "A Royal Ritual."

72. Ibid., 608.

73. Ibid., 608–9.

74. Interview with Isaac Dlamini, Lobamba, Swaziland, 21 August 1985.

75. Kuper, *African Aristocracy*, 232.

76. J. S. M. Matsebula, *A History of Swaziland* (London, 1972).

77. J. S. M. Matsebula, *A Tribute to His Late Majesty King Sobhuza II*

(Mbabane, 1983), 55. See also his *The King's Eye*, 139–40, and H. Kuper, *The Swazi*, 2d rev. ed. (New York, 1986), ix.

78. Bonner, *Kings, Commoners, and Concessionaires*, 293.

79. Swazi *tibongo* are difficult to track down. Apart from the collections by Ginindza and P. A. W. Cook described earlier, they are included in A. J. Kubone, *Umlondulozi* (Pietermaritzburg, 1940); J. J. Nquku, *Bayete* (Mbabane, 1947); J. S. M. Matsebula, *Izakhiwo zamaSwazi* (Johannesburg, 1952); and C. L. S. Nyembezi, *Izibongo zamakhosi* (Pietermaritzburg, 1958). Hilda Kuper's *African Aristocracy* prints a 1947 version of Sobhuza II's *tibongo* by way of preface, while J. S. Zalo, *Akusenjalo* (Pietermaritzburg, 1946), also includes praises of Sobhuza II. A paper by G. N. Mamba, "Group Identity in Swazi Oral Poetry" (in *Aesthetics, Language, and Literature*, eds. S. P. C. Moyo, T. W. C. Sumaili, and J. A. Moody, vol. 2 in *Oral Traditions in Southern Africa*, 4 vols. [Lusaka, 1986], 183–213), contains the praises of Sobhuza II by Mtjopane Mamba on pp. 208–13. Others occur in Bonner's interviews, filed at the Swaziland National Archives. Finally, we are grateful to Carolyn Hamilton for sharing her own recordings and translations. The major gaps are for the period before 1929 and in the 1930s.

80. Ginindza, "SiSwati Oral Poetry," 162.

81. Ibid., 163, 165.

82. Ibid., 168.

83. Ibid., 165, 168–69.

84. See the discussion of the revival of Zulu ethnic consciousness in chapter two, pp. 64–70, above.

85. Ginindza, "SiSwati Oral Poetry," 170. The *imbongi* was Maboya Fakudze.

86. Ginindza Collection, 15.

87. Ibid., 15–16.

88. Ginindza, "SiSwati Oral Poetry," 436–37.

89. Ginindza Collection, 8.

90. Ginindza, "Siswati Oral Poetry," 193.

91. Ginindza Collection, 10.

92. Ibid., 9.

93. Ginindza, "SiSwati Oral Poetry," 191, 194.

94. Ginindza Collection, 28.

95. Ibid., 30–31, 32.

96. Files 830 and RCS 115/14, SNA.

97. Ginindza Collection, 49–50.

98. Mamba, "Group Identity in Swazi Oral Poetry," 212–13.

99. Ginindza, "SiSwati Oral Poetry," 461.

100. Ibid., 465.

101. Ibid., 461, 462–63, 465.

102. Ibid., 463, 465.

103. Such a shift in the nature of Xhosa *izibongo* has also been noted in Opland, *Xhosa Oral Poetry*, 234–71, as a consequence of the forces of the

contemporary state being brought to bear against any possible criticism of the state and its policies.

104. E.g., O. B. Dube, *The Arrow of King Sobhuza II: A Book of Poems and Tributes to the Crown Prince Makhosetive and King Sobhuza II* (Mbabane, 1986). Our thanks to A. Booth for a copy of this book.

6

"Paiva":
The History of a Song

"José de Paiva Raposo . . . just and generous, high-spirited, speaking accurate chiSena and Maganja . . . possessing a special knack of dealing with the Africans, who adored him."
—J. de Azevedo Coutiho, Memorias de um Velho Marinheiro e Soldado de Africa

"Then on Sundays, when they stopped work, they used to say that Paiva was only an ordinary stupid man. We got his money for him, yet we got paid so little. So they made a song about him."
—Group interview, 20 September 1978, Mopeia, Quelimane district, Mozambique

From 1890 to 1978, the lower reaches of the Zambezi River, from its confluence with the Shire River down to the coast, were in varying degrees dominated by a single sugar company that was known from 1920 as Sena Sugar Estates, Ltd. This chapter combines oral and archival sources to trace the development over a corresponding period of a single satiric protest song directed against the company. The examples were collected in Mozambique's Zambezi delta in 1975 and 1976. At that time, Sena Sugar Estates operated at Luabo and Marromeu, some forty miles from the Indian Ocean, but its first plantations had been farther upstream, at Mopeia and Caia, where the company still retained land rights. From the number of widely scattered villages and compounds where examples were recorded and from oral testimony about where it had been sung, it is clear that the song was well-known throughout this whole area and, despite its ribald content, regarded with reverence as "a map" (*mappa*) of the people's whole experience:

> This song can't be forgotten. Even our children will have to know it. Because Paiva was the one who made people suffer. This song, whatever may happen, we have to know. That's because it's about what people suffered. All the children will have to be told of the suffering we went through here on earth, and this is the song that we used to sing.[1]

Of the 120 work songs we collected at the same time, no others were spoken of in such terms.

The simplest and apparently oldest version of the song was sung by a group of men who had worked for the company as field laborers in Mopeia. The lines were divided between a lead singer and the remainder of the group, who, grinning with anticipation between the long *Wo—o—o, Wo*s, shouted the final two words with tremendous emphasis:

Paiva—ay,
  Wo—o—o, Wo—
Paiva—ay,
  Wo—o—o, Wo—
Paiva—ay,

Paiva—ay,
  Wo—o—o, Wo—
Paiva—ay,
  Wo—o—o, Wo—
Paiva—ay,

Paiva, ndampera dinyero ache.

  Nsondo wache!

Paiva—ay,
  Wo—o—o, Wo—
Paiva—ay,
  Wo—o—o, Wo—
Paiva—ay,

Paiva—ay,
  Wo—o—o, Wo—
Paiva—ay,
  Wo—o—o, Wo—
Paiva—ay,

Paiva, I have killed his money for him.

  His penis![2]

On this as on five similar occasions, the lines were sung only once in the context of a formal interview, so it is difficult to be certain how the men would have originally performed it as a worksong in the cane fields or on those Sundays when they were not working. Something can, however, be concluded from the actual form of the song, which is very common on the lower Zambezi. Over one-third of the Sena work songs collected shared this basic structure: a topic, usually a name, proclaimed three times by the lead singer and followed by an epigrammatic choral comment. In the following example, José Guillerme, one of Sena Sugar Estate's agents in the compulsory cotton-growing scheme of the 1940s and 1950s in which the company was one of the largest concessionaires, is being mocked by the women cultivators for his bullying behavior. In the song, Guillerme is called by a nickname, "Makwiri," referring to a boast that he could not be harmed by witchcraft:

Makwiri,
  Ay—ay—o—ay
Makwiri, mwanawe
  Ay—ay—ay—ay
Makwiri, mwanawe
  Nafuna ndibale mwana!
  Ndivale ndanda yanga!
  Nkongo wambuyako, zololo!!

Makwiri,
  Ay—ay—o—ay
Makwiri, you young man
  Ay—ay—ay—ay
Makwiri, you young man
  Can I pick my child up!
  Can I pull my knickers up!
  You grandmother's cunt,
    standing there!![3]

The choric epigram is sacrosanct, but the lead singer can, as here, modify the earlier lines, even dropping the name altogether in order to substitute appropriate comments. It seems a reasonable guess that the early Mopeia performances of *Paiva* would similarly have been expanded in the same way with additional remarks about the Paiva of the period.

Songs of this kind, being concerned with particular individuals, are necessarily ephemeral, losing their relevance when the object disappears from the scene. The survival of *Paiva* over such a long period of time can be attributed to an unusual combination of events that extended its life by broadening its meaning. There are three reasons for believing it to have been some eighty years old at the time of our research in 1975. Sena Sugar Estates began life as the Companhia do Assucar de Moçambique in 1890, with plantations at Mopeia, a refinery, and a labor force of some 2,000 workers recruited from the Sena villages in the immediate neighborhood. In 1905, some workers were sent across the Zambezi River to its south bank to open up new cane fields at Caia, where production began in 1908. Two years later an offshoot of the same company took over the plantations located downstream at Marromeu, which had been run since 1902 by a French firm, the Sociedade Açucareira de Africa Portuguesa. Finally, in 1922, field laborers from Marromeu were transferred to build levees and to plant new cane fields at Luabo. Four plantations belonging to the same company were each opened or expanded in turn by a transfer of laborers. Starting in Mopeia, oral testimony declares, the workers carried the song with them, "teaching others . . . until it came to Luabo."[4] If taken quite literally, this gives us a date of before 1905 for its beginning, with this Sena song moving downstream in partial fulfillment of the missionary Torrend's prediction in 1900 that the Sena language would expand and would soon supplant the old Podzo language of the Zambezi delta area.[5]

Second, the singers' own testimony that this is "a very old song" is reinforced by the content of other songs offered by the same informants and described as equally old:

Shamwale, ngawona!　　　　　　　My friend, look at this!
　O—ay—ay—ay　　　　　　　　　　O—ay—ay—ay
Shamwale, ngawona!　　　　　　　My friend, look at this!
　O—ay—ay—ay　　　　　　　　　　O—ay—ay—ay
Shamwale, ngawona!　　　　　　　My friend, look at this!
　O—ay—ay—ay　　　　　　　　　　O—ay—ay—ay

Shi!	*Shi!*
Yalu!	*Yalu!*
Shamwale, ngawona!	My friend, look at this!
Shi!	*Shi!*
Yalu!!	*Yalu!!*[6]

Shamwale, ngawona was the name given to a four-pronged "hoe" introduced by the company in 1890 for planting the first cane in Mopeia. *Shi* and *Yalu* are ideophones expressing the sounds of the hoe piercing the earth and the soil being turned over, the rhythm of the whole song imitating the regimented movements of the laborers planting cane to numbers chanted by an overseer.

Third, there is the content of the *Paiva* song itself. Informants among the retired field laborers who once worked at Mopeia were unanimous in identifying "Paiva" with José de Paiva Raposo, who was appointed administrator of *Prazo* Maganja Aquem Chire, the area of land occupied by the company, in 1889 and who left Mozambique for good in 1900 to marry a Portuguese heiress.[7] José de Paiva Raposo was nineteen years old in 1889. He was the second son of Ignacio José de Paiva Raposo, who had made a fortune as the largest ivory trader in Lourenço Marques in the 1860s.[8] In 1874, having gambled away his wealth in Lisbon and fathered five sons, he was granted a concession of 20,000 hectares in *Prazo* Maganja Aquem Chire to grow and process opium. One other *Paiva* song, remembered only by a single aging informant, may just possibly refer to this senior Paiva Raposo, who introduced to his poppy plantations the first irrigation machinery ever used on the lower Zambezi River.

Paiva,	Paiva,
O—ay	*O—ay*
Paiva,	Paiva,
O—ay—ay	*O—ay—ay*
Watekenya makina!	*He has set the machine shaking!!*[9]

Whether this song refers to the father or to one of his sons, there is a significant resonance present in the use of the verb *kutekenya,* "to make shake." In the 1850s the same area had been the territorial base of Paul Marianno Vas dos Anjos, a slave trader of Goan origin whose private army of mercenaries devastated the whole of the Shire valley and whose activities David Livingstone publicized in 1860. As was the case with the whole of the Zambezi valley, this area was theoretically under Portuguese sovereignty, with the land actually subdivided into substantial parcels known as *prazos*, which the state rented to individuals. In actuality, however, the authority of the Portuguese government was almost nonexistent, and the *prazo*-holders were able to function as independent barons beyond official control. As such, they were able to exact taxes and labor from the people who lived on their *prazos*, with the tribute paid part of an implicit bargain between patron and client, ruler and ruled, which exchanged protection for such support.

One of these powerful *prazo*-holders was Paul Marianno Vas dos Anjos. He was twice dislodged by Portuguese forces who were helped by slave traders who were his rivals, in 1858 and 1861, but he was able to reestablish his kingdom near the Ruo River's confluence with the Shire. His successors were strong enough to continue to raid their neighbors, finally destroying the Opium Company in 1884. Paul Marianno's African nickname was "Matekenya," the "causer of trembling." [10]

Before Ignácio de Paiva Raposo died in 1887, his Opium Company defunct for three years, he secured a renewal of his concession on the *prazo* for a further thirty years. Two men arrived to take it up on his behalf: his son José and his son-in-law John Peter Hornung, an Englishman of Hungarian descent who had married into the Paiva Raposo family in 1884. After attempting to revive the opium scheme under the auspices of the short-lived Mozambique Produce Company, they secured Portuguese capital for the new Companhia do Assucar de Moçambique in 1890. Hornung was the driving force behind this latter venture, and he was fortunate in having a number of advantages that had been denied to his father-in-law. He came to Zambesia at a time when, after fifty years of intermittent warfare, the Portuguese were at last succeeding in establishing military control. His crop was more suited than opium to the climate and to the type of manual labor that was available. The recent opening up of the port of Chinde gave him a handy port at the mouth of the Zambezi. Reforms of the *prazo* system in 1890 granted to companies prepared to invest capital in the area a monopoly of the labor supply in the area of the conceded *prazos* and also curtailed competition from the peasant agriculture that has grown up in the 1880s after the area had been opened to foreign traders. [11] The growth of powerful new companies—the chartered Companhia de Moçambique, which controlled the area south of the river, and the ambitious Companhia da

Zambesia north of the river—made it impossible for the villagers to escape the new labor laws by migrating within Mozambique. The net of control had tightened, and Hornung was ready to take advantage of the new situation.[12]

Equally important, however, were his Portuguese family connections. At a time when the Portuguese government was particularly sensitive to British activities in the southern half of Mozambique and in the adjacent areas near Lake Malawi, Hornung was able to work behind the Paiva Raposo name, already well-known and officially accepted as having a valid claim in the district. The appointment of José de Paiva Raposo as administrator of the sugar company's *prazo* in 1889 is a case in point. The principal duty of the administrator was to collect an annual head tax of 800 reis, money that could be earned only by working for the company. In rapid succession in 1890 and 1891, he became administrator of the recently subdued *Prazo* Massingiri, and then of *Prazos* Caia, Inhamunho, and Chupanga on the south bank of the Zambezi, into which the company was later to expand. When other members of the family arrived to join the company, Hornung continued to employ this advantage. The first 10,000 hectares of land rented at Luabo, where the new factory was to be opened in 1924, were initially ceded in 1911 to Tomás de Paiva Raposo, who then transferred them to the company in 1927, when he became its general manager. Ignácio de Paiva Raposo, José's elder brother, had a tobacco plantation in Angonia, on Mozambique's eastern border with the Nyasaland Protectorate. In 1914 he transferred his rights in Angonia to the sugar company, which from then on, until the *prazo* system was abolished in 1930, employed large numbers of Ngoni contracted migrant laborers. Ignácio himself served as the company's general manager from 1915 to 1925. As late as 1926, when more land was required for expansion at Mopeia, the additional land was first secured in the names of Artur, Tomás, and Ignácio de Paiva Raposo.

Hornung was immensely successful. At first, in the 1890s, he cashed in on the lucrative liquor trade in the Witwatersrand. Later, after the institution of the Portuguese Labor Code of 1899, he profited from its repressive regulations and then from a dramatic rise of 900 percent in the price of sugar between 1914 and 1919. But he operated more and more from a distance, content to live in a Nash house purchased at West Grinstead in Sussex, where he established a racehorse stud and became master of the hounds. He visited his holdings on the Zambezi only every three years, coming for the last time in 1912, when he distributed "cast-off pink hunting coats" which were "much appreciated" by the Africans.[13] To the people who lived and worked on the sugar company's land, the company remained Paiva Raposo's: "When Hornung came out here, he came as an employee of Paiva Raposo. Nobody knew that this company was an English company. We all thought it was a Portuguese company. Hornung worked just like an employee and he started having his own children . . . but the name which was famous was Paiva Raposo."[14]

This not-very-accurate statement throws a great deal of light on the complaint embedded in the *Paiva* song. For although informants knowledgeable about the area's history who could distinguish between Ignácio, José, Artur, and Tomás insisted that it is José who is the Paiva of the song, thus giving us a starting date of 1890, Paiva is clearly more than an individual. "Paiva" from the very beginning is the company itself, the name under which it alienated land, commandeered labor, and collected taxes. Referring to the Sena custom by which the hunter who killed a game animal received a substantial portion of the meat for himself after distributing specified parts of the animal to the chief on whose land the animal was slain (*Paiva, ndampera dinyero ache*. ["Paiva, I have killed this money for him."]), the song is an attack on the monopolist company system, which is viewed as appropriating virtually all the "meat" despite the fact that it did none of the "hunting." The song is, in short, a satire on the disproportion between wages and profits. Those other Paivas, as we shall see, kept the song alive by maintaining its direct relevance, giving exploitation for each successive generation a fresh human face. But the reference goes beyond them to the system itself. If the actual words seem rather meager compared to the more recent elaborations we are about to consider, it must be remembered that what we have discussed so far is no more than a memory, a skeleton of a performance, an echo of protest.

When we did our research, every village throughout the area had its own preferred version of the *Paiva* song, versions that all preserved the rhymed epigram, which had "to stay like that" because "it came from our fathers."[15] The following example was recorded at Pirira, a village ten kilometers downstream from Luabo and outside the company's concession area. The lead singer was dressed for dancing, with amulets and anklets, a grass skirt and goatskin cap with a squirrel's tail attached, and with a fly whisk in his right hand. He was accompanied by two small hourglass-shaped drums called *njene* and *sugula,* and by women clapping or shaking tin rattles called *machacha.* Normally, we were later informed, there would have been dancing as well—"We imitate the way Paiva walked or the way he talked, just to make people laugh"[16]—but on this occasion, just a few weeks after the country's independence, the atmosphere was more somber:

Paiva,
  Paiva, ndachipita.
Paiva,
  Paiva, ndadungunya.
Paiva,
  Paiva, ndadungunya.
Paiva,
  Mbira ndiyinadumbira.
Paiva,
  Paiva, baba, ndalira.
Paiva,
  Paiva, enda mbalira.
Paiva,
  Paiva, enda mbalira.
Paiva,
  Paiva, ndadungunya.
Paiva,
  Paiva, ndagwa pamoto!
  LUABO!!
Paiva,
  Paiva, ndadungunya.
Paiva,
  Paiva, ndamatama.
Paiva,
  Paiva, ndamatama.
Paiva,
  Paiva, ndalira lero.
Paiva,
  Paiva, ndadungunya.
Paiva,
  Paiva, ndagwa pamoto!
Paiva,
  Paiva, enda mbalira.
Paiva,
  Paiva, ndagwa pamoto!
  PAIVA, LUABO!!

Paiva,
  Paiva, I've felt it!
Paiva,
  Paiva, I've complained.
Paiva,
  Paiva, I've complained.
Paiva,
  The mbira *is my witness.*
Paiva,
  Paiva, father, I've wept.
Paiva,
  Paiva, going weeping.
Paiva,
  Paiva, going weeping.
Paiva,
  Paiva, I've complained.
Paiva,
  Paiva, I've fallen on a fire!
  LUABO!!
Paiva,
  Paiva, I've complained.
Paiva,
  Paiva, I'm speechless.
Paiva,
  Paiva, I'm speechless.
Paiva,
  Paiva, I've wept today.
Paiva,
  Paiva, I've complained.
Paiva,
  Paiva, I've falled on a fire!
Paiva,
  Paiva, going weeping.
Paiva,
  Paiva, I've fallen on a fire!
  PAIVA, LUABO!![17]

It may not be immediately apparent that this is the same song, but after a repetition of the above lines with many of the words replaced by vocalizations, the following emerged, repeated twenty-odd-times:

> O—o—o
>   *O—o—o*
> O—o—o
>   *O—o—o*
> O—o—o
>   *O—o—o*
> *Paiva, ndampera dinyero ache.*
> *Nsondo wache!*[18]

The triple denunciation of the essential germ of the song those three "Paiva's" by the lead singer before the choral epigram—has been expanded into a long introductory solo with a response of its own, a solo that imitates the original version in three ways. It retains the denunciatory repetition of Paiva's name. And finally, the rhyme of the epigram, the device that gives it its punch, is reflected in a virtuoso exhibition of sound patterning and verbal play—the splendid pun of *Mbira ndiyinadumbira,* echoed in the rhymes and half rhymes of *Paiva, baba, ndalira* and *Paiva, enda mbalira,* and later manipulation of the stop consonants in:

> *Paiva, ndamatama,*
>   *   *   *
> *Paiva, ndagwa pamoto!*

The singer described how he learned this version from his father, who had come up from the coast to work in the cane fields of Luabo: "When he went to the garden to dig, he'd be digging and he'd be singing at the same time, and I used to come and stand beside him. Whatever he was singing about, or whatever he said, I used to listen to." It may well be that the reference to the *mbira* is a clue to his father's performance of the song as a solo. Certainly, the handling of the language in these devices, which are described as "making the words stronger" and "making the song flow faster," shows his father to have been a skilled poet.[19]

Most striking of all, however, is a distinct shift in the song's meaning. Obviously, the Paiva whose speech and walk would be imitated in the dance cannot be the Paiva of the 1890s or, indeed, any Paiva of the days when the company was centered at Mopeia, for the song is located very firmly in Luabo. At the same time, the emphasis of the words is less on the economic inequalities castigated in the epigram than on an intensely personal suffering—grief, pain, endurance—for which an individual Paiva is held responsible. Satire implies a certain buoyancy, but at this performance no one laughed. The extra words take the song beyond satire to lament, and it was this version of the song that the singers described as "a map" of suffering that "our children will have to know."

The first of the Paiva Raposos to have an interest in the Luabo area was, as we have seen, Tomás, a nephew of José, who was ceded land at the modern Luabo in 1911. Ostensibly, he was to grow sugarcane there himself, but there is no record of any being planted until Hornung moved his operations downstream in 1924. By this stage, Hornung's empire was enormous. The area over which he exerted economic control in one form or another—land ceded directly to the company, land under his personal administration, and land to which he held monopoly labor rights—comprised some 16,000 square miles. His labor force on his four plantations reached 30,000, made up of local Sena and Podzo people from the Zambezi valley, but also including Ngoni from northwest Mozambique and Nyasaland, and Lomwe and Chuabo people from the part of Mozambique northeast of the valley. He had a chain of company stores stretching from Chinde to Tambara and staffed by Indian employees, owned a 50 percent share in the river transport companies, and was, de facto, the sole market for crops grown by peasant farmers in the area. His power persisted until 1930, when the *prazo* system and its concessions were finally ended and a Portuguese administration was established throughout the Zambesia area. Until then, not surprisingly since Sena Sugar Estates was by now fully capitalized with British investments, Hornung found it convenient to continue to operate behind the facade provided by the Paiva Raposo name—this despite the fact that Ignácio, general manager from 1915 to 1925, was embezzling money, and that Tomás, general manager from 1927 to 1930, was diverting labor from the plantations to work on the construction of a great new bridge across the Zambezi.[20]

Thus, what descended on Luabo in 1922–24 was a company administration with near absolute power acting under the name of Paiva Raposo, the actual authority being delegated to Artur, another brother who was responsible for marking out the new cane fields.

Charles Speller, an Englishman who worked for the company very briefly in Luabo in 1923, gave a graphic account of how that power was exercised:

> The youthful labour clerk (Portuguese) was resident magistrate and inflicted with the assistance of a band of cut-throat retainers—"Raposo's men"—what seemed to me a terrible punishment with an instrument called a "Palmaterio." This thing was the shape and size of a ping-pong bat but much thicker and was perforated with holes like a colander. The hand of the victim was seized and many blows were struck on the palm; then the other palm and then the buttocks. On one occasion I saw the instrument handed over to a second retained to carry on. The result of this treatment is to leave the victim in agony which must endure for a considerable time and renders him completely collapsed. The action of the instrument is that when a blow is struck the skin is drawn up into the many holes and a certain amount of force appears necessary to pull or twist the thing away from the flesh.[21]

In these circumstances, it is not surprising that the *Paiva* song from Mopeia should have found a receptive audience in the new area, or that its meaning should have become modified in the manner already noted.

There is one other detail of the Pirira performance that has not yet been discussed, but that is present in all our remaining examples of the song:

Paiva,	Paiva,
Ay—ay	*Ay—ay*
Paiva,	Paiva,
Ay—ay	*Ay—ay*
Paiva ndi Mama	Paiva is Mother
Ay—ay	*Ay—ay*
Paiva, ndampera dinyero ache.	*Paiva, I have killed his money for him.*
Nsondo wache!	*His penis!*[22]

This version was recorded in the same village as our first example, but from the women, including wives of the retired laborers. The differences are slight, but nonetheless merit attention. As at Pirira, the last line has been flattened into a single utterance sung entirely by the chorus and no longer divided, as the words would seem to require, between the lead singer and the chorus. An extra chorus line has been added. And, third, the extra words *Paiva ndi Mama* ("Paiva is Mother") by the lead singers draws on the metaphor of kinship to make a bitter comment on Paiva's failure to fulfill the company's responsibilities to the area's people in its assumed role as "parent."[23]

These changes seem to be linked to the demands of performance. The song was sung this time with many repetitions as the accompaniment to dancing—the extra chorus line and the flattened epigram making *Paiva* more exactly similar to other women's dance songs, such as *Makwiri*, quoted above. The women stood in a circle, bending forward from the waist and clapping or clacking pieces of wood or shaking tin rattles. One at a time they performed brief solos, dancing on the spot or backing slowly round the circle, eyes fixed on the ground slightly to the left and with elbows crooked, shaking their buttocks to the rhythm. This dance had no particular name, and it apparently made no special reference to the words of the song, as other songs were danced in an identical manner.[24] The verses were repeated as long as the supply of individual performers lasted, in this instance for about twelve minutes, while the lead singer introduced further variations:

Verse 2	Paiva ni baba.	Paiva is father.
Verse 3	Paiva tabusa.	Paiva makes us suffer.
Verse 4	Paiva, dinyero.	Paiva, money.

From this point onward, while the song continued, members of the group, including the male audience, began shouting their own allegations against Paiva:

WOMEN:

Kititabuse iwe,	You are making us suffer,
Nakundimenya,	Beating me up,
Nakundimenya, iwe!	You, beating me up!
Nyamachende, iwe!	Mr. Balls-Owner, you!
Mboli yako!	Your penis!
Kutitabusa peze.	You are making us suffer for nothing.
Ine trabayere peze.	I am working for nothing.
Mbatiwona nyatwa na misale.	We have seen sufferings with the sugar.
Ona, tambira mbondo ziwiri basi!	Look, we're receiving just two hundred—that's all!

Tambira mikuruzado mitato basi,
   mboli yako!!

Getting three small crusados only,
   your penis!!

MEN:

Ngamala dinyero ache nkabe
   kuyiona tai.

After everything, you can't see
   your money at all.

Ndima ziwiri zanyankwira,

Two whole tasks of earthing-up
   [the cane],

Kotoka kotoka antu mbasiyale.

People knocking off, knocking off
   at suppertime,

Kotoka na midiya yamasiku,

Knocking off in the middle of the
   night,

Ngamala tempo yache nkabe
   kuyiona tai.

After everything, you can't see
   your time at all.

Paiva! Mpika chita Paiva!

Paiva! That's what Paiva did!

It will be seen that the women complained mainly about ill-
treatment and the men about poor pay and long working hours.
When the song reemerged from the shouting, some interchange of
words had taken place between the lead singer and the chorus:

Paiva!
   Tampera dinyero ache!

Paiva!
   *We have killed his money for
      him!*

Paiva!
   Tampera dinyero ache!

Paiva!
   *We have killed his money for
      him!*

Paiva!
   Tampera dinyero ache!

Paiva!
   *We have killed his money for
      him!*

   Tampera dinyero ache!

   *We have killed his money for
      him.*

   Nsondo wache!
Nsondo wache!
   Paiva ndi Baba—ay
Nsondo wache!
   Paiva ndi Baba—ay
Nsondo wache!
   Paiva ndi Mama—ay
   Paiva, mdampera dinyero ache.

   Nsondo wache!

   His penis!
His penis!
   Paiva is Father—ay
His penis!
   Paiva is Father—ay
His penis!
   Paiva is Mother—ay
   *Paiva, I have killed his money
      for him.*

   His penis!

It is in this form, as a women's extended dance-song, that the majority of the examples we collected appear and that the song seemed to be most popular. Since the mid-1950s, in fact, *Paiva* has become a women's song—the takeover being illustrated in one performance when an old man sang the original version, breaking the epigram into two sections, only to be forced to change, from the second verse onward, by the women who insisted on joining in. To understand this development, we must look again at the area's history.

After the end of the *prazo* system and the imposition of direct Portuguese administration in 1930, the company's connections with the Paiva Raposo family were gradually broken off. Tomás left in 1930, replaced as general manager by Max Thurnheer, and after Artur's death in 1932 no Paiva Raposo held a managerial position with the company. There were no more advantages to be wrung from the name. However, the changes of 1930 had also altered the problem of finding adequate supplies of labor. The old *prazos* has been, in effect, labor pools, and the *prazo*-holder had privileged access to their labor. From 1930 onward, labor became competitive, applications for it being channeled through the new Portuguese district administrators and *chefes do posto*. Sena Sugar Estates immediately lost its best Ngoni labor to Southern Rhodesia but, using a newly instituted bribery allowance, was for the time being able to recoup its supply from areas in which the Lomwe people lived.

But then came two fresh crises. In 1936, following a collapse in world sugar prices, the company was forced as part of its policy of retrenchment to close down its operations at Caia and Mopeia, and two years later, with the creation of a government Cotton Export Board, instructions went out to all district administrators to give priority to growing cotton to supply the Portuguese textile industry.[25] Effectively anticipating this move, Hornung had in 1936 acquired the recently demarcated cotton concessions for the entire area from Luabo westward to the Shire River. His aim in securing this concession was not to diversify production. And it emphatically was not to give the local African people an alternative way of making a living. General Manager Thurnheer explained in 1942 the company's thinking:

> Contrary to the system established and observed by us within our concession area (where only the women receive the seed but never the men), seed is in all other sections also distributed to the male population, making them cotton growers and as such giving them a legal rea-

son not to work, notwithstanding the fact that it is always the women that grow the cotton, even in respect of the seed distributed to men. . . . However, one thing is sure and that is that this company must retain its present cotton concession while there is a government controlled cotton scheme—profit or no profit—because on its retention depends the control of so much needed local labour for our sugar plantations.[26]

The company undertook to run the local cotton concession to prevent anyone else from running it and thereby acquiring access to local labor. While some labor continued to be available from other districts, Hornung's old empire had in effect shrunk to the borders of the cotton concession, within which he retained monopoly rights. This policy had a disastrous impact on the African population. Under the cotton regulations, seed was distributed free to the growers, and then the cotton was bought at a fixed price, was transported at fixed rates in Portuguese ships only, and was sold in Lisbon at prices fixed below world-market prices. The only means by which the concession holder could increase his own profits was by increasing the actual amount of cotton wrung from the growers. In the case of Sena Sugar Estates, this meant cotton produced by women and children whose husbands and fathers were already forced to work on the sugar plantations. The sufferings of the period, including famine and sexual assaults, are recorded in a number of songs about the cotton scheme, including the following, in which Paiva is again mentioned in two out of ten verses:

Paiva, Mama, ndagopa!   Paiva, Mother, I'm scared!
Ine, Paiva, ndamangiwa.   Paiva, I've been tied up.
Ine, Paiva, ndiri perezo.   Paiva, I've been in prison.
  Mama, tamanqua ife!   *Mama, we've been beaten!*
Paiva, ndagona.   Paiva, I'm worn out.
Paiva, ndagopa.   Paiva, I'm scared.
Paiva, ndagopa.   Paiva, I'm scared.
  Mama, tamangwa ife!   *Mama, we've been beaten!*[27]

The new dependence on local labor in the cane fields and the use of women as cotton growers affected the original *Paiva* song in two ways. By this stage a new Paiva Raposo had appeared on the scene. This was Alberto, a nephew of José and a brother of Tomás. He had worked in the labor office at Mopeia until, following a riot provoked by his brutal treatment of field-workers, extreme even by the standards of the time, he followed his uncle Ignácio into the Zambezi Bridge construction project. In 1940, however, he returned to the sugar company as general factotum and troubleshooter, beginning with the labor office. His return to the cane fields was a signal for a revival of the *Paiva* song, which, while still of general relevance to the company as a whole, had had no specific human target since 1932: "They used to get excited when Paiva was coming to the field. Paiva used to go on a motor trolley to the field. When they saw that he was coming, they would start singing. With these things he didn't get cross. You could swear at him and he just smiled."[28] Stories about his activities were legion—of beatings and cheatings, of his embezzlement of cotton-concession money, of three-day orgies on the company's paddle steamers, moving slowly downstream to Chinde and stopping occasionally to take on fresh women and girls.[29] His nickname was *Chibeket* (meaning "bucket"), which referred to his toothless and pendant lower jaw, and it was his mannerisms that would have been imitated in the dance accompanying the Pirira version of the *Paiva* song.

Meanwhile, the cotton concession continued its operations. Responsibility for seeing that the women cultivated their obligatory half hectare of land lay, not with the concession holder, but with the local Portuguese authorities—the administrator at Mopeia and the *chefe do posto* at Luabo. This was another of the company's complaints about the whole business. As long as cotton growing had the backing of the authorities, the company could rely on a small annual profit, usually averaging some £7,000. By the early 1950s, however, when Mozambique as a whole was producing 32,000 tons of cotton annually, thereby supplying 95 percent of Portugal's needs,[30] the pressures began to relax, and Sena Sugar Estates found itself facing a series of substantial losses, estimated by 1954 as between sixty and seventy thousand pounds sterling—far too heavy a price to be paid for the labor monopoly that, nevertheless, the company could not afford to give up. The man given responsibility for reversing these losses was Alberto de Paiva Raposo. The Portuguese authorities turned a blind eye while *Chibeket*, reemploying men like José Guillerme, who had worked earlier in the Mopeia administration, succeeded in recreating in the cotton fields the atmosphere of the early 1940s. It was at this time that *Paiva* became a women's song that placed special emphasis on beatings and arrests and the hardships of famine.

Thus, as a consequence, it became adapted in yet another way, for to speak of women's songs is not to speak only of words and music for dancing. One of the most popular forms of expression on the lower Zambezi was the song that broke off halfway through, permitting an improved drama enacting the song's main themes to be performed. The song framed the drama. This happened most frequently in songs that satirized particular individuals—a policeman, a cotton overseer, a *chefe do posto*, or a state-appointed village headman. The stage was the circle of singers that remained unbroken, and anyone, it seemed, could perform, the actors frequently being replaced halfway through by women who felt that they could do better. The audience was the remaining women, who screamed with laughter at the caricatures of the rapes and briberies and beatings. The subjects varied—the administrator drunk in his litter, police brutality during a raid for illegally distilled alcohol, the cotton overseer mistreating women under his charge. The following is an example of one such song-with-drama. It describes the local *chefe do posto* providing forced labor to one Dona Anna d'Oliveira, a small-scale planter and trader:

Dona Anna, ay—ay	Dona Anna, ay—ay
Ay—ay—ay	*Ay—ay—ay*
Ay—ay, Dona Anna,	Ay—ay, Dona Anna,
Ay—ay	*Ay—ay*
"Bwera uke!" ntekume,	Telling us, "Go there!"
"Bwera kunu!" ntekume,	Telling us, "Come here!"
Dona Anna, ay—ay	Dona Anna, ay—ay
Ay—ay—ay	*Ay—ay—ay*
Ay—ay, ndikamangewa,	Ay—ay, I used to be tied up.
Ay—ay—ay	*Ay—ay—ay*
"Bwera uku!" ntekume,	Telling us, "Go there!"
"Bwera kunu!" ntekume,	Telling us, "Come here!"
Nakamangewa, ay—ay	Used to be tied up, ay—ay
Ay—ay—ay	*Ay—ay—ay*
Ay—ay, mangewa nankambala.	Ay—ay, tied up with a rope.
Ay—ay	*Ay—ay*
"Bwera uku!" ntekume,	Telling us, "Go there!"
"Bwera kunu!" ntekume	Telling us, "Go there!"

* * *

POLICEMAN: Lima, lima, lima [ari]! Menya, menya, menya muntu [ari]! Menya, menya! Feda puta,

POLICEMAN: Dig, dig, dig! [sobbing]! Beat her, beat her, beat her [sobbing]! Beat her, Beat her! Son of mwanamba, feda puta! Nkhabilima tai polola tai. Nakugona lero, nakugona lero, nakugona lero [ari]. Nkhazi asafuna goniwa uyu. Ndakupata lero.

a bitch, you dog, son of a bitch! You haven't worked today, you lazy bitch. I'll fuck you today, I'll fuck you today, I'll fuck you today [sobbing]! This woman wants to be fucked. I've caught you this time.

WOMAN: Nkabi nyo nyo nyo pianga! Goniwa kwene mbwene.

WOMAN: No, I don't want to be beaten! It's better to be screwed.

POLICEMAN: Feda puta!

POLICEMAN: Son of a bitch!

* * *

Dona Anna, baba,
  Ay—ay—ay
Ay—ay, tikamangewa, baba!

  Ay—ay
"Bwera uku!" ntekume,
"Bwera kunu!" ntekume.

Dona Anna, father!
  Ay—ay—ay
Ay—ay, we used to be tied up father!
  Ay—ay
Telling us, "Go there!"
Telling us, "Come here!"[31]

The *Paiva* song was also used to frame such dramatizations. In the following example, unusual in that no one is directly subjected to violence, the song is halted to allow a scene from the cane fields to be enacted, the women taking the parts of cane cutters and the overseer [*capitão*]:

Ay—ay
Paiva ndi Mbuya
Ay—ay
Paiva, ndawona nyatwa.
  Ay—ay
Paiva—ay
  Paiva, ndampera dinyero ache

  Nsondo wache!
  Ay—ay
Paiva—ay
  Ay—ay
Paiva, ndinamangiwa.
  Ay—ay
Paiva—ay

Ay—ay
Paiva is Protector.
Ay—ay
Paiva, I've seen suffering.
  Ay—ay
Paiva—ay
  Paiva, I've killed his money for him.
  His penis!
  Ay—ay
Paiva—ay
  Ay—ay
Paiva, I'm being arrested
  Ay—ay
Paiva—ay

Paiva, ndampera dinyero ache.

Nsondo wache!
Ay—ay
Paiva—ay
Ay—ay
Paiva ndi Mama,
Ay—ay
Kumanga pika chitwa.
Paiva—ay
Paiva, ndampera dinyero ache.

Nsondo wache!

Paiva, I've killed his money for him.

His penis!
Ay—ay
Paiva—ay
Ay—ay
Paiva is Mother,
Ay—ay
Arrests used to be made.
Paiva—ay
Paiva, I've killed his money for him.

His penis!

* * *

FIRST MAN: Nzungo anativinganya. Nzungo! Asakuti mala Horsi. Asakuti mala—Hair! Misale! Uyu, nyansondo wamache! Uyu wakuchena uyu. Anatipasa nyatwa maningi uyu. Ono, nyankongo wamache dona uyu. Ninyi mache anatisanya ono nyankongo wa mache one. Uwi! Uwi! Uwi! Ndatemeka ine nasupada. Capitão! Ali kupi capitão?

FIRST MAN: The white man's always harassing us. The white man! Horst's finishing us off. He's finishing us off—Hair! Sugar! This one, Mr. Mother's Cunt! That other one is alright. That one gave us a lot of trouble. That one, Mr. Lady's Mother's Cunt. His mother's cunt! He's harassing us, that one. Ouch! Ouch! Ouch! I've cut myself with a cane knife. Capitão! Where is the capitão?

SECOND MAN: Hedi! Hedi! Iwe, capitão! Iwe, capitão! Iwe! Iwe! Iwe!

SECOND MAN: Head! Head! You, capitão! You, capitão! You! You! You!!

CAPITÃO: Nkongo wamako uyu. Unakala mbutisanya. Mwachota tane tenepo? Mwachita tane nsali? Agora imwe musagopa! Azungo nkabe kugopa. Kuti chinchino anabwera nkabe. Agora iwe unasiya nsali kwenda katema mwendo! Koberi zinatambirewe parwezi brinkadera iwe? Usastragari tai?

CAPITÃO: Ah, you, you mother's cunt! You're always causing trouble for us. How did you do that? How were you chopping the cane? Now you're scared! The white men don't get scared. He won't come now just for that. Now you'll be leaving the cane to go and cut your leg! With the money you are paid in a month, do you think it's just a game? You're really ruining things!!

SECOND MAN: Kinyentu zishanu basi!!

FIRST MAN: Kinyentu ziwiri!!! Apima ndima kumi na zinai. Muntu mbodzi ine kapaji kuzitema?

SECOND MAN: Koberi sache! Koberi sache mbisikala kinyento zishanu basi!

CAPITÃO: Agora iwe waziwa koberi sache kinyento zishanu. Tenkitema utome langana misali dretu. *Não podi* jombesa ife macapitao tai. Poso inadyefe nkinapaswa nayiwe tai!

FIRST MAN: Terefache njene idapangiswa. Ndinachitatane ine pano? Ndapangiwa tenepa konta yandima ndi zenezi.

CAPITÃO: Nkazi, tenkiteme tenepa. Tenepa!

*   *   *

Ay—ay
Paiva—ay
Ay—ay
Paiva, ndawone nyatwa.
Ay—ay
Chokera na machibesi.
Paiva, ndampera dinyero ache.

Nsondo wache!
Ay—ay
Ay—ay
Paiva—ay
Ay—ay
Kudya nkabe
Ay—ay

SECOND MAN: Only five shillings!!

FIRST MAN: Two shillings! He measured out fourteen tasks. Can one person like me cut all that?

SECOND MAN: The money! The money comes to only five shillings!

CAPITÃO: Now, you know his money is five shillings! To cut cane you must first look at it properly. Don't make us *capitães* pay! The food that we eat is not supplied by any of you!

FIRST MAN: This is the task I have given myself. How can I do it here all by myself? I've been told that the task's size is like this!!

CAPITÃO: Woman, you must cut the cane this way. This way!

[Chopping sounds]

*   *   *

Ay—ay
Paiva—ay
Ay—ay
Paiva, I've seen suffering.
Ay—ay
Starting from early morning.
Paiva, I've killed his money for him.
His penis!
Ay—ay
Ay—ay
Paiva—ay
Ay—ay
Without food!
Ay—ay

Paiva, ndinamangiwa.   Paiva, I'm being arrested.
Paiva, ndampera dinyero ache.   *Paiva, I've killed his money for*
                                           him.
Nsondo wache!   *His penis!*[32]

It should now be apparent how complete is the cycle of meanings invoked by this performance. The complaints in the drama about conditions of work in the cane fields (about poor pay and large assigned tasks, about the attitudes of plantation managers and the black *capitães*, as revealed in the lack of concern over an accident) are supplemented by the complaints in the song itself about forced labor, hunger, beatings, and arrests.[33] All these meanings are contained in *Paiva*, a man significantly described as *Mbuya* ("Protector" or "Lord") because, though briefly reincarnated in the 1940s and 1950s, he is more than an ordinary man. Alberto de Paiva Raposo died in 1957, and, after his death, no further Paiva Raposos worked for Sena Sugar Estates in Mozambique. Yet *Paiva* was being sung in 1975 and 1976, and sung not only by the older women who recalled the cotton songs like *Makwiri* at our request, but also by newly married girls with young babies, to whom questions about Paiva's physical identity were questions without meaning. The name had become a symbol, the different strands of experience under José, Ignácio, Tomás, Artur, and Alberto de Paiva Raposo uniting in a single word that had come to stand for the system as a whole under which the people suffered for some seventy years or more.

Hence, in our final example, sung by a young woman in her twenties, Paiva's defeat is a recent occurrence:

Ay—ay   *Ay—ay*
Paiva, para—ay!   Paiva, stop—ay!
Ay—ay   *Ay—ay*
Paiva, baba—ndine Julia   Paiva, father, it's me—Julia
Ay—ay   *Ay—ay*
Nyatwa, nyatwa, kweyiwa!   Suffering, suffering, pushed
                                           around!

Paiva, ndampera dinyero ache.   *Paiva, I've killed his money for*
                                           him.
Nsondo wache!   *His penis!*
Ay—ay   *Ay—ay*
Paiva—ay   Paiva—ay
Ay—ay   *Ay—ay*
Paiva, mwanawe   Paiva, young man
Ay—ay   *Ay—ay*

6. Old-style migrant laborers' huts at the Sena Sugar Estates' Luabo plantation, still in use in 1977. (Photo by Leroy Vail.)

Paramatoria
Paiva, ndampera dinyero ache.

Nsondo wache!
Zona Forenca
Zona Machuane
Secretário Jolijo
Secretário Luis Gomes
Ay—ay
Paiva, mwanawe
Ay—ay
Paiva ndioyipa.
Ay—ay
Chinchino tapulumuka!
Takamangiwa na nkhabala
    kunduli!
Ay—ay
Baba—ay
Ay—ay
Baba, ndamwa koropu!

Ndalezera—ay
Ay—ay
Paiva, ndampera dinyero ache.

Nsondo wache!

Palmatoria
*Paiva, I've killed his money for
    him.*
His penis!
Forenca zone
Machuane zone
Secretary George
Secretary Luis Gomes
Ay—ay
Paiva, young man
Ay—ay
Paiva is diabolical.
Ay—ay
Now we have escaped!
We used to be tied up with rope.

Ay—ay
Father—ay
Ay—ay
Father, I've drunk *koropu* [cashew
    fruit wine]
I'm drunk—ay
Ay—ay
*Paiva, I've killed his money for
    him.*
His penis!

Zona Forenca	Forenca zone
Zona Machuane	Machuane zone
Secretário Jolijo	Secretary George
Secretário Luis Basto	Secretary Luis Basto[34]

The *zonas* to which the singer refers were the new administrative subdivisions of the area, and the *secretários* were the new FRELIMO party officials. "Paiva is diabolical," but "Now we have escaped": in this version of the song, Paiva has been at last overthrown by FRE-LIMO.

We began by describing *Paiva* as a satiric protest song directed at Sena Sugar Estates, noting later that it modulates in at least one version into a lament. The problem remains of trying to understand why the words of this song have such a strong hold on the imagination of the people of the area, which in turn raises the question of precisely what kind of song we are dealing with here. Clearly, in spite of the verbal felicity of the Pirira version or the comic vitality of the drama, this is not a song that is cherished for primarily artistic reasons. The words, meaning in practice the epigram, were preserved because "they came from our fathers" and "say what they suffered."[35] Without this explicit reference outside the text to the social and economic background, they say little. There is no attempt to portray the social injustices as a whole in the work that is autonomous and self-explanatory. Thus, instead of using the song to throw light on the history of the region, one must use a fairly detailed knowledge of the history itself to make much sense of the song. This applies not only to the epigram itself, and to those generalized metaphors for suffering ("I've fallen on fire" or "I've seen hardship"), but even to the drama version where, though the cane-field incident is complete in itself, the song of which it is a part speaks of beatings and arrests and hunger: complaints by the women that cannot be understood fully without at least some reference to the workings of the compulsory cotton-growing scheme.

At the same time, the song is clearly critical. Though at first glance the oldest version of the song seems little more than a jeer, it is a jeer that springs from an intellectual rejection of economic injustice; and although the later women's versions may seem only complaints, they are complaints that refer back to a vision of an ordered village society where people might grow their own crops, tend their children, brew drink, and earn their money without the constant interference of the company as policeman, magistrate, or *capitão*. These images are not established within any version of the song itself, but they emerge naturally from the attempt to relate it to known historical circumstances. It is in this sense that we have used the words *satire, protest,* and *lament.*

But there are difficulties. The versions of the song considered so far are five of the most interesting of fourteen examples. Yet even in these, the proportion of repetitive obscenity is very high. It is hard to share the conviction that *Nsondo wache* is effective no matter how often it is sung, or to find much interest in these performances that spend eight or ten minutes cataloging Paiva's private parts. Even the protest element has its dubious aspects. When the men's version was being sung for Paiva's benefit in the Luabo cane fields, we are told that he "just smiled." The quotation continues: "You could swear at him and he just smiled. Because people are working. You can sing what you want. When he comes, he just smiles and after a while he goes away. . . . From there it went to the village. And when they used to sing their dance, *Paiva* had to be sung, to show it to the women and children—to say that this is the song we sing for Paiva in the cane field."[36] The complaint was laughed off by a labor overseer who knew the men would work with better heart now that they had insulted him. In the words of another informant, "We like [the song] so much that we do the work with strength."[37] Work song and protest song, in the context of a system of forced labor, would seem a contradiction in terms, and there are, in fact, other work songs in which the "protest" is directed against fellow workers for not pulling their weight. A final difficulty is that last comment, about taking *Paiva* home to the village for the women and children to hear, as though some victory had been gained!

It is a problem faced by all writers on Mozambique. In the short stories of Bernardo Honwana, a recurring theme is the impatience of the young at the apparent futility of the old. One story, "Dina," describes a situation that, though set in the extreme south of Mozambique, in Ronga territory, closely parallels that on the sugar estates of the Zambezi River valley. Madala, a field laborer, seems incapable of revolt. His work is long and hard, the overseer is a sadistic bully, his daughter is assaulted before his eyes. But when the young leader of the neighboring work gang urges him to take the lead in violent protest, Madala shrugs his shoulders, accepts a bottle of wine for his daughter's violation, and goes meekly back to work—while the young man spits and calls him "Dog!" In others of Honwana's stories the problem is taken into the family, with fathers desperately trying to conceal from their sons the brutal facts of the colonial world, and the sons losing affection and respect for their fathers, who often curse—but never to the white man's face. Honwana pursues the consequences for the younger generation—a loneliness and cruelty, born of frustration and bordering on sadism, expressed most often in the mistreatment of animals.[38]

What are we to make of *Paiva* in this context? The song was apparently cherished for some eighty years. During this time, it was constantly recreated in new forms. Even after independence, in 1976, the children were expected to learn it for its record of past hardship. But its protest against economic injustice never was expanded into strikes or open rebellion, and its only practical effect seems to have been to make the laborers do the company's work more efficiently.

Part of an answer seems to lie in the origins of the form of the song. We have taken *Paiva* back to the 1890s, but obviously it did not appear without some precedents. A form presumably existed to control the idea to be expressed, and assumptions existed about the kind of material to be expressed and about the type of expression appropriate to the genre. Unfortunately, very little material is available from the nineteenth century to substantiate this point. No Portuguese travelers, for whom the area with which we are dealing lay on the direct route from Quelimane to the interior of the Zambezi valley, ever bothered to say more than that "the natives are fond of music." While British missionaries and administrators who traveled in the area were usually more curious, often noting down fragments of canoe or palanquin-carrying songs, their comments are of limited value. Most of them, on their first arrival in Africa, were ill-equipped to understand what they were hearing, and they seem capable of believing anything. The famous canoe song *Sina Mama, sina Baba, sina mama wakulema naye / Mama ndiwe Mariya* ("I have no mother, I have no father, I have no mother to nurse me / My mother is Maria.") was universally understood to be an ancient Jesuit hymn, a relic of the ruined mission at Zumbo that David Livingstone had described in his *Missionary Travels*. It became one of the tourist attractions of the journey to Nyasaland, rivaling a visit to Mary Livingstone's grave in Chupanga. In fact, however, the reference is to Senhora Maria at Chimaura, mother (or aunt) of the notorious warlord Matekenya and herself the owner of a large contingent of slaves.[39] Even odder are some of the translations of the palanquin-carrying songs:

> We travel by night, to court the moon,
> Quickly, quickly trot.
> The river has gone to find the sea,—
> Waters of salt, waters of salt.
> The mudfish sleeps, he has no wings,
> The birds are peeping to see us pass,
> As the white man sleeps.[40]

One can only speculate how many *Nsondo wache*s an embarrassed interpreter had to eliminate to produce such a piece of decadent romanticism.

More helpful are comments from journals kept by members of Livingstone's Zambezi expedition. Livingstone gives an example of a canoe song from Mazaro, "*Uachingere kale,*" which he translates as "You cheated me of old," explaining that it refers to the canoe men's insistence on payment in advance. Alice Werner heard the same song some forty years later as *Wachenjera, Wachenjera, Wachenjera kale.*[41] The connection with *Paiva* is slight but suggestive. In both cases, the complaint is about pay, and the full meaning emerges—as also in *Sina Mama*—after the initial topic has been stated three times. Another aspect of the form into which *Paiva* originally fitted is described in James Stewart's diary: "The canoemen relieve the tedium of paddling by singing. There is little in their songs. Anything serves for a rhyme. Sometimes the songs are not remarkable for their purity. This morning as they were pulling they sang lustily at a song, the refrain of which was *Mkongo ako* [your penis]. I put a stop to that." Stewart's canoe men were also from Mazaro, close by what later became Mopeia, and his high-minded remark about the obscene content of some of these songs is supported by Richard Thornton, who again gives examples.[42] The interesting point here is that many of the work songs used on the sugar plantations had their origin as canoe songs, and in some cases were still used both on the river and in the cane fields, their rhythm being appropriate for both kinds of work:

Asikana mwe,	You young girls,
O	*O*
Pankhotamu	When bending over
Pana ntombwe wanyini!	*That's where the balm of cunt is!*
Kwewa! Kwewa!	Heave! Heave!
O	*O*

Pankhotamu	When bending over
Pana ntombwe wanyini!	*That's where the balm of cunt is!*
Kuba gareta!	Push the trolley!
O	*O*
Pankhotamu	When bending over
Pana ntombwe wanyini!	*That's where the balm of cunt is!*
Kwewa mwadiya!	Pull the canoe!
O	*O*
Pankhotamu	When bending over
Pana ntombwe wanyini!	*That's where the balm of cunt is![43]*

There is nothing surprising about this association of obscenity with manual labor. The palanquin carriers on the Blantyre-Zomba road in 1890 sang songs of the "smoking room" variety,[44] and the same phenomenon has been noted in many other parts of eastern and southern Africa.[45] What matters is that the obscenity of *Paiva* is a normal and accepted feature of the form. The criticism of Paiva, given the work song context in which the idea is expressed, more or less has to be obscene if it is to fulfill all the requirements of the genre. These phrases that become somewhat tedious when carried over into the extended village versions of the song must be understood as part of a convention that, not unnaturally, associates them with hard work.

This is not to say that the words are not obscene. Only within such songs is such language freely permitted. There is a much larger point contained here, however, than straightforward obscenity. In the example we have been considering, the complaint is aimed at an individual, or a series of individuals, personifying the company in its various aspects. Once again, it is the form that legitimizes the criticism. "You could swear at him and he just smiled." To say such things outside the song "would be just insulting him . . . just provoking him," but so long as it was done through singing, "there will be no case."[46]

It has become normal in writing of protest within African societies under colonial rule to emphasize forms of protest understandable in European terms—strikes, demonstrations, stone throwing, letters to newspapers, resolutions from political associations, and finally armed rebellion. What we have in the *Paiva* song is a protest against capitalism expressed in precapitalist terms, using an established form of etiquette, expressing criticism in what the people themselves conceive of as the legitimate channel.

Judging the company by comparing its practices to the customs governing the division of the gains from hunting game, the song reproaches "Paiva," the company, for demanding too much and for providing too little in return. Beyond this, the song does not challenge the existing hierarchy in and of itself. Indeed, in many versions of the song, Paiva is one addressed as a "protector." After the abolition of the *prazo* system in 1930 and the arrival of the Portuguese administration, the people of the area continued to look to the company as patron. The extremes to which such attitudes could be carried are illustrated by one recollected version of the state's takeover in which the whole problem of the violence that followed is attributed to an error in judgment made by the Africans themselves:

> Now, when the government came, we were called to the Company. They told us that the Company was no longer going to deduct taxes from us, because now there was a white government. "You can choose, if you wish to stay with the Company, or if you want to move over to the government. But we will no longer be responsible for any complaints." And then, we all voted to go to the government. And then the Company said to us, "You've now chosen to go the government, but I can tell you in future you are going to cry for the Company." The government was really bad! Our hands are all swollen with this *palmatoria*. Then we went to the Company and said, "We're being beaten up." And then the Company said, "Didn't we tell you? You chose the government, now go to the government. Don't come here to complain about it!"[47]

The *Paiva* song, in its many variations, continued after 1930 to invoke the relationship of client to patron that the people had, with some success, imposed on the company when it was first founded as successor to the earlier *prazo*-holders. Paiva is addressed as "father" and "mother," as though company and workers were bound by kinship relations, and the whole thrust of the song is an appeal that Paiva should have pity. In other instances, as we have seen, Paiva is also addressed as *Mbuya*, "Great One," or "Protector," or "Lord," giving even greater acknowledgment of the acceptance of a patron-client relationship by the area's people.

There are, however, limits to the satisfaction to be gained from such anthropological explanations. The *Paiva* song long ago transcended the form in which it was originally devised, and, given the kind of regime prevailing on the lower Zambezi, one would have thought that the assumptions it embraces and the etiquette it practices would long ago have come to seem irrelevant.

> The reason we sang about Paiva was because of the suffering he made us go through. It's because of the work he used to want us to do, going to work in the sugarcane. A long time ago there was no machinery, and we used to carry the cane on our shoulders. Some were cutting it, some were carrying it to put it on the truck. At the truck there used to be a *capitão*. The *capitão* would give you a cane knife and then when you had filled the truck right up to the top . . . then the *capitão* would take the same knife, go up to the top of the cane truck and start chopping the cane so it would all sink down again. Then you would have to try to fill up the truck again. It would take some time before you finished. If he sees it's getting late, he'll write off your whole day's work. You've spent all that time and you wouldn't get your ticket. . . . Then there were our friends who worked at the factory. The sugar used to be carried in the truck. It used to go from there to the *gombe* [beach, jetty] in a train. Now at the *gombe*, if one of the bags burst . . . you were supposed to carry the bag all the way back to the factory. Then you take a good bag, put it back on your shoulders, and carry it all the way back to the *gombe*. . . . At that time, many people died. That's why we started singing. The owner of the company was called Paiva.[48]

It is this harassment and petty persecution that gives us our clue. In addition to the larger brutalities that were indicated in the earlier part of this chapter, there was a ceaseless day-to-day pressure, exerted in the company's name, that allowed the people no residue of dignity, nothing that they could call their own or that was not in some respect subject to the company's intrusion. Paiva was "the store, the factory, the railway line, the compounds, the cane fields."[49] Everything, in fact, was Paiva—not just in the physical sense but also as an all-pervading essence, the framework of life itself. The recurring phrases "Paiva is father, Paiva is mother," with their disturbing echo of "My mother is Maria" (the slave trader), have a double ring to them, hinting that, despite the protest, complete servitude is always a temptation. One might, as a final degradation, actually accept the company's self-assumed role as "father" and "mother."

The song achieved nothing positive, only occasionally becoming art, and it never emerged into a strike or open rebellion. But, at the very least, it *did* preserve a sense of distance: Not (in the overused and hackneyed metaphor) by acting as a "safety valve" for social pressures, which might express the company's own view of the song but hardly explains its importance as an inheritance to the singers themselves, but by defining a tiny area in which the laborers and their families have a separate identity. As one of the fathers in Honwana's stories put it:

> "Do you know, my son," Papa spoke ponderously, and gesticulated a long time before every word. "The most difficult thing to bear is that feeling of complete emptiness . . . and one suffers very much . . . very, very, very much. One grows with so much bottled up inside, but afterwards it is difficult to scream, you know. . . ."
>
> Mama was going to object, but Papa clutched her shoulder firmly. "It's nothing, mother, but, you know, our son believes that people don't mount wild horses, and that they only make use of the hungry docile ones. Yet when a horse goes wild, it gets shot down, and it's all finished. But tame horses die every day. Every day, d'you hear? Day and day after day—as long as they can stand on their feet." [50]

There are circumstances in which the greater courage can be to go on from day to day, apparently docile yet preserving in an image or slogan or even a curse one small region of the mind that refuses to capitulate completely. The *Paiva* song catered to this, and in a manner that was more than individual. We have been considering it as a text in order to achieve a historical perspective, but the emphasis in all descriptions is naturally on performance. The tune, the drumming, the clapping, the dancing, the technical devices that make the words stronger, were all necessary to bring the performance to life. The singer of *Paiva* belonged to a community of singers, both in the cane fields, where the lead line demanded a response, and at home, with every village having developed its own version of the song. But the community was not only of the living. When the words were sung to this tune with that rhythmic background, when the song appeared in its true form, the link was established with those performances of the past when "our fathers" expressed what "they suffered." What is secured in *Paiva* is not just a private rebellion but a whole tradition of rejection. It is in the song that the people's identity is preserved.

Notes

1. Group interview, Pirira village, Luabo, 25 October 1975. All interviews and songs were recorded in Quelimane district, Mozambique.

2. Sung by Charlie Bicente and the men of Chimbazo village, near Mopeia, 13 August 1975. Other examples of the song not used in this chapter were recorded at Missongue, Murriwa, Cocorico, and Madumo villages, and at the Muidi, Checanyama, Enhaterre, and Caoxe village compounds of the Sena Sugar Estates, Ltd., and also at the Luabo jetty. In this chapter italics within songs indicate choruses.

3. Sung by Mikayera Jasse and Minoria Gwengwe and the women of Chimbazo village, near Mopeia, 13 August 1975. A slight variation was recorded at Madumo village on 17 August 1975.

4. Interview with Jiwa Todo, Madumo village, 2 November 1976.

5. J. Torrend, S. J., *Grammatica do Chisena* (Chupanga, Mozambique, 1900), 2.

6. Sung by Charlie Bicente and the men of Chimbazo village, near Mopeia, 13 August 1975.

7. A *prazo* was a substantial tract of land leased to a private company or individual for a set term of time. For a discussion of the nature of the *prazo* system in the area, see L. Vail and L. White, *Capitalism and Colonialism in Mozambique: A Study of Quelimane District* (London and Minneapolis, 1980), 11–87 passim.

8. D. F. das Neves, *Itinerário de uma Viagem a Caça das Elephantes* (Lisbon, 1878), 200; B. Collin, *J. P. Hornung* (privately printed, foreword dated 1970), 22–23.

9. Sung by Maria Fashe, Anna Tennis, and Laurinia Nicolos, Madumo village, 17 August 1975, after being taught it by Jiwa Todo.

10. M. D. Newitt, *Portuguese Settlement on the Zambesi* (London, 1973), 175–86.

11. Vail and White, *Capitalism and Colonialism*, 58–69.

12. Ibid., 83–90.

13. Collin, *J. P. Hornung*, 79.

14. Interview with men at Mopeia, 10 September 1975.

15. Interview with Jiwa Todo, Madumo village, 2 November 1976.

16. Group interview, Pirira village, 25 October 1976.

17. The *mbira* mentioned in line 8 is the hand piano, a musical instrument often used to accompany solo renditions of songs. Luabo is the place where one of the largest of the company's plantations was situated.

18. Sung by Fernando Nicolas with women of Pirira village, 5 August 1975.

19. Group interview, Pirira village, 25 October 1976.

20. Thurnheer to Hornung, 27 December 1930 and 3 January 1931, file

133, "Recruiting: Quelimane and Angonia," Sena Sugar Estates, Ltd., Archives, Luabo, Mozambique.

21. Charles Speller to J. Harris, 26 February 1927, FO 371/11989, Public Record Office, London.

22. Sung by Minoria Joaquim and women of Chimbazo village, near Mopeia, 13 August 1975.

23. For a discussion of this relationship, see L. Vail and L. White, "Forms of Resistance: Songs and Perceptions of Power in Colonial Mozambique," *American Historical Review* 88, no. 4 (1983): 898–906.

24. Of course, in its original context as a work song, it had no dance or drumming accompaniment. When it was taken to the village and performed for the sake of its words, it is referred to as *Nyimbo de Paiva*, "The Song of Paiva."

25. For a fuller treatment of the history of the cotton-concession scheme, see L. Vail and L. White, "*'Tawani, Machembero!'*: Forced Cotton and Rice Cultivation in the Zambezi," *Journal of African History* 19, no. 2 (1976): 239–64.

26. Report for 1942, file 440, "Final Cotton Reports," Sena Sugar Estates, Ltd., Archives, Luabo, Mozambique.

27. Sung by Virginia João at Mapangane village compound, Luabo, 10 August 1975.

28. Group interview, Pirira village, 25 October 1976.

29. Interview with José Nogueira da Silva, Luabo, August 1975.

30. *Boletim Geral das Colonias*, nos. 341–42 (November-December 1953): 5.

31. Sung in Sena by Julia Manico and the women of Mapangane village, Luabo, 10 August 1975.

32. Sung in Sena by Vittoria Camacho and women of Muanavina village compound, Luabo, 24 August 1975.

33. The plantation managers mentioned in the song's drama are Gerald Horst and his successor, Robert Hair. The speaker hesitates before mentioning Hair and then immediately withdraws criticism of him.

34. Sung by Julia Manica, Mapangane village compound, Luabo, 10 August 1975.

35. Interview with Jiwa Toda, 2 November 1976.

36. Group interview, Pirira village, 25 October 1976.

37. Interview with Jiwa Toda, 2 November 1976.

38. B. Honwana, *We Killed Mangy Dog and Other Mozambique Stories*, trans. Dorothy Guedes (London, 1969).

39. For a musical transcription of "*Sina Mama*," see A. Werner, *The Natives of British Central Africa* (London, 1906), 217. See also Duff MacDonald, *Africana, or the Heart of Heathen Africa* 2 vols. (London, 1882), 2:50; J. de Azevedo Coutinho, *Memorias de um Velho Marinheiro e Solidado de Africa* (Lisbon, 1941), 113–14; and Newitt, *Portuguese Settlement*

on the Zambesi, 279. Senhora Maria is mentioned in another song that originated in the Zambezi, published as no. 6 in E. T. Chakanza, "Nyasa Folk Songs," *African Affairs* 49 (1950): 61.

40. A. Swann, *Fighting the Slave Hunters in Central Africa* (London, 1910), 151. Swann is describing his arrival in Africa in 1883.

41. D. Livingstone and C. Livingstone, *Narrative of an Expedition to the Zambesi and Its Tributaries* (London, 1865), 30; Werner, *Natives of British Central Africa*, 218. (The title from Werner in text translates: "You cheated me, you cheated me, you cheated me of old.")

42. J. Stewart, *The Zambesi Journal of James Stewart*, ed. J. P. R. Wallis (London, 1954), 89; R. Thornton, *The Zambesi Papers of Richard Thornton*, 2 vols., ed. E. C. Tabler (London, 1963), 2:188–89.

43. Sung by Luis Dias, Caoxe compound village, Luabo, 31 August 1975.

44. A. H. Maw, "Transport and Travelling in British Central Africa 1899," *Nyasaland Journal* 8, no. 2 (1955): 13. The editor of the journal, G. D. Hayes, adds the comment that some of these songs later became marching songs of the Kings Africa Rifles.

45. As, for example, in E. E. Evans-Pritchard, "Some Collective Expressions of Obscenity in Africa," in his *The Position of Women in Primitive Societies and Other Essays in Social Anthropology* (Oxford, 1965), 76–101.

46. Interview with Jiwa Todo, Madumo village, 2 November 1976.

47. Group interview, Mopeia, 20 September 1975.

48. Group interview, Pirira village, Luabo, 25 October 1976.

49. Interview with Luiza Drennon, Luabo, November 1976.

50. Honwana, "Papa, Snake & I," in *We Killed Mangy Dog*, 47–48.

7

The Possession of the Dispossessed
Songs as History Among Tumbuka Women

Vimbuza is a type of spirit possession occurring among Tumbuka speakers in Malawi and Zambia.[1] For decades, its incidence has overwhelmingly been among women, and it appears, on the basis of three village censuses, that between 70 and 75 percent of Tumbuka women experience it, most of them poor and uneducated.[2] It is, therefore, a significant phenomenon.

Vimbuza has several phases, beginning with a period in which the symptoms appear.[3] These might include apathy, lassitude, and unexplainable chills and aches in the body, all classic indicators of psychological depression. But, far more tellingly, they might also include rejection of basic patterns of culture. Thus a woman might eat raw or tabooed food instead of cooked food; she might carry her baby upside down on her back or injure it through negligence; she might sleep in the wild bush instead of in the village; she might wander about naked; and, significantly, she might refuse to do the work expected of her as a wife and mother. When a woman exhibits such symptoms, people decide that she is possessed by a wild spirit (*muzimu*, pl: *mizimu*) and needs treatment.

In the possession's second phase, the afflicted woman consults a previously possessed person who is also considered an expert in advising about the herbal medicines (*mankhwala*) appropriate for helping the spirit to "mature" and become articulate. On prescribing the proper medicine, this expert becomes the afflicted woman's *mbuya*, or "spiritual protector." The third and most important phase then takes place, when the *mbuya* organizes a public therapeutic dance attended by the possessed woman and numbers of her female "friends." One large drum (*mphanje*, or *kamango*) and two smaller drums (*mphoza*; *mphiningu*) are beaten in complex rhythmic patterns to "arouse" (*kuwuska*) the spirit so that it might speak and identify itself. Each spirit has its own unique drumming rhythm.

Once the drummers hit upon the right one through trial and error, the woman goes into a trance and the spirit becomes articulate.[4] The woman is then attired in a costume of goatskin or monkey-skin strips (*madumbo*), with small jingling bells (*mangwanda*) attached to her legs. Significantly, she also carries a small ax (*mphompho*) and a herbally treated fly whisk (*litchowa*), symbols of chiefly power among the Tumbuka.[5] Thus costumed, she dances and sings what is in effect a dramatic presentation of her plight in a ceremony that usually lasts several hours.

Two aspects of spirit-possession ceremonies common elsewhere in Africa have especially caught observers' attention. First, glossolalia, or speaking in tongues, typically has been viewed as crucial for legitimizing the ceremonies by "proving" the presence of spirits. Second, great stress has been placed upon the fact that the afflicted person receives a "gift."[6] *Vimbuza* is no different in these respects, and during the ceremony glossolalia occurs and the woman is presented with a gift intended to placate the spirit. At a person's first *vimbuza* dance, this gift is a goat or chicken, and the afflicted person drinks the blood (*chilopa*) directly from the opened neck of the animal. Once this blood sacrifice (*kusawiska*) is consumed, the spirit is appeased and its burden upon the patient eased. Such pacification of the spirit is usually relatively short-lived, however, and in the ceremonies that occur subsequently throughout the victim's life the afflicted person is given a wide range of material things meant to appease the spirit or, in some cases, multiple spirits. The spirits themselves are viewed with ambiguity for, while they are said to cause pain and distress, they are also thought to be able to protect the afflicted against other illness and even witchcraft.

What we find most striking in *vimbuza* ceremonies, however, is the astonishingly self-confident—even arrogant—attitude that the possessed woman shows towards her relatives and neighbors, an attitude said to reflect the anger (*ukali*) of the spirit possessing her. Allied with the spirit world, the woman is recognized as possessing special power, if only briefly. She may threaten people with her ax or contemptuously dismiss the drummers as mere incompetents. And, related to the general argument developed in this book, she may denounce through the candid lyrics of her songs the treatment she has received from those exercising power over her. Although many songs are of only liturgical significance—intended to welcome the spirit, for example, or to encourage the drummers and dancers, whose skills are deemed essential for a successful ceremony—the most im-

7. Tumbuka woman dancing while possessed by a *vimbuza* spirit, Lusaka, Zambia, 1982. (Photo by Leroy Vail.)

portant songs are those that present the complaints of the possessed in the authoritative voice of the spirit. It is also significant that such songs are almost always in the form of a set of stanzas and choruses, with the latter sung by other women of the community. These women are in a structural position within society similar to that of the afflicted woman and are considered her "friends," and a ceremony cannot be performed without their presence to reinforce the songs' messages.[7] The following is typical of such songs, with the in-laws of the possessed person targeted for their presumed evil intentions:

Ŵalwani mbakaya ŵene,	Our relatives are the enemies,
Mwana wane!	My child!
Yayi, nakana nagona!	*No, I refuse to sleep here!*
Ŵalwani mbakaya ŵene,	Our relatives are the enemies,
Mwana wane!	My child!
Yayi, nakana nagona!	*No, I refuse to sleep here!*
Nawera ine!	I am going home!
Ŵatinigunyire kasima.	*They will cook me porridge there!*
Nawera ine!	I am going home!
Nditimyokotolelenge kadendi.	*I will eat good relish with it!*
Nawera ine!	I am going home!
Yayi, nakana nagona!	*No, I refuse to sleep here!*[8]

Possession is, in sum, a form of social therapy that is initiated through the power of poetic license, but it is now especially used by women who, because of their personal insecurity in local society, need to have their message reinforced both by the presence of the supernatural and the supportive participation of sympathetic members of their community. In response, the community is expected not merely to give the woman a material gift during the ceremony itself but also to take steps to meet her complaints and thereby to reintegrate her into the community afterwards. After the completion of the ceremony, the woman generally claims to remember nothing of what has transpired during her trance or what songs she has sung, as they are considered the spirit's utterances.

Our own interest in *vimbuza* has extended over twenty years, and it was while recording performances in Lusaka in 1985 that two songs particularly caught our attention. The first was a boast of defiance against the Ngoni political elite, a foreign group whose origins—like those of Mzilikazi's Ndebele—lay in the turmoil that occurred in Natal in the 1820s and who, after migrating into central Africa, conquered the Tumbuka around 1856.

ŵaNgoni!—Nhkuŵopa yayi 'ne!	The Ngoni!—*I don't fear them!*
Nhkuŵopa yayi 'ne!	*I don't fear them!*
ŵaNgoni!	The Ngoni!
Nhkuŵopa yayi 'ne!	*I don't fear them!*
ŵaNgoni!	The Ngoni!
Nhkuŵopa yayi 'ne!	*I don't fear them!*[9]

The second song was an unequivocal insult to the Jere family, the chiefly family of the Ngoni of Malawi.

aJere! Mugezeenge!	You, Jere! You should take a bath!
Eee—ndimwe azereza!	*Eee—You are a fool!*
aJere! Munkhwapa mukununkha!	You, Jere! Your armpits stink!
Eee—ndimwe azereza!	*Eee—You are a fool!*[10]

Two things seemed remarkable about these songs. First, they were being sung decades after the Ngoni elite or the Jere family actually exercised much power over ordinary Tumbuka. Second, and even more interesting, they were being sung in Zambia, far from the Tumbuka homeland of northern Malawi, where the Jeres were chiefs. More than a century after the arrival of the Ngoni in the Kasitu River valley of northern Malawi and their conquest of the Tumbuka, women in Zambia remembered—and still complained.

We were by no means the first outsiders to be intrigued by *vimbuza*. During the early 1920s, the Scottish missionaries in northern Malawi became increasingly worried by the unexpected appeal that a revived *vimbuza* was then having for many Christian women.[11] More and more women, explaining that they were attending religious ceremonies, were taking part in the "heathen dances" of the *vimbuza* ceremony, which, the missionaries felt, should have died out by then. The missionaries did not know much about these dances, but they *did* know that the dances were accompanied by much loud drumming and that they occurred at night, always a time perilous for African morality. This was ominous not merely because they valued women as faithful church members but, far more importantly, because the upbringing of the young was shaped by the example of their mothers and aunts and grandmothers. The increasing "backsliding" into superstition was a real threat to the successes that had come to typify the mission's work.

Erring women were expelled from the church. But this was clearly no solution. On consulting local Christian men, the missionaries discovered that they, together with the Ngoni chiefs, all agreed that the *vimbuza* ceremonies, with their vulgar emotionalism and their attacks on authority, should be suppressed. The "diseases" (*nthenda*) were but figments of overworked imaginations; the dances gave women the opportunity to flaunt their bodies so as to entice men into adultery while their husbands were away; those who claimed to be able to cure the disease were in fact sorcerers; and the ceremonies wasted valuable time. Thus encouraged, the missionaries appealed to the British authorities to suppress the "heathen dances." As the authorities both respected the missionaries and suspected heterodox African religious innovations of having dangerous political over-tones, they banned *vimbuza* in 1924.[12] Supported by the state's power, the missionaries thought their enigmatic problem with the women was solved.

To understand *vimbuza*'s appeal for Tumbuka women at the time it attracted missionary disapproval and government action, one must situate the spirit possession in general, and *vimbuza* in partic-ular, within the context of the historical changes that transformed Tumbuka society from the mid-nineteenth century onward. At mid-century, before the Ngoni conquest, most Tumbuka speakers lived in isolated homesteads scattered widely through a set of small chief-doms on the lightly wooded plateau between the Luangwa River on the west and northern Lake Malawi on the east. Political and cul-tural variations among them had produced a division into distinct northern and southern sections.[13] Among both groups religious shrines provided an element of unity in particular areas, with spirit possession a central element in the rites of these territorial shrines.[14] Men and women were possessed by the spirit [*ciŵanda*, pl: *viŵanda*] of a god or nature sprite, and once possessed, they served as the priests and priestesses at the spirit's shrine. Whatever their gender, they were known as "the wives of the spirit." In times of ecological crisis—such as drought or epidemic—these "wives" went into trance, communed with the spirit, and then instructed the people in the shrine's area on how to restore harmony between man and nature.[15]

When the Ngoni conquered the Tumbuka, most Tumbuka leaders

were killed or displaced, and the large numbers of ordinary people who failed to escape to the west or north as refugees were absorbed into the new Ngoni state as much-exploited *bafo*—"serfs" or "slaves." Their contribution to the economic base of the state was great, and many of the younger men became members of its armies.[16] As the Ngoni wanted nothing less than total cultural hegemony, they suppressed many Tumbuka customs and practices, including centralized worship at the territorial shrines. Institutionalized Tumbuka religion based on such shrines largely died away.

The Ngoni not only vanquished the southern Tumbuka but also changed previous patterns of land usage and residence in the area. The Kasitu River valley, the heartland of the southern Tumbuka, seemed an ideal home to the travel-weary Ngoni. It was free of tsetse fly, had good pastures, and was blessed with perennial streams. The Ngoni settled in the valley and, like the Ndebele of Mzilikazi, the Chopi of Mozambique, and many other peoples of southern Africa, they responded to the region's political instability by creating a new militarized state stoutly defended against possible attack. To enhance security, the Ngoni leaders concentrated their people and cattle in the central part of the valley, an area roughly fifty miles long by thirty miles wide, and turned the lands around this redoubt into depopulated buffer zones that quickly filled with bush and wild animals.[17]

Before the Ngoni conquest, the Tumbuka had maintained the soil's fertility by using a system of shifting cultivation to grow their principal staple, finger millet (*Eleusine coracana*). This crop was exceedingly demanding on the fragile soil, which had to be allowed to lie fallow for up to twenty or twenty-five years between periods of use that themselves lasted only three to five years.[18] Only if the population remained small enough to ensure that, at any one time, the great bulk of land was fallowing could the soil's long-term fertility be guaranteed.[19] By the late 1870s, however, human and animal populations were too large for the limited resources of the core area. Land was being used for too long, and to give vitality to the rapidly depleting soils the people had to cut down and burn the area's trees and bushes to obtain ashes to fertilize their gardens. This deforestation led, in turn, to the drying up of perennial streams and a sharp fall in agricultural productivity. The declining material conditions in the valley sparked a series of rebellions by the Tumbuka and others in the late 1870s and early 1880s.[20]

Changes in both the form and the nature of spiritual life occurred at the same time. Deprived of economic, political, and social power as well as of their institutionalized prophetic tradition located at shrines, the subordinate Tumbuka, together with other dependents of the Ngoni, began to employ spiritual means to resist Ngoni domination, in effect creating alliances between themselves and the spirit world. These new alliances took two principal forms. First, there was a great increase in witchcraft accusations against the Ngoni elite. The Ngoni aristocrats (as with most African peoples) believed that when unexplained misfortune occurred, it could be attributed to the evil intentions of their personal enemies. This belief meant that they respected similar beliefs of those they incorporated into their new state, and they gradually accepted the local Tumbuka poison (mwavi) ordeal as effective in detecting and punishing witches.[21] As the ecological health of the Kasitu valley deteriorated, social tensions grew and, as a symptom of heightened tensions, witchcraft accusations against the aristocracy and the use of the mwavi ordeal both became increasingly common.[22]

The second manifestation of the new alliance between the southern Tumbuka and the spirit world is the one with which we are most concerned in this chapter. There was a great proliferation of spirits that could possess ordinary people and strengthen their voices of protest. Before the Ngoni conquest, possession among the Tumbuka had been localized at the area's principal shrines in the form of the benevolent prophecy of nature spirits associated with rainfall. After the destruction of the shrines, however, such centralized spirit possession disappeared, and a host of new and strange spirits appeared, apparently accompanying the new peoples the Ngoni brought with them. In the cultural mix of the Ngoni state, with its frequent interethnic marriages, these spirits lost their ethnic valences and began to possess people randomly, without regard to their cultural identity.[23]

From a taxonomic perspective, the new spirits fell into three broad categories, determined by the type of problem being confronted through the possession. First, there was *vimbuza* itself, which involved possession by the spirits of warriors slain in the endemic warfare of the latter nineteenth century and who, lacking proper burials, could find no rest and thus sought out people in whom to dwell. *Vimbuza* spirits dealt with social problems. A second, and apparently indigenous, type of spirit was known as *vilombo* (powerful animal and reptile spirits). Such spirits included those of lions, leopards, and pythons, and dealt with cosmological problems. Finally, there was a third form, *vyanusi*, which was the most disquieting. This occurred when people who had been powerful witch-finders during their own lifetimes returned as spirits after their death to possess people. The name for these spirits, *vyanusi*, was derived from the Ngoni word for witch-finders, *izanusi*. In a society in which belief in witchcraft was central to the consciousness of people at all social levels, it was dangerous for powerful *vyanusi* spirits to be abroad, possessing people and accusing others of witchcraft and dealing with problems of evil arising from presumed witchcraft. Under the Ngoni supremacy, then, spirit possession came to be deinstitutionalized, democratized, and transformed into a form of spiritual resistance to the changed political, social, and economic situation in which the southern Tumbuka and other dependents of the Ngoni found themselves. With the passage of time, the various forms of possession were grouped under the umbrella term of *"vimbuza."*

In the first quarter century of its existence, the state was largely kept isolated from the wider world by Ngoni defenses, and the severe problems it faced arose largely from changing local conditions. In the late 1870s, however, Scottish merchants seeking ivory and Scottish missionaries seeking souls appeared in the area, earnest harbingers of greater changes. In 1878, at Bandawe, on the western shore of Lake Malawi, Presbyterians of the Free Church of Scotland founded the Livingstonia Mission. During the 1880s they negotiated permission to open stations in Ngoni country itself.[24] The missionaries were not merely seeking converts to Christianity, however, but rather converts to a Western way of life, and, with their churches, they brought clinics and schools and carpentry workshops and a host of Victorian ideas and values. The Ngoni state was already in a state of economic decline and political crisis when they began evangelizing, and they found many people willing to listen to their message. The mission's early successes opened a period of rapid change in the area, with the transformative forces of colonial capitalism soon added to the mission's own impact.

The changes that occurred in the decades after 1878 greatly gratified the missionaries. In the late nineteenth century their parish had been at the very center of the still-thriving slave trade to the Indian Ocean coast.[25] British pressures had gradually ended the trade, however, and with the annexation of neighboring Tanganyika from a Germany defeated in World War I, Britain's authority in central Africa was at its zenith.[26] In 1878 virtually every African in the area had been nonliterate, but the area's peoples were now becoming among the best educated in all of Africa and were clamoring for more and better schools. In the 1880s few of the area's people had been Christians, but by the 1920s the mission had turned the region into one of the most Christian in all of Africa. It was not surprising, perhaps, that most of the earliest converts had come from among those Tumbuka and Tonga who had been conquered by the Ngoni and had their culture suppressed. They were naturally willing to listen to new ideas.[27] But many converts had also been made from among the Ngoni aristocrats themselves, and it seemed only appropriate that when at the retirement of Walter Elmslie, one of the most important missionaries and the author of *Among The Wild Ngoni*, a book recounting his early experiences in the country, these Ngoni converts should have presented him a memorial declaring that: "When judging how our country has been brought from darkness and a barbarous state to the light of the Gospel and civilization through your efforts, we see that the results and the progress are most wonderful. Your living among the wild Angoni, for all this time, has made our country to experience great changes, both spiritually and materially, so that now, you leave behind you not the Wild Angoni, but, a domesticated and loyal people."[28]

Economic progress also seemed obvious. While the people had survived in the nineteenth century by raiding others and scratching a doubtful living from a recalcitrant soil, by the early 1920s the area's men were, like to many other of southern Africa's people, working in ever-increasing numbers as labor migrants in European enterprises and building the region's economy. It was clear that the mission's advocacy of the Gospel of Work had succeeded as well as its preaching of the Gospel of Christ.

Yet despite the general satisfaction these changes produced among the Livingstonia missionaries, the Africans had more mixed feelings. Doubtless the ending of the slave trade and the coming of Western education and modern medicine were highly desirable, but they seemed to have been accompanied by more than proportionate travails that had accelerated the decline already begun before 1878. In the mid-1890s, for example, the great pan-African rinderpest epizootic almost wiped out the people's cattle herds, plunging the area into a severe economic depression.[29] This was followed by poor harvests and a period of famine.[30] Then, in 1906, the British ended local political independence and made the area part of the Nyasaland Protectorate, abruptly subjecting its people to the full demands of colonial political economy dominated by the emergent industrial and agrarian economies of southern Africa.[31] Central among these demands was that of earning money to pay newly imposed taxes as well as to pay for bridewealth (*lobola*), school fees, and any goods that might be desired. Because local opportunities for earning money were almost nonexistent, these needs could be met only by the men migrating to work elsewhere. This migrancy had begun as early as the 1890s, when men began to trickle south in search of short-term jobs on the newly established plantations in the southern part of the colony.

Initially, before World War I, people developed strategies to sustain village life. Certain men would go away to earn enough money for several of their friends or relatives to use, for example, and those left at home would attend to village affairs, going away for their share of migrancy labor later, after their friends or relatives had returned.[32] But between 1912 and 1923 a succession of blows wrecked such attempts to come to terms creatively with the necessity of labor migrancy. An outbreak of bovine pleuropneumonia in 1912 resulted in an embargo on the cattle trade from the Kasitu valley, which had earlier been important in supplementing earnings from labor migrancy.[33] During World War I large numbers of men were drafted to serve for periods of up to three years as porters in the British army or as laborers on the plantations in southern Nyasaland, and the shortage of male labor drastically curtailed village food production.[34] At the same time, the army commandeered large amounts of food and cattle from the people, placing still greater burdens on village women seeking to feed their families.[35] The destruction of the war years was followed by the great worldwide Spanish influenza pandemic of 1919, which killed thousands of local people, and then by an outbreak of bubonic plague. A heavy round of inflation and a doubling of the tax rate in 1920 reduced people to wearing animal skins and bark cloth for the first time in decades, and a severe famine in 1923 seemed to deliver the coup de grace to village life.[36] The impact of all these events, taken together with the continuing demand for labor throughout southern Africa, resulted in an abrupt increase in the emigration of the male population, with as many as 70 percent of the men typically being absent from their homes at any one time.

The prolonged shortage of male labor dating from the war years resulted in a fresh assault upon women's position in local society. This occurred at both the emotional and the material level. Migrant husbands would frequently stay away for eight or ten or twelve years or longer, becoming "lost ones," or *machona* (sing., *lichona*), while their wives were left behind in the villages, largely unsupported in solving the problems of everyday survival.[37] Furthermore, almost the entire burden of agricultural work fell upon the women. While women were able to plant and weed and cultivate, having done so for decades, they were less able to clear brush for new gardens or to chop down trees and drag their branches to be burned in established fields for their fertilizing ashes, both tasks considered the work of men. Tumbuka country was well on its way to becoming a gigantic rural slum.

It was at the start of this marginalization of Tumbuka-speaking women that striking changes occurred in the incidence of *vimbuza* spirit possession. First, it began to spread out of its southern Tumbuka core area in the Kasitu valley into adjacent areas to the south, west, and north. Because of the ecological decay and increasing poverty and hunger in the old Ngoni core area, families left it in search of better land.[38] *Vimbuza* moved with them and soon came to be accepted by other Tumbuka-speaking people among whom they settled.[39] Thus it became less and less a strictly southern Tumbuka phenomenon.

The second, more significant, change was its shift of genders. In the period before World War I, when the oppressing "other" had been the Ngoni elite, it had been an experience of both men and women.[40] As colonial capitalism affected the area, however, the men, by obtaining an education at the Livingstonia mission's schools, or by becoming labor migrants, or by doing both, removed themselves from direct subordination to the Ngoni political elite and assumed a greater share in village-level political and economic life through their control over land, cattle, and whatever money entered local society. In this way, non-Ngoni men were able to liberate themselves, at least partially, and to abandon *vimbuza* to the area's women.

It was this shift in power between the sexes that resulted in *vimbuza*'s becoming both more common and an almost exclusively female experience during the late 1910s and early 1920s, much to the surprise and annoyance of the Livingstonia missionaries. Their perplexity about why so many women were backsliding may be explained in terms of the wildly different interpretations of local history held by the two principals. As Victorian Scottish Presbyterians, the missionaries ardently believed in nineteenth-century liberal notions of improvement and uplift through hard work, and they were convinced that they had been instrumental in transforming an ignorant and benighted African society along just such progressive lines. They were equally confident that increased education and literacy, the spread of Christianity, and the replacement of the old subsistence economy by the new colonial cash economy would continue the modernization that they had themselves initiated in 1878.

Yet their Eurocentric perception of local history diverged profoundly from that held by most Tumbuka-speaking women, who were far less cheerful about colonial capitalism's impact and far more sensitive to the advantages of the past. It was this divergence of opinion about the nature of the historical changes that had taken place over the previous several decades that lay behind both the unexpected appeal that the "heathen dances" of *vimbuza* had for ever-larger numbers of "good" Christian Tumbuka women from the late 1910s onward and the missionaries' disillusion with those women.

By the early 1920s the women of the area clearly perceived men and the male-dominated colonial society as *their* opposing "other."[41] In effect, they used the licensed voices of the spirits as a way of seeking a measure of spiritual power and as an avenue of protest and resistance in an increasingly stressful world dominated by others.[42] A full panoply of powerful *vilombo, vimbuza,* and *vyanusi* spirits began to possess the area's women, with men only occasionally affected.[43] It was in response to this change that the missionaries, local men, and the colonial government united in 1924 in an effort to throttle *vimbuza*.

This effort proved a vain one. This was partly because the state simply lacked the ability to enforce its ban. But there were three more substantive reasons for *vimbuza*'s survival and subsequent spread. First, with local society enduring an period of especially traumatic stress, there was a perception of increased Evil. Witchcraft beliefs grew in response to this situation.[44] Prior to the establishment of British colonialism, the *mwavi* ordeal, in which the accused drank poison (*mwavi*) had been used to deal with alleged witchcraft. If innocent, he or she would vomit; if guilty, no vomiting would occur. As a central tenet of their newly imposed colonial legal system, however, the British both suppressed the *mwavi* ordeal as "morally repugnant" and, even more importantly, made it a criminal offense to accuse a person of practicing witchcraft.[45] Outlawing the ordeal meant that the principal means of controlling an apparently growing threat to society had been removed. With its component of *vyanusi*—possession by the spirits of great witchfinders of the past—

the *vimbuza* ceremony quickly moved in to meet, at least partially, a deeply felt need for the control of witches and their evil deeds.[46] Through the licensed songs of *vimbuza*, which, after all, were sung by "spirits," one could violate without fear the law forbidding accusations of witchcraft and thereby bring great public pressure against alleged malefactors. The following song, which was recorded in 1985, is typical of *vyanusi* songs. In it, the singer, a woman, in violation of the law as well as in violation of domestic etiquette, publicly accuses her father-in-law of practicing witchcraft against her:

Ndibabe mwana, mwalya!

"Yeŵo, tawonga!"

   Nkhalelenkhu mwana.

   Uyu mwana?

   "Yeŵo, tawonga!"

Ati ndipoke nthumbo, mwamwa!

Ndibabe mwana, mwalya!

"Yeŵo, tawonga!"

   Nkhalelelenkhu mwana.

   Uyu mwana, pakuti

   Wadada mbahaŵe?

   "Yeŵo, tawonga!"

When I bear a child, you eat it!

"Oh, thanks so very much for it!" [you say]

   How can I raise my child,

   This child?

   "Oh, thanks so very much for it!" [you say]

When I get pregnant, you drink it!

When I bear a child, you eat it!

"Oh, thanks so very much for it!" [you say]

   How can I raise my child.

   This child, as

   My father [in-law] is a wizard?

   "Oh, thanks so very much for it!" [you say][47]

A second factor shielding *vimbuza* was the way in which Christianity developed in the area. By the first decade of the twentieth century heterodox and separatist Christian sects had begun to challenge the supremacy of the mission's staunchly orthodox Victorian Presbyterianism.[48] By the 1920s those Tumbuka speakers who wanted to be considered Christians but who were dissatisfied with the mission's message had a variety of Christian churches from which to choose. These lay on a spectrum of doctrinal orthodoxy and social respectability from the Presbyterians to the Jehovah's Witnesses and the Zionists.[49]

Most important in the Tumbuka area, where, despite early successes, the Jehovah's Witnesses had difficulties establishing themselves and to which Zionism came fairly late,[50] were separatist churches set up by groups of dissident Christians who broke off from the Livingstonia Mission explicitly to create a more emotionally satisfying liturgy and a greater tolerance towards African customs. These early churches included the Last Church of God and His Christ, established in the mid-1920s as a church for polygynists, and the African National church, founded in 1929 specifically to be more accommodating to African customs in general.[51] The constitution of the latter was explicit in its rejection of the Eurocentric demands of the Livingstonia Mission: "We believe the commission of the Christian Church to Africa was to import Christ and education in such a way as to fit in with the manners and customs of the people and not that it should impose upon the Africans the unnecessary and impracticable methods of European countries, such as having one wife, *etc.*, which have no Biblical authority."[52]

The membership of the new, more latitudinarian churches was drawn mostly from those people to whom the hard doctrines of the Presbyterian church gave little solace and who found little allure in the ideals of sobriety, hard work, education, and upward mobility preached by the Livingstonia Mission. In 1929 a colonial official wryly noted that the members of the Last Church of God and His Christ were "baptised without any previous novitiate" and that "They seem to consist chiefly of uneducated and simple people who are glad to hear that they may go to heaven in spite of having 2 or 3 wives and who like to attend services where they are not condemned as adulterers. Educated natives who have left the Mission will not join the sect and laugh at them for their simplicity and lack of organization."[53] As a consequence of the availability of these new Christian churches, the poorer, less educated people who had less exposure to the orthodoxy of the mission and who were ardent believers in spirit possession were able to find respectable spiritual homes.

But there was a third factor involved. Thus far, our analysis has been based on missionary memoirs, archival sources, and oral testimony derived largely, though not exclusively, from interviews with men. The themes have been military conquest, political reorganization, religious and educational change, land distribution and usage, and the growth of labor migrancy and its local impact, themes that also seem important to contemporary historians of southern Africa. To turn from the written sources and the largely male testimony to the actual *vimbuza* songs is to encounter a very different historical emphasis. Taken as a group and treated as contemporary documents, *vimbuza* songs constitute a specific reading by women of Tumbuka

history from the mid-nineteenth century to the present, with particular concern for changing relations between men and women within
the context of the household.

The songs we are describing, which number over four hundred,
were collected over a period of twenty years and over a wide area.
Because they are still current and because they are difficult to date
exactly, we are treating them as contemporary documents—though
with the proviso that some appear to be many decades old. Comparisons with other groups of recordings of *vimbuza* songs—the small
sample collected by Hugh Tracey in 1948 and a series collected by
the Federation of Rhodesia and Nyasaland's Broadcasting Service
during the 1950s—reveal only a few songs present in our collection.
Tracey's collection was a very small one, however, while the Federal
Broadcasting Service's collection was dominated by a single performer.[54] Despite the difficulty in dating most of the songs, there is
strong evidence for the continuity of many of them. Credible testimony attests to many songs having originally derived from a particular area and then spread geographically, with such songs being encountered in widely separate places.[55] The fixed liturgical nature of
the *vimbuza* ceremonies also guarantees a measure of continuity.
Finally, the situations described in the *vimbuza* songs are limited in
scope, and it is recognized that not all people possessed by *vimbuza*
spirits are creative artists. Hence a number of well-known songs are
available to sufferers to use in articulating their particular messages.
Songs composed decades ago may still be used if regarded as appropriate to the current situation. One may, therefore, view the songs of
the *vimbuza* ceremony as analogous to the hymns of the Livingstonia Mission: the messages are stereotyped, but the songs nonetheless reflect the singers' deepest personal concerns. While new
songs are being composed all the time, certain old songs are kept
alive because of their continuing relevance.

One should not be misled by two initial impressions these songs
might give. The first is that some of them are of limited poetic interest. Andrew Smith, it will be remembered, had this impression
about some of the songs he heard performed for Mzilikazi, noting
that they were more "barren of ideas" than the official praise poems
and more "vulgarly expressed." Yet he recognized that they still
served the purpose of the king's becoming "acquainted with the sentiments, views and wishes of his subjects."[56] *Vimbuza* sufferers have
not been, of course, primarily concerned with making poetry and,
although their complaints are presumably more effective if ex-

pressed eloquently and memorably, in the last resort it is the opportunity for licensed expression under the protection of spirits that make the ceremonies socially efficacious. In this context, many of the songs can appear to be nothing more than purely literal statements:

Iyayi lelo, ŵaNyilongo!	Alas, Mr. Nyilongo, you! It's
Gozoli wamala mphapo!	gonorrhea that has finished your semen!
Lekani kundidelela!	Don't go blaming me!
Iyayi lelo, ŵaNyilongo,	*Alas, Mr. Nyilongo. It's*
Gozoli wamala mphapo!	*gonorrhea that has finished your semen!*
Lekani kundidelela!	*Stop blaming me for it!*[57]

This song can be placed in its social and historical contexts and held to be "typical," with Nyilongo having brought back gonorrhea from his stint as a migrant laborer and his wife, refusing to be blamed for the consequent childlessness, denouncing him in licensed song. But its significance may initially appear to be individual and documentary rather than general and symbolic.

The second misleading impression is that there is a great variety of themes represented in these songs. There are indeed songs about conquest and political reorganization, about gender struggle, and about labor migration, though, as one would expect from the nature of the *vimbuza* ceremony in which individual women articulate personal distress to an audience of relatives or neighbors, these issues tend to be presented in highly personal rather than in abstract terms. In the last resort, however, these songs are very much more than a documentary survey of the various pressures put on individual Tumbuka women since the last third of the nineteenth century. By tracing common preoccupations across a wide spectrum of song performances, a consistent, overarching emphasis becomes apparent.

The songs invoke not merely an alternative interpretation of history but also an alternative vision of how life *ought* to be lived. They refer repeatedly and explicitly to Ngoni overrule, to patrilineal marriage, to polygyny, and to the effects of labor migrancy. The central themes are the collapse of the matrilineal extended family, the weakening of village life, and the resulting marginalization of women. But the vision invoked by recurrent metaphors, even in the most documentary of the songs, is of a time when stable and harmonious relationships, freedom from poverty, disease, and possession, and a degree of personal happiness and fulfillment were all guaranteed by the stability of the matrilineal extended family.

In effect, this vision is a utopian vision of a pre-Ngoni, precolonial, precapitalist past when southern Tumbuka customs prevailed unchallenged. As history it is every bit as artificial a construct as the Ngoni elite's own ethnically chauvinistic and largely mythical version of the area's history, which stresses heroic migrations, conquest, and governing skill. It is also as artificial as the similarly ethnically inspired notion of a pre-Ngoni Tumbuka empire that was fabricated with the help of Livingstonia missionaries by Tumbuka men as a response to their double conquest by Ngoni and British.[58] Yet despite its artificiality, the vision generated in the woman's songs is a powerful one and remains alive in areas as far apart as the rural villages of northern Malawi and the urban slums of Lusaka. It permits Tumbuka women, undeniably marginalized by events of the past century, to interpret their history in the light of a single utopian perspective as a sustained, multifaceted assault on the matrilineal family, and to demand changes from those in positions of control over their lives.

We suggest that women have insisted on maintaining *vimbuza* because it has been one of the few places where they could express *their* view of what the area's history was all about. Rejecting the optimistic views of European missionaries about the value of "progress" and finding little comfort in the ethnic boastings of local men, women have used *vimbuza* as their own public voice. From their alternative reading of the area's past arose the values that informed the protests and complaints in the songs they sang while possessed. *Vimbuza*'s role as a condensation of historical and moral truths has been an important factor ensuring its survival in the face of broad-based male hostility. As it is believed that a refusal to deal with a possessing spirit will result in a woman's insanity, men find it impossible to deny women their ceremonies or refuse to pay for them even though *vimbuza* has been very much a woman's weapon in the area's gender conflict. As a consequence, through *vimbuza*, deprived and marginalized women have been able to exercise at least a measure of autonomy and power in an otherwise desperate situation.

The matrilineal household of the southern Tumbuka prior to the Ngoni supremacy provides the template for the reading of history that one finds in current *vimbuza* songs. There are compelling messages in this vision of the past as a time when both the status of women and women's role in the family were superior. Prior to the conquest, the southern Tumbuka had followed matrilineal descent and inheritance practices, with social position and material goods inherited by a man's sister's son, not by his own biological son.[59] Marriages were contracted only gradually. Initially, the bridegroom went to live with his bride's family, remaining there for several years to complete a term of brideservice and to demonstrate that he was a hardworking and dependable provider. After some years, when the wife's family was satisfied with her husband, a hoe and a white bead (*chimalo*) symbolizing the completion of the brideservice were transferred to the wife's family, and the marriage was considered firm. Only then were the husband and wife free to move away and establish their own household. Marrying wives from different families was rare because of the difficulty in completing several terms of brideservice. Polygyny is said to have been relatively rare except in the cases of chiefs. Cases of nonchiefly polygyny that did exist are explained as the results either of a wife's younger sister being "given" freely as a reward to a man who proved to be an exceptionally good husband or of a man inheriting the widow of a deceased brother.

The southern Tumbuka had had to cope with a poor economy based on the hoe cultivation of millet and sorghum grown through a system of shifting agriculture. Cultivation was primarily the responsibility of women, although the initial clearing of fields was the task of men. Women thus occupied a central position in the local economy as guarantors of their families' survival through staple-food production. Although not enjoying great power, women nonetheless did have a secure social status that was guaranteed by their brothers, who served as their jural guardians. Should a divorce occur, a woman retained control over both her children and the land she worked, and the husband had to set out in search of a new life.

The Ngoni conquest is seen to have wholly changed the structure of the southern Tumbuka family and household. Women recall that the initial assault on the matrilineal system was an Ngoni one. This responsibility is implicit in the two generalized insults cited earlier in this chapter and also in this more explicit song about the source of polygyny:

ŵayowoya ndimuNgoni!   The Ngoni has decreed it!
   ŵayowoya ndimuNgoni—eee!   *The Ngoni has decreed it—eee!*

Kanakazi kamoza nkhaulanda!	Having but one wife is a misery!
ŵayowoya ndimuNgoni—eee!	*The Ngoni has decreed it—eee!*
Kanakaza kamoza	*Oh, having only one wife*
nkhaulandaye!!	*is indeed a misery!![60]*

The song's attribution of an increase in polygyny to the Ngoni is accurate. In early nineteenth-century Natal, where the Ngoni had originated, the acquisition of women had been considered vital for increasing the size and power of individual families in a competitive situation. Polygyny was, therefore, very much a cultural ideal for them. Then, during their long anabasis through central and east Africa, Ngoni raiding of other peoples for women and children for incorporation into the group created a sexual imbalance that further strengthened polygyny. At the time of the conquest itself, the Ngoni victors abruptly shattered the matrilineal, uxorilocal, and monogamous expectations of large numbers of Tumbuka women by considering them booty and seizing them as concubines. The later incorporation of young Tumbuka men into the new state's military regiments meant that, following the practice established decades earlier by the Zulu king Shaka in Natal, the age of marriage was postponed until much later than had been the case earlier—perhaps until thirty or more.[61] This left a large cadre of unmarried younger local women available for polygynous unions.

The initial Ngoni introduction of polygyny as a cultural ideal was followed in subsequent years by sustained attacks on a range of southern Tumbuka marriage and residence practices as part of Ngoni policies aimed at entrenching their cultural hegemony. The Ngoni were patrilineal, with descent and inheritance transmitted from father to son. They practiced exogamy, with the gradual transfer of lobola cattle from the husband's family to the wife's family an essential component of the marriage process. Immediately after the initial stage of the marriage process, the women moved from her family to live with her husband's family, where she sought to prove herself a good wife.

Southern Tumbuka men, well aware of Ngoni contempt for their customs, quickly adopted Ngoni practices as they were incorporated into the Ngoni state. In addition to wanting to be like the Ngoni, however, an important economic factor was pushing them toward change. Scholars have long been aware of latent tendencies in matrilineal systems for biological fathers to seek closer relations with their sons then they strictly should have were a fully effective and internally consistent matrilineal system to be in operation.[62] A matrilineal system generally functions in accordance with its so-called rules for as long as women remain central to the primary productive endeavor of subsistence hoe agriculture. When other forms of wealth or value become important, men tend to dominate these and to acquire greater relative economic power, which then enables them to work toward the actualization of patrilineal relationships. New forms of wealth, then, open the way for new types of relationships of power within families as well as for new patterns of power within the wider society.[63]

Cattle were one such form of wealth. From 1856 onward, the Ngoni, who considered cattle as the epitome of wealth, introduced large herds into the southern Tumbuka area for the first time, with men entirely controlling their ownership, care, and use.[64] The Ngoni used cattle to fulfill their lobola obligations, and whenever an Ngoni man married a southern Tumbuka woman, he insisted that her family accept lobola and took her away at once to live with his family.[65] As southern Tumbuka men acquired cattle, they gained the ability to substitute lobola for the expected period of brideservice, to adopt patrilineal descent and inheritance practices, and even to begin embracing polygyny. If a southern Tumbuka man wanted to marry any woman who was herself not southern Tumbuka, the expection was that he would transfer lobola cattle.[66] Only when southern Tumbuka married one another could the earlier form of brideservice marriage be practiced, but by the 1890s even these remnants of the old ways had largely ended.[67] In this way, among the southern Tumbuka a new patrilineal-virilocal family structure rapidly supplanted the early matrilineal-uxorilocal norms.

Wives who had previously dwelt in the midst of a supportive network of their own matrikin were abruptly brought into the new situation of living in the strange villages of their husbands' families. Women, now viewing themselves as outsiders in their husbands' villages, were acutely conscious of the limitations on their influence, their grim isolation, and their fragile social positions. In the following song, the metaphors for this predicament are extraordinarily bitter:

Ta, ŵalanda lero,   We, today's orphans,
   Ta, ŵalanda lero,   *We, the orphans of today,*
Ta, ŵalanda lero,   We, today's orphans,
   Ta, ŵalanda lero,   *We, the orphans of today,*

Ta, ŵalanda tikufwachi?   Why are we orphans dying?
  Liyele!   *Liyele!*
  A-hiye—lero!   *A-hiye—today!*
  E—yayi!   *Oh, no!*
  Ta ŵalanda pera!   *We are just orphans!*
Tikufwa misunga yinga!   We are dying as guarded wanderers.
  Liyele!   *Liyele!*
  A-hiye—lero!   *A-hiye—today!*
  E—yayi!   *Oh, no!*
  Ta ŵalanda pera!   *We are just orphans!*[68]

With the passing of the matrilineal system, women describe themselves as orphans without kin and as "guarded wanderers" (*misunga yinga*), a powerful image evoking landlessness, homelessness, and imprisonment. Patrilineal marriage is not viewed as a new form of marriage. It is a form of slavery.

Distant from the graves of protecting ancestors, they were easy targets for the attacks of *vimbuza* spirits:

Nthenda zukola bweka!   The diseases attack at random!
  Eee yaileee eee!   *Eee yailee eee!*
Nthenda! eee yaileee eee!   Oh, the diseases! eee yailee eee!
  Eee yailee eee!   *Eee yaileee eee!*
Lude ee mainga-mainga.   Lude is a nomad.
  Lude ee mainga-mainga.   *Lude is a wanderer.*
Nthenda zukola ine!   The diseases attack me!
  Eee yaileee eee!   *Eee yaileee eee!*
Ine amama nilije!   Here I have no mother!
  Lude ee mainga-mainga.   *Lude is a wanderer.*[69]

For a brief period, in the late 1890s and first years of the twentieth century, the new ways seemed threatened by the rinderpest epizootic's decimation of the area's cattle herds, the coin of the bridewealth system.[70] Then, in the late 1890s, the lands of the empty buffer zones surrounding the Ngoni state were opened up after forty years of fallowing. Many impoverished people fled close Ngoni oversight, reoccupied newly opened lands, and established new villages and gardens.[71] Finally, in 1906, the new British colonial administration placed the Ngoni elite under colonial control. The threat to the survival of Ngoni cultural practices was soon negated, however, as the area's cattle herds were rapidly rebuilt after rinderpest had ended and as the British refused to recognize long-displaced Tumbuka chiefly families in the newly occupied lands. Instead, the Ngoni aristocrats were permitted to extend their powers into the new lands, where they used their courts to cement in place their policies regarding land usage, marriage, and inheritance.[72]

With the decline of women's economic position came the erosion of women's social role. Southern Tumbuka women came to be seen primarily as workers who sustained the family into which they married and as producers of children for their husbands' families. As an "unprotected wanderer," a wife was subject to exploitation by her husband's family and to incessant criticisms of her work:

"Kwela! Kwela!"	"Climb up! Climb up!"
—Mama ine, nikwele uli?	—My mother, how can I climb?
"Kwela! Kwela!"	"Climb up! Climb up!"
—Mama ine, nikwele uli?	—My mother, how can I climb?
Mwana nabapila, mama ine,	With a child on my back, my mother,
Nikwele uli?	*How can I climb?*
Jembe pamutu, mama ine,	With a hoe on my head, mother,
Nikwele uli?	*How can I climb?*
Nthumbo kumutina, mama ine,	Pregnant up to my heart, my mother,
Nikwele uli?	*How can I climb?*
Nikwelenge, mama 'ne!	Oh, I will try to climb, oh, my mother!
Nikwele uli?	But how can I climb?
Nikwele uli?	*But how can I climb?*[73]

The complaint is comprehensive. The woman is doing all expected of her in the new patrilineal system—working in the garden with a hoe and producing children for her husband's family—yet her mother-in-law presses her to do more, despite her full pregnancy ("up to my heart"). By the repeated use of the phrase *mama ine* ("my mother"), she points to her mother-in-law's glaring departure from the ideals of protection and caring usually associated with mothers.

Yet being possessed, as we have already stressed, licenses a woman to go beyond such criticism through lamentation to strong and explicit rebuke even of those so lofty that she might not speak to them in ordinary day-to-day life. In this way, she can fearlessly condemn a whole range of relatives and fellow villagers, including that most powerful and awesome figure, the head of her husband's family, her father-in-law:

Adada vijala ŵakuninena nane.	My father-in-law slanders me.
Niŵanene!	I shall do the same!
Lili mujira zirimu.	He is a mad fool!
Adada viyala ŵakunituka nane.	My father-in-law insults me.
Niŵatuke!	I shall insult him also!
Lili mujira zirimu!	*He is a mad fool!*
ŵayamba ndiwo!	*It's he who started it!*
Aye aye aye!	*Aye aye aye!*
Aye aye aye!	*Aye aye aye!*
Lili mujira zirimu!	*He is a mad fool!*
ŵakhala kumphala.	He is at the chief's court there.
Nkhaŵaguze mwembe!	I will pull his beard!
ŵayamba ndiwo!	*It's he who started it!*
Aye aye aye!	*Aye aye aye!*
Aye aye aye!	*Aye aye aye!*[74]

With the purpose of lobola clearly stated as being "to purchase the woman's uterus" (*kugala mphapo*), a woman's status is now defined in terms of the children she produces for her husband's family, and any failures to do so is indeed dangerous.[75] A miscarriage is especially traumatic, for it not only is a personal tragedy but can also leave a woman without social standing:

N'telelani ine!	Help me!
Adada, n'telelani 'mwe!	Father, help me!
Amama, n'telelani 'mwe!	Mother, help me!
Akeyala!	*Alas!*
Ŵantenwelenkhu?	How will they love me?
Nkhate ni namwana wamdumbu waŵo.	I believed I'd borne their brother's baby.
Akeyala!	*Alas!*
Niwelelenkhu ine, mama?	Where can I go, mother?
Akeyela!	*Alas!*
Wantenwelenkhu?	How will they love me?
Nkhate ni namwana wamdumbu waŵo.	I believed I'd borne their brother's baby.[76]

In such a situation, a woman often sees her "failure" as the consequence of witchcraft practiced against her by one of her husband's family or one of her own jealous cowives. The following song, for example, accuses a cowife of having procured the ingredients needed for sorcery against her on a recent visit to her family's home.

Awoliŵanyane!   Oh, my cowife!
   Aheeee, ya—ya—yee   *Aheeee, ya—ya—yee*
Nyanga hee!   Herbs for bewitching!
   Nyanga zikwandabweka.   *Bewitching herbs are found*
                                          everywhere.

Walikuya kwaŵo.   She went home to her parents!
   Aheeee, ya—ya—yee   *Aheeee, ya—ya—yee*
Nyanga hee!   Herbs for bewitching!
   Nyanga zikwandabweka.   *Bewitching herbs are found*
                                          everywhere.

Walikujilenga!   She disgraced herself there!
   Aheeee, ya—ya—yee   *Aheeee, ya—ya—yee*
Nyanga hee!   Herbs for bewitching!
   Nyanga zikwandabweka.   *Bewitching herbs are found*
                                          everywhere.[77]

Perhaps the song we have collected that is most extreme in condemning the virilocal system is one in which a woman perceives her isolation as so total and the hostility of her in-laws so overwhelming that it is impossible for her to raise her child in the village. Once again, the legal prohibition of witchcraft accusations is violated:

Nkhalalenkhu mwana?   Where can I raise my child?
Nkhalalenkhu mwana?   Where can I raise my child?
Apa ŵadada mbakaŵi!   Here my father [in-law] is a wizard!
   Iyaya—yalero!   *Oh, alas, the ways of today!*
   Nkhalalenkhu mwana?   *Where can I raise my child?*
Apa ŵadada mbakaŵi!   Here my father [in-law] is a wizard!
Nkhalalenkhu mwana?   Where can I raise my child?
Mbaya nwana wane!   Oh, my poor child!
Apa ŵamama mbahaŵi!   Here my mother [in-law] is a
                                          witch!

   Iyaya—yalero!   *Oh, alas, the ways of today!*
   Nkhalalenkhu mwana?   *Where can I raise my child?*
Apa ŵamama mbakaŵi!   Here my mother [in-law] is a
                                          witch![78]

Some of the greatest problems within the new household structures arise from the acceptance of polygyny, and a great many of the songs collected are concerned with this topic. When situated in a polygynous situation women often find themselves in bitter competition with cowives for both the material support and the sexual attentions of their husband. Although competition and jealousy are very real, they contradict the frequently repeated male assertion that cowives live together in ideal harmony. *Vimbuza* songs belie this assertion of harmony both generally and specifically. In the *vimbuza* songs there are many unequivocal condemnations of polygyny as an institution, as in the following song where a woman declares that she would rather have no husband, despite the disdain and mockery generally evoked by such a state, than accept a polygynous marriage:

Ningaŵa chiwuya ine,	Even if I were an old maid,
Kumitala mingayako yayi!	I'd not marry a polygynist!
Ningayako yaye-yawa!	*Indeed I would not go into it.*
Wanolonoleta!!	*You have destroyed all!!*
Ningaŵa mwale ine,	If I were a unmarried maiden,
Kumitala mingayako yayi!	I'd not marry a polygynist!
Ningayako yaye-yawa!	*Indeed I would not go into it!*
Wanolonoleta!!	*You have destroyed all!!*[79]

Complaints usually address the problems of polygyny more specifically, so that a woman's husband and cowives will know exactly what they are doing to offend. Jealousies about the unequal distribution of a husband's time and sexual attentions among cowives are commonly expressed. In the following example, the singer describes her husband as a "blanket" that she must share with other women. "Blanket" is a complex metaphor with many resonances. It suggests, of course, warmth, comfort, intimacy, and protection. But it suggests a good deal more. Cloth and clothing feature in many *vimbuza* songs in association with civilization and decency and a degree of wealth—one of the possible symptoms of possession is that a woman might strip naked and run into the wild bush. Finally, "blanket" is associated with labor migration, usually being the first item a returning laborer will bring home. The singer sees no reason why she should share her "blanket" with other women.

Asweni ŵane ŵayankhu?	Where has my husband gone?
Ŵamgona kwaNyaBanda!	*He has gone to sleep with that*
	Banda woman!
Asweni ŵane ŵayankhu?	Where has my husband gone?
Ŵamgona kwaNyaBanda!	*He has gone to sleep with that*
	Banda woman!

Mayilo nkhatuma mwana ŵize
namacelo-celo.

—"Ine?!—Yayi!!""Ine?!—Yayi!!"
Gombeza lane—eee!!
Nidikechi ine?
"Lelo ŵamgona mwane!"
 Amama, kunozga!!
"Lelo ŵamgona mwane!"
 Amama, kunozga!!
Gombeza lane—eee!!
Nidikechi ine?
Gombeza lane layankhu?
 Lamgona kwaNyaBanda!

Gombeza lane layankhu?
 Lamgona kwaNyaBanda!

Mayilo nkhatuma mwana ŵize
namacelo-celo.

—"Ine?!—Yayi!!""Ine?!—Yayi!!"
Gombeza lane—eee!!
Nidikechi ine?
ŵamgona kwanyaPhiri.

 Amama, kunozga!
ŵamgona kwanyaMwale.

 Amama, kunozga!
Gombeza lane—eee!!
Nidikechi ine?

Yesterday I sent a child to him to
 tell him to come to me, if only
 in the early morning.
—"Me?!—No!!" "Me?!—No!!"
My blanket—alas!!
With what shall I cover myself?
"Tonight he'll sleep with *me!*"
 Mother, how nice!!
"Tonight he'll sleep with *me!*"
 Mother, how nice!!
Oh, my blanket—alas!!
With what shall I cover myself?
Where has my blanket gone?
 *Gone to sleep with that Banda
 woman!*
Where has my blanket gone?
 *Gone to sleep with that Banda
 woman!*
Yesterday I sent a child to him to
 tell him to come to me, if only
 in the early morning.
—"Me?!—No!!" "Me?!—No!!"
My blanket—alas!!
With what shall I cover myself?
He will sleep with the Phiri
 woman.
 Mother, how nice!
He will sleep with the Mwale
 woman.
 Mother, how nice!
My blanket—alas!!
With what shall I cover myself?[80]

In the women's view, the problems of virilocal marriages based on the transfer of lobola cattle and of polygyny began in the days of the Ngoni supremacy and its assault on the status of women in Tumbuka society. But these problems were greatly complicated when the events during and immediately after World War I enmeshed them firmly in the realities of the colonial political economy, its demand for widespread migrant labor, and the steady impoverishment of the rural areas. Together, as we have seen, these constituted a second assault on women, and this too is documented in the songs of *vimbuza*. Women are aware of the poverty of the rural areas and of their and their children's hunger, and they see the pull of the urban labor markets—symbolized in the songs by "Harare" (Zimbabwe) and "Joni" (Johannesburg's gold mines)—as irresistible as the charms of witchcraft:

Harare ŵayowoya.   Harare has spoken.
  He—ya—ye!   *He—ya—ye!*
  Harare ŵayowoya   *Harare has spoken!*
  He—ya—ye!   *He—ya—ye!*
Harare ŵanadole!   Harare has wonders.
  He—ya—ye!   *He—ya—ye!*
  Harare ŵanadole!   *Harare has wonders!*
  He—ya—ye!   *He—ya—ye!*
Wananyanga yamoto!   It has charms of fire.
  He—ya—ye!   *He—ya—ye!*
  Wananyanga yamoto!   *It has charms of fire!*
  He—ya—ye!   *He—ya—ye!*[81]

The contradictory nature of labor migrancy vexes women. On the one hand, a man *has* to leave his village behind if he is to raise sufficient money for the payment of lobola and to provide his family with the necessities of life. Women recognize this as a fact of life. In the following song the contrast between a life with money earned by such migrancy and one without it is expressed by the metaphorical opposition that we have already seen of clothing, civilization, and maturity contrasted with lack of clothing, the bush, and immaturity:

Nivwalechi naŵo?   What will I ever wear with him?
Nivwalechi naŵo?   What will I ever wear with him?
Nivwalechi naŵo?   What will I ever wear with him?
Mama 'we! Boyi lane!!!   Oh, mother! My boyfriend!!!
  aJere, eeeee   *Mr. Jere, eeeee*
  Boyi lane!!!   *My boyfriend!!!*
Anyinu ŵakuya kuJoni   Your friends go to Johannesburg
Kukagula suti.   So that they can buy suits.
Imwe mukuya susanga.   *You* go into the bush
Kukagima mbeŵa.   To dig for rats.
Zingano wamulasaninge   A needle can prick you through
Mukabudula.   Your thread-bare shorts!
  Boyi lane!   *My boyfriend!*
  Boyi lane!   *My boyfriend!*
Nitole chikumba chambeŵa   Should I use a *rat's* skin

Nibapile mwana?	to tie my baby onto my back?
Nitole mutu wambeŵa	Should I use a *rat's* skull
Nimwelama maji?	to drink my water from?
Boyi lane!	*My boyfriend!*
Boyi lane!	*My boyfriend!*[82]

On the other hand, those women who are married to migrants are profoundly dissatisfied with their conditions. Dwelling apart from their husbands for long periods of time causes many problems that are cataloged in the songs of *vimbuza* and indicate the type of life they have endured since the early 1920s.[83] With a man primarily concerned with surviving in "Harare," or South Africa, and with his family's elders taking care of his interests back at home, the migrant laborer is likely to neglect his far-distant family in central Africa. The metaphor of clothing recurs once again in this context:

Imwe, mukuya kuJoni,	You, who are leaving now for Jo'burg,
Mukaŵaphalirengeko ine nkhule!	Tell him when you get there that I am naked!
Ŵanyinamwe nkhule!	*Your mother is naked too!*
Ine nkhule! Ine nkhule!!	I am naked! Oh, I am naked!!
Wanyinamwe nkhule!!	Your mother is naked too!
Mwana wayegha m'manja!	Your child must be carried in hands [for lack of cloth].
Ine nkhule!!	Oh, I am naked!!
Ŵanyinamwe nkhule!	*Your mother is naked too!*[84]

Furthermore, with her husband far away from her for years at a stretch—perhaps even as a *lichona*—a wife experiences deep sexual jealousies and fears. On the one hand, there is a realization on the part of the rural woman that her husband might marry an urban woman of greater sophistication than herself and that he might support that woman in preference to his distant, unlettered, unsophisticated Tumbuka wife:

Ati kuJoni, yee!	Oh, hear me, you there in Jo'burg!
Ninjani wanihale?	Who is to marry me *now?*
Amama, heliyaye!	*Oh, mother, save me!*
Watola nyaPagilo, amama!	He has married "Miss Posh," mother!
Nyumba yamalata, amama!	*She* now has a house with a corrugated iron roof, mother!

Chijalo capadiloku, amama!   And even a padlocked door,
                                              mother!

  Amama, heliyaye!   *Oh, mother, save me!*[85]

In the absence of her husband, a woman might well be subject to
the sexual demands of her husband's relatives. It is Ngoni custom for
a man suffering impotence to make his wife available to a relative so
that he might impregnate her to bear a child in her husband's name.
During the colonial period the belief grew up that a migrant husband
could return to the village at night as a winged spirit and impregnate
his wife. The combination of the custom and the belief cleared the
way for his acceptance of children borne by his wife in his absence
as his legitimate children. However, it also opened the way for sexual
predation on the part of male relatives of an absent man, and the
songs of *vimbuza* provide an arena for the woman to complain about
unwelcome advances:

Apongozi, fumanimo lero,   Father-in-law, leave now so
Nizunule yumo pela-hola!   that I might reveal who did it!
  Ehee—yawa!!   *Ehee—yawa!!*
Oleee!   Oleee!
  Eeeeeeee!   *Eeeeeeee!*
  Eeeeeeee!   *Eeeeeeee!*
  Eeeeeeee!   *Eeeeeeee!*
Amdala, fumanimo lero,   Old man, get out now so that I
Nizunile imwe pela-hola!   may reveal that it was *you* who
                                        were the one!

  Ehee—yawa!   *Ehee—yawa!*
Oleee!   Oleee!
  Eeeeeeee!   *Eeeeeeee!*
  Eeeeeeee!   *Eeeeeeee!*
  Eeeeeeee!   *Eeeeeeee!*[86]

For a woman left behind in the village, her neglect might end only
at death. Returning to the metaphor of clothing, the following song
observes that the only time she can count on having a decent cotton
dress will be when she dies and, according to custom, the community will have to buy a new dress for her burial:

Salu yamaluwa ndayivwala kale!   Oh, yes, I've worn a flowered print
                                         dress!

Salu yamaluwa ndayivwala kale!   Oh, yes, I've worn a flowered print
                                         dress!

Salu yamaluwa ndayivwala kale!

Oh, yes, I've worn a flowered print
   dress!

Ndayaivwalira kumanda—eee!

I've worn it in the grave—eee![87]

The bitter image of the grave returns when Johannesburg, cardinal symbol of everything labor migrancy has meant to the Tumbuka area's women, is depicted as equivalent to death: the death of the man, perhaps, by accident in the mines or sickness; the death of the marriage with his wife through neglect; the death of village society itself:

Eleli! Mama, adada ŵalikuya,

Eleli! Mother, father has gone,

Eleli! Mama, ŵalikuya kuJoni.

Eleli! Mother, he has gone to
   Jo'burg.

Eleli! Mama, kuJoni nkhumalaro!

Eleli! Mother, Jo'burg is a
   graveyard!

Naliona ine!

Oh, I have seen that!

Ha hee! Nithelekeni hee!

Ha hee! Help me, hee!

Hee! Naliona ine!

Hee! I have seen that!

Ha hee! Nithelekeni hee!

Ha hee! Help me, hee![88]

Not all migrants become *machona*, however. Many return, but women fear that, while away, their lonely husbands might have patronized the prostitutes who throng the work sites of southern Africa:

Imwe, mukuya kuJoni,
mukamuphalirengeko Binwell
uhule ŵaleke ŵafwirenge
muthowa!

You, who are leaving for Jo'burg,
tell Binwell there that he
should leave the whores alone
lest he die in a foreign land!

   Binwell, uhule wuleke!

   Binwell, leave the whores alone!

   Binwell, uhule wuleke!

   Binwell, leave the whores alone!

ŵafwirenge munthowa!

Ah, he will die in a foreign land![89]

Concern with the possibility that her migrant husband might patronize prostitutes arises not only from the wife's wish that he be faithful to her and not waste his money but from her knowledge that men introduce venereal diseases into the rural villages on their return:

Mayoliyoli, 'mwe!

Whoring, oh you!

   Ahe—yayi!

   Ah—no!

Mayoliyoli ngaheni!   Whoring is evil!
 Ahe—hole—yayi!   *Ah—alas—no!*
 Mayoliyoli ngaheni.   *Whoring is evil.*
 Kalasa m'jiso.   *It has afflicted the eye.*
Mayoliyoli, 'mwe!   Whoring, oh you!
 Ahe—yayi!   *Ah—no!*
Mayoliyoli ngaheni.   Whoring is evil!
 Ahe—hole—yayi!   *Ah—alas—no!*
 Mayoliyoli ngaheni.   *Whoring is evil.*
 Kalasa m'jino.   *It has afflicted the tooth.*
Mayoliyoli, 'mwe!   Whoring, oh you!
 Ahe—yayi!   *Ah—no!*
Wawona, mlamu wane!   You have seen it, my in-law!

Ahe—hole—yayi!   Ah—alas—no!
 Mayoliyoli ngaheni.   *Whoring is evil.*
 Kalasa m'jino!   *It has afflicted the tooth!*[90]

In a society in which, as we have seen, bearing children is cardinal to the fulfillment of a woman's expected social role, to be unable to give birth is more than ample grounds for divorce by her husband. In this song, as with the song *Iyayi lelo, ŵaNyilongo,* quoted above, a woman shifts blame from herself and publicly accuses her husband of importing the disease that has rendered him impotent or sterile or made her barren.

Experiencing loneliness, neglect, jealousies, psychological tensions, and exploitation, it was natural that some women should wish to obtain divorces. Divorce had been common among the matrilineal southern Tumbuka before the Ngoni conquest, and it is well known that it is readily available to women both in neighboring matrilineal areas and in urban areas. The songs of *vimbuza* allow a woman to threaten the divorce of an unsatisfactory husband to shame him:

Garu-garu!   You dog, you!
Mwagaruka mwaŵonachi?   What makes you behave this way?
 Garu-garu!   *You dog, you!*
Mwagaruka mwaŵonachi?   What makes you behave this way?
Mwaŵona mwatora ŵalelo!   It's because you've married a fresh
                                                 new wife!

Ine, nimalayilano!   For me, it's "Farewell!"

Ine yayi!!	I won't take it!!
Ine yayi!!	I won't take it!!
Ziduke!	Watch out!
Zizamkomola ng'ombe!	The cattle [of bridewealth] are going to be returning![91]

Despite such threats, however, divorce has been neither easy to obtain nor a really viable alternative. It violates the norms of the patrilinial and virilocal marriage system introduced by the Ngoni, the ideals of Christianity in an area overwhelmingly Christian, and all men's perceived need to exercise firm social control over women.[92] Men absent from their homes for long periods of time have sought to maintain their position at home in the rural village partly by increasing their control over the women whom they have left behind.[93] They have found powerful allies in their opposition to divorce. First, both families linked by the marriage are usually set against divorce. The woman's family oppose it on grounds of scandal and because they probably would have to refund the bridewealth for a wife deemed unsatisfactory.[94] The husband's family oppose it because they desire to retain control over the woman and her labor in a situation of acute labor shortage caused by the absence of men and, especially, because they want her to produce children for the family.

Local chiefs, who have long adjudicated divorce cases in their courts, have been a second force opposed to divorce. They have considered stable family life as vital to the continued existence of a rural society deeply wounded by labor migrancy and poverty, and, as such, they have felt it crucial to control the movements of women. In 1936, for example, they established the compulsory registration of marriages as a means to that end.[95] Furthermore, during the colonial period, the gifts returning migrants usually gave to chiefs were a principal source of their income, and they naturally hesitated to jeopardize this income by granting divorces to wives of absent migrants.[96]

The area's Europeans have similarly opposed divorce. The influential Scottish Presbyterian and Roman Catholic missionaries have argued against it on religious and moral grounds, while the British administrators (and the contemporary Malawian state), as part of their efforts to maintain the social health of rural areas, championed the stability of family life and supported the chiefs.[97]

With such a set of allies ranged against them, women have found it difficult to obtain a divorce—so common in the pre-Ngoni period—and if they did obtain it, the children are retained by the husband's family and the woman must leave her home to seek a new life.[98] Women are well aware that the cards have been stacked against them and that they have had to endure the conditions of their marriage whether they like it or not:

NyaPhiri wakuti, "Ngwane!"
NyaBanda wakuti, "Ngwane!"
Kumwanalume yumoza nakana!
   Lya-ya-ye, nyumba yathenga
     njihi
Aenya eee, nikapeleko madando.
Ningaluza ŵana ŵane ine.

Nakana!!
Mulala wakuti, "Ngwane!"
Mudoko wakuti, "Ngwane!"
Kumwanalume yumoza nakana!
   Lya-ya-ye, nyumba yathenga
     njihi
Aenya eee, nikapeleko madando.
Ningaluza ŵana ŵane ine.

Nakana!!

NyaPhiri says, "He's mine!"
NyaBanda says, "He's mine!"
I reject this man!
   Lya-ya-he, where is the
     government court?
Yes, I want to take my complaint to the court. But I will lose my children if I do.
I cannot do it!!
The old one says, "He's mine."
The young one says, "He's mine!"
I reject this man!
   Lya-ya-he, where is the
     government court?
Yes, I want to take my complaint to the court. But I will lose my children if I do.
No, I cannot do it!![99]

When the colonial period ended in Malawi and Zambia in 1964, *vimbuza* was still, despite the long history of male hostility to it, a vital phenomenon ready for further changes in both its form and its incidence. Political independence was crucial to *vimbuza*'s development for several reasons. First, and of immense importance, the new governments gave official approval to *vimbuza* for the first time in its history. After decades of missionary contempt for and condemnation of "native dancing" as a hotbed of superstition, sensual vice, and immorality, African politicians identified dancing as a centrally important element in what they were trying to define as a new public culture. As the crucial part of the *vimbuza* ceremonials consisted of intricate dancing in striking costumes, *vimbuza* dancing soon was detached from the therapeutic exorcism ceremonies and incorporated, qua dancing, in the formulations of the new, allegedly "national" cultures. This type of dancing quickly came to be a source of income, as it was considered "entertainment" that could command payment, and it was speedily taken over by men, emptied of its spiritual content, and established as something parallel to "real" *vimbuza*. It became a common feature of officially organized displays for tourists and of officially patronized national cultural festivities, and Zambian postal authorities even placed a male *vimbuza* dancer on one of its postage stamps. (See fig. 8.)

Exponents of the new dance-as-entertainment form of *vimbuza*,

8. A male *vimbuza* dancer depicted on a Zambian postage stamp of 1968 as part of the effort to appropriate *vimbuza* spirit possession to be part of a new Zambian "national" culture.

such as the famous Siyayo Mkandawire, a Malawian who enjoyed perhaps the most successful dancing career in Zambia, began literally to sing the praises of their new governmental patrons, thereby reversing the long-established tradition of tart complaint in the songs. In the following "entertainment" *vimbuza* song, Siyayo Mkandawire moves from *vimbuza*'s usual concerns to articulating banal praises for Malawi's President Banda ("Ngwazi") and Zambia's President Kaunda and his United National Independent party for bringing independence to Nyasaland and Northern Rhodesia, respectively:

Mundovwire kulira!   Help me to cry out!
Mundovwire kulira!   Help me to cry out!
Nkhufuma kuMalawi.   I come from Malawi.
   Ee—yaye—ee ayee!   *Ee—yaye—ee ayee!*
   Ee—yaye—ee ayee!   *Ee—yaye—ee ayee!*

Mwana wane, Madando,   My child, Madando,
Mwana wane, mwana wane.   My child, my child!
Nkhufuma kuMzimba.   I come from Mzimba.
   Ee—yaye—ee ayee!   *Ee—yaye—ee ayee!*
   Ee—yaye—ee ayee!   *Ee—yaye—ee ayee!*

Mundovwire, Mwase Kasungu.   Help me, Mwase Kasungu!
Nkhufuma kuMalawi.   I come from Malawi.
   Ee—yaye—ee ayee!   *Ee—yaye—ee ayee!*
   Ee—yaye—ee ayee!   *Ee—yaye—ee ayee!*

Wanangwa! Wanangwa!   Freedom! Freedom! Freedom!
   Wanangwa!
Wanangwa waMalaŵi.   Freedom of Malawi!
Wanangwa waUNIP.   Freedom of UNIP.
   Ee—yaye—ee ayee!   *Ee—yaye—ee ayee!*
   Ee—yaye—ee ayee!   *Ee—yaye—ee ayee!*

Nachema kwaKaunda!   I have called to Kaunda!
Nachema kwaKaunda!   I have called to Kaunda!
Nachema kwaKaunda!   I have called to Kaunda!
Wanangwa kwaKaunda   The freedom of Kaunda
Ngwazi kuMalaŵi   And of the Ngwazi in Malawi!
   Ee—yaye—ee ayee!   *Ee—yaye—ee ayee!*
   Ahole—kwenda kwaSiyayo!   *Ahole—oh, [look at the dance]*
                                            movements of Siyayo![100]

The splitting of *vimbuza* dancing away from the exorcism ceremony as a result of official governmental advocacy established parallel dance traditions in both Malawi and Zambia, and, confusingly,
both streams are known as *vimbuza*. Those who believe in the
therapeutic role of *vimbuza* see dancing-as-entertainment, a part of
the recently forged "national" cultures and a realm of greatly increasing male endeavor, as wholly bogus. Such people are contemptuous of the new *vimbuza* dance groups, often hotly dismissing
them as "just culture," meaning that they are the trivialized crea-
tures of the Ministry of Culture and have no living roots among ordinary people.[101]

Yet official advocacy of *vimbuza* affected the other, "real" *vimbuza* tradition as well, in that it led rapidly to the weakening of
church opposition to it. Most Christian leaders have been pressed by
the independent governments to cease their long opposition to most
aspects of "African Culture" and have decided that it is only politic
to end their open opposition to *vimbuza*. This has been so especially
in the case of European missionaries who have been sensitive to
charges of insensitivity to African customs, and they have been
quick to agree—at least publicly—with the new governments. Now
they claim to see *vimbuza* as "just dancing" and hence posing no
moral or religious problems.[102] As a Presbyterian minister has remarked, while in times past those claiming to be possessed by *vimbuza* would be suspended from the church, "today that is not the
case because religion has become mixed with politics and it would
be politically bad to suspend people from the church."[103]

As a consequence of the official protection afforded to possession
as a component of a recently fabricated "African Culture," *vimbuza*
has come out of the closet and changed a great deal in the past two
decades. The changes have taken three forms: professionalization,
privatization, and Christianization. The professionalization has
stemmed directly from the tradition of the itinerant witchfinders
(*nchimi*) who, from the 1910s onward, periodically gained notoriety
and broad support as prophets. In the colonial period these *nchimi*
were relatively few in number and often incurred overt governmental hostility and suppression. Since independence, however, a new
generation of *nchimi* has thrived, and they are now proliferating rapidly. The granting of legitimacy to a vaguely defined—or a wholly
undefined—corpus of "African customs" by the state won the
nchimi official governmental registration during the 1970s as "Afri-

can healers," even though they are not primarily herbalists (*ng'anga*), dealing as they do primarily with the spirit world. The *nchimi* now emulate Western-type physicians, competing among themselves for customers, with the more successful having opened their own ostentatiously bureaucratized "clinics." They have become the successful psychiatrists of the Tumbuka medical world.

As this has occurred the *nchimi* have energetically moved into *vimbuza* to appropriate for themselves the task of exorcising *vimbuza* spirits and of mediating the messages of *vyanusi* spirits, usurping the role of the nonprofessional village herbalists who, in former times, acted as the *mbuya* of those suffering from possession. More and more, *nchimi* are serving as paid masters of ceremony for exorcism dances that previously were informally organized by a woman, her *mbuya*, and her friends and acquaintances.

With the rise to power of the professional *nchimi* has come another important change in *vimbuza's* incidence. Despite the fact that the Presbyterian and Roman Catholic churches have been compelled by political circumstances to mute their disapproval of spirit possession, they still frown on church members' dancing, and both still maintain—though rarely exercise—the right to suspend communicants who have danced at public ceremonies.[104] To widen its appeal, then, the *nchimi* have developed a new form of *vimbuza* wherein when one is possessed by a spirit, it may be "sealed off" and dealt with by a combination of herbal remedies and private prayer rather than through public dancing.[105] In a complete break with its earlier history of being a social phenomenon, *vimbuza* is currently in the process of becoming, at least partly, a private affliction similar to a psychological problem in Europe or America. Many respectable Christians—men and women alike—now say that they have *vimbuza* but claim that it is being dealt with discretely, without the need for the all-too-obvious—and increasingly costly—public ceremonies in which drumming and dancing are central.[106]

Finally, *vimbuza* is becoming Christianized at the hands of the *nchimi*. On the one hand, the *nchimi*, encouraged by government recognition as exponents of African culture, are now willing to attack the established orthodox churches and claim religious equality with them:

Waliska, mwe!	You priests, hear!
Waliske, mwe mama!	You priests, hear me!

Waliska mwe, lekani	*You priests, stop your*
kudemwera.	*backsliding.*
Uyo Mwenecho	That Owner
Wangamanya nyengo zose,	*Is able at all times,*
Wangamanya kupoka!	*Is able to take your life!*
Madikoni, mwe!	You deacons, hear!
Madikoni, mwe mama!	You deacons, hear me!
Madikoni, lekani kudemwera.	*Deacons, stop your backsliding.*
Uyo Mwenecho	That Owner
Wangamanya nyengo zose,	*Is able at all times,*
Wangamanya kupoka!	*Is able to take your life!*
Walala, mwe!	You elders, hear!
Walala, mwe mama!	You elders, hear me!
Walala mwe, lekani	*Elders, stop your backsliding.*
kudemwera.	
Uyo Mwenecho	That Owner
Wangamanya nyengo zose,	*Is able at all times,*
Wangamanya kupoka!	*Is able to take your life!*[107]

On the other hand, earlier linkages between *vimbuza* and heterodox separatist Christian churches, such as the African National church, have been strengthened and formalized in two ways. First, the *nchimi* have introduced into the possession liturgy formal prayers at its start and finish that invoke the Christian God's help in controlling the spirit that is troubling the afflicted. Second, the *nchimi*—or, perhaps, the afflicted persons themselves—have also introduced a new type of song into the ceremonies. These new songs are often directly derived from hymns sung in churches, and their use creates a wholly new atmosphere of Christian supplication into the *vimbuza* ceremonies:

Musayilani mwana,	Plead for the child,
Musayilani—	Plead—
Muzina linu, Chiuta,	*In your name, Oh God,*
Muzimu Mutuŵa,	*Oh, Holy Spirit,*
Musayilani—eyi—yaya	*Plead for her—eyi—yaya*
Musayilani mwana,	Plead for the child,
Wachindi makola,	So that she will dance well
Musayilani—	Plead—
Muzina linu, Chiuta,	*In your name, Oh God,*
Muzimu Mutuŵa,	*Oh, Holy Spirit,*
Musayilani—eyi—yaya.	*Plead for her—eyi—yaya.*[108]

A final example of the new songs gives an indication of how far the process has proceeded in moving *vimbuza* toward being a Christian ceremony and one that, conceivably, might in the future move away from being a social phenomenon toward being a form of Christianity itself, with the *nchimi* as its priests:

Apa mukukana Chiuta,	As you reject God,
Kudindi mwamukhala nanjani?	In the grave with whom will you stay?
Eya—a—Yesu, mwe!	*Eya—a—Jesus, hear!*
Apa mukukana Chiuta,	As you reject God,
Kudindi mwamukhala nanjani?	In the grave with whom will you stay?
Eya—a—Yesu, mwe!	*Eya—a—Jesus, hear!*
Yesu, mwamphanji yane!	Jesus, you are my rock!
Eya—a—Yesu, mwe!	*Eya—a—Jesus, hear!*
Ndibisame mwa imwe!	Let me hide myself in you!
Eya—a—Yesu, mwe!	*Eya—a—Jesus, hear!*
Ndopazo zinafuma!	Oh, the blood that was shed!
Eya—a—Yesu, mwe!	*Eya—a—Jesus, hear!*[109]

In sum, then, *vimbuza* showed its persistence in the face of decades of hostility during the colonial period by both engaging with historical change and providing women with an interpretation of that history based on the ethical truths perceived as existing in the matrilineal system as it existed before 1856. During the colonial period, it used these truths pungently to criticize those in power over women and to suggest alternatives to the marginalization and mistreatment that were so often the lot of women. But it was never rigid, and its flexibility helped it to survive into the postcolonial period. Since independence in 1964 it has continued to change, perhaps more rapidly than ever, adjusting to a new world of increased bureaucracy and greater tolerance. This being the case, it is virtually certain that *vimbuza*—together with other spirit-possession phenomena—will continue as a prominent marker on the spiritual and intellectual landscape of central Africa regardless of whatever "modernization" might occur. Studies of possession ceremonies—and especially of the songs sung in them—will continue to be useful in shedding light on the consciousness of poor and marginalized women as they attempt to deal with the problems they encounter daily.

Notes

1. Abbreviations used in the note citations for this chapter include those for the Public Record Office, London (PRO), the National Library of Scotland, Edinburgh (NLS), and the Malawi National Archives, Zomba (MNA).

2. One of these censuses was carried out in northern Malawi in 1967 and the others in eastern Zambia and northern Malawi in 1985.

3. Details about *vimbuza* are derived from direct observation, from over two hundred interviews done in Malawi and Zambia, and from analysis of the songs sung in the possession ceremonies.

4. For a discussion of the role of music in inducing trance, see J. Jaynes, *Origins of Consciousness in the Breakdown of the Bicameral Mind* (Boston, 1977), 364–73.

5. For an interesting discussion of the interrelationship between symbolism and power relations, see A. Cohen, *Two-Dimensional Man* (London, 1974).

6. Cf. I. M. Lewis, *Ecstatic Religion: An Anthropological Study of Spirit Possession and Shamanism* (Harmondsworth, 1871), 79–85.

7. Interview with P. Nkhata et al., Kayimbone village, Lundazi district, Zambia, 10 May 1974.

8. Sung by Siyayo Mkandawire apparently sometime in the 1970s. Original tape generously supplied by Mr. Alfred Kankanda from the archives of the Zambia Broadcasting Service without specific details. Italicized sections are those that are choruses. All translations from the Tumbuka are the responsibility of the authors.

9. Sung by Joyce Banda, Lusaka, Zambia, 30 August 1985.

10. Song sung by NyaChihame, Ezuleni village, Lundazi district, Zambia, 29 July 1985.

11. The two paragraphs that follow are based on S. S. Ncozana, "Spirit Possession and Tumbuka Christians, 1875–1950," Ph.D. diss., University of Aberdeen, 1985.

12. B. J. Soko, "Stylistique et Messages dans le Vimbuza," thesis for a doctorate of the third cycle, University of the Sorbonne, Paris, 1984, 45.

13. L. Vail, "Suggestions towards a Reinterpreted Tumbuka History," in *The Early History of Malawi*, ed. B. Pachai (London, 1972), 151–53.

14. For a discussion of Tumbuka religion, see L. Vail, "Religion, Language, and the Tribal Myth: The Tumbuka and Chewa of Malawi," in *Guardians of the Land: Essays on Central African Territorial Cults*, ed. M. Schoffeleers (Gwelo, Zimbabwe, 1978), 209–34.

15. Ibid., 214–18.

16. D. Fraser, "The Zulu of Nyasaland: Their Manners and Customs," *Proceedings of the Philosophical Society of Glasgow* 32 (1900):66–70; J. Henderson, "Northern Nyasaland," *Scottish Geographical Magazine* 16, no. 2

(1900):86–87; Anonymous, "The Tumbuka Tribe," *Aurora* 5, no. 25 (1901); A. C. Simpson, "Early Days on the Zambesi, Shire, and Lake Nyasa," *Central African Times*, 24 December 1904.

17. J. Stewart, "Report on Journey of Exploration, September to December 1879" (Edinburgh, n.d.), 2; Steele to Laws, 9 November 1891, MS 7895, NLS; Sharpe to Elgin, 17 October 1906, CO 525/14, PRO; report of 28 June 1932, "Native Administration, Mzimba, 1932–34," NN 1/20/B, MNA.

18. *Baraza* of 31 October 1935, "Tours of H. E. the Governor, 1935–38," S1/62/35, MNA; S. G. Wilson, "Agricultural Practice among the Angoni-Tumbuka Tribes of Mzimba (Nyasaland)," *East African Agricultural Journal*, October 1941, 89–93.

19. A. Young and P. Brown, *The Physical Environment of Northern Nyasaland* (Zomba, 1962). See also *The Report on the Economic Survey of Nyasaland, 1958–1959* (Salisbury, n.d.), 209–10, which reports the Ngoni area as extremely marginal agricultural land.

20. Interview with Zakeyo Soko, Embangweni village, Mzimba district, Malawi, 1 August 1970; W. A. Elmslie, *Among the Wild Ngoni* (Edinburgh and London, 1901), 31–32; Elmslie to Laws, 6 June 1887, MS 7890, NLS.

21. Interview with Inkhosi yamaKosi Mbwelwa III and councillors, Edingeni, Mzimba district, Malawi, 19 September 1971.

22. Elmslie, *Among the Wild Ngoni*, 59–67; D. Fraser, *Winning a Primitive People* (London, 1914), 183.

23. Interview with Chief Kapichila Banda et al., Ndande village, Lundazi district, Zambia, 28 April 1975.

24. J. McCracken, *Politics and Christianity in Malawi, 1875–1940* (Cambridge, 1977), 57–109.

25. E.g., Granville to Foreign Office, 19 March 1885, and Goodrich to Foreign Office, 24 April and 1 June 1885, FO 84/1702, PRO.

26. It should be noted that the Mission hoped that its own graduates would take the lead in moving the Protectorate toward greater African participation in politics, and it helped sponsor the early Native Associations that are now considered the forerunners of anticolonial politics.

27. Cf. the *Aurora* (Livingstonia, Nyasaland), 1 February and 1 June 1897.

28. Letter from Association to Elmslie, 13 June 1924, "Mombera's Native Association, 1924–29," S1/1365/24, MNA.

29. Laws to Smith, 10 September 1894, MS 7877, NLS.

30. Henderson, "Northern Nyasaland," 82–89; the *Aurora*, 1 October 1897; "Annual Report (Chinteche) 1902," NNC 3/1/1/, MNA.

31. For a general discussion of this change, see L. Vail, "The Political Economy of East Central Africa," in *History of Central Africa*, ed. D. Birmingham and P. M. Martin, 2 vols. (New York, 1983), 2:200–211.

32. See, for example, E. P. Makambe, "The Nyasaland African Labour 'Ulendos' to Southern Rhodesia and the Problem of African 'Highwaymen,' 1903–1923: A Study in the Limitations of Early Independent Labour Migration," *African Affairs*, no. 317 (1980):548–66.

33. "Major Pearce's Confidential Notes on Nyasaland," GOA 5/3//3, MNA.

34. Fraser to Chief Secretary, 24 April 1920, "Hut Tax, 1919–26," S1/1365/19, MNA.

35. "Annual Report, Mombera, 1918," S1/1008/19, MNA.

36. Interviews with Mopho Jere, Ekwalweni village, Mzimba district, Malawi, 22 September 1971, and with Timoti Zimba et al., Mjulu village, Lundazi district, Zambia, 11 May 1974; "Annual Report, Mombera, 1918," S1/1008/19, MNA; "Nyasaland Civil Servants Asscn.: Petition to Secretary of State for Improved Conditions of Service, Fraser to Chief Secretary, 24 April 1920, "Hut Tax, 1919–26," S1/1365/19, MNA; Smith to Churchill, 29 August 1921, and enclosures, CO 525/97, PRO.

37. District Commissioner, Mzimba, to Provincial Commissioner, Northern Province, 26 June 1937, "Administration, 1936," NNM 1/14/6, MNA.

38. Report for Lundazi district, "Annual Report—East Luangwa, 1933," ZA 7/1/16/4, Zambia National Archives, Lusaka. Report of Fairfax-Francklin, 1 November 1930, "Report on Economic Resources of the Northern Province," S1/1361/30, MNA; Report for Mzimba, "Annual Reports, 1937," S1/18/38, MNA; D. C., Mzimba, to Mbelwa, 3 February 1938, "Mombera District Council, 1937/39," NNM 1/16/4, MNA.

39. Interview with P. Nkhata et al., Kayimbone village, Lundazi district, Zambia, 10 May 1974.

40. Interview with Adam Mkandawire et al., Chewe village, Lundazi district, Zambia, 30 March 1974; Ncozana, "Spirit Possession and Tumbuka Christians," 212–14.

41. Interview with Zaona Nkhoma et al., Chewe village, Lundazi district, Zambia, 30 March 1974; Soko, "Stylistique et Messages," 44–45.

42. See Jaynes, *The Origin of Consciousness,* 347–49, for a discussion of the role of stress in provoking spirit possession.

43. The fact that an occasional man is affected does not detract from *vimbuza's* having been primarily a women's phenomenon over the past seventy years. It merely underscores the fact that it is a phenomenon of the dispossessed—not women qua women—with most of the dispossessed being women.

44. Interview with the councillors of Inkhosi yamaKosi Mbwelwa III, Edingeni village, Mzimba district, Malawi, 19 September 1971.

45. M. Chanock, *Law, Custom, and Social Order: The Colonial Experience in Malawi and Zambia* (Cambridge, 1985), 85–102.

46. Interview with P. Nkhata and P. Nyirongo, Kayimbone village, Lundazi district, Zambia, 10 May 1974; Soko, "Stylistique et messages dans le vimbuza," 44.

47. Sung by Mulota Nyirenda, Kayowoyera village, Rumphi district, Malawi, September 1985.

48. See, for example, G. Shepperson and T. Price, *Independent African: John Chilembwe, and the Origins, Setting, and Significance of the Nyasa-*

land Native Rising of 1915 (Edinburgh, 1958), 147–59; K. P. Lohrentz, "Joseph Booth, Charles Domingo, and the Seventh Day Baptists in Northern Nyasaland, 1910–12," *Journal of African History* 12, no. 3 (1971):461–80; and McCracken, *Politics and Christianity in Malawi*, 184–220.

49. For the Jehovah's Witnesses, see R. I. Rotburg, *The Rise of Nationalism in Central Africa* (Cambridge, Mass.: 1967), 135–42; for the Zionists, see Jean Comaroff, *Body of Power, Spirit of Resistance: The Culture and History of a South African People* (Chicago and London, 1985), 195–251, passim.

50. "Reports by Residents in the Northern Province on the Watch Tower Movement," S2/1/24, MNA; Report of Resident, Karonga, to Provincial Commissioner, 5 November 1924, "Native Controlled Missions, 1922–25," NN 1/20/2, MNA.

51. "Native Controlled Missions, 1925–31," NN 1/20/3, MNA; D. C., Karonga, to Provincial Commissioner, 13 March 1929, S2/20¹/23, "Reports on Watch Tower," MNA.

52. Quoted in enclosure in D. C., Karonga, to Provincial Commissioner, 21 March 1929, "Native Controlled Missions, 1925–31," NN 1/20/3, MNA.

53. D. C., Karonga, to Provincial Commissioner, 13 March 1929, "Reports on Watch Tower," S2/20¹/23, MNA.

54. Tracey's songs were recorded for appearance in his *Music of Africa* series of gramophone records, and the master tapes are housed at the Library of African Music, at Rhodes University, Grahamstown, South Africa. The Federal Broadcasting collection, on 78 RPM disks, is housed in the Sound Archives section of the Zambian Broadcasting Services, Lusaka, Zambia.

55. E.g., interview with Sellah Msiska, Kayowoyera village, Rumphi district, Malawi, 27 September 1984.

56. *Andrew Smith's Journal of His Expedition into the Interior of South Africa—1834–36*, ed. W. F. Lye (Cape Town, 1975), 238–39.

57. Sung by NyaKamenya, Chiwono village, Rumphi district, Malawi, 8 September 1984.

58. For a discussion of both these ethnically framed male interpretations of the area's history, see L. Vail and L. White, "Tribalism in the Political History of Malawi," in *The Creation of Tribalism in Southern Africa*, ed. L. Vail (London and Berkeley, 1988), 151–66.

59. The information in the five paragraphs that follow is derived from a host of field interviews, including those with Ching'anya Mkandawire, Mzalangwe area, 13 March 1970, and with Nelson Nkhata, Thombololo village, 4 August 1970, both in Mzimba district, Malawi; and those with Gideon Ntirenda et al., Matheza village, 10 April 1974; David Lunda et al., Chambalesese village, 18 April 1974; James Dokowe, Mphamba village, 1 May 1974; and Chintembo Nyirenda et al., Chintembo village, 9 May 1974; Chief Mwase Lundazi et al., Nthembwe village, 25 April 1974; and Chief Kapachila Banda et al., Ndanda village, 28 April 1975, all in Lundazi district,

Zambia. We are grateful to John Comaroff for clarifying some of the anthropological technicalities for us.

60. Song sung by a group at Thunda village, Livingstonia, Rumphi district, Malawi, 1 January 1984.

61. Interview with David Sibande, Emoneni village, Mzimba district, Malawi, 14 September 1971; also T. C. Young, *Notes on the Customs and Folklore of the Tumbuka-Kamanga Peoples* (Livingstonia [Nyasaland], 1931), 56, and Y. M. Chibambo, *My Ngoni of Nyasaland* (London, n.d.), 40–41.

62. Cf. D. M. Schneider and K. Gough, eds., *Matrilineal Kinship* (Berkeley and Los Angeles, 1961), 21–24.

63. See, for example, C. S. Lancaster's account of the Goba people of the Zambezi valley, *The Goba of the Zambezi: Sex Roles, Economics, and Change* (Norman, Okla., 1981), and L. Holy, *Strategies and Norms in a Changing Matrilineal Society: Descent, Succession, and Inheritance among the Toka of Zambia* (Cambridge, 1986).

64. Fraser, "The Zulu of Nyasaland," 70–71; interviews with David Sibande, Emoneni village, 14 September 1970, and with Inkosi Mzukuzuku and councillors, Embangweni village, 16 September 1971, both in Mzimba district, Malawi.

65. Interview with Zacharia Mwandila et al., Chijemu village, Lundazi district, Zambia, 27 March 1974.

66. Interviews with Daniel Mtonga et al., Chinyumba village, 6 April 1974, and with James Zimba et al., Chifwiti village, 25 March 1974, both in Lundazi district, Zambia.

67. Interview with S. Ng'oma et al., Munonda village, Lundazi district, Zambia, 14 April 1974. See also Young, *Customs and Folklore,* 62. The one exception to this general rule seems to have been in the Mbalachanda area to the west of the South Rukuru River, where the presence of tsetse fly prevented the keeping of cattle. In these areas one could still find "traditional" matrilineal-uxorilocal marriages in the 1960s.

68. Sung by NyaChisi, Chimpeni village, Lundazi district, Zambia, 25 March 1975.

69. Sung by Mutundwatha Nyakando and Felida Nyirenda, Mutendere compound, Lusaka, Zambia, 16 August 1985. It is widely believed in the area that rootless wanderers are peculiarly liable to attacks by spiritual forces.

70. Laws to Smith, 10 September 1894, MS 7877, NLS.

71. Henderson, "Northern Nyasaland," 82–89; *Aurora,* 1 October 1897; "Annual Report (Chinteche) 1902," NNC 3/1/1, MNA.

72. Sharpe to Elgin, 17 October 1906, CO 525/14, PRO.

73. Sung by Flora Mbale, Kaunda Square, Lusaka, Zambia, 25 July 1985.

74. Sung by Mutunduwatha NyaKandaba, Mutendere compound, Lusaka, Zambia, 16 August 1985.

75. Interview with Gidion Nyirenda et al., Matheza village, Lundazi district, Zambia, 10 April 1975.

76. Sung by Loveness Mtonga, Kalingalinga compound, Lusaka, Zambia, 30 July 1985.

77. Sung by Mulacheta Mwale, Ezuleni village, Lundazi district, Zambia, 7 August 1985.

78. Sung by Esther Mulenji Betela, Kamutu Msyali village, Rumphi district, Malawi, 8 September 1984.

79. Sung by Elina NyaMhango, Kayowoyero village, Rumphi district, Malawi, 26 September 1984.

80. Sung by Tamalanji NyaPhiri, Chingala village, Lundazi district, Zambia, 7 September 1982. The phrase "Amama, kunozga" is ironic, and perhaps a better translation would be "Mother, what a shame!"

81. Sung by NyaMphande, Chasimpha village, Lundazi district, Zambia, 25 March 1973.

82. Sung by NyaManda, Kalingalinga compound, Lusaka, Zambia, 31 July 1985.

83. Cf. Read, "Migrant Labour in Africa," 624, where she notes that: "'I must have a man to help me,' was the constantly reiterated cry of the women whose husbands were away, and the poignant refrains of the songs they sang about their absent husbands were more on the theme of their having to live alone than of their wanting more children."

84. Sung by B. K. Nyilongo, Mbulunji village, Rumphi district, Malawi, 15 January 1984.

85. Sung by N. E. T. Nyirenda, Mzokoto village, Rumphi district, Malawi, 14 January 1984.

86. Sung by Tamalanji NyaPhiri, Chingala village, Lundazi district, Zambia, 7 September 1982.

87. Sung by Nyamayuni Msiska, Wayungwa village, Rumphi district, Malawi, 4 January 1984.

88. Sung by Eliza NyaMtonga, Jimusanga village, Lundazi district, Zambia, 16 August 1985.

89. Sung by B. K. Nyilongo, Mbulunji village, Rumphi district, Malawi, 15 January 1984.

90. Sung by Angelina Msyali, Chadimba village, Rumphi district, Malawi, 7 September 1984.

91. Sung by Tamala NyaPhiri, Chimpeni village, Lundazi district, Zambia, 25 March 1973.

92. E.g., Report on meeting of 8 January 1925, "West Nyasa Native Association," S1/2065/19, MNA.

93. As with Chopi workers from Mozambique, it was legally impossible during the colonial period for a man from colonial Malawi to bring his wife and family to the workplace, which was seen as for temporary laborers only. Hence a man had no choice but to migrate without his family.

94. This is discussed in Chanock, *Law, Custom, and Social Order.* See also Read, "Migrant Labour in Africa," 612.

95. Report of meeting of 16 December 1936, "Mombera District Council, 1937–39," NNM 1/16/4, MNA.

96. Tour Report no. 12 of 1938, in "Tour Reports, Fort Jameson, 1938/39," vol. 3, SEC/NAT/36, Zambia National Archives, Lusaka.

97. See, for example, I. Linden, *Catholics, Peasants, and Chewa Resistance in Nyasaland, 1889–1939* (London, 1974).

98. E.g., Report of meeting of 22–24 June 1937, "Mombera District Council, 1937–39," NNM 1/16/4, MNA.

99. Sung by Selina Nyirenda, Garden compound, Lusaka, Zambia, 30 August 1985.

100. Sung by Siyayo Mkandawire and recorded by the Zambian Broadcasting Service at Mwase Lundazi village, Lundazi district, Zambia, 25 September 1965. The recording is stored on disk in the Sound Archives of the Service in Lusaka.

101. E.g., interview with NyaNdaŵadata, Mtendele compound, Lusaka, Zambia, 24 August 1982.

102. Interviews with priests at Nkhamenya Mission, Mzimba district, Malawi, September 1985, and with Father Vaughn, Lumezi Mission, Lundazi district, Zambia, 13 September 1985.

103. Interview with the Reverend Mr. Jere, Lundazi, Lundazi district, Zambia, 12 September 1985.

104. Interviews with the Reverend Mr. Jere, Lundazi, Lundazi district, Zambia, 12 September 1985, and with Father Vaughan, Lumezi Mission, Lundazi district, Zambia, 13 September 1985.

105. Interviews with the Reverend Mr. Jere, Lundazi, Lundazi district, Zambia, and with B. P. Msiska, Mpachi village, Rumphi district, Malawi, 23 September 1985.

106. In connection with this change, we have been informed by Ann-Lise Quinn that more and more men are now being afflicted by *vimbuza* (personal communication, 20 July 1990). Pending further research, one can only wonder if this change is connected with the sharp reduction in the possibility of male labor migrancy to the mines of South Africa.

107. Sung by Mulota Nyirenda, Kayowoyera village, Rumphi district, Malawi, September 1985.

108. Sung by NyaMbuza Msiska, Chiwono village, Rumphi district, Malawi, 7 September 1984.

109. Sung by Milita Mkandawire, Kayowera village, Rumphi district, Malawi, 23 September 1984.

8

Of Chameleons and Clowns
The Case of Jack Mapanje

On 25 September 1987, Jack Mapanje, Malawi's most accomplished poet, was arrested in Zomba by police units acting for Malawi's Special Branch. He was taken in handcuffs to the University of Malawi, where he is head of the English department. His office was searched and various manuscripts were confiscated, including drafts of recent poems and the text of an address delivered at a conference at Stockholm in 1986 under the title "Censoring the African Poem: Personal Reflections," which included a blow-by-blow account of his dealings with the Malawi Censorship Board.[1] Mapanje was then taken to his house, where a further search was made and where his three children were forbidden to telephone their mother, Mercy, a midwife absent in Lilongwe, Malawi's capital, completing a course in community nursing. Finally, he was removed to Mikuyu Maximum Security Detention Centre near Zomba, where he was held in the company of a mixed group of detainees, at least one of whom has been imprisoned without trial for more than twenty years. For eighteen months no visits were permitted by his wife or his priest or by friends or colleagues. He was eventually released on 10 May 1991. No charges were ever brought against him.

Mapanje is best known for his volume *Of Chameleons and Gods*, a selection of poems written between 1970 and 1980 and published in 1981.[2] But he is also chair of the Linguistics Association of SADCC Universities, has worked intermittently for the British Broadcasting Company, and has twice served as a judge for the Commonwealth Prize for poetry. He has published other books, including an important anthology of African oral poetry,[3] and he is editor of *Kalulu*, a Malawian journal devoted to oral literature. One effect of his detention is that the Malawian authorities discovered for the first time the scale of his international reputation. Mapanje was made a Prisoner of Conscience by Amnesty International and an honorary member of P.E.N. American Center. Selections from *Of*

9. Jack Mapanje, Malawi's foremost poet, around 1981, when his *Of Chameleons and Gods* was published. (Courtesy of Heinemann Educational Books, Ltd.)

Chameleons and Gods were read by British playwright Harold Pinter outside the Malawi High Commission in London, and the reading was broadcast on the BBC Africa Service and heard in Zomba by Mapanje's children. His most recent work has been published in *Index on Censorship*, the *Literary Review*, and *Stand*.[4] In June 1988, he was the winner of the Poetry International Award in Rotterdam, and the award was accepted on his behalf by the Nobel Prizewinner Wole Soyinka.

For most of the people who have protested to Malawi's Life President, H. Kamuzu Banda, and his agents over Mapanje's arrest, the issues are straightforward. A much admired poet, living in a dictatorship, was detained without trial, with the government having no discernible intention of bringing charges against him. As the English poet David Constantine puts it, in a poem known to have been read by Mapanje in his detention, "Some things are black and white: laws against poems."[5] The banning of poetry touches some hidden wellspring in most of us, and Mapanje's case was taken up by thousands of readers who had heard little of him until the Malawian authorities were foolish enough to attempt to silence him.[6]

Yet to those who know both Mapanje and Malawi, the case against the Malawian government is both more complex and more outrageous. No poet in southern Africa in recent years has worked more assiduously and self-consciously in terms of the aesthetic we have been describing and illustrating in this book. No poet has more deliberately confronted the issues of poetry and power. His work and his arrest demonstrate two things appropriate to the concluding chapter of this book. On the one hand, they illustrate the imaginative possibilities of adapting the aesthetics of oral poetry to the English language and the printed word. On the other, they demonstrate the ambiguities of that aesthetic in the jungle of postindependence African politics.

Mapanje first came to prominence in the early 1970s as a founder member of the Malawi Writers' Group. This group, which met weekly, was similar to other groups throughout the world in that it provided its members with a small but usually sympathetic audience for their own poems and stories. Two features of the Malawi Writers' Group, however, gave its meetings an unusual importance. The first was that they succeeded in avoiding the control of the official government censor. The Malawi Censorship Board was established in 1968 by an act of Parliament that made it an offense to publish anything or handle any publication "likely to give offense to the religious convictions or feelings of any section of the public, bring anyone into contempt, harm relations between sections of the public or be contrary to the interests of public safety or public order."[7] As if these clauses were not sufficiently comprehensive, the act also makes provision that any member of the public could complain, anonymously if they wished, about material that had caused offence. The effect of this provision has been to make successive censors particularly zealous in order to preserve their positions. For reasons that remain unexplained, however, and that were certainly not anticipated, weekly meetings of the Writers' Group were treated in practice as part of the University of Malawi's teaching program. Although the group was by no means confined to the university—attracting contributions from journalists, teachers, and businessmen—the poems and short stories circulated for discussion were regarded as teaching materials and became, inadvertently but invaluably, a medium of uncensored publication.

The second distinctive feature followed from the first in that, in the circumstances then prevailing at the university, the Writers' Group became the only forum in which Malawian affairs were habitually discussed. The university had a football club, together with various religious societies and an embryonic student branch of the Malawi Congress party (MCP), but there were no political or sociological debating societies of the kind that flourished at other African universities. Even the student newspaper, a four-page broadsheet run off fortnightly on an arthritic duplicator, had to be supervised by a member of the staff whose principal function was to clear its contents with the government censor. The result was that, as the Writers' Group began to establish itself, it attracted to its meetings young intellectuals whose interests would normally have been diverted into other channels but who found in poems and short stories a rare permitted outlet for their concerns. Within weeks of the group's formation in April 1970, up to four hundred copies of the materials to be discussed at each meeting were being circulated within and outside the university.

It was soon obvious that poetry was the favored medium of expression and communication. Poems, these young writers discovered, could be brief and safely obscure, apparently without any sacrifice of literary merit. In part, such assumptions reflected the atmosphere of the English Department's practical criticism classes, but they quickly acquired a more urgent purpose. Over the weeks, a code of imagery began to evolve. Any poetic references to *dawn* or *cockcrow* were immediately taken as metaphors for the Malawi Congress party, the official flag of which contains a symbol of sunrise and whose Life President, H. Kamuzu Banda, proclaims *"Kwacha!"* ("Dawn!") at the beginning of all official speeches. *Kwacha* and *tambala* ("cockerel") are also the names of the units of Malawi's currency, adding conscious irony to all those poems proclaiming their disillusion with roosters and daybreak.[8]

Another recurring metaphor dealt with Chingwe's Hole. The reference is to a natural fault on the top of Zomba Plateau, a cleft in the rock face descending some hundred and fifty feet. In colonial mythology—though not in historical fact—Chingwe was described as a Yao chief who had executed his enemies by hurling them down the crevass. In 1897, Captain Brake and Mr. Gouch of the British Central Africa Rifles descended the cleft on a rope and found only that, like similar clefts throughout the Shire Highlands, the hole had been used previously as a burial site.[9] The myth, however, survived Nyasaland's entire colonial period to be adopted by poets in the Writers' Group as a metaphor for detention without trial in President Banda's Malawi. Every Malawian poet worth his salt has a poem about Chingwe's Hole, including Mapanje, whose own detention has naturally provoked further poems on the theme.

In the early 1970s, therefore, it appeared that the distinctive features of Mapanje's poetry, as that of his contemporaries such as Lupenga Mphande, Geoff Mwanja, and Felix Mnthali, had been determined by the circumstances in which he had begun to discover himself as a writer, namely as a member of the Writers' Group. Social and political concerns were central to his work because the group, his sole audience, functioned in part as the one forum available for such discussion, while a style characterized by subtlety and indirection was necessary to outwit the government's censor. In 1972, however, Mapanje left Malawi to continue his studies at the University of London, and two years later, while still writing poetry, he completed a Master of Philosophy thesis entitled "The Use of Traditional Literary Forms in Modern Malawian Writing in English."[10] This thesis describes the evolution of Malawian writing in general and the genesis of his own work in particular from a very different perspective.

His point of departure is a discussion of the predicament of writers in many parts of Africa—Anglophone and Francophone—who have

10. President Hastings Kamuzu Banda of Malawi, Rumphi, August 1969, just before the Malawi Writers' Group was formed in April 1970 at the University of Malawi. (Photo by Leroy Vail.)

found themselves increasingly, and even violently, at odds with their societies:

> While some writers have had to make a painful re-assessment of their "hoped-for-roles" in Independent Africa by an unhappy accommodation of their moral and aesthetic principles within their new political situation, others have inflicted upon themselves some sort of exile, while still others have been forced into exile by the embarrassed politicians who look at the writer's critical approach to life as an impediment to their remaining in power for as long as they would like.
>
> It is no wonder then that African writers should feel alienated in their societies today. . . . To keep their sanity . . . they have to write what politicians regard as subversive literature or obscure works either directed towards a literary coterie or meant as therapy for their psychological crises.[11]

These words anticipated by seven years the Introduction to *Of Chameleons and Gods*, where Mapanje speaks of writing verse "as a way of preserving some sanity" and of the recurring temptation "where personal voices are too easily muffled" to be like the chameleon and "bask in one's brilliant camouflage."[12] The passage from his 1974 thesis continues by identifying the dangers in this: "All this points to the possibility of the development of the doctrine of art for art's sake. If politicians do not tolerate writers this development is predictable in certain African countries, for, as the Russian Georgi Plekhanov's experience shows, art *per se* develops when the artists feel a 'hopeless contradiction between their aims and the aims of the society to which they belong.'"[13] The results may be "therapeutic," but Mapanje has larger ambitions than to direct encoded signals to small embattled communities of the like-minded.

The way forward, Mapanje argues, is for the writer to learn from the "traditional" artists of his society, and the remainder of the thesis is devoted to examining the forms of oral literature available within Malawi. Two central arguments are developed about oral culture that both throw a great deal of light on his own poetic practice and clarify just how fundamental is the nature of his challenge to President Banda's own appropriation of Malawi's history and culture.

Mapanje appeals first for a return to "traditional literature and modes of thought as the source of metaphor and inspiration."[14] In suggesting this, he is not, as it may appear, advocating a nostalgic or neotraditional literature of drums and masks and fly whisks and rain shrines. He means that he wishes the new generation of young Malawian artists to have available, even when writing in English, something of the range of devices and density of metaphor the oral poet shares with his audience. At the center of his argument is a long section on the art of riddling, a subject that has long fascinated him. Riddling, he argues, is at the heart of all new metaphors. The "rebellious nature of the riddle" lies in the fact that it surprises the audience into realizing that things are not "patterned as they appear": "Riddles push the audience into seeing relationships between the verbal world and the world behind it. Herein lies the role of the riddle challenger, if seriously taken, as a poet. Riddling is an intellectual process of creating symbols and metaphors. Need we ask the use of riddles to young writers today?" [15]

Mapanje firmly rejects the notions, still current in some discussions of writing from East and Central Africa, that oral modes are simple and unsophisticated or that wit and polish and complexity in a writer are signs of Western influence. Unfashionably for 1974, he criticizes Okot p'Bitek's *Song of Lawino,* which then enjoyed cult status as a revolutionary text, for "language so simple and ideas so naive that the work fringes on triteness." [16] To Mapanje, the language of the oral poet is sophisticated and mischievous, dense with history refined to metaphor, yet capable of dynamic effects of communication precisely because those metaphors are understood and have achieved currency. To recreate in Malawian English a language of such local resonance, recapturing the toughness and complexity of oral poetry and especially its capacity for intellectual rebellion, has become his literary program. From this perspective, the coded metaphors of the poems he contributed to meetings of the Writers' Group in the early 1970s were not primarily the product of circumstances in which the group came together. They were the offspring of a marriage of the English language with a Malawian oral aesthetic.

But the appeal to oral models carries a second implication. Mapanje's thesis of 1974 also lays claim to the authority of the oral poet in interrogating the powerful. He describes how this license operated in Malawi with a range of examples extending from the praise poet assessing the character and conduct of chiefs to the ordinary woman at her mortar pounding millet and singing satirically about her husband's laziness or neglect or declining virility. Under President Banda's regime, however, oral poetry—like dancing—has increasingly been appropriated for purposes of elementary propaganda useful in forging an officially backed public culture. It is used by agricultural-extension workers coaxing village farmers into buying fertilizers, by social workers addressing issues of rural hygiene,[17] and even by the Christian churches, which have stolen many of the best tunes. What Mapanje terms the most "dangerous" of these tendencies is that politicians have "changed the old traditional war song . . . to watered down propaganda to praise the new leaders with very little poetic insight. . . . What the new praise-song lacks is an element of constructive criticism of either the leadership or the society. The criticism was necessary in the original song because it was one way of helping the chief or the traditional leader to improve. It was also a way of knowing what the people think about the leadership. . . . What we would like to see is a critical praise-poem to bring about sanity where it is rare to find."[18] As we described in chapter two of this book, this is an argument that has been deployed by South African poets from A. C. Jordan onward. But Mapanje is the first poet in an independent country in central or southern Africa to appeal to this aesthetic as his license in questioning power.

By proposing a return to the modes and conventions of oral literature, Mapanje finds an escape from the dangers implicit in the work of the Writers' Group, the dangers of writing for a small coterie from an art-for-art's-sake stance. In its vigorous language and public themes, *Of Chameleons and Gods* fulfills this poetic program, and the embarrassed reception of the book in Malawi and its subsequent fate, having never been cleared for sale, illuminate murky corners of the country's political culture. Before these points are demonstrated in an analysis of the individual poems, however, there is one other claim made in Mapanje's 1974 thesis that needs examination. It is the statement that "the most tragic event" in Malawi's history was the Cabinet Crisis of 1964, when "the intellectuals who had made independence possible were discredited."[19]

What has come to be called the Cabinet Crisis erupted within days of Malawi's independence in July 1964.[20] It began on 26 July with a speech by President Banda, on his return from the Cairo summit of the Organization of African Unity, in which he attacked unnamed members of his cabinet for questioning his policies. In foreign affairs, Banda was moving toward a trade agreement with Portugal, the colonial power in neighboring Mozambique, and toward friendly relations with the Republic of South Africa. At home, Banda sought to impose charges for outpatients at government hospitals and to set strict limits to the pace of Africanization, especially in the civil service. Banda justified these measures on economic grounds, but their political base was revealed by his refusal to accept a soft loan of £10 million from the People's Republic of China in return for an end to Malawi's two-Chinas policy.

At the cabinet meeting of 27 August, Banda was attacked on all these issues and apparently offered his resignation. Over the next twelve days, however, he prorogued Parliament, identified a loyalist faction in the cabinet, and dismissed "rebel" ministers Kanyame Chiume, Orton Chirwa, Augustine Bwanausi, and Rose Chibambo, an action that forced Yatuta Chisiza and Willie Chokani to resign in sympathy. In a recalled Parliament on 8 September, he demanded and received a vote of confidence. The ministers in disagreement with Banda, now including Henry Chipembere, who had earlier been absent in Canada, never recovered the initiative and returned to their constituencies or left Malawi for neighboring countries. The following February, Chipembere attempted an insurrection from his base in Fort Johnson (Mangoche) but was easily defeated at Liwonde. Later, in October 1967, Yatuta Chisiza launched a small invasion from Tanzania, but he was killed and his mutilated body publicly displayed in Blantyre. It was clear by that stage that the dissident ministers commanded little popular support.

Accounts of the Crisis have stressed clashes of age and personality between Banda and his lieutenants. As early as 1959, less than a year after Banda's triumphal return to Nyasaland at the invitation of the young radicals, these clashes were evident. The young activists had decided that the anti-Federation struggle needed a mature figurehead who could command wider support than their constituency among the educated, and they devoted much effort to building Banda's reputation. By 1961, however, Dunduzu Chisiza, who had strong claims to being the Congress party's only genuine intellectual, was reflecting on the dangers of messianic cults in African politics, effectively anticipating the power struggles that would follow Malawi's independence.[21] It was certainly true that the crisis of September 1964 was caused in part by Banda's contemptuous dismissal of his ministers as "boys" whose only role was to carry out his instructions. However, such descriptions do not explain why the dissident ministers were able to mobilize so little support. Behind the personal and generational quarrel lay structural divisions within the Congress party that had been concealed by the nature of the campaign for independence.

One of the most surprising features of Malawian nationalism, given the long history of education in the country and the long contact between Malawian workers and the labor markets of southern Africa, was its intellectual poverty. By contrast with the analyses of colonialism that were developed, for example, in the 1960s by Julius Nyerere and in the 1970s by Samora Machel, Banda has been able to offer only his own theatrical character feebly supplemented by his building contractor's vision, allegedly revealed to him while in Gwelo Prison, of a national university, a road along the shore of Lake Malawi, and a new capital city atop a hill.

Part of the problem seems to lie in the nature of Malawi's antico-lonial struggle. The imposition by Britain in 1953 of the Federation of Rhodesia and Nyasaland influenced Malawian nationalism in two ways. First, it made its most powerful manifestation, the struggle against federation, an essentially negative force. The fight was less for independence than against a transfer of power from London to Salisbury. Second, it created a temporary and precarious unity be-tween sections of Malawian society that, in their class and ethnic interests, were fundamentally divided. The campaign to, as Presi-dent Banda put it, "break the stupid Federation" became the basis and focus of a coalition of protest that concealed deep differences of vision concerning the form that an independent Malawi might take and that could not survive the transition to independence. From this perspective, the least surprising feature of the Cabinet Crisis was the speed with which it erupted.

For northern Malawi, where Scottish missionaries had opened schools as early as the late 1870s and where money earned through labor migrancy to the gold mines of the Witwatersrand had long been invested in education, politics were essentially a matter of advance-ment within the colonial structures. In 1964, northerners looked to the rapid Africanization of the civil service and the professions and to the development of a benign bureaucracy not unlike those emerg-ing in Tanzania and Zambia. For southern Malawi, with its history of land alienation and the immigration of Lomwe people from Mo-zambique, aggravated by the legacy of the long *thangata* (labor rent) system, politics was a complex blend of land hunger and ethnic in-security. In 1964, southerners looked to swift land reform and the opportunity to establish fresh village communities, sustained by cash cropping and by improved facilities for wage labor within Ma-lawi and southern Africa.

By further contrast, for the Central Region of Malawi, which had never experienced labor migrancy on the scale of the north nor land alienation on the pattern of the south, politics was about racial restrictions on African farming and commerce. In 1964, Africans from President Banda's own Central Region looked to the chance to grow crops forbidden to them in the colonial period and to engage in trade. In practice, of course, these regional divisions were more complex. Within each region were further divisions of class and ethnicity, and compounding them all were conflicts of gender and religion. Briefly, however, African clerks and schoolteachers, peasant farmers and some chiefs, tenants and residents on Trust lands, Christians of all denominations and Muslims, men and women, the northern, central, and southern provinces, could all find common ground in resisting the entrenchment of a new, more repressive form of colonial rule from Southern Rhodesia.

In September 1964, as this coalition fell apart in the wake of independence, President Banda was effectively faced with the collapse of the Malawi Congress party. Though its subordinate sections—the Youth League, the Women's League, the Young Pioneers—remained loyal, the party itself could not function as an organ of government. However, the structures of administration that Banda had inherited from the colonial period remained intact. From the 1930s onward, Nyasaland's colonial governors, advised by the Legislative Council and assisted by a civil service, had presided over a hierarchy of Provincial and District Commissioners and of Higher Native Authorities, Native Authorities, and Village Headmen. To the three categories of "native" authorities had been devolved responsibilities for collecting taxes, maintaining local order, administering local justice, and assisting in labor recruitment under the system of indirect rule. For the nine years following September 1964, while Banda rebuilt the party to his own specifications, Malawi was governed in the fashion of the late colonial period.

There were advantages for Banda in this. Chiefs and headmen had been selected or created by the colonial authorities in accordance with a neotraditional interpretation of Nyasaland's history that resonated comfortably with Banda's own neocolonial conservatism after 1964. Even since the days of the Chilembwe Rising, in 1915, there had been tensions between certain chiefs and the educated young men emerging from mission schools, and by the 1940s these tensions were aggravated by the sheer number of Malawians who, through education, or the experience of labor migration, looked for opportunities outside and beyond the ethnically based structures of power. In 1964, when the young intellectuals were outmaneuvered or driven into exile, the chiefs as a group could seem Banda's natural allies, offering him an established hierarchy of administrators and informers reaching into the smallest and most remote village. In 1966, when Banda changed himself from Prime Minister responsible to Parliament to President responsible only to himself, he was effectively merging the posts of colonial governor and paramount chief. In 1971, when people he declared to be dissidents were acquitted in the High Court for "lack of evidence," it was the chiefs to whom he turned, empowering the "traditional" courts that were controlled by the chiefs to impose the death sentence.[22] Since then, all Banda's opponents have been tried by panels of chiefs in accordance with absurdly lax rules of evidence.[23]

Not all chiefs were loyal to Banda, however. Many of them had given their support to the Federation and had come into conflict with the Malawi Congress party under Banda in the disturbances of 1959. Some of them were educated men who sympathized with the dismissed cabinet ministers, while others felt disadvantaged in the ethnic competition for national resources that had always been a feature of indirect rule and that intensified when Banda, a Chewa from the central region, became Life President in 1971. Most disturbing of all, they owned their legitimacy, such as it was after the manipulation of "traditions" by the colonial authorities, to inheritance and not to Banda's personal patronage. They were capable of asserting, as did Chief Mwase Kasungu in 1973, that by Malawian custom he was chief for life and could not be asked to abdicate.

Chief Mwase Kasungu's declaration appeared in a circular letter to other chiefs in response to Banda's assertion of the refurbished Congress party's authority over the chiefs at the party convention of September 1973. By then, nine years after the Cabinet Crisis, the party had been rebuilt at all levels, with a pyramid of party appointees at the village, district, provincial, and national levels overlapping precisely the pyramid of administration. All that remained was to bring the chiefs firmly into line.

Banda's opening address to the 1973 convention dealt with the fate of the exiled "Capricornists," Malawians who had served in the Federal Assembly in the 1950s or in other federal institutions. Among these was the sad figure of Wellington Manoah Chirwa, who had petitioned to return from exile in London to be allowed to die in his home village in Nkhata Bay district. The impression was created that delegates were free to debate the matter openly, and several chiefs, including some from Banda's home area, fell into the trap of recommending that Chirwa should be allowed to return home. Banda's closing address denounced them as traitors, and, as the chiefs left the convention building, they were slapped and kicked by the Young Pioneers and several were subsequently jailed. At a special district conference summoned in Kasungu in February 1974, the role of chiefs in Malawian society was explained. Under colonial and federal administration, the chiefs had sold out, becoming little more than messengers for the oppressors. President Banda, however, had restored chiefs to their rightful status, and they owed everything to him. No chief had anything to fear as long as they cooperated with the party. The conference concluded by replacing Mwase Kasungu, despite his great prestige as an energetic opponent of federation, with a malleable twenty-year-old student from the University of Malawi, subchief Kawomba.

From 1973, when, from Banda's point of view, the problems of the Cabinet Crisis were finally resolved, Malawi has been over-governed as never before in its history. President Banda occupies the pinnacles of two rival systems of authority, capable as Life President of both the party and the state of playing off at any level one set of officials against the other as circumstances have demanded. The party has the power to discipline the administration, but, if the party's members get out of line, as occurred in the serious plot of a coup d'etat in 1975, the chiefs could be used to discipline the party. Thus, when the Secretary-General of the party, Albert Muwalo, and the Head of the Special Branch, Focus Gwede, were sent to be tried for treason, it was before a panel of chiefs.

These political structures have remained intact to the present day. They have come under intense pressure as a result of three circumstances: from the "politics of succession," as, from 1980 onwards, potential heirs to the nonagenerian Banda have maneuvered for position; from the politics of destabilization from South African-backed RENAMO forces operating freely with Malawi against the government of neighboring Mozambique; and from the economic intervention of the World Bank and the International Monetary Fund, which, since the collapse of the Malawian economy in the late 1970s, have demolished many of the financial structures that were the sources of Banda's powers of patronage. But the political structures have not been modified—not even in response to Banda's extreme decrepitude—and their origins in the Cabinet Crisis of 1964 have largely been forgotten.

In today's Malawi, the events of September 1964 remain a totally embargoed topic. President Banda's annual rehearsal of his destruction of the "stupid Federation" at Independence Day celebrations makes no acknowledgement of the efforts of Chipembere, Chirwa, Chisiza, and Chiume at organizing the party he inherited, and their names cannot even be mentioned. All Malawians over the age of thirty-five are aware of the falseness of Banda's history, but no one addresses the issue. When we proposed in July 1982 to a gathering of Malawian historians and political scientists that it was time to hold a seminar on the Cabinet Crisis, the response was an appalled silence, and several people left the room. Even at the University of Edinburgh in 1984, at a conference on Malawi's development strategy, a paper on the Cabinet Crisis by an academic with privileged information was suppressed by the organizers.[24]

The exception to this rule of silence has been Jack Mapanje, who has never ceased to argue, in poetry and in prose, that the political rivalries central to the Cabinet Crisis and replicated in the current politics of the succession have been the key to Malawi's intellectual and cultural sterility.

For members of the Writers' Group at the University of Malawi in the early 1970s, the literary agenda set by these political developments was extremely complex. As young intellectuals, many of whom had "thrown stones" as schoolchildren in the disturbances of 1959, it was natural for them to sympathize with the educated ministers defeated in 1964. Where they themselves were to fit into Banda's Malawi was far from clear, the politics of patronage leaving little space for graduates produced by the university from 1969 onward.

Banda's preferred "elite" were the party officials and members of Parliament whom he personally selected, the MPs being subsequently declared as having "won unopposed," before he presented them with the farms and businesses for the management of which they were held accountable to him. It was a system with no room for anyone who had achieved distinction through his or her own efforts, and even being a successful boxer or singer or footballer carried risks. On the eve of the elections of 1971 there were rumors that Dr. Peter Mwanza, Principal of the university's Chancellor College, was willing to be a candidate. Banda's response was to declare that he wanted no "graduates in parliament." The marginalization of the educated seemed complete.

There were more personal reasons for insecurity. Most Malawian students came from rural backgrounds and maintained strong family connections. They were deeply conscious of the gap between their current lives and those of the generations before them, and much of what they wrote was concerned with exploring the nature of their individual missions. An influential text was Wordsworth's pastoral poem "Michael." This tale of an English north-country shepherd who sent his son to earn money in town to redeem a mortgage and who lost everything because of his son's waywardness was read as a contemporary Malawian story, both because of Wordsworth's eloquent celebration of the integrity of the life of Michael's nonliterate ancestors and because of the father's great grief that his son had gone astray in the city. Many poems and stories contributed to the Writers' Group explored such themes. James Ng'ombe's short story "The Leopard" described the sacrifices made by the narrator's elder brother to enable him to gain an education at secondary school and university, sacrifices brought home to him only when his brother is killed by a leopard while defending the parents' tiny herd of goats. The story concluded with a personal confession of betrayal.

There is nothing very surprising in the fact that a group of young writers was concerned with questions of identity. But their difficulties were unusually acute. Malawi's older generation of writers was not at hand to offer any guidance. David Rubadiri, Malawi's best known poet and ambassador to the United Nations, had become yet another casualty of the Cabinet Crisis, and his work was banned. The novelist Legson Kayira had chosen exile in Britain, his crime being that he had duplicated Banda's personal myth in walking many hundreds of miles to obtain an education. Aubrey Kachingwe, Malawi's other published novelist, had opted for the safety of silence. There were, of course, potential African models from farther afield. But the political education of young Malawian writers had been swift and brutal (none of them had forgotten the public display of Yatuta Chisiza's insulted corpse), and the cultural nationalism of Chinua Achebe's *Things Fall Apart*, Ngugi waThiongo's *The River Between*, and Okot p'Bitek's *Song of Lawino*, much admired though these writers were, seemed already to belong to simpler times.

Song of Lawino, a series of satiric songs addressed by an Acoli woman to her alienated, deracinated, Westernized, shame-ridden husband, was especially problematic. At the Universities of Nairobi and Dar es Salaam, the poem was being hailed as a revolutionary text, the authentic voice of the peasantry directed against the new, venal petit bourgeoisie. Further south, in a country well within South Africa's orbit, such appeals to traditional values read more ambiguously. There were students in Malawi's "Banda-stan" who wrote satires in imitation of *Song of Lawino,* attacking the use of lipstick or of hair-straightening and skin-lightening creams, only to suffer the indignity of having their work praised by the government censor! In political practice, Banda had first used the "traditional" chiefs to outmaneuver the graduate ministers, and he had then used traditionalist arguments to outmaneuver the "traditional" chiefs. In Banda's world, Lawino appeared an innocent. So much of what Lawino argues in her songs seemed, in fact, to have been appropriated by President Banda that Malawian students fell into the habit of calling the Women's League members "Banda's Lawinos."

The greatest difficulty for these young writers in creating alternatives to Banda's world, however, was the sheer imaginative appeal of Banda's own symbolic constructions. By the 1970s, and largely as a substitute for political debate, Malawi's political year had evolved into a cycle of presidential rituals—the regional crop inspections, the opening of the tobacco auctions, the president's official birthday, the opening of the Parliament, the opening of the party convention, and so on. For all the intellectual poverty of Malawian nationalism, there was no denying the effectiveness of Banda as theater.

Most resonant of all, and standing by way of illustration of these public performances, were the ceremonials enacted at the international airport whenever President Banda left Malawi or returned home from visits abroad. From first light, many thousands of people would converge on the airport, which was then located at Chileka, outside Blantyre. Prominent among them were members of the Women's League, dressed in the style originally designed on the model of a housemaid's uniform made by Janet Beck, an employee of the Blantyre Mission at the turn of the century, but which President Banda had proclaimed to be a "traditional" style in his war against the miniskirt during the late 1960s. Many of the women had traveled hundreds of miles by open lorry to be present, and while the colors of their dresses represented Malawi's three regions, all displayed Banda's portrait prominently on their clothing as they occupied the ground surrounding the presidential podium. Towards mid-morning, if he was leaving Malawi, the president himself arrived, standing in an open limousine and accompanied by the official "hostess," Cecilia Kadzamira, by the Minister of the Southern Region, and by other high officials. He was dressed, as always, in a long grey overcoat, a three-piece Saville Row suit, and a Homburg hat, wearing dark glasses, his right hand brandishing an ivory-handled fly whisk. As he took his seat on the podium, the overcoat was handed to an official and the proceedings began.

The relative informality of such occasions in the early 1970s needs emphasis, for although armed police were on duty and although the Young Pioneers had played a part in ensuring a large turnout, the atmosphere was not oppressive. First, Banda was entertained by groups of women from different regions and districts, taking their turns to sing and dance his praises. These performances would last for upward of two hours while Banda gesticulated his appreciation and engaged in animated conversation with a bored-looking Ms. Kadzamira. Next came Banda's speech, the central theme of which was usually the need for Malawians to observe the "four corner-stones" of the party, Unity, Order, Obedience, and Discipline, during his absence. Such speeches were invariably in English, enunciated a clause at a time on a rising cadence with pauses while the official interpreter (in those days John Msonthi, later, after Msonthi's disgrace and fall from favor, Ms. Kadzamira's uncle, John Tembo, then head of the Bank of Malawi) translated it into Chewa. Integral to the delivery were moments when Banda would correct the interpreter's Chewa, inviting the audience to ridicule Msonthi's supposedly imperfect knowledge of the language. The presidential party then retreated to the airport's VIP lounge, where, while the crowd still waited outside, the third act of the ceremonials was played out. This was a broadcast press conference, Banda's audience shifting to the worlds' newspapers, his theme—international affairs. Finally, Banda would inspect a small guard of honor of the Malawi Rifles under the command of Brigadier Lewis, their British commander, before advancing down a red carpet to the VC-10 jet that by now, with perfect timing, was roaring impatiently on the tarmac. As Banda advanced, shaking hands with a long line of dignitaries—his ministers, party officials, church officials, ambassadors and high commissioners and cultural representatives, the Papal legate, the university's Vice-Chancellor—the impression was created that he was keeping the plane waiting. The crowd's last glimpse of their president, before the catharsis of the jet's take-off was of a white glove waving from the first-class gangway.

Essentially, what was being recreated at these airport meetings was the welcome engineered at Chileka by the Congress party's young intellectuals (though without their role being acknowledged) on the occasion of Banda's return to Malawi after forty years of exile in July 1958. But the rituals had other resonances. Banda's dress, his ease in

English, his displays of erudition, and his command of limousines and jet airliners, all proclaimed his mastery of the white world of education, technology, and international affairs. His manipulation of politicians and party officials, diplomats, journalists, and the military illustrated different aspects of his competence and powers.

Most significant of all, however, was the time and space allotted to the neotraditional Women's League, whom Banda courted with his chieftain's fly whisk, his apparent expertise in Chewa, and his acceptance of their praises. All these elements were brought together in the subtle and elaborate praise name "His Excellency, the Life President, Ngwazi Doctor H. Kamuzu Banda." But the attention paid to the Women's League was no mere formality. Their praise songs became central to the official speeches, with Banda taking up their themes, reiterating and reinforcing their messages, and accepting their agenda. President Banda would say "as the women sang just now" and then proceed to discuss the issue about which they had commented. The impression was fostered that, in the final analysis, everything that Banda was doing in the large world of power and diplomacy was being done on their behalf.

It was in precisely this nuance of state occasions that the young poets of the Malawi Writers' Group found room for maneuver. Transcribed, translated, and set out baldly on the page, the praise songs of the Women's League can appear to be of very little merit, and it has to be accepted that some of them are feebly expressed and abjectly sycophantic. We noted earlier the complaint in Mapanje's 1974 thesis that older conventions of critical praises have been changed "to watered down propaganda . . . with very little poetic insight":

> All these things
> Belong to Kamuzu Banda.
>
> All the chickens
> Are Kamuzu Banda's.
>
> All the goats
> Are Kamuzu Banda's.
>
> Etc. indefinitely.[25]

But the older conventions were not entirely moribund and could come to life in two ways. First, many of the songs set out very specific reasons why Banda should be praised. He had "taken the country peacefully," had brought roads, clothing, food, schools, and hospitals:

> When Banda came, what did you see?
> When Banda came
> You saw Congo cloth and Zambia cloth.[26]

It was songs such as these that Banda would take up in his speech of response, beginning with "as the women sang just now," and effectively letting the women define his program. For all his self-congratulatory air, there was a sense in which the conditions of praise had been laid down by the women and not himself, so that the praises functioned as a kind of contract between the ruled and their ruler. The women had made it abundantly clear what they expected—peace, improving standards of living—from such homages to power.

Second, there were occasions when the songs contained muted criticism. The usual tactic was to claim that President Banda "had found out" what was going on. President Banda sometimes "didn't know" that money was being embezzled or that land was being appropriated or property confiscated or that famine was prevailing locally, but the songs made everything clear to him. Some of these songs were composed in their home areas by local branches of the Women's League, occasionally in collaboration with their husbands, making the women an important channel of communication with President Banda. One of the best instances of this was a song performed in 1975, when the Secretary-General of the Congress party, Albert Muwalo, and the head of the Special Branch, Focus Gwede, were arrested for plotting to assassinate President Banda in order to prevent power falling into the hands of Cecilia Kadzamira and her uncle, John Tembo. Banda, who was then on tour in his home region, had forbidden all references to the affair, but a group of women performed a song cataloging through several verses Muwalo's abuses of power, each verse having as its chorus line "Kamuzu didn't know!" Banda was stung into an angry speech of self-exculpation.[27]

It was this space for poetry on state occasions, this occasional loophole for poetic license, that provided Mapanje and such contemporaries as Lupenga Mphande and Geoff Mwanja with a possible poetic model. Mapanje in his 1974 thesis quotes with obvious pride one of the Women's League praise songs for Banda after the killing of Yatuta Chisiza:

> Let us thank Ngwazi Banda
> For the work he performed, oh Lord!
> Of killing those rebels
> Who wanted to destroy
> The freedom of Malawi.
>
>   *   *   *
>
> But this is not all, dear Malawians,
> Let us try hard to develop this country,
> Doing all the work with our own hands,
> And we must be very lucky, indeed,
> To have our own life president.[28]

He comments on the song's "noteworthy ironic twist" and, though the irony is not explained, we assume that he is referring to the contrast in the second stanza between "doing all the work with our own hands" and being "very lucky, indeed, / To have our own life president."[29] As this example perhaps demonstrates, Mapanje and other members of the Writers' Group were, if anything, overanxious to track down ironies in the women's songs and to appropriate to their cause anything that had the most innocent of double meanings. They were not alone in doing this. The Simon and Garfunkel song "Cecilia" was so widely relished in Malawi as a description of Banda's much-speculated-upon domestic life with Cecilia Kadzamira ("Cecilia, I'm down on my knees, I'm begging you please to come home") that the recording was officially banned!

Ludicrous as this sounds, it also had its serious side. Assumptions still prevailed in Malawi about the capacity of poetry to make the powerful appear ridiculous. A neotraditional authority could be undermined by a traditional aesthetic. This became the model of Mapanje's *Of Chameleons and Gods*.

The profoundly oral nature of Mapanje's style needs little demonstration. The poems are dominated by the speaking voice, usually in the first person and the present tense. They shift line by line, both in tone and syntax, from bald statement to quiet reflection to satiric gibe to open interrogation. They are intensely dramatic, with strong beginnings and forceful endings and incorporating a good deal of direct speech. These effects are, of course, an achievement of artifice. Mapanje is not, in practice, an oral poet with his audience there before him. He writes his poems in several drafts, working through as many as a dozen versions before hitting on the form and the images appropriate for what he wishes to say. But the direction of these revisions is always toward greater immediacy of impact and variety of tone, the illusion of orality. Equally demonstrable is the extent to which Mapanje has adopted the oral poet's stance of public spokesman. Poem after poem uses the first person plural *we* in a manner not available to postromantic European poets. Of the forty-seven poems in *Of Chameleons and Gods*, no fewer than eighteen end with questions and a further eleven with exclamations. It is the stance of the praise poet, telling the chief what no one else will say and licensed by the medium of which he is master.

What is less obvious, but no less important, is the extent to which Mapanje's metaphors have the precision and accuracy of reference of the oral poems that are his models. To non-Malawian readers, the language of these poems is colorful and highly individual. Mapanje's "voice," reviewers have remarked, is "distinctive" and he has a gift for eloquence, for coining the memorable phrase. To his audience in Malawi, however, the poems are also packed with references to the people, places, and events of Malawi's recent history. A reading of the landscapes of Malawi is also a reading of ethnic tensions and political rivalries. To repeat the words we used of the praise poems discussed in chapter two, these poems represent, not history as code, but history as drama, evaluation, and judgment. They address the agenda that has been set by President Banda since the events of the Cabinet Crisis of 1964, and they seize back Banda's own appropriation of the past by offering an alternative reading of history, custom, and tradition. In the process, they become the best guide available within Malawi to events over the past generation. In a country where intellectual and moral enquiry has been savagely repressed, Mapanje's satire challenges like a conscience.

These are large claims. We shall try to substantiate them by discussing in detail three poems from *Of Chameleons and Gods* and, subsequently, one of his more recent poems. The first is a relatively early composition, "The New Platform Dances," written in 1970, when Mapanje was still an undergraduate, and it was first published in the proceedings of the Writers' Group:[30]

> Haven't I danced the big dance
> Compelled the rains so dust could
> Soar high above like when animals
> Stampede? Haven't I in animal
> Skins wriggled with amulets

Rattled with anklets
Scattered nervous women
With snakes around my neck
With spears in these hands
Then enticed them back
With flywhisk's magic?
Haven't I moved with all
Concentric in the arena
To the mystic drums
Dancing the half-nude
Lomwe dance
Haven't I?

Haven't my wives at mortars sung
Me songs of praise, of glory,
How I quaked the earth
How my skin trembled
How my neck peaked
Above all dancers
How my voice throbbed
Like the father-drum
I danced to
Haven't they?

Now, when I see my daughters writhe
Under cheating abstract
Voices of slack drums, ululate
To babble-idea-men-masks
Without amulets or anklets,
Why don't I stand up
To show them how we danced
Chopa, how IT was born?
Why do I sit still
Why does my speech choke
Like I have not danced
Before? Haven't I
Danced the bigger dance?
Haven't I?

The speaker in this poem, a dramatic monologue, is a Lomwe headman. The Lomwe people migrated to Malawi from Mozambique at
the turn of this century, and following the long years of their settlement under labor-tenant schemes, the notorious *thangata* system,
they today remain among the poorest of Malawi's people. Their cen-

tral role in the revolt organized by John Chilembwe in 1915 made them deeply suspect to the colonial authorities, and ironically, despite Chilembwe's status as a national hero in independent Malawi, the Lomwe have continued to be regarded as potential troublemakers. Rumors of ethnic conspiracy in Malawi invariably refer to the Lomwe in disparaging terms. The Lomwe headman in this poem, therefore, has affinities with the prostitute, the mad person, the prisoner, the Jehovah's Witness, and the old woman selling *thobwa* (sweet millet beer) who appear in others of Mapanje's poems. He is adopting the voice of someone deep inside Malawian society but outside the system that controls it.

Appropriately, the poem's central metaphor is of the *chopa* dance. This is a Lomwe dance of great power and complex symbolism, the function of which is to honor the ancestors and "compel" them to send the rain.[31] To an immense battery of drumming, the men dance in processions around their chief or headman—wielding spears and axes, sometimes even with venomous snakes draped around their necks—while the women dance in an outer circle waving green branches. For its oppositions of male to female, violence to gentleness, hunting to planting, dust to the rains, *chopa* draws it symbolism from the Lomwe creation myth, which tells how the first man and first woman came out of a cave in their Mozambique homeland and brought conflict to a harmonious world through their discovery of fire.

Thus the poem sets up two contrasts. The first is between the old dance, in which the headman's duty was to dance until his power and energy "compelled the rains," and the new dances of politicians on public platforms whom the poem calls, in a sharply compressed neologism, "babble-idea-men-masks." The second contrast is between the praise songs sung by the headman's "wives," which were praises for real achievement, and the dances and ululations accompanied by "slack drums"—drums without resonance—offered to the new leaders. The reference is, of course, to the Women's League. Implicit in these contrasts is the larger one between a coherent world alive with meaning, whose hierarchies have religious sanction, and the new, parallel world of dummy figures with "cheating abstract / Voices." This is not, one should note, a contrast between past and present. The headman is alive and challenging Banda's neotraditionalism *on his own ground*. The metaphor does not demand that Mapanje himself believe in *chopa* or the rituals of rainmaking (he is not himself Lomwe). It is Banda who has assumed the trappings of chief-

taincy and, by the very standards he has invoked, his dance is an
empty one.

Of course, the poem makes no such statement. It was understood
by the Malawi government censor, who cleared it for publication in
1971 and allowed it to be read on the radio, as a defense of "traditional" as opposed to modern styles of dancing with, perhaps, a satire on the early 1970s fashion in Malawi of Western-style platform
shoes.[32] Every sentence throughout the poem is actually a question,
interrogating the reader and drawing him, through his unstated re-
plies, into complicity with intellectual rebellion. There is a further
ambiguity. The headman's final questions are "Why do I sit still /
Why does my speech choke?" etc. The closing lines can be read in
different ways—as a bewildered old man's inability to come to terms
with the new world or as a rhetorical call to arms. There is no real
doubt as to the correct reading—Mapanje chose the latter in his
broadcast of 1971. But one almost feels sorry for the government
censor in having had to cope with such sophisticated dissent.

The second poem we have selected for discussion from *Of Chameleons and Gods* was written ten years later, in the spring of 1980,
when Mapanje was in London working on his doctoral dissertation.
News had come from Malawi about the fall from power of Gwanda
Chakwamba Phiri, the Minister of the Southern Region, Minister for
Youth and Culture, and Leader of the House. Chakwamba had been
one of the most notorious of Banda's ministers, being embroiled particularly in disputes with Catholic missions in the Lower Shire area
over the supply of schoolgirls as companions for visiting dignitaries.
He had been loyal to Banda during the Cabinet Crisis and bore on his
face scars of a bad beating he had endured during the disturbances of
those days. As had happened earlier to the other ministers who stood
by Banda in 1964, Chakwamba was being eliminated by the palace
faction of the Tembo-Kadzamira family as they maneuvered to dominate the Malawian political stage.

Mapanje was staying in Kent with one of the present writers
shortly after Chakwamba's disgrace, and he described a poem he was
writing about the event. The poem dwelt on the irony that the usual
punishment for any politician who fell from power in Malawi was to
be exiled to his home village. There were, in fact, many ironies involved in this, and some Malawian poets would have seen a return to
the village as a kind of cleansing. Mapanje's view was more biting.
Malawi's political elite subsists by sucking wealth from the villages,
and to be condemned to experience the poverty they had themselves

been instrumental in creating was a punishment whose appropriate-ness could be celebrated.[33] The evening after Mapanje's return to London, Landeg White stole this idea and wrote the poem "Minis-tering," later published in his collection, *For Captain Stedman*. Posting it next morning to Mapanje, he received by return mail the poem "Making Our Clowns Martyrs, (or, Returning Home without Chauffeurs)."[34] The two poems are contrasted here because, though dealing with the same event, they illustrate with unusual clarity the effects of writing within contrasting aesthetic traditions. White's poem is as follows:

Ministering

She has watched him rise and now he falls.
The transistor denounces him. He returns
Unchauffeured, Benz-less, trudging the path
From the cotton depot where the lorry dropped him:
His paunch is heavy, his suit sweat-stained, he smells.

The children swagger in his wake. He mutters
At the anthills. It was tribalism, conspiracy,
His typists whoring. There was nothing else,
No reason. He was no different. The President
Would learn things when he got his letter.

The path snakes through the village. What he didn't
See on the ministerial visit, in his soft world
Of secretaries, his bitterness sees now.
The place is full of beggars, primitive, the thatch
Rotting, reeds uncut, thistles in the cotton gardens.

She watched him rise. Now he returns. What accident
Permitted it and what appetites propelled,
She knows. There is nothing to come back to.
The girls have gone, the young men have gone.
At the black door of her hut where burning cowdung

Stuns the mosquitoes, she awaits her son.

It seems fair to claim that this treatment is true to Mapanje's origi-nal idea. The minister's public disgrace, his humiliating return home, and his bitterness at the poverty he confronts for the first time, are all established. The themes of the corruption of the political elite and of the impoverishment of the village—the cotton gardens are abandoned, the young people have left—are explicit. Nevertheless, this is not a public poem. Its feeling is essentially private, focusing on the minister's reception by his mother who is "ministering" to him—a pun that conjures away the public world. Its movement from the opening line stresses her role as the sad but compassionate observer of an inevitable cycle of events. But her marginality is not questioned, and there is nothing to be done. Behind the poem is a tradition of English pastoral celebrating the simplicity, integrity, and intimacy of village culture by contrasting it with the corrupt but energetic and thoroughly *modern* city. Appropriately, the style is simple, the rhythms elegiac. It is not surprising that one reviewer should have been reminded of Chinua Achebe.

Mapanje's version, in sharp contrast, reads more like something by Wole Soyinka. It begins mockingly in the public domain, with the first person plural and with four heavily stressed words, "We all know why." The "We" are the villagers for whom the poet is spokesman, but this village seems as big as all Malawi, and it is by no means depopulated or dying. It is desperately poor: there are mosquitoes here too, and "broken reed-fences" and "poached reed-huts" and "stunted pit-latrines," each adjective in turn rich with significance. Materially, it is not much to come back to after the life of banqueting halls and concubines. But intellectually it is more alive than the city, the "we" of the poem surveying the political scene with an eloquent and raging contempt.

As the poem moves from the swamps of the Shire River valley in the south to the hills and lake waters of the Central Region, the landscape becomes the arena for Malawi's regional and ethnic conflicts. To non-Malawian readers, the imagery may seem merely colorful and vigorous, but within Malawi these metaphors are clearly understood as an evaluation of much recent history. The actors have learned different lessons from the bush where they began, carrying the rules of the jungle into their deadly rivalry. Now that the former "clown" has become a "martyr" ("the orders you once shouted / . . . have now locked you in"), he is advised to learn from "the leopards of / Dedza hills," with their known ruthlessness. All Malawi can identify the leopards with the Tembo-Kadzamira family, which originated there.

It is a fascinating coincidence that both poems end by shifting the focus to women. But the "mad auntie" of Mapanje's version is no mere mother figure, emblematic of the former pastoral virtues. As the "clown" is dispatched home, he is greeted, even in his village, by nervous relatives whose faces are carved "in somebody's image." But the auntie, in her disregarded madness, maintains the village's capacity for questioning, the intellectual vigor that, in Mapanje's conviction, is the inheritance of Malawi's oral culture. Appropriately, then the style of the poem is again profoundly oral though with a rhythmic drive and density of imagery that is an enormous advance on "The New Platform Dances" of ten years earlier. This is not a poem of questions to be answered by the reader, but a series of authoritative, mocking statements characterized by active verbs and strong epithets in heavily stressed sentences manipulating the rhythms of a longer line. The poem that results is akin to the caustic Chopi satires of Katini's or Gomukomu's *migodo* discussed in chapter four:

> *Making Our Clowns Martyrs*
> (or, *Returning Home without Chauffeurs*)
>
> We all know why you have come back home with no
> National colours flanking your black mercedes benz.
> The radio said the toilets in the banquet halls of
> Your dream have grown green creepers and cockroaches
> Which won't flush, and the orders you once shouted
> To the concubines so mute have now locked you in.
> Hard luck my friend. But we all know what currents
> Have stroked your temper. You come from a breed of
> Toxic frogs croaking beside the smoking marshes of
> River Shire, and the first words you breathed were
> Snapped by the lethal mosquitoes of this morass.
> We knew you would wade your way through the arena
> Though we wondered how you had got chosen for the benz.
> You should have been born up the hills, brother where
> Lake waters swirl and tempers deepen with each season
> Of the rains. There you'd see how the leopards of
> Dedza hills comb the land or hedge before their assault.
> But welcome back to the broken reed-fences, brother;
> Welcome home to the poached reed-huts you left behind;
> Welcome to these stunted pit-latrines where only
> The pungent whiff of buzzing green flies gives way.
> You will find your idle ducks still shuffle and fart
> In large amounts. The black dog you left still sniffs
> Distant recognition, lying, licking its leg-wounds. And
> Should the relatives greet you with nervous curiosity

In the manner of masks carved in somebody's image,
There is always across the dusty road, your mad auntie.
She alone still thinks this new world is going shit.
She alone still cracks about why where whys are crimes.[35]

The third poem from *Of Chameleons and Gods* that we discuss was
also written in 1980 and is notable for making the first public acknowledgment in Malawi that President Banda is aging and that he
will eventually have to make way for younger men. The name Kwangala is glossed by Mapanje as a "Yao word for dancing frenetically,"
and the reference is again to Banda's dealings with the Women's
League, in particular, to the "chief's" practice of dancing briefly with
the women on Independence day anniversaries. Once again, too, the
subject of the poem is addressed and interrogated directly.

> *On His Royal Blindness*
> *Paramount Chief Kwangala*
>
> I admire the quixotic display of your paramountcy
> How you brandish our ancestral shields and spears
> Among your warriors dazzled by your loftiness
> But I fear the way you spend your golden breath
> Those impromptu, long-winded tirades of your might
> In the heat, do they suit your brittle constitution?
>
> I know that I too must sing to such royal happiness
> And I am not arguing. Wasn't I too tucked away in my
> Loin-cloth infested by jiggers and fleas before
> Your bright eminence showed up? How could I quibble
> Over your having changed all that? How dare I when
> We have scribbled our praises all over our graves?
>
> Why should I quarrel when I too have known mask
> Dancers making troubled journeys to the gold mines
> On bare feet and bringing back fake European gadgets
> The broken pipes, torn coats, crumpled bowler hats,
> Dangling mirrors and rusty tincans to make their
> Mask dancing strange? Didn't my brothers die there?
>
> No, your grace, I am no alarmist nor banterer
> I am only a child surprised how you broadly disparage
> Me shocked by the tedium of your continuous palaver.
> I adore your majesty. But paramountcy is like a raindrop

On a vast sea. Why should we wait for the children to
Tell us about our toothless gums or our showing flies?

The precise tones of this poem's ironies are extraordinarily difficult to pin down. It was written after the intense political repression
of the mid-1970s had receded, culminating in the arrests of Muwalo
and Gwede, but before the crisis over the succession to the clearly
aging President Banda was to explode in the killings of senior cabinet ministers in 1983. Although the poem clearly insists that Kwangala's time is over, it seems at one level a fairly sympathetic view of
his place in history both as actor and as victim. Stanza two acknowledges the economic change that the chief has brought about, while
at the same time mimicking in a manner always derided in Malawi
the self-denigration of sycophants. Stanza three accepts that other
Malawians (like President Banda) have traveled to South Africa to
bring back regalia for their dancing, though the self-caricatures that
result are saddening. The argument in stanzas one and four is not
that Kwangala has been especially nasty but that he is very old and
that it is time to give way to younger men. More than any other of
Mapanje's poems, "On His Royal Blindness" seems to fit the description of praise poetry given by Andrew Smith in 1835—the *imbongi*'s
poetic license deriving from a broad acceptance of the current hierarchy.

Yet this reading of the poem, carried for the most part (though not
entirely) by the nouns and verbs, is completely undermined by the
epithets. From the beginning the chief's display is "quixotic," his
speeches "long-winded," his constitution "brittle." By the third
stanza, the "European gadgets" central to the dance (President Banda's suit, his Homburg hat, his dark glasses) have become "fake . . .
torn . . . crumpled . . . dangling . . . rusty." In successive readings, the
ironies spread back from the adjectives to the nouns ("golden
breath," "royal happiness," "bright eminence") until the whole text
seems a triumph of delicate mockery, offering praises and in the
same breath reclaiming them. Yet this description, too, needs qualification. The comments in stanzas two and three—"I am not arguing," "How could I quibble?" "Why should I quarrel?"—are entirely
serious and contain no detectable ambiguity. They cannot be otherwise, given the number of deaths involved, deaths from which the
poet cannot detach himself through mockery. Malawians may have
"scribbled our praises all over our graves," but it was not Kwangala
who made "my brothers die there."

It is this semiacceptance of a common destiny with Kwangala in the making of Malawi's present that justifies the poem's conclusion. The charity the poet extends to the chief is not extended by the chief to the poet, who is "only a child surprised how you broadly disparage / Me." There is no room for him in President Banda's Malawi. Yet in a court of sycophants, who else will point out the painful truth about "toothless gums" and his "showing flies"?

In the last analysis, "Of His Royal Blindness" is a poem about the role of the poet in Malawi, demanding to be offered the space and license sanctioned by Banda's own neotraditionalism. There are a number of poems in *Of Chameleons and Gods* that explore related ideas. "Kabula Curio Shop" describes the marginalization of the artist. "Glory Be to Chingwe's Hole" shows how the artists' creations are appropriated for the chief's own purposes. "We Wondered about the Mellow Peaches" reflects, among other things, on the erosion of larger visions by the sheer pettiness of dictatorships. All these themes come together in the paper "Censoring the African Poem," which Mapanje read to the conference in Stockholm in 1986, one of the manuscripts seized by the Special Branch at the time of his arrest, though blessedly too late to prevent publication.

In Malawi, *Of Chameleons and Gods* fell into a limbo by being neither officially proscribed nor officially cleared for sale.[36] Bookshops that displayed it were ordered to return their copies to London, while there were rumors that the Special Branch had bought the last fifty copies in the university bookstore and thrown them down pit latrines. James Ng'ombe, author years before of "The Leopard" and now chairman of Dzuka ["Wake Up"] Publishing Company, proposed to bring out a "Malawian" version of *Of Chameleons and Gods*, omitting those poems that "poke at wounds that are still raw in Malawian history." As Mapanje comments, "the mind still boggles about what the Malawian version of already Malawian verse would be."[37] Dzimani Kadzamira, brother of Cecilia Kadzamira and Principal of the University of Malawi's Chancellor College, widely viewed as a fiefdom of the Tembo-Kadzamira family, used the situation to check on the loyalty of former members of the Writers' Group, inviting them on the Censorship Board's behalf to report in writing whether they considered that Mapanje's book should be banned. Ironically, copies of these reports came into Mapanje's hands in London. The verdict of the majority was "no problem," but he had thus been warned which of his friends were untrustworthy.

In 1984 Heinemann reprinted the book. Plainly, it was selling both at home and abroad, and the censorship board was divided as to which market infuriated it more. In June 1985 the Ministry of Education and Culture issued a circular banning "without delay" its use in schools and colleges. But still the book itself was not banned. Malawians could be prosecuted for possessing a copy of *Animal Farm* or, by this stage, *Song of Lawino*. But it was not an offense to have imported a personal copy of *Of Chameleons and Gods*.

Typically, Mapanje found much to amuse him in the censor board's discomfiture. He insists that "the objective of most Censorship Boards is first and foremost to protect the censors from dismissal," and recalls with relish the occasion when President Banda recommended to his cabinet a book he had been presented with on his return to Meharry College, the American school where he first trained to be a doctor, only to find it was on the list of banned books. Even Dzimani Kadzamira's elaborate maneuver had had its positive side: it was the first time the censors had solicited the opinion of Malawi's intellectuals and the idea might, perhaps, catch on! As for the imaginative effects of censorship, the challenge to outwit the authorities could be stimulating. He quotes the Polish novelist Tadeusz Konwicki to the effect that censorship "forces the writer to employ metaphors which raise the piece of writing to a higher level" and wrings humor from the suggestion that the Malawi censorship board has actually improved his poems. As these comments make clear, his reflections are both balanced and subtle. But his evident good humor only lends greater weight to his main charge, driven home by examples, that "censorship ultimately protects African leadership against truth."[38]

There is no doubt that *Of Chameleons and Gods* did circulate widely among Malawi's teachers, professionals, and civil servants. By the early 1980s, the uncertainties generated by the politics of the succession to Banda were beginning to create a new coalition of resistance, Malawians of all ages and regions and classes coming together once again under the auspices of the Malawi Congress party to oppose the ever-growing pretensions of the Tembo-Kadzamira family. Mapanje's poems were informally enlisted in this cause, at least to the extent that people found stimulus in the eloquence of his questioning. There is evidence, too, that some of his poems circulated orally. His metaphors were featured in semipublic discussions, and it was possible to sit in bars and hear people talking about "Chingwe" or "the leopards of Dedza" or about the merits of "drink-

ing at the source," Mapanje's sardonic image for traveling to the
United Kingdom. Nor was there any doubt about his growing reputation both outside and within Malawi. One of the reasons given for
not formally banning *Of Chameleons and Gods* was the risk of preventing him from returning to Malawi. Another was the risk of making him a hero. When he did return, after completing his Ph.D. in
April 1983, he was asked to deliver a public lecture at Chancellor
College in Zomba. His thesis had been on "Aspect and Tense in
ChiYao, ChiChewa, and English," and he chose for his lecture the
most rarefied and abstruse of linguistic topics. Yet it drew an audience so large that the venue had to be shifted to Kamuzu Hall, the
new theater built for presidential convocations.

By April 1983, however, it was also plain that the literary project
to which he was committed and through which he had discovered
his identity as a poet had no future. The poem he wrote describing
his return begins as follows:

> Another Fools' day touches down, another homecoming.
> Shush. Bunting! some anniversary: they'll be preoccupied.
> Only a wife, children and a friend, probably waiting.[39]

There is no longer the public voice of the oral poet speaking for the
community. The motif "Shush" recurs throughout the poem, the
poet anxious not to disturb the "they" who are preoccupied with
other matters than his arrival, and the consolations of return are entirely private and familial. *Of Chameleons and Gods* had conjured
the illusion of the oral poet speaking for his society, making comments that were licensed by his oral aesthetic. In poetic terms, this
metaphor served Mapanje extremely well. In the difficult circumstances in which he had tried to find his poetic voice, it gave him
a public style and helped to shape poems of great dramatic power.
Politically, however, he was *Out of Bounds*—as the title of his
projected second volume of poems expresses it. In theory, he had
identified a space for satirical poetry within Malawi's political culture. In practice, he had set up an unacceptable challenge to the regime.

There are four reasons for the government's opposition to Mapanje. The first and most banal, given the intellectual poverty of Malawian nationalism, is that there was no room for poems that recorded with such moral precision the main events of Malawian

history since 1959. No other Malawian writing within Malawi has dared to discuss the anti-Federation struggle and its links with the Cabinet Crisis, the attempted coup of 1975, and the struggle for the presidential succession. Like Wole Soyinka in comparable circumstances, Mapanje has become the conscience of his nation. But there are further reasons why his poetry gave offense, arising out of the ambiguities of the enterprise itself.

In the earliest account we have of poetic license, Andrew Smith's description of Mzilikazi in 1835, Smith had emphasized the role of oral poetry in allowing people to present their comments and requests to the king, who was by this means kept in touch with popular sentiment. But no matter how sharp the criticism, no challenge was intended to the ruler's legitimacy. The very act of performance implied an acceptance of clientage in Mzilikazi's nascent state. Mapanje, however, together with his Malawian readers, had moved beyond the simpler forms of the politics of patronage. By virtue of the education that had made them so fluent in English, they had a claim to status in their own right. That in itself caused offense in Banda's Malawi, where the lines of communication remain as paternalistic as under colonialism—the landowner dealing with his peasants, the master with his servants, the president with his people.

Exacerbating this problem was the fact that Mapanje's poems had been printed. The terms of the relationship between ruler and ruled changed when the ruled was able to ensure the permanency of his complaint through writing. Finally, and compounding every offense, was the fact that the poems had been published in London and in English by a scholar employed at the Tembo-Kadzamira-dominated university. When the confrontation of the praise poet and the paramount chief was played out before an international audience in the capital of the former colonial power, it could indeed seem that the poet was merely "poking at raw wounds."[40]

Mapanje has shown himself aware of these contradictions. Even in his 1974 thesis, where the notion of poetic license was elaborated, he refers also to the benefits of publication abroad. "Writers," he remarks, "are a threat to African leadership because having been published abroad they are usually given international recognition and hence international protection."[41] The license implicit in this statement is conferred, not by an oral aesthetic, but by publication in London, Paris, or New York. Significantly, *Of Chameleons and Gods* concludes with a section entitled "Assembling Another Voice." In the nine poems of this section, Mapanje shows some impatience with the pettiness of local politics ("All this fuss about conspiracies and goats")[42] and contemplates poems on broader issues (Soweto, Wiriyamu, Kampuchean children) and even a nonpolitical art:

> I should have set up votive slabs from Mphunzi
> Hills, chalked the rude walls with gentle
> Gazelles and the lore about sweet fondlings—
> To while away my temper.[43]

From his return in April 1983, Mapanje regarded himself as licensed only in the sense that he had a London reputation and that his creation, The Linguistics Association of the SADCC countries' universities, was generating some foreign exchange for Malawi. His paper on censorship, first delivered in November 1986, makes no mention of the oral poet's license. That stance has been abandoned. By then, however, the political murders of May 1983 had confirmed in appalling fashion the need for "another voice."[44]

The constitution of Malawi provides that on the President's death the Secretary-General of the Congress party will become Acting President, with the responsibility to summon within three months a party convention at which a new president will be elected. Given the widespread hatred in Malawi of the Tembo-Kadzamira family, both inside and outside the Congress party, together with the fact that the Malawi Army backs the constitution, these provisions appear to lay down insuperable obstacles to John Tembo's or Cecilia Kadzamira's securing the succession.[45] Tembo by 1982, contrary to party policy, had already forged, with South Africa's backing, an alliance with RENAMO forces that were operating freely within Malawi against neighboring Mozambique.[46]

In May 1983, President Banda planned a bizarre maneuver that would have furthered the Tembo-Kadzamira family's ambitions. He proposed to spend a year's "sabbatical" in Britain, leaving Cecilia Kadzamira in charge of the government during his absence. Recognizing this scheme as an attempt to circumvent the constitution, both the cabinet and the Congress party resisted. Precisely what happened next has been the subject of many different rumors, but the outcome was clear. Dick Matenje, the Secretary-General of the Congress party, Aaron Gadama, the Minister for the Central Region, and two members of Parliament, were assassinated, probably by police units in Tembo's pay. Banda never took his sabbatical, and the post of Secretary-General of the party remains unfilled to this day.[47]

Seven months after these events, Mapanje wrote to England for the first time about the murders:

> I am sorry for having taken so long to write to tell you about what is happening here. I arrived safely but everybody who matters wasn't in fact expecting me to return because of the poem "Making our clowns martyrs." So the philosophy is if you come from Zomba and you are important, I shouldn't write a poem about Zomba!
>
> And then the murders happened! And there were supposed to be more people to go with them. The village is so shocked that these days only a handful of women go dancing. Right now everyone is waiting and waiting, watching the road where the event is going to happen from. The rains are about to fail. We had in November two weeks of water rationing, the first in the history of this country. It has never happened in anybody's lifetime. The poets are revising their myths about Napolo! The interpretation that everybody is giving is obviously that the Gods are "laughing at us for our callous deaths which were not necessary at all!"
>
> Do you remember watching Idi Amin off Tottenham Court Road in 1973? Well, those shootings were so remote. They looked like jokes. I did not realise that ten years later the story'd get home. And it was so painful that I could not work or think for months![48]

Mapanje had shed no tears over Gwanda Chakwamba's fall from power and subsequent imprisonment. But Dick Matenje and Aaron Gadama were men of altogether different mettle. Not only did they embody the constitutional means of defeating the Tembo-Kadzamira family, they had in the two years prior to their murder been signaling the need for greater openness in Malawian politics. Gadama in particular had made courageous speeches insisting that the whole point of a mass party was to involve the masses in discussion, and though the discussions over which he presided were somewhat formulaic, emphasizing the reasons why Malawians should be grateful to Banda, there were promises implicit in his campaign. His and Matenje's murders killed off the hopes they had inspired of a peaceful transition to a more open and democratic state.

The themes of most of the poems Mapanje has written since 1983 are present in embryo in his letter about the murders. Fear is one dominant motif. In part, this is the personal, physical fear of "being accidentalized," for the murder of the ministers was disguised as an

automobile crash,[49] but equally it is the fear of the social violence
that, in the absence of any provision for the presidential succession,
now seems unavoidable in Malawi. As Mapanje wrote in the letter
quoted above, "We can't afford to be too wild in our treatment of
ourselves as if the nation was not meant to survive." A closely related motif is what Mapanje sees as the final and absolute suppression of all debate inside Malawi. Not only is the poet himself *Out of
Bounds;* even the Women's League no longer bothers to turn out to
sing Banda's praises, their patron-president now being out of touch
with events, impervious to all influence from below. Significantly,
the dominant metaphor of these recent poems is of drought. Malawi
has experienced two droughts and a famine since 1983, but, as in
Mapanje's letter about the murders, the famine of these poems is
more than literal and is fertile with meanings.

The following example is representative of a wealth of poems that
exist mainly in manuscript. It describes Kadango village, in Mango-
chi district, on the eastern shore of Lake Malawi close by the border
with Mozambique. This is Mapanje's home village, where he spent
his childhood and where he still has close relatives. Though with
typical restraint he does not flaunt this fact before the reader, it remains the key to the poem's tightness and sad anger.[50]

> *Kadango Village: Even Milimbo Lagoon Is Dry*
> —For Landeg and Alice

> In the cracking heat of October, a village market.
> A queue of skeletal hands reaching out for the last
> Cowlac tin of loose grain, falters, against hope.

> In the drought, a frail dog sniffing his lover's arse
> Goes berserk, barking at the wave of grey eddying
> Between the mountain boulders and the shrivelling lake.

> Scurvy children kicking the grit, scud beachwards,
> Their wobbly feet digging in for possible cassava
> Where even such tubers are now hushed in shoot.

> Rocky geckos, blue tongues hanging out, scuttle on
> The hot sand but bil-tong, belly up, before the beach.
> Fish eagles suspended, swoop down for grasshoppers.

> Even Milimbo lagoon is dead; no oar dips in anymore.
> Those fishermen who dreamt up better weather
> Once, no longer cast their nets here, and their

> Delightful bawdy songs to bait the droughts are
> Cloaked in the choking fumes of dawn, banned. But
> Our fat-necked custodians despatch another tale.

The images are of sterility, fear, and repression. The drought is a real one, the villagers starving and dependent on food handouts. The "cracking heat" is too much, even for the land's natural survivors—the dogs that go berserk, the cassava tubers that are "hushed in shoot," and the lizards that are turned to biltong by the sand's heat. Only the fish eagles, swooping from far above, feed well. These images of a cursed, silenced, and preyed-upon village are almost surreal in their intensity. But the poem's real meaning emerges in the final two stanzas. The drought could have been "baited" by the fishermen's "delightful bawdy songs." As with "The New Platform Dances," there is no need to take the rainmaking metaphor literally. The drought is an image of the nation's sterility, and what matters is that the fishermen's songs are now "cloaked in the choking fumes of dawn." It seems a slightly awkward metaphor until we remember the coded images deployed at meetings of the Writers' Group in 1970: "dawn" referring to *kwacha*—the opening exortation at each public meeting attended by President Banda—and to the "freedom" gained in 1964.

An early draft of this poem was entitled "On Approaching Forty," suggesting a poetical stocktaking. The project begun at those meetings of the Writers' Group has finally been "banned." There is now no means in Malawi of "compelling the rains," of challenging the version of history prolugated from above by "our fat-necked custodians."

Notes

1. J. Mapanje, "Censoring the African Poem: Personal Reflections," in *Criticism and Ideology*, ed., K. Holst-Petersen (Uppsala, 1986), 104–11.

2. J. Mapanje, *Of Chameleons and Gods* (London, 1981).

3. J. Mapanje and L. White, eds., *Oral Poetry from Africa: An Anthology* (London, 1983). SADCC is the acronym for the Southern African Development Coordination Conference.

4. "Kadongo Village: Even Milimbo Lagoon Is Dry," "Too Late, Creon, to Repair," "Martyrs Day Prayer, 1984," and "Another Fool's Day Touches Down: Shush," in *Index on Censorship* 16, no. 10 (Nov.–Dec. 1987): 23; "Another Fool's Day Touches Down: Shush," in *Literary Review*, January

1988, 25–26; "Moving into Monkey Bay (Balandra North)," in *Stand* 29, no. 3 (Summer 1988): 38.

5. Quoted from David Constantine, "Poem on My Birthday for Irina Ratushinskaya," in his *Madder* (London, 1987), 60.

6. E.g., Amnesty International, *Malawi: Human Rights Violations Twenty-five Years after Independence* (London, 1989), 9; J. Perlez, "Starving Children of Malawi Kill Leader's Boast of Plenty," *New York Times*, 3 April 1990: R. Omaan, "A Malawi Poet under Arrest," *New York Review of Books* 37, no. 16 (25 October 1990): 67.

7. Quoted from J. Gibbs, "Singing in the Dark Rain," *Index on Censorship* 17, no. 2 (February 1988): 19.

8. The history of the symbol of dawn is a long one, and its use in contemporary Malawi is not without its ironies. It begins in the 1890s, when Harry Johnston, the British Commissioner who established the Protectorate and who was a keen believer in the same opposition that Felix Mendelssohn explored in his Second Symphony, chose the Latin phrase *Lux in tenebris* ("Light in the darkness") as the country's motto. Its symbolism was that of the "dawn" of Western civilization in the area heralding the end of African benightedness. The iconographic symbol of a sun rising at dawn was soon incorporated into the Protectorate's official coat of arms, and it was used on Nyasaland postage stamps from 1934 through 1963. Upon Nyasaland's independence in 1964, Harry Johnston's original motto was translated into Chewa and the rising-sun motif was placed on the new country's flag, coinage, and currency.

9. *British Central Africa Gazette* 4, no. 17 (18 October 1897).

10. J. A. C. Mapanje, "The Use of Traditional Literary Forms in Modern Malawian Writing in English," M. Phil. thesis, University of London, 1974.

11. Ibid., 8–9.

12. Mapanje, *Of Chameleons and Gods*, xi.

13. Mapanje, "Use of Traditional Literary Forms," 9.

14. Ibid., 2.

15. Ibid., 136.

16. Ibid., 16.

17. D. Kerr, "Community Theater and Public Health in Malawi," *Journal of Southern African Studies* 15, no. 3 (April 1989): 469–85.

18. Mapanje, "Use of Traditional Literary Forms," 29–30, 32–33.

19. Ibid., 25.

20. Much of the material in this section derives from John Hooper, "The Politics of Patronage: An Assessment of the Political Economy of Malawi since Independence," M.A. thesis, University of York, 1984. See also P. Short, *Banda* (London, 1974), 197–230; Williams, *Malawi*, 196–229; and L. Vail and L. White, "Tribalism in the Political History of Malawi," in *The Creation of Tribalism in Southern Africa*, ed. L. Vail, (London and Berkeley, 1989), 151–52, 178–84.

21. D. Chisiza, *Africa: What Lies Ahead?* (New Delhi, 1961).

22. Williams, *Malawi*, 252–60.

23. Thus, during the trial of Albert Muwalo, in 1977, anonymous letters were accepted as "evidence" on the grounds that the "traditional Malawian saying" declares "there is no smoke without fire."

24. Andrew Ross, "The Malawi Cabinet Crisis of 1964." This paper was subsequently presented to a research seminar at the University of York in 1985.

25. W. Van Zanten, "Traditional Malawi Music," MSS collection in the University of Malawi Library, Zomba, Malawi (1970–71), no pagination.

26. Ibid.

27. Other instances of public protest through song were an occasion in 1966 or 1967, at Kamuzu Stadium in Blantyre, when women from Ncheu sang a song to President Banda complaining that Muwalo had murdered one of their local chiefs, and another when, after Chewa had been made the national language in 1968, the songs sung to welcome the president when he visited the Northern Region included one in which the local people complained that their language, Tumbuka, was being killed as a result (unattributable letters to authors).

28. Mapanje, "Traditional Oral Forms," 32.

29. Ibid., 31.

30. Mapanje, "The New Platform Dances," in *Of Chameleons and Gods*, 12–13.

31. See L. White, *Magomero: Portrait of an African Village* (Cambridge, 1987), 106–8.

32. See *Mau: Thirty-nine Poems from Malawi* (Blantyre, 1971).

33. See L. Vail, "The State and the Creation of Colonial Malawi's Agricultural Economy," in *Imperialism, Colonialism, and Hunger: East and Central Africa*, ed. R. I. Rotburg (Lexington, Mass., 1983), 72–78.

34. L. White, "Ministering," in *For Captain Stedman: Poems* (Liskeard, Cornwall, 1983), 48; Mapanje, "Making Our Clowns Martyrs (or, Returning Home Without Chauffeurs)," in *Of Chameleons and Gods*, 59–60.

35. Mapanje, "Making Our Clowns Martyrs," 59–61.

36. The paragraphs that follow are taken from Mapanje's "Censoring the African Poem."

37. Ibid., 105–6.

38. Ibid., 105, 104.

39. Mapanje, "Another Fool's Day Touches Down: Shush," in *Index on Censorship* 16, no. 10 (Nov.-Dec. 1987): 23.

40. Mapanje, "Censoring the African Poem," 105.

41. Mapanje, "Traditional Literary Forms," 10.

42. From "We Wondered about the Mellow Peaches," in *Of Chameleons and Gods*, 70.

43. Ibid.

44. Mapanje, *Of Chameleons and Gods*, 63.

45. See *Africa Confidential* 30, no. 14 (7 July 1989): 6–7.

46. For a discussion of Malawi's relations with RENAMO and Mozambique, see D. Hedges, "Notes on Malawi-Mozambique Relations, 1961–1987," *Journal of Southern African Studies* 15, no. 4 (October 1989), especially pp. 635–44.

47. When this chapter was written, in mid-1990, Maxwell Pashani had been appointed acting secretary-general, but, as such, he had no constitutional authority.

48. Private letter from Mapanje to Landeg White, 12 December 1983.

49. Austin Madinga, who succeeded John Tembo as governor of the Bank of Malawi after Tembo was removed in 1982 at the insistence of the International Monetary Fund, also died in a car crash. *Africa Confidential* 30, no. 14 (7 July 1989): 6–7. "Being accidentalized" was a term used by ordinary Malawians in reference to being killed in a mysterious automobile accident.

50. Mapanje, "Kadango Village: Even Milimbo Lagoon Is Dry," in *Index on Censorship* 16, no. 10 (Nov.-Dec. 1987): 23.

Conclusion
A Polemic

The argument of this book has been that the oral poetry of south-central Africa, in its different genres and many languages, is linked by a common aesthetic, a shared set of assumptions concerning the nature and purpose of poetry. Central to this aesthetic is the concept of poetic license, the convention that poetic expression is privileged expression, the performer being free to express opinions that would otherwise be in breach of other social conventions. This aesthetic has itself, at different times and in different societies, been the subject of historic struggle. It has occasionally been appropriated, in its role as a medium for commenting on power, by those in power and used as a vehicle of propaganda on behalf of ruling groups. As a consequence, poetic license appears in different guises and has at times needed to be reinforced by notions of the privileges due to artistic expression or by the belief in spirit possession. But even in states as authoritarian as Lobengula's Ndebele or Salazar's Mozambique or Banda's Malawi, it has remained precariously in the culture as a medium of dissent preserving readings of history alternative to the official one.

The advantages of this argument are that it establishes the continuity of a particular poetic tradition over a wide area of southern Africa and over a long period of time, linking together types of poetic performance—praise songs, entertainments, satires, work songs, possession songs—that have hitherto been described separately. It provides vivid access to the past and present intellectual life of communities whose ideas have largely had to be inferred, passively and statically, from the analysis of institutions and observed patterns of behavior. It strengthens and makes more specific the customary claim that oral poetry is a type of social action by showing that in southern Africa poetry is valued precisely because it is a privileged form of expression. It makes redundant the distinction between text

and context, between formalist analyses of literary devices and social analyses of content, in short between poetics and history, by offering us a corpus of poetry whose content is legitimized by its
forms. Finally, it enables us to recognize important lines of continuity between oral and written poetry in southern Africa.

Before the quality of this poetry can be appreciated, however, it is
necessary to lay aside the theories which have dominated the study
of oral poetry for the last three decades. The dubious antecedents of
oral formulaic theory were examined in detail in chapter one, but
the main points are worth repeating. Human history did not begin
with the inventions either of the alphabet or of moveable type, and
there are no fundamental distinctions to be made between oral and
literate man. The oral poetry of south-central Africa is not, in general, composed in performance, and its essence cannot be understood through an investigation of the mechanics of its performance.
It is not dominated by the "formula," whether in Parry's terms as an
aid to improvisation or in McLuhan's and Ong's as a constraint on
thought. It is emphatically not the expression of societies locked in
cycles of intellectual repetition, incapable of change unless released
by missionaries or traders bringing "signs." On the contrary, its governing convention—the aesthetic of poetic license—makes it the
primary means by which both oral intellectuals and ordinary men
and women express, within the existing structures of power, their
versions of history. The resulting "maps of experience" open up the
intellectual, emotional, and moral life of the region's societies more
clearly and dramatically than any other source.

The range of historical themes discussed in the separate case studies of this book is considerable. Those most directly addressed have
been military conquest and resistance, state formation, the invention of tradition, the origins of ethnicity, the impact of forced labor
and labor migrancy, patron-client relations, worker consciousness,
and gender struggle. But it has been no part of our argument that the
songs and poems that embody these themes are in themselves definitive readings of history. Metaphor, like theory, is a means of transcending the particular, of rising above "mindless empiricism." But
its sources are imaginative, its methods intuitive; its statements are
concrete, not abstract. This is what gives the poems their greatest
force, their sense of springing from authentic experience. But one
cannot deduce from material whose effects are rhetorical and whose
purpose is to give intellectual and emotional satisfaction a straightforward reading of historical facts. For these reasons, each of our

chapters has combined literary material with evidence from oral and archival sources. With a history as complex and many-sided as the history of southern Africa over the past century and a half, this combination of different voices in a complex dialogue is essential.

Our separate chapters have shown poetic license operating in the poetry of six different countries (Malawi, Mozambique, South Africa, Swaziland, Zambia, and Zimbabwe) and in eight different languages (Chopi, Ndebele, Sena, Sotho, Swazi, Tumbuka, Zulu, and Malawian English). One chapter offers the history of a single form (the Chopi *ngodo*), while two others show traditions of praising developing in response to historical change (Ndebele and Swazi). One deals with the evolution of a single song over a period of eight decades (*Paiva*); one with recurrent themes in a wide range of examples (*vimbuza* spirit possession); and one with the work of an individual poet writing in English within the tradition (Jack Mapanje). We have discussed songs and poems from opposite ends of the political spectrum—from the official court praises of Zulu, Ndebele, and Swazi kings, but including highly critical material, to the poetic complaints of representatives of the region's most exploited and marginalized peoples, the forced laborers of colonial Mozambique and the Tumbuka women. Finally, our chapters have shifted geographically between rural villages and stockaded towns and worker compounds to the townships of contemporary Lusaka, and they have moved in time from the third decade of the nineteenth century, through the different phases of capitalist penetration and colonial overrule, to the contrasting circumstances of contemporary Zambia and Malawi. We believe that we have demonstrated some of the huge variety of circumstances in which the aesthetic we have been describing can flourish in arenas of struggle and that our historical approach illuminates not only the region's literature but also its history.

These are large claims. We hope indeed that this book will prove innovative, affecting profoundly the way history and the oral literature of southern Africa—and further afield—is studied in future years. But it would be inappropriate to end the book on this note. We have already indicated in chapter two that none of our individual chapters can be regarded as definitive. Our discussion of the development of forms, essential to the mapping of literary history, has been inhibited by the poverty and dubious provenance of nineteenth-century recordings, so that chapters such as three, on Ndebele praises, and five, on Swazi praises, have had to be tentative and partly hypothetical in their conclusions. The book's very scope, following on our contention as to the existence of a common aesthetic over a wide area and a long period of time, has meant that we have frequently had to work with translations. To repeat our earlier words, if poetry is "what is left out in translation," then many of our comments and interpretations must await the intervention of scholars "versed" in the languages concerned to whom the poems speak from deep inside their own cultures.

But there is more at stake here than our own limitations. We have argued elsewhere that literary criticism has been the Cinderella of African studies, producing little scholarship that can match the commitment and intellectual vigor of debates in related disciplines. Part of this failure seems to lie in its origins in the New Criticism of the 1950s, when a stress on the study of the "text as artefact," as "verbal icon" or "well-wrought urn," led all too easily to the assumption that there was some special virtue in isolating literature from its social and historical setting. The perfection of art involved its timelessness, and timelessness could be demonstrated by ignoring time. As applied to written African literature, the earliest to be discussed, this frequently meant that critics set themselves no larger tasks than reportage and simple exposition, a mixture of content summary and praise. It became part of critical strategy to apologize for the assumed anthropological orientation of African novels and to set up such status-claiming parallels as that Wole Soyinka uses language like James Joyce, that Camara Laye is Kafkaesque, that Armah shares Swift's excremental vision, and that Amos Tutuola's novels are, like *Wuthering Heights*, a kind of sport. Forced by the very nature of such literature to look a little further, critics have been content to take their image of Africa from the literature itself and then praise the literature for its truth, operating with such simple concepts as "the traditional African way of life," the "clash between African and European cultures," and the "corruption following independence," concepts that seem strangely innocent to the historian or to the social or political scientist. More recently, and in strong reaction to this, there have been attempts to marry literary criticism to underdevelopment or to neo-Marxist paradigms.[1] The result has been a criticism in which *literary* concerns hardly appear, the writers being judged by the company they keep—their publishers, their audiences, the prizes they have won—or by the approximation of their themes to a predetermined agenda. Such books and articles are much livelier than those that preceded them, and they contain some excellent individual work. But they draw their judgments from narrowly political criteria and have not succeeded in demonstrating the value of a literary dimension to African studies.

At the heart of this failure has been criticism's inability to come to terms with Africa's dominant literature, that is, its oral literature. The New Criticism, as Isidore Okpewho pointed out a decade ago, was by definition ill-equipped to discuss oral literature in which, as we have seen, there is no such thing as artifact or established text to be defended from such heresies as the biographical or intentional fallacies. Nor have the New Criticism's successors, in structuralism or poststructuralism, found ways of assimilating the kind of material that is the subject of this book. Structuralism preserved the notion of a fixed text, a closed system insulated from history, while poststructuralism has returned the unstable text to history only by undermining the authority of the poem's language, an authority basic to the aesthetic we have been describing.

The problem goes deeper. It is sobering to reflect that after well over a century of collecting material and two decades after Finnegan's *Oral Literature in Africa* cleared the ground for further research, there is still not a single African society whose literature we possess as a whole. There are collections of Akan dirges and Yoruba *ijala* (hunter poems) and Xhosa narratives and Venda riddles and Bagamoyo cattle songs—and so on almost indefinitely, so that it seems at times that researchers are implicitly suggesting that every "tribe" has cornered the market in a specialized genre and is doing its own thing to its own rules. But in no instance throughout sub-Saharan Africa is it yet possible to situate such material in a comprehensive literary record of the region or the society. By this we mean an account of the various literary forms practiced with a substantial selection of examples of each, an account of the relative value placed by performers and audiences on the different genres and on the aesthetics of performance, including a clear sense of the fluidity of genres with material flowing easily between them, and finally an appreciation of how each form, again with a number of examples, has developed under the impact of individual imaginations in response to social and historical change since, say, the early nineteenth century.

Or even the twentieth! There is little excuse for this situation now, beyond the sheer labor of collection, transcription, translation, and interviews with informants. The evidence has been available to enquirers prepared to listen since the late 1950s, when African studies first became truly African-centered. But unlike the anthropologists whose work we criticize in chapter one of this book, a generation of historians, social and political scientists, and literary critics who have studied Africa has been unembarrassed to work in ignorance of African languages, and material that has a profound intrinsic value of its own and that is essential to the understanding of social and historical change, has been shunted to the sidelines of folklore, structural linguistics, or the hunt for the formula.

Finally, and most fundamental of all, is the complaint voiced recently by Olabiyi Yai about the unequal relations between oral poets and academic critics. Quoting T. S. Eliot to the effect that the dialectic between poetic creativity and criticism is taken for granted in both Western and oriental literary traditions, Yai continues:

> Paradoxically, the state of the art in oral poetry criticism is a negation of Eliot's dictum. No communication seems to exist between the production/consumption of oral poetry and its criticism. More precisely, communication is unidimensional. When the creator of oral poetry and his academic critics are contemporaries the terms of the critical exchange are unilaterally set by the critic. The poet is thus degraded from his status of creator to that of an informant. He can only make such contributions as required by the initiatives of the critic.[2]

No expatriate students of African oral literature can be entirely confident of having avoided this charge. The way forward is to listen, and listen again.

Notes

1. E.g., C. Amuta, *The Theory of African Literature: Implications for Practical Criticism* (London and Atlantic Highlands, N.J., 1989).
2. Olabiyi Yai, "Issues in Oral Poetry: Criticism, Teaching, and Translation," in *Discourse and its Disguises: The Interpretation of African Oral Texts*, eds. K. Barber and P. F. de Moraes Farias (Birmingham, U.K., 1989), 52.

Select Bibliography

Ackerman, Ronald. *J. G. Frazer: His Life and Work*. Cambridge, 1987.

Amuta, Chidi. *The Theory of African Literature: Implications for Practical Criticism*. London and Atlantic Highlands, N.J., 1989.

Anonymous. "The Tumbuka Tribe," *Aurora* 5, no. 25 (1901):

Apter, Andrew. "In Dispraise of the King: Rituals 'against' Rebellion in South East Africa," *Man*, n.s. 18, no. 3 (1983): 521–34.

Asad, Talal, ed. *Anthropology and the Colonial Encounter*. New York, 1973.

Axtell, James. *The Invasion Within: The Contest of Cultures in Colonial North America*. New York and Oxford, 1985.

Baines, Thomas. *The Goldfield Diaries of Thomas Baines*. Edited by J. P. R. Wallis. 3 vols. London, 1946.

Barber, Karin. "Documenting Social and Ideological Change through Yoruba *Oriki*: A Stylistic Analysis," *Journal of the Historical Society of Nigeria* 10, no. 4 (1981): 39–52.

Beemer, Hilda. "The Swazi Rain Ceremony (Critical Comments on P. J. Schoeman's article)," *Bantu Studies* 9 (1935): 273–80.

Bernal, Martin. *The Fabrication of Ancient Greece, 1785–1985*. Vol. 1 in *Black Athena: The Afroasiatic Roots of Classical Civilization*. London, 1987.

Boas, Franz. *The Mind of Primitive Man*. New York, 1911.

Bonner, Philip. *Kings, Commoners, and Concessionaires: The Evolution and Dissolution of the Nineteenth Century Swazi State*. Cambridge, 1983.

Boon, James A. *Affinities and Extremes*. Chicago, 1990.

Booth, Alan R. "Homestead, State and Migrant Labor in Colonial Swaziland," *African Economic History* 14 (1985): 107–45.

———. "Capitalism and the Competition for Swazi Labour, 1945–1960," *Journal of Southern African Studies* 13, no. 1 (October 1986): 125–50.

Botelho de Carvalho Araujo, José. *Relatório do Governador do Districto de Inhambane, 1917*. Coimbra, 1920.

Brown, Donald E. *Hierarchy, History, and Human Nature: The Social Origins of Historical Consciousness*. Tucson, Ariz. 1988.

Bryant, A. T. *Olden Days in Zululand and Natal*. London, 1929.

Bynum, David E. *The Daemon in the Wood: A Study of Oral Narrative Patterns*, Cambridge, Mass., 1978.

Cabral, Augusto. *Raças, Usos, e Costumes dos Indígenas do Districto de Inhambane.* Lourenço Marques, 1910.

Caldas Xavier, Alfredo A. "O Inharrime e as Guerras zavallas," *Boletim de Sociedade da Geographia de Lisboa,* 2d ser., nos. 7–8 (1880): 479–528.

Cardoso, Augusto. *Relatório do Governador do Districto de Inhambane, 1906–1907.* Lourenço Marques, 1907.

———. *Relatório do Governador do Districto de Inhambane, 1907–1909.* Lourenço Marques, 1909.

Carothers, J. C. *The African Mind in Health and Disease.* Geneva, 1953.

Chadwick, H. M., and N. K. Chadwick. *The Growth of Literature.* 3 vols. Cambridge, 1932–40.

Chanock, Martin. *Law, Custom, and Social Order: The Colonial Experience in Malawi and Zambia.* Cambridge, 1985.

Chibambo, Yesaya M. *My Ngoni of Nyasaland.* London, n.d.

Chisiza, Dunduza. *Africa: What Lies Ahead.* New Delhi, 1961.

Churchill, William. *Report for the Year 1891 on the Trade of the Consular District of Mozambique.* Consular Series no. 995, C.6550. London, 1892.

Clarence-Smith, W. Gervase. *The Third Portuguese Empire, 1825–1975: A Study in Economic Imperialism.* Manchester, U.K., 1985.

Clifford, James M. *The Predicament of Culture: Twentieth-Century Ethnography, Literature, and Art.* Cambridge, Mass., 1988.

Cobbing, Julian. "The Ndebele under the Khumalos, 1820–1896." Ph.D. diss., University of Lancaster, 1976.

———. "The Mfecane as Alibi: Thoughts on Dithakong and Mbolompo," *Journal of African History* 29, no. 3 (1988): 487–513.

Cohen, Abner. *Two-Dimensional Man.* London, 1974.

Cohn, Bernard S. "History and Anthropology: The State of Play," *Comparative Study of Society and History* 22, no. 2 (1980): 198–221.

Collin, Bertha. *J. P. Hornung.* n.p., n.d. [1970].

Comaroff, Jean. *Body of Power, Spirit of Resistance: The Culture and History of a South African People.* Chicago and London, 1985.

Connah, Graham. *African Civilizations.* Cambridge, 1987.

Cook, P. A. W. "History and Izibongo of the Swazi Chiefs," *Bantu Studies* 5 (1931): 181–202.

Cope, Trevor. *Izibongo: Zulu Praise Poems.* Oxford, 1968.

Coplan, David B. *In Township Tonight: South Africa's Black City Music and Theatre.* New York, 1985.

———. "The Power of Oral Poetry: Narrative Songs of the Basotho Migrants," *Research in African Literature* 18 (1987): 1–35.

Correira de Matos, Maria Leonor. "Origens d Povo Chope Segundo a Tradição Oral," *Memorias do Instituto de Investigação Científica de Moçambique,* 10, ser. C (1973): 1–85.

Correira Henriques, C. *Relatório do Governador do Districto de Inhambane, 1913–1915.* Lourenço Marques, 1916.

Cosentino, Donald J. *Defiant Maids and Stubborn Farmers: Tradition and Invention in the Mende Story Performance.* Cambridge, 1982.

Crush, Jonathan. "Colonial Coercion and the Swazi Tax Revolt of 1903–1907," *Political Geography Quarterly* 4, no. 3 (1985): 178–90.

———. *The Struggle for Swazi Labour, 1890–1920.* Kingston and Montreal, 1987.

Curtin, Philip D. *The Image of Africa: British Ideas and Actions, 1780–1850.* Madison, Wis., 1964.

da Cruz, Daniel. *Em Terras da Gaza.* Porto, 1910.

d'Almeida Saldanha, E. *Desnacionalização de Moçambique.* Lourenço Marques, 1911.

Damane, M., and P. B. Sanders. *Lithoko: Sotho Praise Poems.* Oxford, 1974.

Darwin, Charles. *The Origin of Species by Means of Natural Selection, or, The Preservation of Favoured Races in the Struggle for Life.* 1859; rep. Harmondsworth, 1968.

da Silva Cunha, J. M. *O Trabalho Indígena: Estudo de Direito Colonial.* 2d ed., Lisbon, 1955.

das Neves, Dioclesiano F. *Itinerário de uma Viagem a Caça das Elephantes.* Lisbon, 1878.

de Almeida Garrett, T. *Um Governo em Africa: Inhambane, 1905–1906.* Lisbon, 1907.

de Azevedo Coutinho, Joachim. *Memorias de um Velho Marinheiro e Soldado de Africa.* Lisbon, 1941.

de Bettencourt, Tristão. *Relatório do Governador-Geral de Moçambique, 1940–42.* 2 vols. Lisbon, 1945.

de Figueiredo Gomes e Sousa, Antonio. "Recolonizacão de Distrito de Inhambane," *Boletim da Sociedade de Estudos da Colonia de Moçambique* 5, nos. 31 and 32 (1936): 171–87; 282–92.

Deng, Francis. *The Dinka and their Songs.* Oxford, 1973.

Depelchin, Henri, S.J., and Charles Croonenberghs, S.J. *Journey to Gubulawayo.* Bulawayo, 1979. English translation by Moira Lloyd of *Trois Ans dans l'Afrique Australe: Le Pays des Matabélés debuts de la Mission du Zambèse.* Brussels, 1882.

Diamond, Stanley. *In Search of the Primitive.* New Brunswick, N.J., 1974.

dos Santos, Carlos Afonso. *Relatório do Governador do Distrito de Inhambane nãos annos 1931, 1932, 1933, e 1934.* Lisbon, 1937.

dos Santos, P. Luiz Feliciano. *Gramatica de Línqua Chope.* Lourenço Marques, 1941.

Dundes, Alan. *Interpreting Folklore.* Bloomington and London, 1980.

Earthy, Dora. *Valenge Women.* London, 1933.

Eggan, Frederick. "One Hundred Years of Ethnology and Social Anthropology." In *One Hundred Years of Anthropology,* edited by J. O. Brew. Cambridge, Mass., 1968.

Elmslie, Walter A. *Among the Wild Ngoni.* Edinburgh and London, 1901.

Elton, Frederick. "Journal of an Exploration of the Limpopo River," *Journal of the Royal Geographical Society* 42 (1872): 1–48.

Enes, Antonio. *Moçambique.* 3d edition. Lisbon, 1946.

Erskine, St. Vincent. "Journey of Exploration to the Mouth of the River Limpopo," *Journal of the Royal Geographical Society* 39 (1869): 233–67.

———. "Journey to Umzila's, South-East Africa, in 1871–1872," *Journal of the Royal Geographical Society* 45 (1875): 45–125.

———. "Third and Fourth Journeys in Gaza, or Southern Mozambique, 1873 to 1874, and 1874 to 1875," *Journal of the Royal Geographical Society* 48 (1878): 25–26.

Etherington, Norman. *Preachers and Politics in South Africa, 1835–80.* London, 1978.

Evans-Pritchard, Edward E. "Some collective expressions of obscenity in Africa." Pp. 76–101 in his *The Position of Women in Primitive Societies and Other Essays in Social Anthropology.* Oxford, 1965.

———. *A History of Anthropological Thought.* New York, 1981.

Fabian, Johannes. *Time and Other: How Anthropology Makes Its Object.* New York, 1983.

Fereira Cabral, José Ricardo. *Relatório do Governador do Districto de Inhambane, 1910–1911.* Lourenço Marques, 1912.

———. *Relatório do Governador do Districto de Inhambane, 1911–1912.* Lourenço Marques, 1912.

Finnegan, Ruth. *Limba Stories and Storytelling.* Oxford, 1967.

———. *Oral Literature in Africa.* Oxford, 1970.

———. *Oral Poetry: Its Nature, Significance, and Social Context.* Cambridge, 1977.

———. "What is Oral Literature Anyway?". Pp. 123–54 in *Oral Literature and the Formula,* edited by B. A. Stolz and R. S. Shannon. Ann Arbor, 1976.

First, Ruth. *The Mozambican Miner: A Study in the Export of Labour.* Maputo, 1977.

Fransman, Martin. "The Colonial State and the Land Question in Swaziland, 1903–1907." Pp. 27–38 in University of London, Institute of Commonwealth Studies, *The Societies of Southern Africa in the Nineteenth and Twentieth Centuries,* vol. 9. London, 1978.

Frazer, Donald. "The Zulu of Nyasaland: Their Manners and Customs," *Proceedings of the Philosophical Society of Glasgow* 32 (1900): 66–70.

———. *Winning a Primitive People.* London, 1914.

Fuller, Charles E. "An Ethno-Study of Continuity and Change in Gwambe Culture." Ph.D. diss., Northwestern University, 1955.

Fuze, M. M. *The Black People and Whence They Came: A Zulu View.* Pietermaritzburg, 1979.

Geertz, Clifford. *Local Knowledge.* New York, 1983.

Gibbs, James. "Singing in the Dark Rain," *Index on Censorship* 17, no. 2 (February 1988): 19–20.

Ginindza, Thokozile T. *Tibongo teMakhosi netetiNdlovukazi*. London, 1975.

————. "SiSwati Oral Poetry." Ph.D. diss., International College, Los Angeles, 1985.

Gluckman, Max. "Social Aspects of First-Fruit Ceremonies among the South-Eastern Bantu," *Africa* (1938): 25–41.

————. "Analysis of a Social Situation in Modern Zululand," *Bantu Studies* 14, nos. 1 and 2 (1940): 1–30, 147–74.

————. "Rituals of Rebellion in South East Africa." Pp. 110–36 in his *Order and Rebellion in Tribal Africa*. New York, 1963.

Goody, John R. *The Domestication of the Savage Mind*. Cambridge, 1977.

————. *The Logic of Writing and the Organization of Society*. Cambridge, 1986.

Gould, Stephen J. *The Mismeasure of Man*. New York and London, 1981.

Grant, E. W. "The Izibongo of the Zulu Chiefs," *Bantu Studies* 3, no. 3 (1927–29): 201–44.

Grout, L. *Zululand: Or Life among the Zulu-Kafirs of Natal and Zululand*. 1864; rpt. London, 1970.

Grunner, Elizabeth. "Ukubongo Nezibongo: Zulu Praising and Praises." D. Phil. diss., University of London, 1984.

Guy, Jeff. *The Destruction of the Zulu Kingdom*. London, 1979.

Harries, Patrick. "Slavery, Social Incorporation, and Surplus Extraction: The Nature of Free and Unfree Labour in South-East Africa," *Journal of African History* 20, no. 3 (1981): 309–30.

Harris, William V. *Ancient Literacy*. Cambridge, Mass., 1989.

Havelock, Eric A. *Preface to Plato*. Cambridge, Mass., 1963.

Haviland, Emma H. *Under the Southern Cross: or, A Woman's Life Work for Africa*. Cincinnati, 1928.

Hedges, David. "Notes on Malawi-Mozambique Relations, 1961–1987," *Journal of Southern African Studies* 15, no. 4 (October 1989): 617–44.

Hemans, T. J. "Praises Given to the King of the Amandebele," *NADA* 10, no. 3 (1971): 94–96.

Henderson, James. "Northern Nyasaland," *Scottish Geographical Magazine* 16, no. 2 (1900): 86–87.

Hodza, A. C., and George Fortune. *Shona Praise Poetry*. Oxford, 1979.

Hoenigswald, Henry. "On the History of the Comparative Method," *Anthropological Linguistics* 5 (1963): 1–11.

Holy, Ladislaw. *Strategies and Norms in a Changing Matrilineal Society: Descent, Succession, and Inheritance among the Toka of Zambia*. Cambridge, 1986.

Honwana, Bernardo. *We Killed Mangy Dog and Other Mozambique Stories*. Translated by Dorothy Guedes. London, 1969.

Hooper, John. "The Politics of Patronage: An Assessment of the Political Economy of Malawi since Independence." M.A. thesis, University of York, 1984.

Horton, Robin. "African Traditional Thought and Western Science," *Africa* 37 (1967): 50–71, 155–87.

Isaacman, Allen, et al. "Cotton Is the Mother of Poverty: Peasant Resistance to Forced Cotton Production in Mozambique, 1938–1961." *International Journal of African Historical Studies* 13, no. 4 (1980): 581–615.

Jaynes, Julian. *Origins of Consciousness in the Breakdown of the Bicameral Mind.* Boston, 1977.

Jeeves, Alan H. *Migrant Labour in South Africa's Mining Economy: The Struggle for the Gold Mines' Labour Supply, 1890–1920.* Kingston and Montreal, 1985.

Johnston, Harry Hamilton. *Report for the Year 1889 on the Trade of Mozambique and District.* Consular Series no. 742, C.5895. London, 1890.

Jordan, Archibald Campbell. "Towards an African Literature," *Africa South* 2, no. 1 (October-December, 1957): 104–5, and 3, no. 2 (January-March, 1959): 74.

———. *Towards an African Literature: the Emergence of Literary Form in Xhosa.* Berkeley and Los Angeles, 1973.

Junod, Henri A. *The Life of a South African Tribe.* 2 vols. 2d, rev. ed. 1927; rpt. New York, 1962.

Junod, Henri Philippe. "Some Notes on Tshopi Origins," *Bantu Studies* 3, no. 1 (1929): 57–71.

———. "The Mbila or Native Piano of the Tshopi Tribe," *Bantu Studies* 3, no. 3 (1929): 275–85.

Katzenellenbogen, Simon. *South Africa and Southern Mozambique: Labour, Railways, and Trade in the Making of a Relationship.* Manchester, U.K., 1982.

Kerr, David. "Community Theater and Public Health in Malawi," *Journal of Southern African Studies* 15, no. 3 (April 1989): 469–85.

Kerr, W. Montague. *The Far Interior* 2 vols. London, 1886.

Kidd, Dudley. *The Essential Kafir.* London, 1904.

Koljevic, S. *The Epic in the Making.* Oxford, 1980.

Kunene, Mazisi. *Emperor Shake the Great.* London, 1979.

Kuper, Adam. *Anthropology and Anthropologists: The Modern British School.* 2d, revised edition. London, 1983.

———. *The Invention of Primitive Society: Transformations of an Illusion.* London and New York, 1988.

Kuper, Hilda. "The Swazi Reaction to Missions," *African Studies* 5, no. 3 (1946): 177–88.

———. "A Ritual of Kingship among the Swazi," *Africa* 14 (1944): 230–57. Reprinted as chapter 13, pp. 197–225, of her *An African Aristocracy.* London, 1947.

———. "A Royal Ritual in a Changing Political Context," *Cahiers d'etudes africaines* 12, no. 48 (1972): 593–615.

———. *Sobhuza II, Ngwenyama and King of Swaziland.* London, 1978.

————. *The Swazi.* 2d, revised edition. New York, 1986.

Lancaster, Chester S. *The Goba of the Zambezi: Sex Roles, Economics, and Change.* Norman, Okla., 1981.

Lévi-Strauss, Claude. *La Pensée Sauvage.* Paris, 1962.

————. *Tristes Tropiques.* London, 1973.

Lévy-Bruhl, Lucien. *How Natives Think.* New York, 1926. English translation by L. A. Clare of *Les Fonctions Mentales dans les Sociétés Inférieures* (Paris, 1910).

Lewis, Ioan M. *Ecstatic Religion: An Anthropological Study of Spirit Possession and Shamanism.* Harmondsworth, 1971.

Liesegang, Gerhard. "Notes on the Internal Structure of the Gaza Kingdom of Southern Mozambique, 1840–1895." Pp. 178–209 in *Before and After Shaka: Papers in Nguni History,* edited by Jeffrey Peires. Grahamstown, South Africa, 1981.

Lincoln, Bruce. "Ritual, Rebellion, Resistance: Once More the Swazi Ncwala," *Man,* n.s. 22, no. 2 (1987): 132–56.

Linden, Ian. *Catholics, Peasants, and Chewa Resistance in Nyasaland, 1889–1939.* London, 1974.

Livingstone, David, and Charles Livingstone. *Narrative of an Expedition to the Zambesi and Its Tributaries.* London, 1865.

Lohrentz, Kenneth P. "Joseph Booth, Charles Domingo, and the Seventh Day Baptists in Northern Nyasaland, 1910–12," *Journal of African History* 12, no. 3 (1971): 461–80.

Lord, Albert B. *The Singer of Tales.* Cambridge, Mass., 1960.

————. "Perspectives on Recent Work in Oral Literature," *Forum for Modern Language Studies* 10 (1974): 187–210.

MacDonald, Duff. *Africana, or the Heart of Heathen Africa.* 2 vols. London, 1882.

McCracken, John. *Politics and Christianity in Malawi, 1875–1940.* Cambridge, 1977.

McGrane, Bernard. *Beyond Anthropology: Society and the Other.* New York, 1989.

McLuhan, Marshall. *The Gutenburg Galaxy.* Toronto, 1962.

————. *Counterblast.* London, 1970.

Macmillan, Hugh. "Decolonisation and the Triumph of 'Tradition,'" *Journal of Modern African Studies* 23, no. 4 (1985): 643–66.

————. "A Nation Divided? The Swazi in Swaziland and the Transvaal, 1865–1986." Pp. 289–323 in *The Creation of Tribalism in Southern Africa,* edited by Leroy Vail. London and Berkeley, 1988.

Mafeje, Archie. "A Chief Visits Town," *Journal of Local Administration Overseas* 2 (1963): 88–99.

————. "The Role of the Bard in a Contemporary African Community," *Journal of African Languages* 6, no. 3 (1967): 193–223.

Makambe, E. P. "The Nyasaland African Labour 'Ulendos' to Southern Rhodesia and the Problem of African 'Highwaymen,' 1903–1923: A Study in the Limitations of Early Independent Labour Migration," *African Affairs*, no. 317 (1980): 548–66.

Mamba, G. N. "Group Identity in Swazi Oral Poetry." Pp. 183–213 in *Aesthetics, Language, and Literature*, vol. 2 in *Oral Traditions in Southern Africa*, edited by S. P. C. Moyo, T. W. C. Sumaili, and J. A. Moody. 4 vols. Lusaka, 1986.

Mapanje, J. A. C. "The Use of Traditional Literary Forms in Modern Malawian Writing in English." M. Phil. thesis. University of London, 1974.

Mapanje, Jack. *Of Chameleons and Gods*. London, 1981.

———. "Censoring the African Poem: Personal Reflections." Pp. 104–11 in *Criticism and Ideology*, edited by K. Holst-Petersen. Uppsala, 1986.

———, and Landeg White, eds. *Oral Poetry from Africa: An Anthology*. London, 1983.

Marchand, Philip. *Marshall McLuhan: The Medium and the Messenger*. New York, 1989.

Marcus, George E. and Michael M. J. Fischer. *Anthropology as Cultural Critique: An Experimental Moment in the Human Sciences*. Chicago and London, 1986.

Marks, Shula. *Ambiguities of Dependence in South Africa: Class, Nationalism, and the State in Twentieth Century Natal*. Baltimore and London, 1986.

———. "Patriotism, Patriarchy, and Purity: Natal and the Politics of Zulu Ethnic Consciousness." Pp. 215–40 in *The Politics of Tribalism in Southern Africa*, edited by Leroy Vail. London and Berkeley, 1988.

Marques, Belo. *Musica Negra: Estudos de Folclore Tonga*. Lisbon, 1943.

Marwick, Max. *Sorcery in Its Social Setting*. Manchester, U.K., 1965.

Mathers, E. P. *Zambesia: England's el Dorado in Africa*. 3d edition. London, 1895.

Matsebula, J. S. M. *A History of Swaziland*. London, 1972.

———. *The King's Eye*. Cape Town, 1983.

———. *A Tribute to the Late His Majesty King Sobhuza II*. Mbabane, 1983.

Maw, A. H. "Transport and Travelling in British Central Africa 1899," *Nyasaland Journal* 8 no. 2 (1955): 11–15.

Merriam, Alan P. "Song Texts of the Bashi," *African Music Society Journal* 1 (1954): 1–35.

Mhlagazanhlansi. *My Friend Kumalo*. 1944; rpt. Bulawayo, 1972.

Mitchell, J. Clyde. *The Kalela Dance*, Rhodes-Livingstone Paper number 27. Manchester, U.K., 1956.

Moffat, Robert. *Missionary Labours and Scenes in Southern Africa*. 6th edition. New York, 1844.

———. *The Matabele Journals of Robert Moffat, 1829–1860*. Edited by J. P. R. Wallis. 2 vols. London, 1945.

Moore, Sally Falk. *Social Facts and Fabrications: "Customary" Law on Kilimanjaro, 1880–1980*. Cambridge, 1986.

Mosse, George L. *Toward the Final Solution: A History of European Racism.* New York, 1978.

Mozambique. *Cultura Industria e Comércio Arroz.* Lourenço Marques, 1941.

Mozambique. *Department of Agriculture: Bulletin no. 1.* Lourenço Marques, 1909.

Mudimbe, Valentine Y. *The Invention of Africa: Gnosis, Philosophy, and the Order of Knowledge.* Bloomington, Ind., 1988.

Mueller, Martin. *The Iliad.* London, 1984.

Munro, J. Forbes. *Africa and the International Economy, 1800–1960.* London, 1976.

Mzamane, Mbulelo V. "The Uses of Traditional Oral Forms in Black South African Literature." Pp. 147–60 in *Literature and Society in South Africa,* edited by L. White and T. Couzens. Harlow, Essex, 1984.

Ncozana, S. S. "Spirit Possession and Tumbuka Christians, 1875–1950." Ph.D. diss., University of Aberdeen, 1985.

Newitt, Malyn D. *Portuguese Settlement on the Zambesi.* London, 1973.

Okpewho, Isidore. *The Epic in Africa: Towards a Poetics of the Oral Performance.* Revised edition. New York, 1979.

Omer-Cooper, John D. *History of Southern Africa.* Portsmouth, N.H., 1987.

Ong, Walter J. *Ramus, Method, and the Decay of Dialogue.* Cambridge, Mass., 1958.

———. *Orality and Literacy: The Technologizing of the Word.* London and New York, 1982.

———. "McLuhan as Teacher: the St. Louis Years." Pp. 25–31 in *Marshall McLuhan: The Man and His Message,* edited by George Sanderson and Frank Macdonald. Golden, Colo., 1989.

Opland, Jeff. "*Imbongi nezibongo:* the Xhosa Tribal Poet and the Contemporary Poetic Tradition," *PMLA* 90 (1975): 185–208.

———. "Caedmon and Ntsikana: Anglo-Saxon and Xhosa Transitional Poets," *Annals of the Grahamstown Historic Society* 2, no. 3 (1977): 56–65.

———. "The Installation of the Chancellor: A Study of Transitional Oral Poetry." Unpublished paper presented at the Conference on Literature and Society in Southern Africa, University of York, U.K., 8–11 September 1981.

———. *Xhosa Oral Poetry.* Cambridge, 1983.

———. "The Isolation of the Xhosa Oral Poet," Pp. 175–95 in *Literature and Society in South Africa,* edited by L. White and T. Couzens. Harlow, Essex, 1984.

Packard, Randall. "Maize, Cattle, and Mosquitoes: The Political Economy of Malaria Epidemics in Colonial Swaziland," *Journal of African History* 25, no. 2 (1984): 189–212.

Parry, Milman. *L'Epithète Traditionnelle dans Homère: Essai sur un Problème de Style Homèrique.* Paris, 1928.

———. *Les Formules et la Métrique d'Homère*. Paris, 1928.

———. *The Making of Homeric Verse: The Collected Papers of Milman Perry*. Edited by Adam Parry. Oxford, 1971.

Pélissier, René. *Naissance du Mozambique: Résistance et Révoltes Anticoloniales (1854–1918)*. 2 vols. Orgeval, France, 1984.

Penniman, T. K. *A Hundred Years of Anthropology*. 2d, revised edition. London, 1952.

Penvenne, Jeanne M. "A History of African Labor in Lourenço Marques, Mozambique, 1877 to 1950." Ph.D. diss., Boston University, 1982.

Pery, G. A. *Geographia e Estatistica de Portugal e Colonias*. Lisbon, 1875.

Phimister, Ian, and Charles van Onselen. "The Political Economy of Tribal Animosity: A Case Study of the 1929 Bulawayo Location 'Faction Fight,'" *Journal of Southern African Studies* 6, no. 1 (October 1979): 1–43.

Pirio, Gregory R. "Commerce, Industry, and Empire: The Making of Modern Colonialism in Angola and Mozambique, 1890–1914." Ph.D. diss., University of California, Los Angeles, 1982.

Pona, A. P. deP. *Dos Primieros Trabalhos dos Portugueses no Monomotapa*. Lisbon, 1892.

Portugal. *Pautas das Alfandegas de Provincia de Moçambique: Comprehendando as de Lourenço Marques e Cabo Delgado: Approvados por Decreto de 29 de dezembro de 1892*. Lisbon, 1893.

Potholm, Charles P. "The Ngwenyama of Swaziland: The Dynamics of Political Adaptation." Pp. 129–59 in *African Kingships in Perspective*, edited by René Lemarchand. London, 1977.

Price, Richard. *First Time: The Historical Vision of an Afro-American People*. Baltimore, 1983.

Radin, Paul. *Primitive Man as Philosopher*. New York, 1927.

Ranger, Terence O. *The African Voice in Southern Rhodesia, 1898–1930*. London, 1970.

Rasmussen, R. Kent. *Migrant Kingdom: Mzilikazi's Ndebele in South Africa*. London, 1978.

Rich, Paul B. *White Power and the Liberal Conscience: Racial Segregation and South African Liberalism, 1921–60*. Johannesburg, 1984.

Rita-Ferreira, Antonio. " 'Timbilas' e 'Jazz' entre os Indigenas de Homoine (Mozambique)," *Boletim Investigagação Cientifica, Mozambique* 1, no. 1 (1960): 68–79.

Roberts, Ray S. "The End of the Ndebele Royal Family." Seminar paper, History Department, University of Zimbabwe, 1988.

Rocha, Ilidio. *A Arte Maravilhosa do Povo Chope*. Lourenço Marques, 1962.

———. "A Morte dos *Ngodo* Chopes—Uma Dramática Forma de Resistência Cultural." In Institute of Anthropology, University of Coimbra, *Moçambique: Aspectos da Cultura Material*. Coimbra, 1986.

Rodney, Walter. "The Year 1895 in Southern Mozambique: African Resistance to the Imposition of European Colonial Rule," *Journal of the Historical Society of Nigeria* 5, no. 4 (1971): 509–36.

Rosaldo, Renato. *Ilongot Headhunting, 1883–1973.* Stanford, Calif. 1980.

Ross, Andrew. "The Malawi Cabinet Crisis of 1964." Paper presented at Edinburgh University in 1984.

Rotburg, Robert I. *The Rise of Nationalism in Central Africa.* Cambridge, Mass., 1967.

Rycroft, David, "An 1842 Version of Dingana Eulogies," *African Studies Journal* 43, no. 2 (1984); 249–74.

Sahlins, Marshall. *Islands of History.* Chicago, 1985.

Said, Edward. *Orientalism.* New York, 1979.

Samuelson, R. C. A. *Long, Long Ago.* Durban, 1929; rpt. Durban, 1974.

Schapera, Isaac. *Praise-Poems of Tswana Chiefs.* Oxford, 1965.

Scheub, Harold. *The Xhosa "Ntsomi."* Oxford, 1975.

Schnapper, G. *La Politique et le Commerce Français dans le Golfe de Guinée de 1838 à 1871.* Paris, 1961.

Schneider, David M. and Kathleen Gough, eds. *Matrilineal Kinship.* Berkeley and Los Angeles, 1961.

Schoeman, P. J. "The Swazi Rain Ceremony," *Bantu Studies* 9 (1935): 169–75.

Scott, James C. *The Moral Economy of the Peasant: Rebellion and Subsistence in Southeast Asia.* New Haven, 1976.

———. *Weapons of the Weak: Everyday Forms of Peasant Resistance.* New Haven, 1985.

Sharp, John. "The Roots and Development of *Volkekunde* in South Africa," *Journal of Southern Africa Studies* 8, no. 1 (1981): 16–36.

Shepperson, George and Thomas Price. *Independent African; John Chilembwe, and the Origins, Setting, and Significance of the Nyasaland Native Rising of 1915.* Edinburgh, 1958.

Shive, David. *Naming Achilles.* New York and Oxford, 1987.

Short, Philip. *Banda.* London, 1974.

Smith, Andrew. *Andrew Smith's Journal of his expedition into the interior of South Africa—1834–36.* Edited by W. F. Lye. Cape Town, 1975.

Smith, Andrew. *The Diary of Dr. Andrew Smith, ?, 1834–36.* Edited by P. R. Kirby. 2 vols. Cape Town, 1939–40.

Soko, Boston J. "Stylistique et Messages dan le Vimbuza." Thesis for a doctorate of the third cycle, University of the Sorbonne, Paris, 1984.

Spence, C. F. *Moçambique (East African Province of Portugal).* Cape Town, 1963.

Stanton, William. *The Leopard's Spots: Scientific Attitudes towards Race in America, 1815–1859.* Chicago, 1960.

Stepan, Nancy. *The Idea of Race in Science: Great Britain, 1800–1960.* London and Hamden, Conn., 1982.

Stevens, Richard P. "Swaziland Political Development," *Journal of Modern African Studies* 1 (1963): 327–50.

Stewart, James. *The Zambesi Journal of James Stewart.* Edited by J. P. R. Wallis. London, 1954.

Stocking, George W. Jr. *Race, Culture, and Evolution: Essays in the History of Anthropology.* 1968; rpt. Chicago, 1982.

———. *Victorian Anthropology.* New York and London, 1987.

Street, Brian V. *The Savage in Literature: Representations of "Primitive" Society in English Fiction, 1858–1920.* London and Boston, 1975.

Swann, Alfred. *Fighting the Slave Hunters in Central Africa.* London, 1910.

Thomas, T. M. *Eleven Years in Central South Africa.* London, 1872.

Thornton, Richard. *The Zambesi Papers of Richard Thornton.* Edited by E. C. Tabler. 2 vols. London, 1963.

Torgovnik, Marianne. *Gone Primitive: Savage Intellects, Modern Lives.* Chicago, 1990.

Torrend, J. *Grammatica do Chisena.* Chupanga, Mozambique, 1900.

Tracey, Andrew, and Gai Zantzinger. *A Companion to the Films "Mgodo wa Mabanquzi" and "Mgodo wa Mkandeni."* N.p. [Roodepoort, South Africa], 1976.

Tracey, Hugh. *Chopi Musicians: Their Music, Poetry, and Instruments.* London, 1948.

———. *African Dances of the Witwatersrand Gold Mines.* Johannesburg, 1952.

Trapido, Stanley. "'The Friends of the Natives': Merchants, Peasants, and the Political and Ideological Structure of Liberalism in the Cape, 1854–1910." Pp. 247–74 in *Economy and Society in Pre-Industrial South Africa,* edited by Shula Marks and Anthony Atmore. London, 1980.

Tylor, Edward. *Anthropology.* New York, 1881.

Vail, Leroy. "Suggestions towards a Reinterpreted Tumbuka History." Pp. 148–67 in *The Early History of Malawi,* edited by B. Pachai. London, 1972.

———. "Religion, Language, and the Tribal Myth: the Tumbuka and Chewa of Malawi." Pp. 209–234 in *Guardians of the Land: Essays on Central African Territorial Cults,* edited by M. Schoffeleers. Gwelo, Zimbabwe, 1978.

———. "The Political Economy of East Central Africa." Pp. 200–250 in *History of Central Africa,* edited by David Birmingham and Phyllis M. Martin. Vol 2. New York, 1983.

———. "The State and the Creation of Colonial Malawi's Agricultural Economy." Pp. 39–88 in *Imperialism, Colonialism, and Hunger: East and Central Africa,* edited by Robert I. Rotburg. Lexington, Mass., 1983.

———, and Landeg White. "'Tawani, Machembero!' Forced Cotton and Rice Cultivation in the Zambesi," *Journal of African History* 19, no. 2 (1976): 239–64.

———, and Landeg White. *Capitalism and Colonialism in Mozambique: A Study of Quelimane District.* London and Minneapolis, 1980.

———, and Landeg White. "Forms of Resistance: Songs and Perceptions of Power in Colonial Mozambique," *American Historical Review* 88, no. 4 (1983): 883–919.

———, and Landeg White. "Tribalism in the Political History of Malawi." Pp. 151–92 in *The Creation of Tribalism in Southern Africa. Studies in the Political Economy of Idealogy*, edited by L. Vail. London, Berkeley, and Los Angeles, 1989.

Vaughan, Michael. "*Staffrider* and Directions within Contemporary South African Literature." Pp. 196–212 in *Literature and Society in South Africa*, edited by L. White and T. Couzens. Harlow, Essex 1984.

Wainwright, A., P. McAllister, and P. Wallace. *The Xhosa Imbongi (Praise Poet) as a Conveyer of Social Criticism and Praise in the Mining Industry*. Research Report 39/78. Johannesburg, Chamber of Mines and South Africa Research Organisation, 1979.

Webster, David J. "Kinship and Cooperation: Aganation, Alternative Structures, and the Individual in Chopi Society." Ph.D. diss., Rhodes University, Grahamstown, South Africa, 1975.

———. "Migrant Labour, Social Formations, and the Proletarianization of the Chopi of Southern Mozambique," *African Perspectives* 1 (1978): 157–74.

Werner, Alice. *The Natives of British Central Africa*. London, 1906.

White, Landeg E. "Power and the Praise Poem," *Journal of Southern African Studies* 9 no. 1 (1982): 8–32.

———. *Magomero: Portrait of an African Village*. Cambridge, 1987.

Wilensky, A. H. *Portuguese Overseas Legislation for Africa*. Braga, 1968.

Williams, Raymond. *Keywords: A Vocabulary of Culture and Society*. London, 1976.

Williams, T. David. *Malawi: The Politics of Despair*. Ithaca, N.Y.: 1978.

Wilson, Brian R., ed. *Rationality*. Oxford, 1970.

Wilson, S. G. "Agricultural Practice among the Angoni-Tumbuka Tribes of Mzimba (Nyasaland)," *The East African Agricultural Journal*, October 1941, 89–93.

Wolf, Eric. *Europe and the People without History*. Berkeley and Los Angeles, 1982.

Wundt, Wilhelm. *Völkerpsychologie*. Berlin, 1900.

———. *Elements of Folk Psychology: Outlines of a Psychological History of the Development of Mankind*. London and New York, 1916. English translation by E. L. Schaub of *Elemente der Völkerpsychologie* (Berlin, 1912).

Yai, Olabiyi. "Issues in Oral Poetry: Criticism, Teaching, and Translation," in *Discourse and Its Disguises: The Interpretation of African Oral Texts* (Birmingham, U.K., 1989).

Young, A., and P. Brown. *The Physical Environment of Northern Nyasaland*. Zomba, 1962.

Young, Thomas Cullen. *Notes on the Customs and Folklore of the Tumbuka-Kamanga Peoples*. Livingstonia [Nyasaland], 1931.

Index